Dane & Thomas: How to Use a Law Library

AN INTRODUCTION TO LEGAL SKILLS

AUSTRALIA
The Law Book Company
Brisbane : Sydney : Melbourne : Perth

CANADA
Carswell
Ottawa : Toronto : Calgary : Montreal : Vancouver

AGENTS
Steimatzky's Agency Ltd, Tel Aviv
N.M. Tripathi (Private) Ltd, Bombay
Eastern Law House (Private) Ltd, Calcutta
M.P.P. House, Bangalore
Universal Book Traders, Delhi
Aditya Books, Delhi
MacMillan Shuppan KK, Tokyo
Pakistan Law House, Karachi, Lahore

Dane & Thomas: How to Use a Law Library

An Introduction to Legal Skills

FOURTH EDITION

by

PHILIP A. THOMAS
Professor of Socio Legal Studies, Cardiff Law School, University of Wales, Cardiff

JOHN KNOWLES
Sub-Librarian (Law and Official Publications), Queen's University Belfast

with contributions by:

Jennefer Aston
Consultant Librarian, Law Library, Dublin

Maria Bell
Assistant Librarian, London School of Economics

David R. Hart
Law Librarian, University of Dundee

Paul Norman
Institute of Advanced Legal Studies, London

LONDON
SWEET & MAXWELL
2001

First Edition 1979
Second Impression 1980
Second Edition 1987
Second Impression 1992
Third Edition 1996
Fourth Edition 2001

Published in 2001 by
Sweet & Maxwell Limited
100 Avenue Road
Swiss Cottage
London NW3 3PF
(http://www.sweetandmaxwell.co.uk)
Typeset by Mendip Communications Limited,
Frome, Somerset
Printed in England by Clays Ltd, St Ives plc

No natural forests were destroyed to make this product, only farmed timber was used and
replanted

A CIP catalogue record for this book is available from the British Library

ISBN 0421 744103

Preface

As a new law student you will quickly discover that you are required to spend considerable time in the law library. At secondary education level you may have been prepared carefully for state examinations by teachers who provided you with the essential information for the examination. The responsibility for learning was possibly a shared function: one between you and your teachers with the teachers taking the principal role. The balance within this relationship changes on entering university as an undergraduate. The emphasis of higher education study is on self preparation leading to self learning. You must not rely on your lecturers to "tell you all the law". If you do you will be sadly disappointed. Guidance, ideas, principles and support should come from the staff via lectures and seminars but ultimately the responsibility of coming to terms with legal knowledge belongs with you: the student.

Thus, the law library is your "laboratory" where you will prepare for a seminar, read references provided in lectures, or research an essay topic. Legal studies are essentially a library based exercise. Learn how to use the library wisely and effectively. It is a resource to be used properly. Inefficient use will result in you wasting valuable time and your academic work will suffer. Acquiring a proper working knowledge of the law library is a skill which will carry you through your degree programme and beyond into legal practice. Increasingly, skills training is recognised as an essential and important element of legal education. Skills acquisition is commonly found in the undergraduate syllabus and is also located in the post graduate courses which all potential legal practitioners are obliged to undertake. Remember that lawyers carry only a certain amount of legal knowledge in their heads and even that information might be incomplete, wrong or out of date. A lawyer who relies only on memory is one who is in danger of being subject to a negligence claim from the client! The law is dynamic and fast moving. No person knows it all and a clever lawyer will admit to knowing only a little law. A good lawyer is one who knows where and how to look for the relevant law and is able to understand and apply it in the best interests of the client. The library skills that you learn now will stand you in good stead for the future. Develop proper techniques and good habits about library usage now and the benefits will be both immediate and long term.

Since the last edition of this book, prepared in 1995, libraries have undergone a fundamental change. The virtual library sits alongside the print library. The growth of electronically held information is dramatic. Library users are now faced with a super-abundance of information either held in the library, accessible via the library or, indeed, from outside the library by using the library's subscription to access databases that are subscription based. In addition we identify websites on the internet which are free to you. Do remember that this is a fast-changing area of library development and you are advised to update this book for yourself as you discover new sources of information. Consequently, the book has been restructured to recognise these major changes. Finding relevant information can be done either electronically or through print sources. We clearly identify the search techniques for both "electronic" and "print" sources. Sometimes electronic is faster or easier and sometimes print is preferable. We give you advice on which one is currently better for the new researcher. The fast and ever changing shape and substance of law means that you must keep up to date, whether as a student, lecturer, or practitioner. There is no escaping the dynamic nature of law. You cannot hope to keep abreast of change through legal gossip, looking at other people's notes, reading a standard text, which by definition is out of date by the time it is printed, hoping the lecturer has got it right and that, in turn, you have written down your notes from lectures correctly and fully. Ultimately the responsibility for learning the law rests with you and the most appropriate and efficient way is through a careful and informed use of the law library. It is there that you will find the latest information on changes to the law.

The principal purpose of this book is to provide you with basic information about how a law collection is organised and how you can access the information that is contained within the library. In a sense, this book is a labour saving device. Use it as a reference book throughout your student days and indeed probably thereafter should you decide to enter legal practice. It is not intended to be treated as a textbook and thereby associated with a particular course. It is a reference aid to be consulted when you have a problem. Consequently, you might use the book selectively, referring to those sections which are useful at a particular point in your studies, or when recommended to look up a case, statute or issue by a member of the teaching staff. This book is essentially a handy tool, it is a practical work which tells you how to use library materials properly. Thus, the obvious place to use it is in the library itself.

The book concentrates on the law in England and Wales. However, Scotland, Northern Ireland and the Republic of Ireland are covered. In addition, chapters are provided on European Union law and public international law. The recent constitutional changes in Northern Ireland have resulted in a major rewrite as has the introduction of devolution in Scotland and Wales. The European Union continues to develop at a pace, acceptable to many but not all, and therefore that chapter has also been heavily amended. The introduction of the Human Rights Act 1998 made us consider adding a separate section on that Act but we decided that our approach would be integrative rather than discrete.

Your introductory library tour, valuable though it is, usually takes place during the first hectic weeks of your new life as a student. We hope that you will supplement this introduction by regular reference to this book. Some of the most important reference works can be difficult to use. To help you, we have provided summaries of the steps to be taken when consulting them and, in some cases, we have also provided algorithms (flow-charts). Both the summaries and the flow-charts are intended to be used in conjunction with the main text. Remember that the library staff are there to help you. If, after consulting this book, you are still unable to find what you want, do not hestitate to ask for assistance or information.

May, 2001   *Philip A. Thomas*
                                                                                                      John Knowles

Acknowledgments

The authors and publishers would like to thank the following for granting permission to reproduce material included in this book:

BAIILI
Bowker-Saur (Lawyer's Law Books: a Practical Index to Legal Literature. By Donal Rainstrick: with a foreword by Lord Mackay of Clashfern. 3rd ed. East Grinstead: Bowker-Saur 1997. © K. G. Saur, München.)
Butterworths & Co. (Publishers) Ltd
Department of Justice, Dublin
EUR-OP Office for Publications
Her Majesty's Stationery Office
Incorporated Council of Law Reporting
Legal Information Resources Ltd
Sarah Carter, University of Kent
Scottish Council of Law Reporting
SLS Publications
Stationery Office, Dublin
Sweet & Maxwell
The Stationery Office
The United Nations
Westlaw UK

While every care has been taken to establish and acknowledge copyright, and contact the copyright owners, the publishers tender their apologies for any accidental infringement. They would be pleased to come to a suitable arrangement with the rightful owners in each case.

Contents

5. JOURNALS

8. SCOTS LAW

1 | Using a Library

INTRODUCTION

1–1

Large libraries may appear confusing to use. Most libraries are, however, arranged on the same basic principles and once these have been mastered you should not experience too much difficulty in finding your way around, even in the largest library. University and college libraries contain two main types of print material: journals (often called periodicals or magazines) and books. Electronic resources are introduced in Chapter 2.

Books

1–2

In some institutions, books on different subjects are housed in separate buildings. For instance, you may find that the law books are placed in a separate law library. If this has not been done, the law books will be collected together in one area of the library.

Arrangement of Books on the Shelves

1–3

Books are usually grouped on the shelves according to their subject. The subject dealt with in each book is indicated by numbers, or letters and numbers, which are usually written on the spine of the book. These symbols indicate the exact subject matter of each volume. They are known as the classification number or classmark and bring together, in one area of the library, all books dealing with the same subject. The classification number serves two purposes: it indicates the subject of the book and tells you where the book is to be found on the shelves.

There may be a number of separate sequences in the library. Some books, such as dictionaries and encyclopedias, are designed by their nature to be used as reference books, rather than as books to be read from cover to cover; these may be shelved in a separate reference collection. Very large books (folios) and very thin books (pamphlets) may be kept in separate sequences. Thus, the size of the book may be important in helping you to find it on the shelves. There will normally be some indication on the catalogue entry (**1–4**) if the book is shelved separately. Parliamentary papers and publications of international bodies, such as the European Union and the United Nations, are often located in areas of the library set aside for this purpose. Most important from your point of view, there may be a separate reserve, short loan or undergraduate collection of basic textbooks which are in great demand. These are normally available only for reference or for loan for a short time. Such a collection may include photocopies of articles from journals and extracts from books on your reading lists. Copies of examination papers set in previous years are usually available.

1–4   Using the Library Catalogue

To find out what books are available in the library, you need to consult the library catalogue. The main catalogue will be held on computer. In some libraries, card catalogues may also be used (see **1–5**). Computers dedicated to catalogue access will be available in prominent places throughout the library building. You can also connect to the catalogue from outside the library, using either the university network or the internet.

Computerised catalogues are usually straightforward to use. Computer terminals within the library building often have simple display screens using single letter commands or keyboard function keys (F1, F2, etc.) to change the catalogue display. If you are connecting to the catalogue from outside the library, you are likely to see a web-based version of the catalogue (see **2–4**). There will be instructions on screen and in most cases, library leaflets, which will help you learn how to search the catalogue.

All computerised catalogues allow you to search for books by the author's name, or the title of the book. If you do not have the exact title, a keyword search enables you to search for words occurring anywhere in the title. Additional searches by subject area or classification are usually possible. If the library has the book you want, the catalogue entry will give you its full details (*e.g.* its publisher, the date of publication and the length of the book in pages) and the classification number, which tells you where to find the book on the shelves. A computerised catalogue also shows you whether the book is out on loan and, if so, when it is due to be returned to the library.

Author searches should be used with care. Even if you are sure of the author of the book, you may need to check a number of author entries before you find the right one. Suppose you have a reference to a book written by John Jackson. If you use the author search and enter "Jackson, J" you will see index entries that might feature the following variations of the name (among others):

Jackson, J.A., John Archer, 1929–
Jackson, J.D, John Dugland, 1955–
Jackson, J.E., John Ellwood
Jackson, John, 1887–1958
Jackson, John E.

You need to start with "Jackson, J.A." and work down the list in order to find the right author. In this case, the second author listed is a writer on legal subjects, but a search using "Jackson, John" would have missed the correct entry. The index display would begin with "Jackson, John, 1887–1958".

If you have a reference to both the author and title of the book you want, it is usually easier and quicker to search by title (ignoring words such as "The" or "A" in the title). Most catalogues also allow a search using a combination of author surname and title, thereby avoiding the problem noted above.

Law books often continue to be known by the name of the original author, even though that author might be dead. This is something you will need to take account of when using the catalogue. Let us take as an example, *Winfield and Jolowicz on Tort*. This is in its fifteenth edition. Winfield has not been involved with the work for many years, but it is still referred to by his name. You will usually find an entry in the author catalogue under Winfield, but in addition, there will also be an entry under Rogers, W.V.H. who is the author of the current edition. If you are using a title search you need to search for "Winfield and Jolowicz on Tort", not "Tort", the original title.

Many law books have been written jointly by two or more authors. You may be referred for example to Craig and de Burca (*EU Law*) or Clayton and Tomlinson (*The Law of Human Rights*). There will be an entry in the catalogue for both authors, and title searches should be for "EU Law" or "Law of Human Rights".

Sometimes a book does not have an individual as the author. It is published by an organisation or society and the organisation is, in effect, the author. In this case, you will find an entry in the catalogue under the name of the body, *e.g.* Law Commission, Law Society, Legal Action Group, United Nations.

Using Microfiche and Card Catalogues   1–5

Details of older books in your library may be held only in a card catalogue. There are usually three main sequences: an author (or name) catalogue, a subject catalogue and a classified catalogue. The author catalogue contains records arranged alphabetically by authors' names. In some libraries, it may also include entries under the titles of books. A subject catalogue usually links a subject heading to numbers or ranges of numbers in the classification scheme. The classified sequence then files details of books by classification number.

Most libraries will have a microfiche copy of the main library catalogue. In most cases, this will be the only copy of the catalogue available if the computer system fails. It is arranged in the same way as a card catalogue and includes title entries.

Finding and Borrowing Books   1–6

The classification number (**1–3**) will appear prominently on the catalogue entry. This number will enable you to trace the book on the shelves. If the library is a large one, there is usually a guide near the catalogue showing you where books with that classification number are found.

If you have any difficulty in understanding how the books are arranged on the shelves, or in using the catalogue, ask a member of the library staff for help.

If the book is not on the shelves it may be:

(a) in use by another reader in the library;
(b) on loan to another reader;
(c) in a separate sequence of books which are larger or smaller than average, or which are in heavy demand (**1–3**);
(d) mis-shelved or missing;
(e) removed by the library staff for some reason, *e.g.* rebinding.

Computerised catalogues are able to show whether the book you want is on loan or is missing. If the book is on loan, it may be possible for you to reserve it, in which case the book will be recalled from its present borrower.

Much of the material in your law library will not be available for loan. Law reports, journals and reference materials, for example, are usually only for use within the library. The library staff will explain which materials are available for loan, how many items you can borrow and for how long. You will need to show your library card every time you borrow books. The staff will stamp the label on the inside cover of the books with the date by which you need to return them, although you may find that you can renew the books if you require them for longer. Remember, you will be fined if you keep the books beyond the stamped return date.

1-7 LAW REPORTS AND JOURNALS

In the course of your studies, you will need to look at the reports of cases which have been heard in courts, both in this country and abroad. These reports are published in a number of publications called law reports. Amongst the best known series of law reports are the *All England Law Reports*, the *Weekly Law Reports* and the *Law Reports*. We shall examine these series in more detail in Chapter 3. There is a standard form of writing references to law reports, and this is explained in **3–3**. The law reports are usually shelved in a separate sequence in the law library and they will often be grouped together by country, so that all the English law reports are together. You may find that the international law reports are shelved separately.

You will also find that you are referred to articles and case notes in journals (periodicals or magazines). Your reading list should give you the author and title of the article, the year, the volume number, the title of the journal in which the article appeared and the first page number on which the article is printed, *e.g.* Buxton, Richard, "The Human Rights Act and private law" (2000) 116 L.Q.R. 48.

The form in which this information is written varies but it is important that you learn to distinguish a reference to a journal article from a reference to a chapter or pages in a book. If you are in any doubt as to the nature of the reference (*i.e.* whether it is a book, a journal article or a law report), ask a member of the library staff for advice. The library catalogue will only include the title of journals. You will need to use other indexes (*e.g.* the *Legal Journals Index*—see **5–4**) to find the location of individual articles within journals.

1-8 Abbreviations

One of the major difficulties facing a new student is the tradition, adopted by lecturers and authors, of referring to journals and law reports only by an abbreviated form of their title. Instead of writing the name of the journal or law report in full, they are invariably shortened to such cryptic abbreviations as: [2000] A.C.; [2001] 2 All E.R.; 136 N.L.J.; 4 L.M.C.L.Q. This may make it very difficult for you to know whether you are looking for a law report or a journal article. Many of the references are confusingly similar, *e.g.* L.R. can be the abbreviation for both "law report" and "law review" (the law reports are shelved together, but separate from law reviews, which are journals). Consequently, you could find yourself looking in the wrong sequence. A common mistake, for instance, is to assume that a reference to a report of a case in "Crim.L.R." means that you must search amongst the law reports for a series entitled the Criminal Law Reports. There is no such series (although there is a series called the *Criminal Appeal Reports*). The reference "Crim.L.R." is to the *Criminal Law Review*, which is a journal, shelved with the other journals. This contains both articles and reports of cases.

There are several publications which list the meaning of abbreviations in common use. These publications are outlined in **3–5**.

1-9 Tracing Journals and Law Reports

To find out if a journal or law report is available, use the computerised catalogue and search for the title of the journal. The catalogue should allow you to select a separate journal title search, so that you only search for journal entries. In some systems there is a "Journal title" search box on the main catalogue screen.

If you are looking for a journal which includes the name of an organisation in its title, you may by unsure of the precise title to use. Is it the *American Bar Association Journal*, for example, or the *Journal of the American Bar Association*? In these cases it is usually possible to search for the journal by the name of the organisation which produces it. If the publication you wish to find has "Bulletin", "Transactions" or "Proceedings" at the start of its title, retain these words when you make your search.

When searching for both law reports and journals, use the full title, not the standard abbreviation (see **1–8**). Drop "The" from the search. For example, if you wish to locate *The All England Law Reports*, use "All England Law Reports", not "The All England Law Reports".

If the journal or law report you require is not available in your own library, the staff may be able to help you to locate a copy in another local library. Alternatively, it may be possible to obtain a photocopy of the article on inter-library loan or through a commercial document supply service. As the services cost money, you may need to obtain prior approval from a lecturer, or alternatively you may have to pay for the service.

OTHER LIBRARY SERVICES   1–10

In addition to the print sources available in your library, and the electronic sources introduced in Chapter 2, you will find some other useful sources of information. The library, for example, may have material (such as old editions of *The Times* newspaper) available only in the form of microfiche or microfilm, and there may be collections of audio-visual material (audio cassettes, videotapes, slides, etc.), press cuttings and other materials which do not form part of the normal collections.

Academic libraries often offer a wide range of other resources. Almost all libraries, for example, provide photocopying facilities. You may find that your library also offers graphic design facilities, a bindery (should you need to bind your dissertation) and fax machines. Most academic libraries also provide computers, allowing you to type up your essays using a word processor, access the campus network or undertake any other computer-related work, while in the library.

WHICH LIBRARIES CAN I USE?   1–11

If you are studying at a university or college, the majority of the books you require should be available in your own institution's library. Remember that there may be more than one library available. For instance, in addition to the main library collection, there may be a smaller collection of books and reports in your department or faculty building. If you are living in a hall of residence, the hall's library may include some textbooks.

You may join the public library in the area in which you live, work or study. Most large towns will have some legal textbooks and law reports in their central library. If what you want is not available, the library staff may be able to borrow the material you require through inter-library loan. This may take some time, so ask for the material well in advance of your actual need.

When you return home for the vacation, the university nearest your home may allow you to use their library for reference. The library catalogues of other universities can be accessed on the internet (see **7–29**), so you may wish to check whether they have the books you require before you go. These catalogues may also give details of the libraries' opening hours and other useful information.

If you are studying for a professional examination, your professional body will have a library, from which you may be able to borrow books (by post, if necessary). The nearest large public library is another possible source of supply, and your employer may have a library to which you can have access.

Students studying for the Bar may also use the library of their Inn. Local public libraries, the libraries attached to the courts and the collections available in chambers are other possible sources. Those training to be solicitors can use the facilities of the Law Society's library, and the collections held by local law societies may be made available to students.

The addresses of libraries can be found in the Library Association's *Libraries in the United Kingdom and the Republic of Ireland*, or the information can be obtained, by telephone or in person, from any public library. U.K. university websites can be found using the Niss Information website (at **www.niss.ac.uk**).

1–12 DICTIONARIES

The newcomer to law rapidly discovers that lawyers have a language of their own, which is a mixture of Latin, French and English. There are several small pocket dictionaries of legal terms which are useful for students, *e.g.* P. G. Osborn, *Concise Law Dictionary* and Mozley and Whiteley, *Law Dictionary*. Students should also consult standard English dictionaries, such as the multi-volumed *Oxford English Dictionary* or one of its smaller versions. W. A. Jowitt, *Dictionary of English Law* is a larger legal dictionary. D. M. Walker, *Oxford Companion to Law*, is another source of information on legal terms, institutions, doctrines and general legal matters. It includes lists of judges and law officers.

Latin phrases and maxims may cause difficulties for students who have no classical languages. Latin phrases appear in most legal dictionaries and a collection of legal maxims appears in H. Broom, *A Selection of Legal Maxims*: see also Appendix II, at the back of this book. If you are carrying out research in legal history, you may need J. H. Baker, *Manual of Law French*.

1–13 Tracing people and addresses

A number of websites and reference works enable you to trace the address of a solicitor, or to find the address of courts, legal firms, professional bodies, etc. Waterlow publishes a *Solicitors' and Barristers' Directory*, which gives alphabetical lists of solicitors and barristers, with their addresses. Lists of Q.C.s, judges, Benchers of the Inns, Recorders and members of the Institute of Legal Executives are also included. The lists of barristers' chambers and solicitors' firms in each geographical area included in the *Directory* can also be searched online (at **www.connectinglegal.com**). If you want to trace a solicitor by name or specialism, the Law Society's *Directory of Solicitors* is available online (at **www.solicitors-online.com**). The *Bar Directory* is published as a joint venture by the General Council of the Bar and Sweet & Maxwell. The sections of the *Bar Directory* covering Chambers by location and barristers in private practice can be searched online (at **www.sweetandmaxwell.co.uk/bardirectory/website**). Legalease publishes both *The Legal 500*, a guide to barristers' chambers and solicitors firms for commercial clients, and *Who's Who in the Law*, which provides professional profiles of barristers and solicitors. Biographical details of prominent members of the legal profession can also be found in *Who's Who*, while *Debrett's Correct Form* provides advice on the correct form of address when writing to, or addressing, members of the judiciary and other eminent people.

Law students looking for training contracts, formerly known as articles, should consult the *Register of Solicitors Employing Trainees (ROSET)*, issued by the Law Society. The addresses of area legal aid offices are found on the Legal Services Commission website (at **www.legalservices.gov.uk**). The Legal Services Commission has replaced the Legal Aid Board. The addresses of many organisations and bodies may be found in the *Directory of British Associations*, and in the companion publication, *Councils, Committees and Boards*. The humble telephone directory should not be overlooked as a source of information. The *Yellow Pages* can be searched online (at **www.yell.co.uk**). The reference collection in your library will contain many other print sources enabling you to trace people and organisations and internet gateways (see **2–16**) provide links to relevant websites. Ask the reference librarian for advice if you need help.

ASSISTANCE FROM LIBRARY STAFF 1–14

Remember that the library staff are there to help you. They will be pleased to explain how the books are arranged on the shelves, to decipher abbreviations, help with difficulties with reading lists and suggest possible sources of information. Do not hesitate to ask them for advice, no matter how busy they may appear to be. They can also help you load your microfilm, show you how to use the CD-ROMs, find an internet website and search online databases for yourself.

Most libraries produce handouts or library guides. You should make a point of reading those which are relevant. They will explain how the books are arranged on the shelves, how to use the library catalogue, how to borrow books, etc. In academic libraries, tours of the library are often arranged at the beginning of the session. If such a tour is available, you should certainly attend, as it will help you to familiarise yourself with the library. You may also find that the law librarian will lead lectures or seminars to introduce you to important legal sources. Those lessons will reinforce the skills you will learn in the following chapters.

2 Using Computers to Access the Law

INTRODUCTION

Information technology means a dramatic change in the availability and scope of information in your law library. Historically, for some access solely to the printed page represented information starvation in a poorly stocked library. Today, for some the electronic age can mean information overload. The modern researcher has access to a range of resources undreamed of a few decades ago and the challenge is to develop appropriate research techniques which will allow you to find the relevant information quickly.

A great deal of the information available in print in the law library is now available in electronic form, both on CD-ROM, and more significantly, on the internet. The law reports mentioned in Chapter 3 can be found, read and printed using a CD-ROM attached to a personal computer (PC) for example, or by using a web browser such as Netscape or Internet Explorer and a connection to the internet. Some printed law journals are also available in full text on the internet, and the number is set to grow. Acts of the U.K. Parliament are available free on the HMSO website.

Expanding electronic information means the law library has become increasingly important as a gateway to resources. It provides services which can help you get to grips with the legal information available. These services include the provision of useful access points on library or information service web pages, as well as the provision of documentation for legal databases and teaching tutorials to help you understand how to use them. The expansion of electronic resources has also meant that the library has also become a gate*keeper* for electronic sources of information, controlling the subscriptions required to access the many commercial services you will want to use. But do remember that librarians remain central to library usage. They continue to provide informal help about using electronic sources in the most efficient manner.

However, electronic resources are limited in their scope and not all libraries can access electronic information. Sometimes it is easier and quicker to use printed materials. Consequently, an appreciation and understanding of both print and electronic resources is necessary. In the following chapters, electronic sources are described alongside print sources as an alternative source of information. Where there is an electronic source, it usually precedes the print equivalent.

At every stage in the chapters that follow, the web address and the names of service providers and CD-ROM titles are given, along with a description of the service. Bear in mind that the way in which electronic services have been made available has changed rapidly in recent years and is likely to continue to change. The precise details of web addresses and access conditions may change and new services will become available. Part of the process of learning to make best use of electronic sources of information is learning how best to keep track of these changes. Do not let a change of an electronic address frustrate you. You need to be able to identify and update your basic tracing information. Fortunately, the internet itself provides the perfect means of keeping up with changes in the availability of information. Paragraph **2–16** of this chapter suggests some useful internet gateway sites that help you monitor important changes in the provision of legal information. Remember, staying abreast of change is an important task which, in turn, helps you access relevant information quickly and easily. To be a successful researcher you also need to be efficient in your research skills. You can even update the text of this book!

2–2 WHY USE ELECTRONIC SOURCES?

The use of computers has made it possible for a large amount of legal information to be held and made available from a single electronic source. New ways of conducting legal research have also been opened up and the time spent in finding legal information greatly reduced. The speed with which information has become available has also increased.

Long-established information providers, such as Lexis-Nexis, and more recently, commercial law publishers, have built databases of full-text material, and have either published the text in the form of CD-ROMs, or provided online access using remote servers. "Full text" literally means that you have access to everything not simply an account, an abridgement or a potted version of the law. The Lexis databases, for example, contain the full text of a very wide range of English law reports commencing in 1945. Access to United Kingdom legislation is also available, and separate files contain United States and Commonwealth case law and legislation. The point has been reached where all but the largest and most well-stocked libraries can match their print holding of the primary sources of law with electronic alternatives. These electronic resources are not only available in the library. Online services can make this large volume of material available to the student working not just at a single PC in the library, but anywhere within the university, perhaps at a time when the library building is closed. Access may also be possible from home, thereby helping part-time students and distance learners. Wherever you are working a substantial body of law source material can be made available to you if you have a network connection. Unlike the print user, you need not suffer the frustration caused by the discovery that the printed volume you sought on the library shelves is in use, missing or mutilated.

Using full-text databases of case law such as those provided by Lexis-Nexis, you can also search, for example, for any combination of words that might be found in a judgment. This is just one illustration of the way new methods of researching have become possible. Assume you are looking for case law on the use of the word "roadway". You are establishing if the access routes of a car park constitute a roadway. You start by constructing your search using the words that might be relevant. Searching for cases in which roads, roadway and car park are in close proximity will provide you with a list of cases to check. With a little imagination you will see that issues as diverse as a particular characteristic of a criminal case (the use of an unusual weapon), a particular phrase used by a judge, or a distinctive place name could all provide a route into the reported case law using keyword searches.

The speed with which legal research can be carried out can be seen in the context of the bibliographic databases described in Chapter 5. It also means that a more thorough research exercise is possible. To take an example used in **2–14**, try using the print volumes of the *Legal Journals Index* to find references to journal articles on the use of provocation as a defence in cases of domestic violence. You will be faced with a painstaking search through a series of annual volumes looking at the entries indexed under the subject headings used for provocation and for domestic violence. Thereafter you must note the details of the relevant articles. The online or CD-ROM version of the index allows you to search in a matter of seconds for articles that match the keywords "provocation" and "domestic violence" and then print the resulting list of references. You can easily modify your search approach, by changing the search words you used, if you discover that your initial search finds too many or too few references to be either useful or plausible.

One of the best examples of the speed with which information can now become available, is provided by the placing of transcripts of judgments on the internet soon after they are handed down. These transcripts are found on websites within a day of delivery. This is a process that began with the House of Lords in 1996 and judgments are available from the Court Service of England and Wales and the Scottish Court Service. Details of these sources are found in Chapter 3. As a result, if you hear of a case that might be relevant to your studies, it is possible to move directly from the media report of the issues raised to an examination of the legal issues as they appear first hand in the full text of the judgment. This means that you can be fully aware of the latest developments in case law. For example, the Court of Appeal made its judgment available electronically concerning the separation of conjoined twins, A (Children) September 22, 2000 (Mary and Jodie), almost as soon as it was delivered in court. Print publication of the judgment in the *All England Law Reports* had to wait for the issue which appeared on December 13, 2000. (The case is cited as *A (Children) (Conjoined Twins: Medical Treatment) (No.1)* [2000] 4 All E.R. 961.)

USING CD-ROMS   2–3

Many of the full-text products of the commercial legal publishers, including the *All England Law Reports*, the *Law Reports* series and *UK Statutory Instruments*, were first made available electronically in CD-ROM form. You may find that your library still has significant holdings of legal information in this form. The use of CD-ROMs enables a large amount of data to be stored on disc and makes possible the use of relatively sophisticated search software. Windows-based software in particular has allowed the construction of relatively helpful display screens. These often make use of graphic icons to start searches and perform various other functions, including the display of search results and the sending of instructions to the printer. Graphic icons and web-like page design have tended to replace the use of menu commands and function keys.

If you wish to use a CD-ROM held by your library you have to borrow the CD from an issue or information desk. As the CD-ROM requires particular search software to be loaded on to a computer before it can be used, you will be directed to a particular PC or workstation on which the search software is loaded. Alternatively the CD-ROM may be pre-loaded on a particular computer and you will need to locate the one that holds the CD-ROM database. This may or may not be located within the law library. Where CD-ROMs have been networked by your university, it may be possible for any machine on a university's local network to use the CD-ROM database, though again the particular machine may need to have CD-ROM search software pre-loaded. When in doubt ask for advice from the library staff about what is located where in the library.

A particular feature of full-text CD-ROMs is that they often make use of "hyperlinking" between search results. A hyperlink takes you from the original underlined reference to a related document. For example, if you are looking for a particular law report in the *All England Law Reports*, or the *Weekly Law Reports*, which makes reference to another case reported in the same series, then clicking the case name link can display the full text of the other case. The text of the reports themselves is designed to print in a way that closely follows the version published in the publisher's printed volumes and the original pagination is retained.

A wide range of legal CD-ROMs is currently available and some of the main publishers are listed in **2–5**. For the most part they provide full-text products, though *Current Legal Information* from Sweet & Maxwell contains a number of bibliographic databases.

2–4   SEARCHING THE INTERNET

Anyone who has used the internet is aware of the enormous diversity of information. What you find when you search the internet is not so much a well-ordered electronic library, but something more like an open and chaotically organised market place. Consequently, finding the information that might be of use to you can be a challenge.

Most of the information on the internet is held on web pages. Indeed, for most people "the web" and the internet are synonymous. The web pages themselves are held on web "servers" and each web page has its own unique web address. Web servers range from the most powerful to the smallest of computers and are found globally. Each of them enables you to copy a page from the host machine on to your own computer. You will find that the web pages held on a particular server are usually organised into a single website, and each website will have its own home page, which serves as a starting point for the exploration of the information held on the site. For example, the HMSO home page (at **www.hmso.gov.uk**) is the starting point, among other things, for the legislation which can be found on the site (the Human Rights Act 1998, for example, is found at **www.legislation.hmso.gov.uk/acts/acts1998/19980042.htm**). The address of an individual page can also be typed into the location bar of a web browser if you wish to go directly to that page, though the unwieldy nature of some of the individual pages means that the home page often remains the best place to begin. In addition, the addresses of particular pages are subject to change as sites are reorganised.

The use of links or hyperlinks between one web page and another, also means it is possible to move from a page on one website to a page held in a completely different location thereby blurring the distinction between one website and another. The experience of surfing the web consists of the process by which you move relatively seamlessly from pages held on one web server to others held elsewhere on the internet. In the course of legal research into the background to the Human Rights Act for example, you might move from some lecture notes on the Act held on a university server to the pages on the Home Office website that contain further information. From there, you might move on to the HMSO site which holds the text of the relevant white paper *Rights Brought Home* (at **www.official-documents.co.uk/document/hoffice/rights/rights.htm**), again held as a collection of web pages on a web server.

One way of exploring the contents of the internet is to surf in this fashion from one web page to another. Another common approach is to use one the general internet search engines, such as Alta Vista (at **uk.altavista.com**) or Excite UK (at **www.excite.co.uk**) and Google (at **www.google.com**). These are powerful computers that index the whole range, or at least a very large number of web pages, and provide a keyword search facility enabling you to search for words in the addresses, titles and text of web pages. The results are presented as a series of web links in which the pages carrying most prominently the word or words you used in your search are listed first. The results can be surprising given the enormous variety of web pages on the internet. The more specific the enquiry you use the more helpful the results page is likely to be. A search that uses the keywords "human genetics advisory committee" is more likely to be of use than one that simply uses "human genetics law". A more structured approach to exploring the contents of the internet is provided by the internet gateways listed in **2–16**. Using an internet gateway that concentrates on law resources alone will mean that you can confine your search to the legal information on the internet and find some guidance on the major sources. This will be a more refined approach than that possible using the internet search engines.

ACCESSING LEGAL DATABASES ON THE INTERNET   2–5

A number of legal publishers which began by publishing CD-ROMs, including Butterworths and Sweet & Maxwell, now provide full-text access to legal material on the internet. In doing so they have joined specialist providers of legal material: Lexis-Nexis, Westlaw UK and Lawtel. Access to the online journal indexes described in Chapter 5 is also possible using the internet, though the services themselves have tended to be the preserve of specialist database providers. However, all these commercial services now use web-based interfaces to grant access to their databases, using the internet to connect you to the database itself.

Finding the home page of a database provider is no different from finding the home page of any other website on the internet. You need a computer connected to the internet, either through an institution's local network, or through an internet connection provided by one of the many internet service providers.

The database home page, once found, looks much like any other web page on the internet, and so too will the search and results pages. One difference is that the web pages you see when you are using one of the online databases are part of a live interactive session in which you are sending questions and commands to the database and receiving information in response. There will be some form of logging on and exit procedure to start and finish your database session and you may also be "timed out" if you leave a page for a long period of time and then wish to restart. Because you are logged on to a remote database it is also not advisable to use the "forward" and "back" commands of your web browser, as this can mean that the pages you are using become out of step with the server at the other end of your search session. The need for a logging on procedure also has the particular consequence that for the most part you will need to have a username and a password before you can gain access to the database you wish to use. Again, contact the library staff. They will have usernames and the password which allow authorised people to access these subscription databases.

Usernames and Passwords   2–6

Online databases provided by legal publishers and commercial database providers cost money. Your university law library must pay a subscription to provide access. Typically access is licensed to staff and students of a university, either for a limited number of simultaneous users, or for unlimited access to any number of users. The licence will have been paid for as part of an annual subscription, resulting in no additional charge made by the database provider for the connection time to the database.

Where databases are licensed, the logging on procedure for the database is important, not just because it provides a way of starting a database query session, but also because it provides a way of confirming that there is a current valid subscription to access the database. The username and the password you enter confirm that the institution has a current subscription.

The importance of usernames and passwords means that in order to gain access to a database, you will have to discover, not only which databases the university has subscribed to, but also which username and which password you will need to use to gain access to a particular database. Library websites and printed guides will usually be able to tell you which databases are available, and you will probably be able to obtain usernames and passwords from library issue and information desks or by attending lectures or tutorials designed to introduce the databases. At this point human resources again become important. Contact the law library staff and ask them for information about these restricted databases.

An unfortunate consequence of this access control is that it threatened to produce a situation in which you are required to record and keep a username and password combination for every single online database you might make use of. Some easing of this difficulty has been made possible however for the United Kingdom academic community by the use of the "Athens" registration system. This system operates as an access broker handling the registration systems of the database providers which sign up to it, so that if you are registered with one Athens username and associated password you will have access to a number of different database services. Butterworths (**2–9**) and Context (**2–10**) are among the database providers making use of the system. Universities have also been involved in initiatives to create local systems which would make it possible for one student logon ID to become the key to all relevant on-site and remote database access.

If you are accessing a database from your institution's local network, you may find that the logging on process is hidden from you, and you do not need to enter usernames and passwords. These will again become necessary if you wish to access a database from a computer that is not part of the institutional network, perhaps a computer connected to the internet in your own home.

2–7 Lexis-Nexis

The Lexis databases, made available by Lexis-Nexis, are historically the earliest established legal databases in the United Kingdom. Their use pre-dates web-based interfaces and the use of internet connections. This has placed them in a special position with regard to access methods. When the service was launched in the 1980s, access to the database demanded the use of a special terminal and a telephone connection to the database, and the use of the database was charged according to the length of time the user was connected to the service. Later versions of Lexis developed this time-costing technique, making use of specialist software loaded on ordinary PCs and connections using the internet. This has been the way Lexis databases have been used for the most part in U.K. universities, and also by the legal profession. Throughout this period, charges for the use of the databases have been based on the length of time the user is connected to the

Lexis databases. Consequently, direct use of Lexis-Nexis in universities has tended to be restricted to academic staff and librarians. Students wishing to make use of the database have had to request that a search be made for them, usually by trained library staff. The search software used has also assumed an "expert" user which meant that the casual or untrained user could be in difficulty and also find that search proved surprisingly expensive.

This system is changing for U.K. universities as Lexis-Nexis have developed a web-based search interface, Lexis-Nexis Professional, and offered site licences along the lines of those used by other database providers. In Great Britain the licence is handled by Butterworths LEXIS direct, a merged service, which has emerged as a consequence of common corporate ownership. Access to the Lexis databases is now possible from the Butterworths LEXIS direct web pages which also contain links to the Butterworths databases, noted in **2–9**.

The Lexis databases continue to hold the widest coverage of primary legal material and full-text, electronic "libraries", including those for case law and legislation for England and Wales. Additional electronic libraries cover E.U. legislation and American, Republic of Ireland and Commonwealth case law. The coverage of the case law of England and Wales, Scotland and Northern Ireland in particular remains unrivalled, including the text of 30 of the law report series from 1945 onwards. These include the major law reports, such as the *All England Law Reports* and the *Law Reports*. Transcripts of a significant number of unreported cases are also included. The databases selected remain the same whichever access method is used. Further details can be obtained from the Lexis-Nexis pages (at **www.lexis-nexis.com**).

Additional Database Providers   2–8

A complete listing of the providers of legal databases is not possible here and even for those listed, the information provided may be subject to change over a short period. However, an awareness of the way different information providers have brought together their databases is useful, as it can be difficult to obtain an overall picture of who is providing what in the legal sphere. It may not always be obvious, for example, that the same basic resource can be found using a number of different routes. A law report published in the *Law Reports* could, for example, be found by using Lexis-Nexis, Justis.com from Context, or Westlaw UK. Its citation could also be checked using Sweet & Maxwell's *Current Legal Information*, Lawtel or Westlaw UK. Specific databases will be referred to throughout this book. The major service providers, apart from Lexis-Nexis are as listed below.

Butterworths   2–9
Butterworths has made available a variety of databases through the Butterworths LEXIS direct service. The service combines access to both Butterworths services and Lexis-Nexis Professional. However, alternative direct access to the Lexis database remains available. The Butterworths databases include *All England Direct*. This makes available the full text of the *All England Law Reports* from 1936. *Legislation Direct* provides access to the full, amended text of all Acts and Statutory Instruments of general application in England and Wales, and *Halsbury's Laws Direct* is an online version of *Halsbury's Laws of England*. A current awareness service includes a legal news feature, a web journal and a number of subsidiary databases including *Is it in Force?* Butterworths also produce a number of CD-ROMs. The text of *Company Law Cases* for example is included in their *Corporate*

Law Service. Further details can be obtained from the Butterworths home page (at **www.butterworths.co.uk**)

2–10   Context

Context initially specialised in the provision of the JUSTIS range of CD-ROMs, although many of its databases are available online through its JUSTIS.com service (at **www.justis.com**). JUSTIS.com provides access to the full text of the *Law Reports* from 1865, known as the *Electronic Law Reports*, while *Weekly Law* provides access to the *Weekly Law Reports* from 1953. Legislation is also available in the form of *JUSTIS UK Statutes*, which offers the full text of statutes since 1235, with links to amended and amending legislation. *UK Statutory Instruments* provides access to statutory instruments from 1987. *JUSTIS Celex* also makes available the content of the European Union's legislation and case law database. Details of the full range of CD-ROMs and a link to the JUSTIS.com service can be found on the Context home page (at **www.context.co.uk**).

2–11   Lawtel

Lawtel is essentially a digest service, making available summaries of developments in legislation and case law along with a daily update which can be sent as an email. The summaries of cases cover a wide range of courts and tribunals and the major law reports from 1980. A particularly useful feature of the service is a legislation database that enables repeals, commencements and amendments to be traced (though the text is not available). Approximately 50 legal and non-legal journals are also indexed. Further details can be found on the Lawtel home page (at **www.lawtel.co.uk**).

2–12   Sweet & Maxwell

Sweet & Maxwell's *Current Legal Information* service (CLI), available both on CD-ROM and as an internet service, provides access to a number of databases which make available the *Current Law* citators in electronic form, along with the *Legal Journals Index* and the *Financial Journals Index*. The CLI databases provide a valuable means of tracing cases and changes to legislation, along with access to the electronic version of the major indexes to U.K. law journals. The databases also appear in a repackaged form as part of the Westlaw UK service. Sweet & Maxwell offer some alerting services free of charge. Further information is available from the Sweet & Maxwell home page (at **www.sweetandmaxwell.co.uk**).

2–13   Westlaw UK

Westlaw UK was launched in 2000 as a subsidiary element of the Westlaw service which has long provided access to United States legislation and case law. Westlaw has joined with Sweet & Maxwell in providing the service. It brings together access to the law reports published by Sweet & Maxwell (in addition to the *Law Reports*), and includes a legislation database covering England and Wales, the *Current Legal Information* databases and the full text of some Sweet & Maxwell law journals. Details are available from the Westlaw UK home page (at **www.westlaw.co.uk**).

2–14   DATABASE SEARCHING

When a database of full text or bibliographic data is constructed, all uses of a word are automatically indexed and tagged according to their place in the document. Words will be

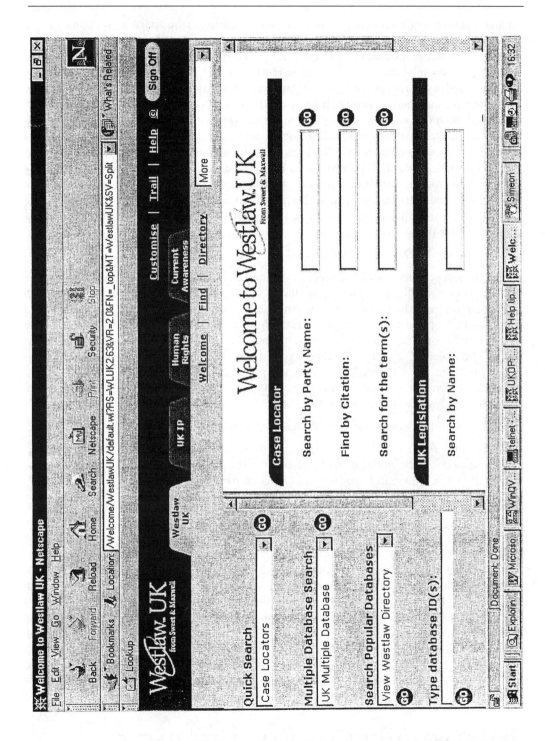

indexed as title words, for example, or as names appearing in the "parties" section of a case report. This will enable searches to be restricted to words in the title or names in the parties section or "field" of the database. If a name, *e.g.* "Hart", is tagged as the name of a party to a case, all cases in which someone called Hart is one of the parties will be listed in the computer index used for party names. If you search for Hart as the party to a case, the name you entered is matched against the database indexes and the relevant documents retrieved. The database index works at this level in much the same way as the index to this book, and the database search software is performing an operation that is equivalent to looking up a word in the index and seeing which pages contain relevant information.

This indexing of words makes so-called Boolean searching a powerful way of retrieving information from a database. Suppose, as in **2–2**, you want to search a bibliographic database in order to find journal references relevant to the issue of provocation as a defence and you are particularly interested in linking the issue to domestic violence against women. Enter the words

Provocation AND domestic violence

in the subject search area of the search page and click the "search" or "go" button. The search software will now retrieve all index entries that are linked to both the term "provocation" and the term "domestic violence". The significance of the "AND" (one of the "Boolean operators") is that it requests this linking of index entries to be made. The result is a list of references which contain both the word "provocation" and the words "domestic violence". In many databases you need to use quotation marks to indicate that you wish "domestic violence" to treated as a phrase.

Another significant Boolean operator is "OR", which acts as a request to group the index entries for two different words. Using

Battered women OR domestic violence

will widen the scope to the references found to include those using battered women, but perhaps not domestic violence. A search putting the previous two together is possible for most databases. The search words would be constructed as:

Provocation AND (domestic violence OR battered women).

Truncation is another useful search feature. Where truncation is employed

Tax*

searches the index entries for other words beginning "tax", including tax, taxes, taxation—and taxi. The truncation symbol varies between databases, so it is worth checking the help pages for the appropriate symbol.

In general, Boolean searches are worth using in a database search as a way of refining the accuracy and scope of a search. Remember, no single search is necessarily comprehensive. It is advisable to reconsider your search words and re-edit them as you read your search results and find, perhaps, much more than you had anticipated, or, indeed, much less. Subject searching for cases is considered at greater length in **7–8** and searching for legislation is discussed in **7–20**.

2–15   FREE SOURCES ON THE INTERNET

The primary sources of law, the judgments made in the courts and the statute law made by the United Kindom's various legislative bodies, are not the property of the legal publishers and database providers listed above. The BAILII (British and Irish Legal Information Institute) website (at **www.bailii.org**) has provided a significant boost to the freeing of the online sources of law by bringing together the publicly available text of U.K. and Irish judgments and legislation on a single website. The site is an extension of the AUSTLII (Australasian Legal Information Institute) website. The site provides access to recent House of Lords Decisions, Court of Appeal and High Court decisions, United Kingdom Employment Appeal Tribunal Decisions, and United Kingdom Social Security and Child Support Commissioner's Opinions. The legislation available at the HMSO site is also included.

The HMSO website itself is another important source of free primary legal material. United Kingdom Acts of Parliament from 1988 are available from the site (at **www.hmso.gov.uk**) along with Statutory Instruments from 1987. Links are also available for Scotland, Northern Ireland and Wales legislation. In addition, the site guides you to the House of Lords judgments that are available directly from the United Kingdom Parliament site (at **www.parliament.the-stationery-office.co.uk**). The judgments are available from 1996. Other key websites are those that bring together primary material from the European Union, and other international organisations. These are noted in Chapters 11 and 12. Further information on finding government or official publications is found in Chapter 6.

Both BAILII and the HMSO sites provide links to full-text material but, in addition, they also provide the possibility of keyword searching using web search engines specific to their sites. These search engines work in the same way as the general internet search engines mentioned in **2–4** above. They allow keyword searches on all the pages held on the website, placing links to the pages which featured your search words most prominently at the top of the results page. As noted in 2–4, the results produced by this kind of relevance ranking can be surprising. For example, if you use the term "Northern Ireland" when searching for Northern Ireland Statutory Rules on the HMSO site you find that the search results highlight legislation in which the words "Northern Ireland" appear most often. As a result, the Northern Ireland Act 1998 will feature near the top of the results list. Where the search engine on a website allows Boolean searching, as is the case for BAILII and the HMSO websites, this can help improve your search. When using web search engines, it is advisable to check the help screens to confirm how to search for a phrase, or how to deal with plurals.

It should be remembered that BAILII and HMSO in particular are collections of documents placed on a web server. They are not online databases. This is a restricted service and means that they do not provide the full searching facilities offered by the commercial databases. Other "value added" features associated with commercial databases are also missing. For example, there are no hypertext links placed within the text of the source documents. More importantly, neither are there the added headnotes and case summaries that are found in the commercially published law reports. It is only the commercial information providers that offer the amended text of legislation or the means to trace amendments and repeals.

The availability of free information from a current law database could become a reality however with the launch of the much postponed Statute Law Database, in preparation from the Lord Chancellor's Department. The database is designed to combine the ability to search for the current state of primary legislation with an ability to discover the amended state of that legislation at any date from February 1991 onwards. The Statutory Publications Office within the Lord Chancellor's Department is currently exploring ways in which the database might be made available. Database preparation should be

British and Irish Legal Information Institute

Comprehensive Access to Freely Available British and Irish Public Legal Information

Find | any of these words ▼ | in | BAILII Databases ▼ |

| | Search |

Tip: To get more control over which BAILII databases you are searching, click on the [Full Search Form] link below.

[Search Help] [**Full Search Form**]

BAILII Cases & Legislation

- England and Wales
- Ireland
- Northern Ireland
- Scotland
- United Kingdom

World Law

- England and Wales
- Ireland
- Northern Ireland
- Scotland
- United Kingdom

Recent Cases & Other Announcements

Last updated 14 April 2001

- Scandecor Developments AB v. Scandecor Marketing AV and Others and One Other Action [2001] UKHL 21 (4th April, 2001)
- International Power Plc v. Healy and Others, Formerly National Power v. Feldon and Others and National Grid Company Plc v. Mayes and Others [2001] UKHL 20 (4th April, 2001)
- Eastbourne Town Radio Cars Association v. Commissioners of Customs & Excise [2001] UKHL 19 (4th April, 2001)
- Amoco (UK) Exploration Company etc. and Others v. Teesside Gas Transportation Ltd and v. Imperial Chemical Industries Plc and others (Consolidated Appeals) [2001] UKHL 18 (4th April, 2001)

- **Past Recent Announcements**

About BAILII
Feedback - Who's Who - Contact
Details - Technical Infrastructure -
Photos - Citing cases on BAILII -
Statistics - Copyright Policy -
Disclaimers - Privacy Policy

Help
Searching Help - Case Law Help -
Legislation Help

BAILII Support
People who have Helped -
Grants

---

completed in 2001 and you are advised to consult the Lord Chancellor's Department website (at **www.open.gov.uk/lcd**) for further developments.

INTERNET GATEWAYS

2–16

One way of discovering the range of legal information available on the web, and also of keeping up to date, is to use an internet gateway or "portal". This is a single website that brings together links to the full range of material highlighted in this chapter and in the references found throughout the book. For United Kingdom law three valuable sites providing links to legal information are Sarah Carter's Lawlinks site on the University of Kent's web pages (at **library.ukc.ac.uk/library/lawlinks**), the Delia Venables site (at **www.venables.co.uk**) and David Swarbrick's site (at **www.swarb.co.uk**).

The websites of many of the university law schools and law libraries offer additional starting points for United Kingdom law. The Faculty of Law at Cambridge (at **www.law.cam.ac.uk**) provides an example of a site with a helpful listing of resources. The NISS Information gateway provides a full listing of all the UK academic sites (at **www.niss.ac.uk**), along with links to publishers and book shops which provide a good starting point for identifying wider resources. Legal material is accessible via the more general UK academic listings provided by the BUBL Information Service (at **bubl.ac.uk**) which links to websites by subject, and the SOSIG Social Science Information Gateway (at **sosig.ac.uk**), which concentrates on evaluating and providing links to a selection of full-text resources.

Going beyond U.K. sources, the U.S. Findlaw site (at **www.findlaw.com**) is a valuable starting point for International as well as U.S. law and the law of individual countries (other sources for International law are identified in chapter 12). Two sites which bring together legal information with a strong slant towards sources relevant to U.S. law are Law.com (at **law.com**) and Hieros Gamos (at **www.hg.org**)

WHEN TO USE PRINT SOURCES

2–17

Compelling as the reasons are for using electronic sources of information in preference to print sources, it should not be assumed that the electronic source is always better. For some tasks, such as checking a citation when the name and year of a case are already known to you, a print source can be quicker and easier to use. In this case, a fast, accurate result can be achieved by using the *Current Law Case Citator* (see **3–14**). The full text of an Act of Parliament, or a House of Lords judgment may run to many pages. Remember, the typeface and layout of the printed versions, combined with the ability to scan and skip easily through the text, can make the printed publication much easier both to read and to handle; especially when the alternative is a stack of pages gathered from a computer printer. There is also a significant time investment in getting to grips with either a CD-ROM or an online source of information. The layout of the web pages needs to be mastered, as does the search software associated with database searching. Of course, you must also have access to a networked computer, or a computer with a CD-ROM before you can even begin. This is not always possible. In addition, you need to obtain usernames and passwords if you wish to use online commercial databases, as noted in **2–6**. These factors have to be weighed against the time taken to use a print source.

As a library user, you will also be faced with a limited choice of available online and

LAWLINKS - Legal information on the internet   http://library.ukc.ac.uk/library/lawlinks/

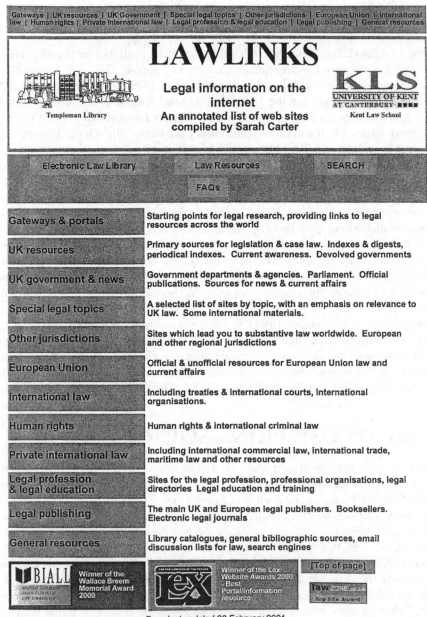

Gateways | UK resources | UK Government | Special legal topics | Other jurisdictions | European Union | International law | Human rights | Private international law | Legal profession & legal education | Legal publishing | General resources

LAWLINKS

Legal information on the internet
An annotated list of web sites compiled by Sarah Carter

Templeman Library

KLS
UNIVERSITY OF KENT
AT CANTERBURY
Kent Law School

Electronic Law Library	Law Resources	SEARCH
	FAQs	

Gateways & portals	Starting points for legal research, providing links to legal resources across the world
UK resources	Primary sources for legislation & case law. Indexes & digests, periodical indexes. Current awareness. Devolved governments
UK government & news	Government departments & agencies. Parliament. Official publications. Sources for news & current affairs
Special legal topics	A selected list of sites by topic, with an emphasis on relevance to UK law. Some international materials.
Other jurisdictions	Sites which lead you to substantive law worldwide. European and other regional jurisdictions
European Union	Official & unofficial resources for European Union law and current affairs
International law	Including treaties & international courts, international organisations.
Human rights	Human rights & international criminal law
Private international law	Including international commercial law, international trade, maritime law and other resources
Legal profession & legal education	Sites for the legal profession, professional organisations, legal directories Legal education and training
Legal publishing	The main UK and European legal publishers. Booksellers. Electronic legal journals
General resources	Library catalogues, general bibliographic sources, email discussion lists for law, search engines

BIALL
BRITISH AND IRISH
ASSOCIATION OF
LAW LIBRARIES
Winner of the Wallace Breem Memorial Award 2000

lex
FOR THE LAWYERS OF THE FUTURE
Winner of the Lex Website Awards 2000 - Best Portal/information resource

[Top of page]

lawZONE.co.uk
Top Site Award

Page last updated 28 February 2001
Feedback: lawlinks-mail@ukc.ac.uk
Editor: Sarah Carter
s.h.carter@ukc.ac.uk

CD-ROM sources. Just as the book and journal coverage of a library is limited by the funds available, so too is access to online and CD-ROM subscription services. Very few libraries have access to anything approaching the full range of services. Where both print and electronic services are available the choice generally depends on the particular resources available, the task you have in mind and, of course, your own personal preferences.

Remember too, that some of the most significant legal resources are still found only in print form. The student textbooks and research monographs, which make up much of a library collection, are currently available solely in print, as are the majority of the authoritative practitioner texts. Most of the journal literature in law is also available only in print, though this is changing as some publishers are providing online access to their journal titles (see **5–2**).

COMBINING PRINT AND ELECTRONIC SOURCES

2–18

It is important to place electronic resources in the wider context of your legal study or research. Electronic resources are an important part of the resources available to you, but you need to learn how to make use of these alongside printed resources. It is not simply the case that "electronic" means "modern" and "paper" means "old-fashioned". Bear in mind that a student textbook usually provides your best starting point when you are new to a subject area. If you wish to find out about the impact of the Human Rights Act 1998 on statutory interpretation, for example, you need to clarify the basic issues. This is often best achieved with the help of a textbook and some quality time to think about the core issues. You will find no shortage of textbooks in this area. Books published as "cases and materials" will offer a valuable quick reference as they contain extracts from leading cases and statute law. Only after you have looked at the textbook material will it probably make sense to go online using an index such as the *Legal Journals Index*. You can then search for references to journal articles that have discussed and developed the issues you have identified in your basic preparation. Online or CD-ROM access to case law might have its place as you search for judgments that have cited what you now know to be the key cases. Having traced journal articles and cases online or on CD-ROM, you may finally need to return to print sources and use the library catalogue to locate particular journals or law reports on the library shelves.

To make the best use of a law library you must learn how to move comfortably between electronic and print resources. The ability to do so will result in better time management and better coverage of the material. The remaining chapters of this book, which place electronic resources beside those in print, are designed to enable you to switch research techniques as and when appropriate.

$\boxed{3}$ Law Reports

INTRODUCTION

Law reports are one of the basic (or "primary") sources of English law. Traditionally, the common law has developed through the practical reasoning of the judges. This is based on the particular facts of the case in question, social forces and previous judicial reasoning when it has a bearing on the case being heard. Legal principles stated in earlier decisions are given effect in later cases by the operation of the doctrine of precedent, which is described in detail in Glanville Williams, *Learning the Law*, chap. 6. The successful development of the common law depends largely upon the production of reliable law reports which carry not only the facts, issues and decision but also, most importantly, the legal principles upon which the judgment is made. Currently, the judiciary spend most of their court time considering the scope and application of particular Acts of Parliament.

Only a very small proportion of cases decided by the courts are reported in print. A case is selected for reporting if it raises a point of legal significance. Just because a case is widely reported in the media, it does not follow that it will appear in law reports.

Judges, to a greater or lesser extent, follow or are influenced by their own previous decisions and those of colleagues and predecessors. Throughout your legal training and practice you will make constant use of law reports. Hence, a thorough working knowledge of them is essential. Glanville Williams (*Learning the Law* (11th ed.), p. 32) offered the following advice to students of law:

> "The great disadvantage of confining oneself to textbooks and lecture notes is that it means taking all one's law at second hand. The law of England is contained in statutes and judicial decisions; what the textbook writer thinks is not, in itself, law. He may have misinterpreted the authorities, and the reader who goes to them goes to the fountainhead. Besides familiarising himself with the law reports and statute book, the lawyer-to-be should get to know his way about the library as a whole, together with its apparatus of catalogues and books of reference."

THE HISTORY OF LAW REPORTS

Law reports have existed, in one form or another, since the reign of Edward I. These very early law reports are known as the *Year Books*. If you wish to see a copy, reprints of a number of these *Year Books* are available in the series of publications published by the Selden Society, in the Rolls Series and in facsimile reprints issued by Professional Books.

After the *Year Books* had ceased, collections of law reports published privately by individuals began to appear. These reports, the first of which were published in 1571, were normally referred to by the name of the reporter or compiler. For this reason, they are collectively referred to as the *Nominate Reports* and they vary considerably in accuracy and reliability (Glanville Williams, *Learning the Law* (11th ed.), p. 35). Few libraries will have a complete collection of these old reports and if you do obtain a copy, you may find that the antiquated print makes it difficult to read. Fortunately, the great majority of these *Nominate Reports* can be found in at least one of the three reprint series, called the *English Reports*, the *Revised Reports* and the *All England Law Reports Reprint*. The most comprehensive of the three series is the *English Reports*, which is examined in detail later in the chapter (para. **3–10**).

In 1865, a body called the Incorporated Council of Law Reporting commenced publication of the *Law Reports*, a single series of reports covering all the major courts. These reports were rapidly accepted by the legal profession as the most authoritative version of law reports and, as a result, most of the earlier series published by individuals ceased publication in 1865 or soon after. Judgments in the *Law Reports* have been checked by the relevant judges before publication and are cited in court in preference to any other series. The *Law Reports* series is described in more detail in **3–8**.

Today, there are over 50 different series of law reports for England and Wales. The *Weekly Law Reports* and the *All England Law Reports*, like the *Law Reports*, cover a wide range of topics and are aimed at the lawyer in general practice. There are also a large number of law reports which cover a specialised area of the law, such as the *Criminal Appeal Reports* and the *Road Traffic Reports*.

A case may be reported in more than one series of law reports. For example, a short report may appear in *The Times* newspaper (under the heading "Law Report") a day or so after the judgment is given. A summary or a full report may be published in some of the weekly legal journals, such as the *New Law Journal* and the *Solicitors Journal*, or a case note may discuss the significance of the new judgment. Several months later, the case may be published in one or both of the two general series of law reports which appear weekly, the *All England Law Reports* and the *Weekly Law Reports*, and in specialist law reports and journals (*e.g. Tax Cases*, the *Criminal Law Review*). Some time later, a final, authoritative version checked by the judges concerned may be published in the *Law Reports*. Thus, if your library does not hold the series of law reports given in the reference you have, it is worth checking whether the case is reported elsewhere (see **3–13**).

A significant development in recent years has been the availability of "unreported" judgments online. These contain the full text of judgments, but not the case summaries, headnotes, etc. which are provided by a law report (see **3–6**). From 1996 onwards unreported judgments have been available free as various courts have placed transcripts of judgments directly on the internet. These unreported judgments are likely to play an increasingly important role as a source of law. However, there are no signs that they will displace conventional law reports. Sources of unreported judgments are described in **3–12**.

3–3 CITATION OF LAW REPORTS

Lawyers often use abbreviations when referring to the sources where a report of a case can be found. These can appear confusing at first, but constant use will rapidly make you familiar with the meaning of most of the abbreviations used. References to cases (called *citations*) are structured as shown in the following example:

Giles v. Thompson[1] [1993][2] 2[3] W.L.R.[4] 908[5].

[1] the names of the parties involved in the case;

[2] the year in which the case is reported. Square brackets indicate that the date is an essential part of the citation. Some series of law reports number the volumes serially from year to year, so the reference is sufficient even if the year is omitted. Round brackets are used if the date is not essential but merely an aid;

[3] the volume number, *i.e.* the second volume published in 1993. Where only one volume is published in a year, the volume number is omitted unless it is essential for finding the correct volume;

[4] the abbreviation for the name of the law report or journal;

[5] the page number on which the case begins.

Thus, in this example, the case of *Giles* v. *Thompson* will be found in the 1993 volumes of the *Weekly Law Reports* (abbreviated to W.L.R.). There are three volumes of the *Weekly Law Reports* containing the cases reported in 1993. The case referred to will be found in the second volume, at page 908.

If you wish to draw attention to a particular phrase or section in the judgment, you should write out the citation for the case, followed by "at" and the page number where the section or phrase is printed, hence:

Giles v. Thompson [1993] 2 W.L.R. 908 at 910.

NEUTRAL CITATIONS 3-4

Since 2001 the High Court and Court of Appeal have adopted a neutral, or common, form of citation for all cases. These "neutral" citations do not distinguish between print and online media and are independent of any of the published law reports. This form of citation has been adopted in order to make it easier to cite and to trace unreported judgments. The neutral form of citation can be seen in the following example:

R. (Ebrahim) v. Feltham Magistrates Court [2001] EWHC Admin 130.

EWHC Admin is the standard abbreviation for the High Court (Administrative Division) for England and Wales. The number 130, placed without brackets after EWHC Admin, tells you that the judgment is judgment number 130 for 2001.

Other abbreviations are EWCA Civ for the Court of Appeal (Civil Division) and EWCA Crim for the Court of Appeal (Criminal Division).

Rather than give page references, these citations use numbers in square brackets which indicate the paragraphs of a judgment, *e.g.*

R. (Ebrahim) v. Feltham Magistrates Court [2001] EWHC Admin 130 at [40]–[42].

When judgments are given in the High Court or Court of Appeal the neutral form of citation is always given at least once, ahead of any other citations. *R. (Ebrahim)* v. *Feltham Magistrates Court* has been reported in the *All England Law Reports*, so the case would be cited as follows:

R. (Ebrahim) v. Feltham Magistrates Court [2001] EWHC Admin 130 at [40]–[43]; [2001] All ER 831 at 841.

The House of Lords adopted a similar form of neutral citation in 2001. The 2001 case *Johnson (AP) v. Unisys Limited*, for example, is cited using the neutral system as:

Johnson (AP) v. Unisys Limited [2001] UKHL 13.

UKHL is the abbreviation for the House of Lords and the number 13, placed without brackets after UKHL, tells you that the judgment is judgment number 13 for 2001. Any numbers in square brackets at the end of the citation represent paragraph numbers, as they do for Court of Appeal and High Court cases.

3–5 HOW TO FIND THE MEANING OF ABBREVIATIONS

If you are faced with an abbreviation for a law report or journal which you do not recognise, look in any of the following works.

> D. Raistrick, *Index to Legal Citations and Abbreviations*;
> *Sweet & Maxwell's Guide to Law Reports and Statutes*;
> *Current Law*;
> *The Digest* (near the front of Vol. 1(1) and the *Cumulative Supplement*);
> *Halsbury's Laws of England* (4th ed., Vol. 1(1) reissue, pp. 15–41);
> *Osborn's Concise Law Dictionary*;
> *Manual of Legal Citations* (Pts I and II);
> *Legal Journals Index* (near the front of any issue).

The simplest source for the beginner is the list which is printed in each issue of *Current Law*. If you do not find the answer here, look in one of the alternative sources. A list of some of the most commonly used abbreviations will be found in Appendix I of this book.

3–6 FORMAT OF LAW REPORTS

Page 29 gives a typical example of the first page of a law report. The citation is *Cleveland Petroleum Co. Ltd* v. *Dartstone Ltd. and Another* [1969] 1 All E.R. 201. Several key points in the illustration are numbered.

1. The names of the parties. In a civil case, the name of the plaintiff (the person bringing the action) comes first, followed by the name of the defendant. The small letter "v." between the names is an abbreviation of the Latin "versus" but when speaking of a civil case, you say "*and*" not "*versus*". A criminal case, on the other hand, might appear as *R.* v. *Smith*. R. is the abbreviated form for the Latin words *Rex* (king) or *Regina* (queen). The charge against Smith, the accused, is brought on behalf of the Crown and this case would be said as "*the Crown against Smith*".
2. The name of the court in which the case was heard, the names of the judges (M.R.: Master of the Rolls; L.JJ.: Lords Justices) and the date on which the case was heard.
3. A summary of the main legal issues of the case. You are advised not to rely on this, as it is not necessarily complete or accurate.

First Page of a Law Report from the All England Law Reports Series

C.A.   CLEVELAND PETROLEUM v. DARTSTONE (LORD DENNING, M.R.)   **201**

A

CLEVELAND PETROLEUM CO., LTD. v. DARTSTONE, LTD. AND ANOTHER. (1)

[COURT OF APPEAL, CIVIL DIVISION (Lord Denning, M.R., Russell and Salmon, L.JJ.), November 26, 1968.] (2)

B   *Trade—Restraint of trade—Agreement—Petrol filling station—Solus agreement—Lease by garage owner to petrol supplier—Underlease to company to operate service station—Covenant in underlease for exclusive sale of supplier's products—Assignment of underlease by licence granted by supplier—Interim injunction to restrain breach of covenant.* (3)

C   S. the owner in fee simple of a garage, leased the premises to the plaintiffs for 25 years from 1st July 1960. The plaintiffs granted an underlease to C.O.S.S., Ltd., by which C.O.S.S., Ltd., covenanted, inter alia, to carry on the business of a petrol filling station at all times and not to sell or distribute motor fuels other than those supplied by the plaintiffs. After several assignments the underlease was assigned to the defendants who undertook to observe and perform the covenants. The defendants thereupon challenged the validity of the ties. The plaintiffs issued a writ claiming an injunction restraining the defendants from breaking this covenant. The plaintiffs obtained an interim injunction against which the defendants appealed. (4)

D

E   **Held:** the appeal would be dismissed, the tie was valid and not an unreasonable restraint of trade because the defendants, not having been in possession previously, took possession of the premises under a lease and entered into a restrictive covenant knowing about such covenant, and thereby bound themselves to it (see p. 203, letters C, F and G, post).

Dicta in *Esso Petroleum Co., Ltd.* v. *Harper's Garage (Stourport), Ltd.* ([1967] 1 All E.R. at pp. 707, 714, and 724, 725) applied.

Appeal dismissed. (5)

F   [As to agreements in restraint of trade, see 38 HALSBURY'S LAWS (3rd Edn.) 20, para. 13; and for cases on the subject, see 45 DIGEST (Repl.) 443-449, 271-297.] (6)

Case referred to:
Esso Petroleum Co., Ltd. v. *Harper's Garage (Stourport), Ltd.,* [1967] 1 All E.R. 699; [1968] A.C. 269; [1967] 2 W.L.R. 871; Digest (Repl.) Supp. (7)

G   **Interlocutory Appeal.**

This was an appeal by the defendants, Dartstone, Ltd., and James Arthur Gregory, from an order of EVELEIGH, J., dated 1st November 1968, granting an interim injunction restraining the defendants from acting in breach of a covenant contained in an underlease made on 1st July 1960 between the plaintiffs, Cleveland Petroleum Co., Ltd., and County Oak Service Station, Ltd., and assigned to the defendants on 30th August 1968. The facts are set out in the judgment of LORD DENNING, M.R. (8)

H

Raymond Walton, Q.C., and *M. C. B. Buckley* for the defendants. (9)
A. P. Leggatt for the plaintiffs. (10)

I   **LORD DENNING, M.R.:** This case concerns a garage and petrol station called County Oak service station, at Crawley in Sussex. Mr. Sainsbury was the owner in fee simple. On 1st July 1960, there were three separate transactions: First, Mr. Sainsbury granted a lease of the entire premises to the plaintiffs, Cleveland Petroleum Co., Ltd., for 25 years, from 1st July 1960. The plaintiffs paid him £50,000 premium and agreed also to pay a nominal rent of £10 a year. Secondly, the plaintiffs granted an underlease of the premises to a company called County Oak Service Station, Ltd. That company was one in which Mr. Sainsbury had a predominant interest. The underlease was for 25 years, less three days from

4. The headnote, which is a brief statement of the case and the nature of the claim (in a civil case) or the charge (in a criminal case). Again, do not rely on the publisher's précis but instead read the case.
5. The court's ruling is stated, with a summary of reasons.
6. In certain reports, *e.g.* the *All England Law Reports*, the major legal points are cross-referenced to *Halsbury's Laws* and *The Digest*.
7. A list of cases which were referred to during the hearing.
8. A summary of the history of the previous proceedings of the case. The final sentence explains where in the report you can find the details of the facts of the case.
9. The names of the counsel (the barristers) who appeared for the parties. Q.C.s (Queen's Counsel) are senior counsel.
10. The start of the judgment given by Lord Denning M.R.

3–7   RECENT CASES

The law is constantly changing, with new cases being reported daily. Therefore be prepared to consult recent cases. This is essential if you are to remain aware of the most recent developments. The most up-to-date law reports are found in the broadsheet newspapers. *The Times*, the *Financial Times*, the *Daily Telegraph* and *The Independent* regularly publish law reports. These newspaper reports appear ahead of the major law report series but, unlike them, do not reproduce the full text of judgments. If you wish to look at the text of a recent judgment before it has been reported, turn to the various sources of "unreported" judgments, described in **3–11**. Recent *reported* cases are found in the following ways:

Electronic
Some, though not all, newspaper law reports are available from the website of the relevant newspaper. For example, law reports from *The Times* are found at the newspaper's website (at **www.thetimes.co.uk**), although some searching may be required at the site. In common with other newspapers, *The Times* places a great deal of information on its home page. To find the law reports, follow the link to the newspaper edition and then to the law section. The current week's reports are located within the law section along with a link to an archive which contains the last three months of reports. The *Daily Telegraph* (at **www.telegraph.co.uk**) is another online source for recent reports through a link to reports provided by Westlaw UK. Reports are updated every Tuesday. Thereafter they are removed. Neither *The Independent* nor the *Financial Times* provides access to law reports from its website, though the law reports published by *The Independent* are available on the CD-ROM version of the newspaper. Your library may hold a number of the major newspapers in CD-ROM form and in the case of *The Times*, *The Independent* and the *Daily Telegraph*, these have the advantage of providing a conveniently searchable archive of law reports. Remember that the CD-ROM version of the newspaper your library holds may be up to three months behind the current print issue, so be prepared to use alternative research tools if your search is focused on the very latest cases.

The *All England Law Reports* and the *Weekly Law Reports* and some of the other specialist series also provide access to recent cases. If you want to find a recent case in the *All England Law Reports*, for example, look for it by logging on to the Butterworths All England Direct service (at **www.butterworths.co.uk**). Then select *All England Law Reports*. You find a contents listing which arranges the most recent cases by year and volume, placing them in the order in which they appear in the printed reports. Similarly, access to the *Weekly Law Reports* from Context's Justis.com service (at **www.justis.com**) enables you to view the contents of the current year of the reports, listing the contents of the printed volumes in reverse order, 3, then 2 and 1. The most recent cases in the database are listed first for each volume. You need to be aware that these databases do not offer access to the very latest reports appearing in the *All England Law Reports* and the *Weekly Law Reports*. The weekly print issues of the *All England Law Reports* publish reports up to three weeks ahead of their appearance in the All England Direct database. The Justis.com versions of the *Weekly Law Reports* can be two to three months behind their printed counterparts. There is also a delay following print publication of between two and three months before the text of an *All England Law Report* or a *Weekly Law Report* is available on the Lexis English case law database (see **2–7**).

Specialist law report series are available from all the online database providers. Justis.com, for example, provides access to the *Family Law Reports*, the *Industrial Cases Reports* and *Lloyd's Law Reports*, though your library needs a separate subscription for each of them. Lexis-Nexis (**2–7**) and Westlaw UK (**2–13**) provide access to a number of titles. Westlaw UK, for example, includes the *Common Market Law Reports* and the *European Human Rights Law Reports* in its database coverage. Cases are sometimes reported in these specialist series ahead of the *All England Law Reports* and the *Weekly Law Reports*. As noted in Chapter 2, do check precisely which databases are available in your library. Bear in mind that, as with the *All England Law Reports* and the *Weekly Law Reports*, it would be wrong to assume that the text of a report from one of these specialist series will appear online before, or even at the same time as, the print version. The print source may be more recent than the electronic report.

A wide range of the specialist law report series is also available in CD-ROM form, from Butterworths (at **www.butterworths.co.uk**) and Context (at **www.context.co.uk**) in particular. These CD-ROMs tend to be updated on a quarterly basis, so the reports you are looking at will be less up to date than either the print or the online sources. They may be up to three months behind those available in print.

Print
The most up-to-date law reports available in print remain those found in the broadsheet newspapers. Your library may keep the daily copies (perhaps bound up into large volumes), or the law librarian may cut the law reports out of the newspaper and file them in folders. Older newspapers, *The Times* in particular, are available on microfilm. In addition many law libraries have a subscription to a separately printed version of the law reports published in *The Times*, kept in folders as *The Times Law Reports*.

If you wish to find a report of a case in the printed *All England Law Reports* or *the Weekly Law Reports* (or indeed most other series of law reports), which has been published in the last few months, you will not find a bound volume on the shelves but a series of paper covered parts, or issues. However, your reference (citation) will make it appear that you are looking for a bound volume. So how do you find it? Page 33 shows the front cover of a weekly issue of the *All England Law Reports*. You will find, at the top of the front cover, the date of this issue, the part (or issue) number, and the year, volume and page numbers covered by this issue, *i.e.*:

[2001] 1 All ER 865–960   Part 11   14 March 2001

This indicates that this issue (Part 11) will eventually form pages 865–960 of the first bound volume of the *All England Law Reports* for 2001. Also on the front cover appears a list of all the cases reported in that part, showing the page number on which each report begins.

Many other law reports are published in a number of parts during the current year. At the end of the year, these are replaced by a bound volume or volumes. Every part will indicate on its cover the volume and pages in the bound volume where it will finally appear.

The *Weekly Law Reports* is a series (which commenced in 1953) that you will consult frequently. The arrangement of its weekly print issues is rather confusing. Three bound volumes are produced each year, and each weekly issue contains some cases which will eventually appear in Volume 1 of the bound volumes for that year, and some cases which will subsequently appear in either Volume 2 or Volume 3. The front cover of each issue shows the contents and the volume in which these pages will eventually appear. For example on the front cover shown on page 34, is printed:

Part 8
2 March 2001
[2001] 1 W.L.R. 385–409
[2001] 2 W.L.R. 457–592

Part 8 therefore contains pages 385–409 of what will eventually form Volume 1 of the *Weekly Law Reports* for 2001, and pages 457–592 of Volume 2. A sheet of green paper is inserted in the issue to mark the division between the pages destined for Volume 1 and those forming part of Volume 2. A list of all the cases included in the part is printed on the front cover, and the volume and page number for each case is shown. You may wonder why the publishers (the Incorporated Council of Law Reporting, who also publish the *Law Reports*) have chosen this method of publishing the issues. The reason is that the cases in Volumes 2 and 3 will be republished, after being checked by the judges and with a summary of counsel's arguments, in the *Law Reports*. Those cases appearing in Volume 1, however, will not reappear in the *Law Reports*.

You may find that the latest issue of each journal and law reports series will be displayed in a separate area of the library. The remainder of the issues for the current year may also be filed in this area, or they may be in a box on the shelves alongside the bound volumes.

3–8 THE LAW REPORTS SERIES

The publication known as the *Law Reports*, which commenced publication in 1865, was originally published in 11 series, each covering a different court. The rationalisation of the court structure since that time has reduced this to four series. These are:

Appeal Cases (abbreviated to A.C.);
Chancery Division (Ch.);
Queen's Bench Division (Q.B.);
Family Division (Fam.).

The *Law Reports* are available online from Westlaw UK (at **www.westlaw.co.uk),** Lexis-Nexis Professional (at **web.lexis-nexis.com/professional**) and Justis.com from Context (at **www.justis.com**). Context also provide the *Law Reports* on CD-ROM. In the case of Lexis-Nexis, coverage is from 1945. Justis.com and Westlaw UK offer full historical coverage.

[2001] 1 All ER 8051950
Part 11
14 March 2001

The
All England
Law Reports

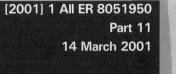

THE WEEKLY LAW REPORTS

[2001] 1 WLR 385–409
[2001] 2 WLR 457–592

2 March 2001

Part 8

Editor ROBERT WILLIAMS *Barrister*

ICLR

THE INCORPORATED COUNCIL OF **LAW REPORTING**
FOR ENGLAND & WALES

INDEX

Annual subscription **£250** (UK)
£280 (overseas)

Megarry House   119 Chancery Lane   London WC2A 1PP
Tel: 020 7242 6471 Fax: 020 7831 5247
postmaster@iclr.co.uk www.lawreports.co.uk

The printed *Law Reports* are usually arranged on the shelves in the series order noted above. Paper-covered parts are issued monthly and are replaced by bound volumes at the end of the year. The monthly issues of the Chancery Division and Family Division, however, are published within the same paper-covered part, although they are bound as separate series.

The location on the shelves of the various earlier series often reflects their relationship to the present four series, for example, the historical predecessors of the present Queen's Bench Division (called the King's Bench Division when a King is on the throne) were the Court for Crown Cases Reserved, the Court of Common Pleas and the Court of Exchequer. These are therefore usually shelved before the Queen's Bench Division reports (because they are its predecessors) but after the Appeal Cases and Chancery Division reports. The same arrangement is applied with the other three current series (*i.e.* reports of the predecessors of the present courts are filed at the beginning of each series).

The figure on page 36 shows the way in which the *Law Reports* are arranged on the shelves in most libraries. The abbreviations used to denote each series are shown, and also the dates during which each series appeared.

Citations for the *Law Reports* have varied over the years as the system of numbering the reports changed. Until 1891, for example, each volume in the various series had its own individual number, running sequentially through the years. The date in the citation is therefore in round brackets, to show it is not essential to the reference. For the *Law Reports* after 1891, however, the date is in square brackets, since the year must be quoted in order to locate the correct volume. The other slight complication in the citation of the *Law Reports* is the use of the abbreviation L.R. (for *Law Reports*) which is placed before the volume number in citations of *Law Reports* before 1875, *e.g. Rylands* v. *Fletcher* (1868) L.R. 3 H.L. 330.

The figure on page 36 clarifies the use of abbreviations and brackets for the *Law Reports*. It is worth noting, however, that the abbreviation H.L. stands for *Law Reports: English and Irish Appeal Cases* and not, as you might guess, Law Reports: House of Lords.

OLDER LAW REPORTS   3–9

We have concentrated upon the modern series of law reports because these are the reports which you will be using most frequently. However, from time to time you will need to look at older cases, that is, those reported in the first half of the nineteenth century or even several centuries earlier. Reports of older cases can be found in several series: the *English Reports*, *Revised Reports*, the *Law Journal Reports*, the *Law Times Reports* and the *All England Law Reports Reprint* series. We shall now look at some of these series in more detail.

The reports published privately by individuals (and known as the *Nominate Reports*) ceased publication around 1865, when the *Law Reports* were first published. If the date of the case you want is before 1865, you are most likely to find it in a series known as the *English Reports*. Many libraries have the *English Reports* in print form. A CD-ROM was launched by JUTASTAT in 2001.

How to Use the English Reports   3–10

If you know the name of the case, look it up in the alphabetical index of the names of cases, printed in Volumes 177–178 of the *English Reports*. Beside the name of the case is printed

Law Reports

TABLE OF THE LAW REPORTS

The mode of citation is given in brackets. In the first, second and third columns, dots (. . .) are put where the number of the volume would appear in the citation. In the fourth column square brackets([ ]) are put where the year would appear in the citation.

1866–1875	1875–1880	1881–1890	1891–present
House of Lords. English and Irish Appeals (L.R. ... H.L.)			
House of Lords. Scotch and Divorce Appeals (L.R. ... H.L.Sc. or L.R. ... H.L.Sc. and Div.) Privy Council Appeals (L.R. ... P.C.)	Appeal Cases (...App.Cas.)	Appeal Cases (...App.Cas.)	Appeal Cases ([ ]) A.C.)
Chancery Appeal Cases (L.R. ... Ch. or Ch. App.) Equity Cases (L.R. ... Eq.)	Chancery Division (...Ch.D.)	Chancery Division (...Ch.D.)	Chancery Division ([ ]) Ch.)
Crown Cases Reserved (L.R. ... C.C., or, ... C.C.R.)	Queen's Bench Division (...Q.B.D.)		
Queen's Bench Cases* (L.R. ... Q.B.)		Queen's Bench Division (...Q.B.D.)	Queen's (or King's) Bench Division ([ ] Q.B. or K.B.)†
Common Pleas Cases (L.R. ... C.P.)	Common Pleas Division (...C.P.D.)		
Exchequer Cases‡ (L.R. ... Ex.)	Exchequer Division (...Ex.D.)		
Admiralty and Ecclesiastical Cases (L.R. ... A. & E.) Probate and Divorce Cases (L.R. ... P. & D.)	Probate Division (...P.D.)	Probate Division (...P.D.)	Probate Division ([ ] P.) Since 1972 Family Division ([ ]Fam.)

* Note that there is also a series called Queen's Bench Reports in the old reports (113–118 E.R.).
† After 1907 this includes cases in the Court of Criminal Appeal, later the Court of Appeal, in place of the previous Court for Crown Cases Reserved.
‡ Note that there is also a series called Exchequer Reports in the old reports (154–156 E.R.).

(Reproduced from G. Williams, *Learning the Law* (11th ed.), p.39.)

the abbreviation for the name of the original nominate reporter, and the volume and page in his reports where the case appeared. The number printed in **bold** type next to this is the volume number in the *English Reports* where the case will be found, and this is followed by the page number in that volume:

> *Daniel* v. *North*[a]   11 East, 372[b]   **103**[c] 1047

[a] name of the case;

[b] volume, name of the original reporter, page number in the original report, *i.e.* the original report of this case appeared in Volume 11 of *East's Reports* p. 372;

[c] the reprint of the report appears in Volume 103 of the *English Reports* at page 1047.

Table of Cases in the English Reports

```
424  DAN (A)        (B) INDEX OF CASES                    (C) .
→ Daniel v. North, 11 East, 372    .      .      .      .      . 103 1047
    —— v. Phillips, 4 T. R. 499    .      .      .      .      . 100 1141
    —— v. Pit, Peake Add. Cas. 238 .     .      .      .      . 170  257
    —— v. Pit, 6 Esp. 74    .      .      .      .      .      . 170  834
    —— v. Purbeck, W. Kel. 97    .      .      .      .      .  25  510
    —— v. Purkis, W. Kel. 97    .      .      .      .      .  25  510
    —— v. Purkurst, 2 Barn. K. B. 214, 220 .   .      .      . 94 457, 461
    —— v. Russell, 14 Ves. Jun. 393 ; 2 Ves. Jun. Supp. 376 . . 33 572 ; 34 1139
    —— v. Skipwith, 2 Bro. C. C. 155 .   .      .      .      .  29   89
    —— v. Sterlin, 1 Freeman, 50    .    .      .      .      .  89   39
    —— v. Thompson, 15 East, 78    .     .      .      .      . 104  774
    —— v. Trotman, 1 Moo. N. S. 123.    .      .      .      .  15  649
    —— v. Turpin, 1 Keble, 124    .      .      .      .      .  83  852
    —— v. Ubley, Jones, W. 137    .      .      .      .      .  82   73
    —— v. Uply, Latch, 9, 39, 134    .   .      .      .      . 82 248, 264, 312
    —— v. Upton, Noy, 80    .     .      .      .      .      .  74 1047
    —— v. Waddington, Cro. Jac. 377.    .      .      .      .  79  322
    —— v. Waddington, 3 Bulstrode, 130   .      .      .      .  81  111
    —— v. Warren, 2 Y. & C. C. C. 290    .      .      .      .  63  127
    —— v. Wilkin, 7 Ex. 429 .     .      .      .      .      . 155 1016
    —— v. Wilkin, 8 Ex. 156 .     .      .      .      .      . 155 1300
    —— v. Wilson, 5 T. R. 1 .     .      .      .      .      . 101    1
  Daniel's Case, 2 Dy. 133 b .    .      .      .      .      .  73  291
    —— Trust, In re, 18 Beav. 309    .   .      .      .      .  52  122
```

You will see that Volume 103 of the *English Reports* has the volumes and names of the *Nominate Reports* which are to be found in that volume printed on the spine. Page 1047 appears in its normal position at the top outer corner of the page whilst the volume and page number of the original report are printed at the inner margin.

Sometimes you may only have a citation (reference) to the original nominate report, *e.g.* 3 Car. & P. (Carrington and Payne); 2 Barn. & Ald. (Barnewall and Alderson). This reference is often printed in an abbreviated form. You do not know the name of the case, so you are unable to look it up in the index to the *English Reports*. Let us suppose, for example, that you have come across a reference to (1809) 11 East 372. Because the date is before 1865, you know that it is likely to be found in the *English Reports*; but you do not know the name of the case. How do you find it? If the name of the report has been abbreviated, *e.g.* 3 Car. & P., you will need to look in Raistrick's *Index to Legal Citations and Abbreviations* or one of the similar reference works (see **3–5**) to find the meaning of the abbreviation. You then turn to the *Chart to the English Reports*. This may be displayed near the *English Reports*, or it may be a slim volume shelved with the *English Reports* themselves. The Chart contains an alphabetical list of the names of all the reporters whose work has been reprinted in the *English Reports*, showing which volume their work appears in. The Chart indicates that Volumes 7 to 11 of *East's Reports* are reprinted in Volume 103 of the *English Reports*. If you open Volume 103 at random, you will see that, at the top of each page (at the *inner* margin) the volume and page numbers of the original report are printed. Find the volume and page reference which most nearly corresponds to your reference. There is no entry at the top of the page for Volume 11 of *East's Reports*, page 372, but there is an entry, at the top inner margin, for page 371. If you look at the figure on page 24, you will see the heading "11 East 371" at the top of the page. There are also numbers printed, in square brackets, in the body of the text. These indicate when the page numbers in the original report changed. For instance, in the original Volume 11 of *East's Reports*, page 371 began with the words "practice, but a specific notice of trial at Monmouth ...". Page 372 began with the case of *Daniel* v. *North*.

3–11   Other Older Law Reports

If the *English Reports* are not available in your library, you may find the case you need reprinted in the *Revised Reports*. The *Revised Reports* has similar coverage to the *English Reports* but is not as comprehensive.

The *All England Law Reports Reprint* series is another useful source for old cases between 1558 and 1935. The cases are reprinted from the reports which originally appeared in the *Law Times Reports*, which commenced in 1843, and from earlier reports. The *Reprint* series contains some 5,000 cases selected principally upon the criterion that they have been referred to in the *All England Law Reports* and in *Halsbury's Laws of England*. There is an index volume containing an alphabetical list of cases and a subject index of the cases included in the reprint.

Chart to the English Reports

8	TABLE OF ENGLISH REPORTS			
Old Reports.	Volume in English Reports.	Abbreviation.	Period covered (approximate).	Series.
Dow & Clark, 1 & 2	6	Dow & Cl.	1827–1832	H.L.
Dowling & Ryland	171	Dowl. & Ry. N.P.	1822–1823	N.P.
Drewry, 1–3	61	Drew.	1852–1859	V.C.
„ 4	62			
Drewry & Smale, 1 & 2	62	Drew & Sm. or Dr. & Sm.	1860–1865	V.C.
Dyer, 1–3	73	Dy.	1513–1582	K.B.
East, 1–6	102			
„ 7–11	103	East.	1801–1812	K.B.
„ 12–16	104			
Eden, 1 & 2	28	Eden.	1757–1766	Ch.
Edwards	165	Edw.	1808–1812	Ecc. Adm. P. & D.
Ellis & Blackburn, 1–3	118			
„ „ 4–7	119	El. & Bl.	1851–1858	K.B.
„ „ 8	120			
Ellis, Blackburn & Ellis	120	El. Bl. & El.	1858	K.B.
Ellis & Ellis, 1	120	El. & El.	1858–1861	K.B.
„ „ 2 & 3	121			
Eq. Cases Abridged, 1	21	Eq. Ca. Abr.	1667–1744	Ch.
„ „ 2	22			
Espinasse, 1–6	170	Esp.	1793–1807	N.P.

Two other series of nineteenth century cases are also referred to regularly: the *Law Journal Reports* and the *Law Times Reports*. The *Law Journal Reports* cover the period 1823–1949. They can be complicated to use because usually two volumes were published each year, both bearing the same volume number. In one volume were printed the cases heard in common law courts, while in the other were printed equity cases. You will need to check both volumes, unless you know whether the case you want is equity or common law. To add to the difficulty, the volume numbering and the method of citation changed during

Sample Page from the English Reports

before ; but they could not agree on the person to be substituted, and therefore the original appointment stood as before.

Per Curiam. Rule absolute.

AMBROSE *against* REES.   Wednesday, June 14th, 1809.   Notice having been given for the trial of a cause at Monmouth, which arose in Glamorganshire, as being in fact the next English county since the st. 27 H. 8, c. 26, s. 4, though Hereford be the common place of trial ; the Court refused to set aside the verdict as for a mis-trial, on motion ; the question being open on the record.

Marryat opposed a rule for setting aside the verdict obtained in this cause, upon the ground of an irregularity in the trial.   The venue was laid in Glamorganshire, and the cause was tried at Monmouth, as the next English county where the King's writ of venire runs (*b*) ; but it was objected that it ought to have been tried at Hereford, according to the general custom that all causes in which the venue is laid in any county in South Wales should be tried at Hereford.   But the rule being that the cause should be tried in the next English county, and Monmouth being in fact the next English county to Glamorganshire, and more conveniently situated for the trial of the cause, there seems no solid ground for impeaching the validity of the trial ; though the practice relied on is easily accounted for by the consideration that Monmouthshire was originally a Welch county, and till it became an English county in the 27th year of Hen. 8, Herefordshire was in fact the next English county to Glamorgan.   And there is no reason for setting aside this verdict on the ground of surprize ; for the defendant had not merely a notice of trial in the next English county, generally, which might have misled him by the notoriety of the **[371]** practice, but a specific notice of trial at Monmouth, to which he made no objection at the time.

Abbott, in support of the rule, relied on the known practice which had always prevailed, as well since as before the Statute 27 H. 8 ; and referred to *Morgan* v. *Morgan* (*a*), where the question arose in 1656, upon an ejectment for lands in Breknock-shire, which was tried at Monmouth ; and afterwards judgment was arrested, on the ground of a mis-trial, as it ought to have been tried in Herefordshire ; for that Monmouthshire was but made an English county by statute within time of memory ; and that trials in the next English county of issues arising in Wales have been time out of mind and at the common law ; so that a place newly made an English county cannot have such a trial.   And he observed, that if this trial were good, all the judgments in causes out of Glamorganshire tried at Hereford have been erroneous.

Lord Ellenborough C.J.   If the question appear on the record, then the defendant cannot apply in this summary manner.   And as he did not object at the time, we shall not relieve him upon motion.

Per Curiam. Rule discharged.

→ **[372]** DANIEL *against* NORTH.   Wednesday, June 14th, 1809.   Where lights had been put out and enjoyed without interruption for above 20 years during the occupation of the opposite premises by a tenant ; that will not conclude the landlord of such opposite premises, without evidence of his knowledge of the fact, which is the foundation of presuming a grant against him ; and consequently will not conclude a succeeding tenant who was in possession under such landlord from building up against such encroaching lights.

[Considered and applied, *Wheaton* v. *Maple* [1893], 3 Ch. 57 ; *Roberts* v. *James*, 1903, 89 L. T. 286.   For *Rugby Charity* v. *Merryweather*, 11 East, 375, n., see *Woodyer* v. *Hadden*, 1813, 5 Taunt. 138 ; *Wood* v. *Veal*, 1822, 5 B. & Ald. 457 ; *Vernon* v. *St. James's, Westminster*, 1880, 16 Ch. D. 457 ; *Bourke* v. *Davis*, 1889, 44 Ch. D. 123.]

The plaintiff declared in case, upon his seisin in fee of a certain messuage or dwelling-house in Stockport, on one side of which there is and was and of right ought to be six windows ; and stated that the defendant wrongfully erected a wall 60 feet high and 50 in length near the said house and windows, and obstructed the light and

(*b*) Vide 1 Term Rep. 313.   (*a*) Hard. 66.

Algorithm designed to show how to look up a case in the English Reports

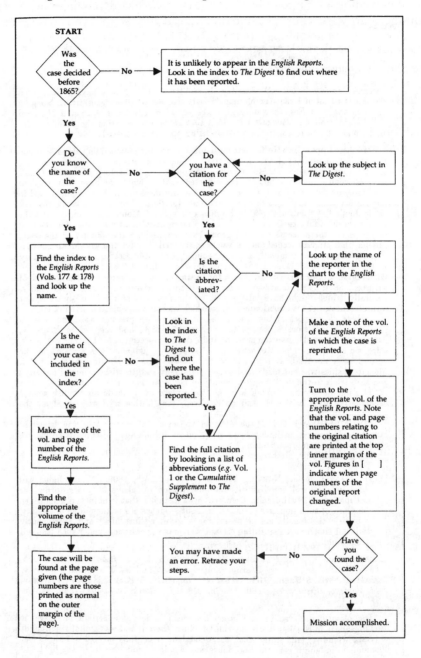

the course of its publication. The first nine volumes (1823–1831) are known as the Old Series (L.J.O.S.). References to the New Series (1833–1949) omit the letters N.S. Citations give the abbreviation for the court in which the case was heard. It is therefore necessary to decide if the court was a court of common law or equity, so that you consult the correct volume. For example, the reference 16 L.J.Q.B. 274 is a reference to Volume 16 of the *Law Journal (New Series)* in the common law volumes (since Queen's Bench was a court of common law), at page 274 of the reports of Queen's Bench. Volume 16 contains law reports from several different courts. Each court's reports have a separate sequence of page numbers. You are looking for page 274 in the sequence of Queen's Bench reports.

The *Law Times Reports* (L.T.) cover the period 1859–1947. Prior to this, the reports were published as part of the journal entitled *Law Times* and these are cited as the *Law Times, Old Series* (L.T.O.S.) which ran from 1843–1860. You may find this Old Series is shelved with the journals, not with the law reports.

UNREPORTED CASES   3–12

Transcripts of judgments made in a very wide range of cases are on the internet, sometimes within hours of the judgment being handed down. Although substantial archives of such transcripts are being created, perhaps the most useful aspect of these databases is the opportunity this gives the law student to find the text of very recent judgments. As noted in **2–2**, where cases have provoked coverage in the newspapers and other media, the availability of judgments on the internet makes it possible for you to examine the legal issues by going directly to the text of a judgment.

This trend towards the public availability of judgments was led by the House of Lords, which made its own judgments available from 1996 on the HMSO Parliament website (at **www.parliament.uk**). As the judgments of the court of final appeal, they are the most influential judgments available free on the internet. The judgments are found in the judicial work and judgments section of the House of Lords site and list the full text of opinions delivered alphabetically by case and year. The search engine for the Parliament site can be limited so that the judgments are the only part of the web site searched. More recently the Privy Council has made its judgments available (at **www.privy-council.org.uk**), providing the full text from 1999 along with a selection of earlier judgments. (The Privy Council complements the role of the House of Lords in its role as the court of final appeal for some Commonwealth countries, the Channel Islands, Isle of Man and United Kingdom overseas territories.)

The Court Service (at **www.courtservice.gov.uk**) provides access to full-text judgments, where the presiding judge concerned feels the text should be made available. The judgments page of the website provides links to the most recent cases. All cases selected for the site from 1999 onwards are on the Court Service Judgments Database. The database allows the judgments to be viewed by date, court, and respondent and a keyword search is available. The link to each judgment displays the first few paragraphs of the judgment. Click an icon at the foot of the page to display the full text. The cases selected come from the Court of Appeal and the High Court and include the Commercial Court of the Queen's Bench Division and the Patents Court of the Chancery Division. Employment Appeals Tribunal cases are also included.

Your university may also have registered for access to the Casetrack database (at **www.casetrack.com**) provided on a commercial basis by Smith Bernal. Smith Bernal is the official reporter to the Court of Appeal and can make a transcript of a judgment available within an hour of the judgment being given. Court of Appeal judgments are available from April 1996, and High Court judgments from July 1998. Cases can be browsed by court and date. Keyword searches can be made on the text of the judgments. Smith Bernal hosts in addition a free archive of Court of Appeal and Crown Office transcripts (at **www.casetrack.com/casebase**). It contains judgments made between 1996 and 1999.

An alternative route to the judgments initially made available in Smith Bernal's Casebase database, along with the judgments selected for internet publication by the Court Service, is provided by BAILII (at **www.bailii.org**) which carries the cases on a single website along with House of Lords and Privy Council judgments. Judgments are listed alphabetically by the name of the first party and keyword searching is available. BAILII also provides access to the judgments provided by the Scottish Court Service (at **www.scotcourts.gov.uk**). The Scottish Court Service provides full-text transcripts of Court opinions from the Supreme Court along with many Sheriff Courts' opinions from 1999 onwards.

Pre-dating these internet sites in making transcripts available, Lexis-Nexis (see **2–7**) has been adding the Smith Bernal transcripts of Court of Appeal judgments to its database since 1980. If the case is not subsequently fully reported the transcript remains in the database along with the full text of reported cases. The Butterworths All England Direct service (at **www.butterworths.com**) provides access to transcripts from 1997 onwards and Westlaw UK (at **www.westlaw.co.uk**) from 1999.

The increasing number of transcripts on the internet is a mixed blessing. Some of these judgments will be reported later, but many will not. About a third of Court of Appeal cases will be reported. As noted in the introduction to this chapter, the aim of law reporting is to make available those cases that raise a point of legal significance. It is unusual for cases which raise a significant legal issue to go unreported. On the other hand, extensive use of unreported judgments may fail to add anything of value to the consideration of a legal issue. The availability of unreported judgments from the Lexis databases led Lord Diplock to suggest in 1982, following the citing of a number of unreported judgments in the case he was considering, that the practice should be discouraged. For his part, he commented: "I gained no assistance from the perusal of any of these transcripts. None of them laid down a relevant principle of law that was not to be found in reported cases." His comments are found in *Roberts Petroleum Ltd* v. *Bernard Kenny Ltd* [1983] 2 A.C. 192, at 200.

3–13   HOW TO FIND A CASE WHEN YOU ONLY KNOW ITS NAME

We will now turn to some of the problems frequently encountered by students and show how these are solved. Often you know the name of a case but you have no idea where the case was reported; or else the reference which you have been given has proved to be inaccurate. How can you find out where a report of the case appears?

The easiest way of tracing a case is to look it up in the *Current Law Case Citators*, especially if you think your case was probably decided in or after 1947. *The Digest* (**3–15**) is the best place to find older cases. In addition, most series of law reports have indexes to cases reported in their publication.

How to Use the Current Law Case Citators

Electronic

The *Current Law Case Citator* is produced by Sweet & Maxwell as part of *Current Legal Information*, either as a web-based service (at **www.smlawpub.jhc.net**) or as a CD-ROM. It is also available as part of the Westlaw UK service (at **www.westlaw.co.uk**). Westlaw UK presents the Citator as the "Case locator" database. Whichever database you are using, the first step of the search is relatively straightforward. Begin by entering the name of one of the parties you have in the search box of the web page or CD-ROM screen. The search box will request a "search term" and here you can enter *e.g.* "Biles" to search for *Biles* v. *Caesar*. Next, click a "go" or "enter" button. If the parties have common names it might be advisable to enter both, *e.g.* "Jones AND Sainsbury's". As with all database searches, you must be careful about the spelling of names, as even the slightest error results in failure to locate your case (in the second case, even dropping the apostrophe in "Sainsbury's" is sufficient to produce a negative response from the database). Be exact and you will succeed, otherwise frustration and ignorance are your rewards.

If a number of cases contain the name you have entered, they will be listed on an index page and you can select a link for the particular case you wish to trace. The information you are presented with is similar, whether you have used *Current Legal Information*, Westlaw UK or for that matter the printed *Current Law Case Citator*. The results for a search for the case *Biles* v. *Caesar* are interpreted below.

Print

The printed version of the *Current Law Case Citator* has an alphabetical list of the names of cases which have been published or quoted in court between the dates specified on the spine. If you have an idea of the approximate date, and easy access to the printed volumes, searching the printed source will often be quicker, and easier than using the databases noted above. The *Citator* is published in a number of parts:

1. *The Current Law Case Citator 1947–1976* is a bound volume covering cases which were reported or cited in court between 1947 and 1976.
2. *The Current Law Case Citator 1977–1988* is a bound volume covering cases which were reported or cited in court between 1977 and 1988.
3. *The Current Law Case Citator 1989–1995* is a bound volume covering cases which were reported or cited in court between 1989 and 1995.
4. In the spring of each year a paperback issue of the *Current Law Case Citator* is produced. It includes references to cases reported or cited between 1996 and the end of the preceding year.
5. The *Citator* is updated monthly in the *Current Law Monthly Digest*. To find cases reported in the current year, look in the Table of Cases in the most recent issue of the *Monthly Digest*. The December issue of the previous year's *Monthly Digest* can be used to find cases in that year, if the cumulative supplement described in point 3 has not yet been published.

The number of parts to the *Citator* may at first seem confusing. It is best to look through the *Citators* in chronological order, as above, in order to ensure that you have looked in all the relevant issues.

You may find your library has copies of the *Scottish Current Law Case Citator* for the periods 1948–1976 and 1977–1988. Despite its name, the Scottish version does contain all the English cases but, in addition, it lists Scottish cases in a separate alphabetical sequence at the back of the volume. The two publications have now merged and the *Current Law Case Citator* volumes since 1989 now also include Scottish cases. Part 1 of the *Citator* lists all the English cases, while the Scottish cases are listed in Part 2. Make sure you look for your case in the right section!

In each of the *Citators*, the cases are listed in alphabetical order. Cases which start with a single letter, *e.g. S.* v. *Cox*, are at the beginning of that letter of the alphabet; criminal cases starting with *R.* v. are at the beginning of the letter R section. If the title of the case is *Re Smith*, or *Ex p. Smith*, look under *Smith*. (See Appendix II for the meaning of *Re* and *Ex p.*) When you have traced the case you require, you will find an entry similar to the following:

```
                         CASE CITATOR 1947-76                              BIN

Bigos v. Bousted [1951] 1 All E.R. 92; [95 S.J. 180; 211 L.T. 346; 67
    L.Q.R. 156] ..........................................................  Digested, 1751
  —— v. J.R.S.S.T. Charitable Trust (Trustees of) (1965) 109 S.J. 273, C.A.  Digested, 65/2206
Bilainkin v. Bilainkin [1959] 1 W.L.R. 139; 103 S.J. 90; [1959] 1 All
    E.R. 161, C.A. .......................................................  Digested, 59/948
Bilang v. Rigg [1972] N.Z.L.R. 954 ......................................  Digested, 72/1886
Bilbee v. Hasse & Co. (1889) 5 T.L.R. 677 ...............................  Considered, 30
Bilbow v. Bilbow and Zandos (October 25, 1957), unreported .............  Reported, 57/1019
Bilcon v. Fegmay Investments [1966] 2 Q.B. 221; [1966] 3 W.L.R. 118;
    110 S.J. 618; [1966] 2 All E.R. 513 ................................  Digested, 66/373
Bildt v. Foy (1892) 9 T.L.R. 34 .........................................  Considered, 67/3093
Biles v. Caesar [1957] 1 W.L.R. 156; 101 S.J. 108; [1957] 1 All E.R.
    151; [101 S.J. 141; 21 Conv. 169], C.A. ...... Digested, 57/1943: Followed, 59/1834:
                                                              Applied, 68/2181: 69/2037
Bilham, Re [1901] 2 Ch. 169 ............................................  Distinguished, 60/3322
Bill v. Short Brothers and Harland [1963] N.I. 1 .......................  Digested, 62/2014
Billage v. Southee (1852) 9 Hare 534 ...................................  Applied, 52/1485: 70/1145
Billam v. Griffith (1941) 23 T.C. 757 ..................................  Applied, 4758
Billericay U. D. C., Plot No. 9a, Pitsea Temporary Housing Site, Re (1950)
    1 P. & C.R. 239, Lands Tribunal ...................................  Noted, 1498
```

Now you are ready to interpret the entry for our main example, *Biles* v. *Caesar*.

Biles v. Caesar

The entry for *Biles* v. *Caesar* gives you a complete "life history" of the case as covered by the *Citator*. It shows you where and when the case was originally reported, where you can find journal articles commenting on the case, and perhaps criticising the decision, and in which cases the decision has been quoted in court; also whether the court to which it was quoted agreed with the decision of the judges in the case. It also notes whether the case was confirmed or overruled or followed. This form of history is important within the doctrine of precedent as well as important for the individual case and the obiter dicta found within it.

Let us look at the information which the *Case Citator* gives you for *Biles* v. *Caesar* in more detail. What does it mean? The illustration is taken from the print version of the *Citator*. The same information is available in the electronic versions, with the exception of the entries noted in (2) below.

(1) After the name of the case (*Biles* v. *Caesar*) there is a list of three places where you can find a full report of the cases:
  (a) [1957] 1 W.L.R. 156—for the year 1957 in the first of the three volumes of the *Weekly Law Reports* at page 156;
  (b) (1957) 101 S.J. 108—for the year 1957 in volume 101 of the *Solicitors Journal* at page 108 (this, as the name suggests, is a journal, shelved with other journals);
  (c) [1957] 1 All E.R. 151—for the year 1958 in the first volume of the All England Law Reports at page 151.

(2) The entries which are enclosed in square brackets in the printed volume—[101 S.J. 141; 21 Conv. 169]—are references to articles or comments in law journals where the case is

discussed in some detail. If you select volume 101 of the *Solicitors Journal*, or volume 21 of *The Conveyancer*, you see articles discussing the case of *Biles* v. *Caesar* (these entries are not present in the electronic versions).

(3) The C.A. after the references to the case tells us that it is a Court of Appeal Decision. If the decision of the court of first instance was reported, references to these reports would have been included after the C.A.

(4) The word *Digested* followed by the figures 57/1943 in both the printed and the electronic *Current Legal Information* version of the *Citator* indicates that you will find a digest (a summary) of the case in the 1957 volume of the *Current Law Year Book* (see **7–12**). Every item in the 1957 volume has its own individual number; you will find that item 1943 is a summary of the facts and decisions in the case of *Biles* v. *Caesar*. If you are using Westlaw UK the text of the digest entry is on screen. If the case you want is dated 1986 or later, you can obtain the text of digest entries using *Current Legal Information* by using the *Current Law Cases* database.

(5) You may also wish to know whether the decision given in a particular case has been subsequently approved, *i.e.* whether the case has been quoted with approval by another judge in a later case. By 1976, when the print *Citatator* volume was published, the case of *Biles* v. *Caesar* had been quoted in three other cases—in 1959, when the decision was followed, and in 1968 and 1969 when the courts applied the decision in the *Biles* case to two other cases, following the doctrine of precedent. If you are using *Current Legal Information*, or the printed *Citator*, you can find the names of the cases in which *Biles* was referred to by looking in the 1959 *Current Law Year Book,* at item 1834, and in the 1968 and 1969 *Year Books*, at the item numbers given. The Westlaw UK database will directly to the *Year Book* entries for the cases. The meaning of terms such as *Applied* and *Followed* is given in the front of the *Cumulative Supplement to The Digest* (**3–15**), under the heading "Meaning of terms used in classifying annotated cases".

If you are using the printed *Citator* and, as in the above example, you find a reference to your case in the *Citator* for 1947 to 1976, it is still advisable to check through the more recent *Citators* to find the present status of the judgment. You can find out whether since 1976, for example, the case has been taken to a higher court or the decision has been approved or overruled in other judgments. For more information on how to trace the subsequent judicial history of a case, see **7–17**.

If you are unable to find the case you require in the *Current Law Case Citators*, it may be that the case is either very old or from another jurisdiction. The next place to look is in *The Digest*.

How to Trace a Case in The Digest   3–15

Older English and Scottish cases can most easily be traced using *The Digest* (formerly known as the *English and Empire Digest*), as can many cases heard in Irish, European and Commonwealth courts. *The Digest* consists of the main work (around 70 volumes), several *Continuation Volumes,* a *Cumulative Supplement*, a *Consolidated Table of Cases* and a *Consolidated Index. The Digest* is in its third edition which is called the *Green Band Reissue* because of the green stripe on the spine. Most of the *Green Band Reissue* volumes have now been updated and reprinted. These volumes say *2nd Reissue* on the spine. The date of reissue of any volume is printed on the title page inside the front cover.

To trace a particular case in *The Digest*, go first to the four-volume *Consolidated Table of Cases*. This contains an alphabetical list of the 400,000 cases summarised in *The Digest* and gives a reference to the volume in which the case can be found. Page 47 shows the entry in the *Consolidated Table of Cases* for the case of *Bell* v. *Twentyman*. This case is included in Volumes 19, 36(1) and 36(2) of *The Digest*, since it is relevant to the law of easements, negligence and nuisance. At the front of each of these volumes, there is another Table of Cases which refers you to the *case* number (or *page* number in older volumes—see the heading at the top of the column) where you can find a summary of the case and a list of citations where the full report can be found. If, for example, you wished to find a summary of the negligence aspects of the case of *Bell* v. *Twentyman*, you would now look up the name of the case in the Table of Cases at the front of Volume 36(1). Alongside the name of the case is the number 133, which refers you to case number 133 in that volume. The entry is shown on page 48. The case number is given in **bold**, followed by a summary of the case and references to where the full text of the report can be found. The case of *Bell* v. *Twentyman* was reported in a number of series. To find the meaning of the abbreviations used, look in the list of abbreviations in the *Cumulative Supplement*.   The *Consolidated Table of Cases* is updated and reprinted every two years. To find the latest cases, you will need to look in the annual *Cumulative Supplement*. There is a Table of Cases at the front of the volume, which indicates where in the *Cumulative Supplement* a summary of the case can be found. For more information on *The Digest*, refer to **7–13**.

3–16   Tracing a Case through the Indexes in Law Reports

In addition to the *Current Law Case Citators* and *The Digest*, there are a number of indexes to the cases in individual series of law reports. For instance, the *All England Law Reports* has published a volume containing a list of all the cases in the *All England Law Reports Reprint* (see **3–11**), which covers selected cases between 1558 and 1935. In addition, there are three volumes containing the *Consolidated Tables and Index 1936–1992*. Volume 1 contains a list of all the cases included in the *All England Law Reports* between these dates. The reference given is to the year, volume and page number. Cases reported since 1992 appear in the annual cumulative *Tables and Index*, updated quarterly by the *Current Tables and Index*.

If you know that the case you are looking for is old, you can turn to the index in Volumes 177 and 178 of the *English Reports*, and this will tell you if the case is printed in the *English Reports* (see **3–10**). Several other series of law reports also publish indexes and these can be useful if you know that a case is reported in a particular series but you have not got an exact reference.

The indexes to the *Law Reports* are very useful. From 1865 to 1949, a series of *Law Reports: Digests* were published. These contain summaries of the cases reported in the *Law Reports*, in subject order, and a list of cases is usually included. From 1950 this has been published as the *Law Reports Consolidated Index* (lettered on the spine *Law Reports Index*), usually referred to as the *Red Index*. Four bound volumes, each covering cases in a 10-year period, have been published for the period 1951–1990. An annual paper-covered *Red Index* is published, containing cases from 1991 to the end of the last year. This is supplemented by the *Pink Index*, which is issued at intervals during the year and lists all the cases published during the current year. The main arrangement of all the indexes is by subject, but there are two alphabetical lists. The list of Cases Reported, at the front of each volume, covers recently reported cases, whilst the separate list of Cases Judicially Considered, at the back of the volume, gives information on older cases which have been mentioned in court during the period covered by the index. In addition to cases published in the *Law Reports* and the *Weekly Law Reports*, the indexes also include cases published in the *All England Law Reports*, the *Criminal Appeal Reports*, the *Lloyd's Law Reports*,

Example Page from The Digest Consolidated Table of Cases A–C

Bell v London & North Western Ry Co (1852) **8(2) Chos**
Bell v London & South Western Bank (1874) **7 Bldg Soc**
Bell v Long (CAN) **21 Exon**
Bell v Love (1883) **11 Comns; 34 Mines**
Bell v McKindsey (CAN) **17 Deeds**
Bell v Macklin (1887) (CAN) **40 S Land**
Bell v McLean (1868) (CAN) **42 Shrffs**
Bell v Manning (1865) (CAN) **6 B of Exch**
Bell v Mansfield (1893) (AUS) **42 Ship**
Bell v Marsh (1903) **21 Estpl**
Bell v Marsh (CAN) **19 Easmt**
Bell v Martin (1831) **11 Confl**
Bell v Matthewman (1920) (CAN) **23 Exors**
Bell v McCubbin (1989) **CVH**
Bell v McDougall (1882) (CAN) **5(1) Bkpcy**
Bell v Midland Ry Co (1861) **17 Damgs; 19 Easmt; 36(2) Nuis**
Bell v Miller (1862) (CAN) **3 Arbn**
Bell v Miller (AUS) **29 Insce**
Bell v Milner (1957) (CAN) **9(2) Coys**
Bell v Moffat (1880) (CAN) **6 B of Exch**
Bell v Montreal Trust Co (1956) (CAN) **45 Stats**
Bell v Murray (1833) (SCOT) **27(2) H&W**
Bell v Nangle (IR) **17 Deeds**
Bell v National Forest Products Ltd, Luttin, Porter (CAN) **26 Guar**
Bell v National Provincial Bank of England Ltd (1904) **28(1) Inc T**
Bell v Nevin (1866) **36(2) Prtnrs**
Bell v New Zealand Rugby Football Union (1931) (NZ) **12(1) Contr**
Bell v Nicholls, ex p Richards (CAN) **21 Exon**
Bell v Nixon (1816) **29 Insce**
Bell v North Staffordshire Ry Co (1879) **37(2) Pract**
Bell v Northern Constitution Ltd (1943) (NI) **32 Libel**
Bell v Northwood (1886) (CAN) **45 Sp Pfce**
Bell v Norwich (Bp) (1565) **19 Eccl**
Bell v Oakley (1814) **18 Distr**
Bell v Ogilvie (1863) (SCOT) **44 Solrs**
Bell v Ontario Human Rights Commission & McKay (1971) (CAN) **CVD**
Bell v Ontario Human Rights Commission and McKay (CAN) **16 Cr Pract**
Bell v Ottawa Trust & Deposit Co (1897) (CAN) **5(1) Bkpcy**
Bell v Parent (CAN) **33 Mags**
Bell v Park (1914) (IR) **50 Wills**
Bell v Parke (1860) (IR) **32 Libel**
Bell v Petry (1897) (NZ) **27(1) H&W**
Bell v Phyn (1802) **36(2) Prtnrs; 50 Wills**
Bell v Pitt (AUS) **19 Easmt**
Bell v Plumbly (1900) **46 Stk Ex**
Bell v Port of London Assurance Co (1850) **22(2) Evid**
Bell v Portland Shire (1876) (AUS) **1(1) Admin L**
Bell v Postlethwaite (1855) **3 Arbn**
Bell v Puller (1810) **42 Ship**
Bell v Quebec Corpn (1879) **49 Water**
Bell v R (1973) (CAN) **CVD**
Bell v Raisbeck (1844) **23 Exors**
Bell v Rea (1852) **1(2) Agcy**
Bell v Reid (1813) **2 Aliens**
Bell v Reuben (1946) **31 L&T**
Bell v Riddell (1882) (CAN) **27(1) H&W**
Bell v Riddell (1884) (CAN) **12(1) Contr**
Bell v Robinson (1824) **18 Distr; 25 Fraud Conv**
Bell v Robinson (1909) (CAN) **5(2) Bkpcy**
Bell v Rogers (1914) (CAN) **6 B of Exch**

Bell v Rokeby (1905) (CAN) **1(2) Agcy**
Bell v Ross (1885) (CAN) **5(1) Bkpcy**
Bell v Rowe (1901) (AUS) **12(2) Contr**
Bell v Ry Comr (1861) (AUS) **2 Animals**
Bell v Sarvis (1903) (CAN) **50 Wills**
Bell v Schultz (1912) (CAN) **39(2) S Goods; 46 Tort**
Bell v Scott (1922) (AUS) **40 S Land**
Bell v Searight, Re Searight (1899) **50 Wills**
Bell v Secretary of State for Defence (1985) **CVG**
Bell v Shuttleworth (1841) **6 B of Exch; 12(2) Contr; 26 Guar; 30 Jdgmts**
Bell v Simpson (1857) **4(1) Bkpcy**
Bell v Skelton (1831) **23 Exors**
Bell v Smith (1826) **22(2) Evid**
Bell v Spelliscy (1932) (CAN) **23 Exors**
Bell v Spereman (1726) **39(1) Recrs**
Bell v Stewart (1842) (IR) **6 B of Exch**
Bell v Stocker (1882) **27(1) H&W**
Bell v Stockton, etc Tramway Co (1887) **39(1) R Traf**
Bell v Stone (1798) **32 Libel**
Bell v Sunderland Bldg Soc (1883) **35 Mtge**
Bell v Tainthorp (1834) **30 Juries**
Bell v Tape (1837) (IR) **11 Const L**
Bell v Taxes Comr (NZ) **30 Land Tax**
Bell v Taylor (1836) **44 Solrs**
Bell v Thatcher (1675) **32 Libel**
Bell v Thompson (1934) (AUS) **2 Animals**
Bell v Timiswood (1812) **23 Exors**
Bell v Toronto Transportation Commission (1926) (CAN) **18 Discy**
Bell v Travco Hotels Ltd (1953) **29 Inns**
Bell v Turner (1874) **22(2) Evid**
Bell v Turner (1877) **48 Trusts**
Bell v Twentyman (1841) **19 Easmt; 36(1) Negl; ← 36(2) Nuis**
Bell v Union Bank (1923) (NZ) **3 Bank**
Bell v Walker & Debrett (1785) **13 Coprt**
Bell v Wardell (1740) **17 Custom; 46 Time**
Bell v Welch (1850) **12(1) Contr; 26 Guar**
Bell v Wermore (CAN) **21 Exon**
Bell v Westmount Town (1899) (CAN) **8(2) Comwlth**
Bell v Wetmore (1880) (CAN) **27(1) H&W**
Bell v Wetmore (CAN) **17 Damgs**
Bell v Whitbread & Co Ltd (1970) **25 Gaming**
Bell v White (1857) (CAN) **7 Bounds&F**
Bell v Whitehead (1839) **13 Coprt**
Bell v Wilson (1865) (1866) **17 Deeds**
Bell v Wilson (1866) **34 Mines**
Bell v Wilson (1900) (CAN) **32 Libel**
Bell v Windsor & Annapolis Ry Co (1892) (CAN) **8(1) Carr**
Bell v Witts, Re Mercer (1894) **48 Trusts**
Bell v Wright (1895) (CAN) **44 Solrs**
Bell v Wyndham (1865) **25 Fish**
Bell, exp (1988) **CVH**
Bell, In the Estate of (1908) **23 Exors**
Bell, In the Goods of (1859) **23 Exors**
Bell, In the Goods of (1878) **23 Exors**
Bell, In the Goods of Hunt v Hunt (1866) **50 Wills**
Bell, R v (1731) **14(2) Crim**
Bell, R v (1737) **14(2) Crim**
Bell, R v (1753) **15 Crim**
Bell, R v (1822) **36(2) Nuis**
Bell, R v (1829) **14(2) Crim**
Bell, R v (1841) **15 Crim**
Bell, R v (1857) (CAN) **28(3) Infts**
Bell, R v (1859) (IR) **14(2) Crim; 15 Crim**

Example Page from The Digest, Vol. 36(1), 2nd Reissue

General Principles of the Law of Negligence   Cases 132–139

ii THE DUTY TO TAKE CARE

1 Necessity for

CROSS REFERENCES See ACTION vol 1(1) (reissue) nos 228, 229 (*injuria absque damno*); no 230 et seq (*damnum absque injuria*)

132 No negligence without duty In an action by the consignor of goods against the proprietor of a general booking-office for the transmission of parcels by coach, etc, charging negligence, whereby consignor lost his goods, it is not sufficient to prove that they never reached their destination or were accounted for. The office-keeper's duty is to deliver to a carrier; and some evidence must be given, showing specifically a breach of that duty. A tradesman, having made up goods by order, delivered them at a booking-office, with the customer's address, and booked them, to be forwarded to him, not specifying any particular conveyance, and no particular mode of transmission having been pointed out by the customer.

Quaere: whether the consignor could maintain an action against the office-keeper for a negligent loss of the goods while under his charge.

Gilbart v Dale (1836) 5 Ad & El 543; 2 Har & W 383; 1 Nev & PKB 22; 6 LJKB 3; 111 ER 1270
ANNOTATION **Apld** Mid Ry v Bromley (1856) 17 CB 372

➤ **133** —— In case for an injury to plaintiff's reversionary interest by defendant's obstruction of a watercourse on his land and thereby sending water upon and under the house and land in the occupation of plaintiff's tenant, defendant pleaded, that the obstruction was caused by the neglect of plaintiff's tenant to repair a wall on the demised land, that in consequence it fell into the watercourse, and caused the damage, and that within a reasonable time after defendant had notice he removed it: *Held* to be a bad plea, it not showing any obligation on the tenant to repair the wall merely as terre-tenant. *Quaere*: whether it would have been good if it had.
Bell v Twentyman (1841) 1 QB 766; 1 Gal & Dav 223; 10 LJQ B 278; 6 Jur 366; 113 ER 1324
ANNOTATION **Distd** Taylor v Stendall (1845) 5 LTOS 214

134 —— A declaration in case stated, by way of inducement, that plaintiff was possessed of a dwelling-house as tenant to defendant, and that defendant, at the request of plaintiff, promised to fit up a cellar for a wine cellar, with brick and stone binns; and then charged that it became the duty of defendant to use due care in fitting up the same, but that he did not, and that the slabs gave way, and broke plaintiff's wine bottles. It was proved that defendant did fit up a wine cellar with brick and stone binns; but that plaintiff afterwards required more binns to be made, and defendant consented to have the partitions carried up to the roof of the cellar. The workmen, however, by plain-

tiff's directions, erected the new partitions upon the centre of the slabs which covered the binns first made, and the slabs then gave way. It was proved that those slabs would have been strong enough to bear the weight of empty bottles; but some of the witnesses thought not that of full bottles: *Held* under these circumstances no breach of duty was shown, defendant having only undertaken to fit up a wine cellar with brick and stone binns, and not one of any particular character.
Richardson v Berkeley (1847) 10 LTOS 203

135 —— The declaration stated that defendants were possessed of a mooring anchor, which was kept by them fixed in a known part of a navigable river, covered by ordinary tides, that the anchor had become removed into, and remained in, another part of the river covered by ordinary tides, not indicated, whereof defendants had notice, and although they had the means and power of refixing and securing the anchor, and indicating it, they neglected so to do, whereby plaintiffs' vessel, whilst sailing in a part of the river ordinarily used by ships, ran foul of and struck against the anchor, and was thereby damaged, etc: *Held* bad, for not showing that defendants were privy to the removal of the anchor, or that it was their duty to refix it and to indicate it.
Hancock v York, Newcastle & Berwick Ry Co (1850) 10 CB 348; 14 LTOS 467; 138 ER 140

136 —— Negligence creates no cause of action unless it expresses a breach of a duty (*Erle, CJ*).
Dutton v Powles (1862) 2 B&S 191; 31 LJQB 191; 6 LT 224; 8 Jur NS 970; 10 WR 408; 1 Mar LC 209; 121 ER 1043, Ex Ch

137 —— Plaintiff, a carman, being sent by his employer to defendants for some goods, was directed by a servant of defendants to go to the counting house. In proceeding along a dark passage of defendants in the direction pointed out, plaintiff fell down a staircase, and was injured: *Held* defendants were not guilty of any negligence; for if the passage was so dark that plaintiff could not see his way, he ought not to have proceeded; and if, on the other hand, there was sufficient light, he ought to have avoided the danger.
Wilkinson v Fairrie (1862) 1 H&C 633; 32 LJ Ex 73; 7 LT 599; 9 Jur NS 280; 158 ER 1038
ANNOTATIONS **Apld** Lewis v Ronald (1909) 101 LT 534 **Consd** Campbell v Shelbourne Hotel Ltd [1939] 2 KB 534

138 —— *Skelton v London & North Western Ry Co* (1867) no 485 post

139 —— Plaintiffs, merchants at Valparaiso, received through defendants a telegram purporting to come from London and addressed to them, ordering a large shipment of barley. No such message was ever in

21

the *Local Government Reports*, the *Industrial Cases Reports*, the *Road Traffic Reports* and *Tax Cases*. If the *Current Law Case Citators* are not available in your library, this index to the *Law Reports* will fulfil a similar function.

HOW TO TRACE VERY RECENT UNREPORTED CASES

3–17

A number of websites are available free of charge. They help you trace very recent unreported cases. If you do not know the precise date of a recent case, or the court in which it was held, these sites help you find cases by name and by the subject matter of the case. The ability to search for cases using general subject terms such as "intellectual property" or "family" provides a way of keeping up with cases which update and perhaps change the law before they appear in legal textbooks and the reported case literature. This means you can stay ahead of printed materials.

A leading example of one of these websites is provided by the *Law Direct* site which forms part of the Butterworths LEXIS direct service (at **www.butterworths.com**). Launched in 2000 it is a non-subscription (free) service, though it has links to the subscription elements of the Butterworths site. The *Cases Database* which forms part of *Law Direct* contains digests and summaries of cases from a wide variety of courts since 1995. Cases can be searched by name and by court and the digests themselves can be searched. This is of great benefit if you know something of the nature of the case, but are unsure of the name of the parties to the case. The conjoined twins case mentioned in **2–2**, for example, which raised difficult legal and ethical issues in the later part of 2000, would not generally have been referred to by case name in the news media, and a clear reference of the Court of Appeal might be missing. A keyword search using "conjoined twins" or "siamese twins" on *Law Direct's Cases* database allows you to find the correct name and court. The sources of judgment transcripts described in **3–11** could be used to retrieve the full text of the judgment. Searches can also be made using general subject searches.

The ability to search for cases by subject, as well as name, date and court, is provided by David Swarbrick's website (at **www.swarb.co.uk**), which maintains an extensive index of cases since 1992. The full index with search facilities is available free on the site.

If your library has a subscription to the Lawtel database (at **www.lawtel.co.uk**), then you have access to a source which provides digests of very recent cases from a wide range of courts and tribunals. The database also offers the particular advantages of hypertext links to summaries of relevant cases cited in a decision, along with links to transcripts for Court of Appeal, Crown Office List and High Court judgments dating back to 1993. References to places in which the case may subsequently be reported are added as they become available.

Remember that, as mentioned in **3–11**, the availability of unreported cases can be a mixed blessing. Though the specialist practitioner, or legal academic, may be able to sift through summaries of recent cases and decide which raise legal issues of significance, this is not easily accomplished by the law student. Finding information and interpreting it are two separate tasks involving different skills and levels of knowledge.

The *Daily Law Notes* service from the Incorporated Council of Law Reporting (at **www.lawreports.co.uk**) offers a useful element of selection, providing what is, in effect, a short cut to recent cases that are likely to be of legal interest but which may not be fully reported. It consists of a selective list of cases, organised by court and major subject heading, that will appear later in the *Weekly Law Reports*. The headnotes to be used in the *Weekly Law Reports* are included.

3–18 HOW TO TRACE VERY RECENT REPORTED CASES

Electronic

Sweet & Maxwell's *Current Law* provides both the leading current awareness service for recent reported cases and also the digest information available in print as the *Current Law Monthly Digest,* available either online (at **www.smlawpub.jhc.net**) or on CD-ROM as the *Current Law Cases* database (part of *Current Legal Information*). The case digests also appear in the *Case Locator* database which forms part of the Westlaw UK service (at **www.westlaw.co.uk**). If you type in the database search box of *Current Law Cases* the name of your case, you will retrieve a summary of the case, along with a note of where it is reported. Cases mentioned in the decision are listed. *Current Law Cases* includes the digests of newspaper law reports published in print as the *Daily Law Reports Index*. If you are using the *Case Locator* database with Westlaw UK, a search for your case by name will link to the full text of either a judgment transcript or a law report, along with the case digest, provided the reports are available in the Westlaw UK database. The Lawtel service, see **2–11**, presents a means of searching for a wide range of both unreported and reported cases and retrieving a case summary which in turn is linked to transcripts of the judgments.

An alternative approach is to go directly to the databases of full-text case law available from Lexis-Nexis and the database providers listed in **2–8**, particularly Westlaw UK. Since these databases combine reports found in a number of different report series, you do not need a full citation in order to find a case by name. The widest range of full-text reported judgments remains the Lexis database. Unless your library has a subscription to Lexis-Nexis Professional though, access procedures usually require you to contact a law librarian who will perform a search on your behalf.

Print

Many of the print indexes already mentioned have regular updates throughout the year. In addition, there are "current awareness" publications that aim to keep their readership as up to date as possible with legal developments. It is in these two types of publication that you will look to find references to very recent cases.

The *Current Law Monthly Digest* includes a Cumulative Table of Cases. Look in the list in the *latest* issue. If the name of your case appears, the reference given is to the monthly issue of the *Current Law Monthly Digest* and to the individual item number within that issue, where you will find a summary of the case and a note of where it has been reported. For example, suppose the Table of Cases gives your case a reference such as: Jan 129. This means that if you look in the January issue of the *Monthly Digest*, item 129 (not page 129) is a summary of the case, with a list of places where the case is reported in full. Scottish cases are included in the Table of Cases, but the reference will lead you to the Scottish law section of the *Monthly Digest.*

The indexes to the *Law Reports* and the *All England Law Reports* can be used to trace recent cases. The *Pink Index* to the *Law Reports* will cover cases reported in several of the major series of law reports; its front cover indicates the exact period it covers. If the case is too recent to be included in here, look inside the latest copy of the *Weekly Law Reports.*

The front cover of the *Weekly Law Reports* lists only the contents of that particular issue. The list inside covers all cases reported in the series since the last *Pink Index* was published.

The *All England Law Reports Current Tables and Index* covers all cases published in the *All England Law Reports* in the current year. A list inside the latest issue of the *All England Law Reports* brings the *Current Tables* up to date. There is also a list of cases to be reported in future issues.

There is usually a delay of several months before a case is reported in law report series such as the *All England Law Reports* and the *Weekly Law Reports*. Reports of cases heard in the past few weeks will only be available in newspapers or weekly journals.

Newspaper law reports are the quickest to appear, with most being published within a week and some appearing the day after the end of the case. Since 1988, an index of newspaper law reports has been published every fortnight. The *Daily Law Reports Index* abstracts law reports from *The Times*, the *Financial Times*, *The Independent*, *The Guardian*, the *Daily Telegraph* and *Lloyd's List*. The entries are ordered by case name and include references to the newspapers which carry the report and a summary of the facts of the case and decision reached. There is also an index listing each party in the cases, should you know only the name of the defendant. The fortnightly loose parts are cumulated into a quarterly bound volume, which includes an additional index listing cases which have been reported by a newspaper and have now been more fully reported in one of the major law report series. An annual bound volume cumulates these quarterly volumes.

Reports of recent cases can also be found in legal journals. Some of the weekly journals, such as the *New Law Journal*, and specialist journals, such as the *Journal of Planning and Environmental Law* and the *Estates Gazette*, produce short reports of relevant cases. References to these reports can be found using the *Legal Journals Index* (see **5–4**).

SUMMARY: HOW TO FIND A CASE

1. If the date is unknown:

    look in the *Current Law Case Citator*, which is available either in print,
    or online and on CD-ROM as one of the *Current Legal Information* databases,
    or as part of Westlaw UK's *Case Locator*;
    an alternative print source is provided by *The Digest*, in the *Consolidated Table of Cases*, and in the *Cumulative Supplement*.

2. If the case is thought to be old look in:

    the *Digest Consolidated Table of Cases*,
    the index to the *English Reports*,
    the index to the *All England Law Reports Reprint*.

3. If the case is thought to be very recent and unreported, use one of the databases described in **3–17**.

4. If the case is thought to be recent, and reported, look in:

    the *Current Law Cases* database within *Current Legal Information*,
    or Westlaw UK's *Case Locator*;
    the print equivalent is published as the *Current Law Monthly Digest*;

the indexes of the *Law Reports*, the *Weekly Law Reports* and the *All England Law Reports* provide further print alternatives.

5. If you know that the case has been reported in one of the leading series, but your reference is incomplete:

search for the case online or on CD-ROM,
or look in the printed index to the series if there is one.

3–19 HOW TO TRACE JOURNAL ARTICLES AND COMMENTARIES ON A CASE

You may want to find journal articles written about a case, or trace comments on a recent court decision. Such articles and comments usually explain the significance of the case and relate it to other relevant decisions. Sometimes writers who disagree with a decision may accept that the case provides a justification for a change in the law. Journal articles can be traced using both electronic and print sources, though this is one area where electronic sources have greatly increased the ease with which useful articles can be identified.

Electronic
The easiest and most comprehensive way to find articles on an English case is via the *Legal Journals Index* (**5–4**). This is available online (at **www.smlawpub.jhc.net**) or on CD-ROM as part of *Current Legal Information*. The *Index* is also available from Westlaw UK (at **www.westlaw.co.uk**). Whichever electronic form of the *Index* is used, if you enter the case name or names you have as your search term, you will retrieve a list of references to journal articles. These, if you are using *Current Legal Information*, are noted as being "articles", "case comment" or "editorial". All references are to sources which provide significant review of your case. A search using the search terms "F AND West Berkshire" for example, will retrieve a list of 20 or so references to articles relating to the case *F.* v. *West Berkshire HA*, which will include, among others, references to "Fam. Law 1989 19(Sep) 367–368" and "S.J. 1989 133(14)". You may then need to refer to the separate listing of abbreviations used in *Current Legal Information*, to confirm that the references are to *Family Law* and the *Solicitors Journal*.

The Articles Index available from Lawtel (at **www.lawtel.co.uk**) provides an alternative source of references to articles on cases. Although coverage of journal (and newspaper) articles is only from 1998, and fewer journals are indexed than is the case for the *Legal Journals Index*, cases mentioned in an article are fully indexed. A summary is provided of each article indexed. To search Lawtel, select the "Articles Index" tab on the home page, then "Focused Search". Case names can then be entered in the "Case Law Cited" box. Searching on the *F.* v. *West Berkshire HA* mentioned above retrieved references to 18 journal articles.

The *Index to Legal Periodicals & Books* (**5–6**) can also be searched online, though fewer English journals are indexed than in the *Legal Journals Index*. It contains references to journal articles dating from 1981 and you can search for cases using a Case Name Index. A search for articles referring to *F.* v. *West Berkshire HA* finds one reference.

Print
Journal articles on a case can be traced by using the *Legal Journals Index* (**5–4**), the *Current Law Case Citators* or the *Index to Legal Periodicals* (**5–5**). If you look again at the specimen

entry (*Biles* v. *Caesar*) from the *Current Law Case Citator* (**3–14**), you will see that the entries which were completely enclosed in square brackets were journal articles on that case. For articles published in the current year, you should look in the Table of Cases in the latest *Current Law Monthly Digest*. If your case appears in *lower* case, it means either that there has been a journal article on the case or that the case has been judicially considered during the year. If you turn to the issue of the *Monthly Digest* indicated and then to the item number, you will either find another case in which your case has been cited or a note of a journal article which has been written about your case.

The easiest and most comprehensive way to find articles on an English case is to use the *Legal Journals Index*, which indexes all the major British legal journals. The Case Index provides details of journal articles and commentaries on the case as well as references to any reports of the case in journals. The printed version of the *Legal Journals Index* is published monthly, with quarterly cumulations and an annual bound cumulative volume.

The *Legal Journals Index* was first published in 1986. If your library does not hold the *Legal Journals Index*, or if you require articles prior to 1986, you may trace articles on your case in the *Index to Legal Periodicals* (**5–6**). Look in the back of the issues under the heading "Table of Cases Commented Upon". Most will be American cases, but important British cases are included, if there has been a lengthy article written about them.

The weekly journals, such as the *New Law Journal* and the *Solicitors Journal*, and many of the specialist journals, such as *Public Law*, the *Criminal Law Review* and *The Conveyancer*, include notes and comments on recent cases. Since these are relatively short, they often do not appear in the list of journal articles printed in *Current Law* or the *Legal Journals Index*. If you know roughly when the case was decided, you may find helpful material by browsing through the contents pages of relevant journals of the time. A quick glance through recent issues is also often rewarding when searching for comments on a case decided within the last month.

TRIBUNALS

3–20

The establishment of the welfare state led to the creation of a large number of tribunals. They were set up to resolve disputes over entitlement to welfare benefits. Subsequently, other areas, such as problems between landlords and tenants, and between employer and employees because of unfair dismissal, have been subject to resolution through tribunals. Tribunals can be extremely busy, hearing many thousands of cases each year, but only a comparatively small number of cases are eventually reported in the law reports. Some law reports, such as the *Industrial Cases Reports* and *Immigration Appeals*, carry reports of appeals from the tribunal to an appeal court but the vast majority of cases heard by tribunals are not reported. However, selected decisions of three tribunals are available from the Court Service website (at **www.courtservice.gov.uk**). Select the "Tribunals" link from the home page. The Social Security & Child Support Commissioners have placed decisions on their web page (see **3–32**). Decisions of the Special Commissioners of Income Tax and VAT and Duties Tribunals are available from 1999. Decisions of the Lands Tribunal are available from 1996.

Social Welfare Law

3–21

The most important decisions taken by the Social Security Commissioners are available online from the Court Service web site (at **www.courtservice.gov.uk**). To find them, select

"Tribunals" and the Court Service home page. The link for "Social Security Commissioners & Child Support Commissioners" leads you to "Starred Decisions". These are the decisions the Commissioners think should be published in print. Starred decisions are listed from 1990 onwards and the full text is available from 1997. A few are available for earlier years. The printed decisions are published individually by Corporate Document Services.

Previously, bound volumes of decisions were published by HMSO, the last appearing in 1993 as *Reported Decisions of the Social Security Commissioner, Vol 13. 1989–1990*. These were reissues of decisions published individually by HMSO. The bound volumes cover the period between 1976 and 1990. Reported decisions between 1948 and 1976 were published in the seven volumes of the *Reported Decisions of the Commissioner under the Social Security and National Insurance (Industrial Injuries) Acts*, known as the *Blue Books* because of their colour.

The form of citation for Commissioners' decisions differs from that used in conventional law reports and references to cases do not include the names of parties. All reported cases since 1950 bear the prefix R, followed, in brackets, by an abbreviation for the series. For example, the prefix R(U) indicates a Commissioner's decision on unemployment benefit, and R(P) a decision on entitlement to pensions. Within each series, reports are cited by the report number and the year: R(U) 7/62 indicates a reported unemployment benefit decision, case number 7 of 1962. The following abbreviations are in use:

R(A)	Attendance allowance
R(DLA)	Disability Living Allowance
R(DWA)	Disability Working Allowance
R(F)	Family allowances and child benefit
R(FC)	Family Credit
R(FIS)	Family Income Supplement
R(G)	General—miscellaneous (maternity benefit, widow's benefit, death grant, etc.)
R(I)	Industrial injuries
R(IS)	Income Support
R(M)	Mobility allowance
R(P)	Retirement pensions
R(S)	Sickness and invalidity benefit
R(SB)	Supplementary benefit
R(SSP)	Statutory sick pay
R(U)	Unemployment benefit

Unpublished decisions are prefaced by C instead of R. For example, CP3/81 is a reference to an unpublished 1981 Commissioner's decision on pensions and CSB 15/82 is an unreported decision on supplementary benefits. Commissioners have "starred" decisions since 1987. The year in these "starred" cases is given in full, *e.g.* CDLA 1347/1999. The R prefix is then used on publication.

Reported cases from 1948 to 1950 had a different method of citation. They were prefixed by C, followed by a letter (*not* enclosed in brackets) representing the area of law covered. Thus, CI denotes an early decision on industrial injuries. Scottish or Welsh cases were prefixed with CS and CW respectively. The cases were numbered in sequence. However, only a minority were printed, which has resulted in gaps in the numerical sequence. For example, CWI 17/49 is followed by CWI 20/49. Cases numbered 18 or 19 of 1949 are unreported. The abbreviation (KL) after the citation is an indication that the case has been reported, whilst the suffix (K) denotes a decision of limited value.

Decisions on a particular subject can be traced using *Neligan: Social Security Case Law: Digest of Commissioner's Decisions*. The *Digest* is available from the Department of Social Security's website (at **www.dss.gov.uk**). To find the publication, use "Quick Search" and search for "Neligan". The two-volume print version of *Neligan* is published by Corporate Document Services. This publication summarises the majority of the reported decisions, under appropriate subject headings. Appendix 3 provides a list of decisions numbers which will allow you to trace the summary of a particular case should the full report of the Commissioner's decision be unavailable. A general subject index is also provided.

TSO publishes a general guide to social security law, *The Law Relating to Social Security*, as an 11-volume looseleaf work. The volumes are updated by periodic supplements and contain the text of relevant statutes and regulations. HMSO became TSO (The Stationery Office) following privatisation in 1996.

REPORTED DECISIONS OF OTHER TRIBUNALS

3–22

The wide range of tribunals makes a complete guide impossible within the available space. What follows is selective.

Immigration appeals are covered by *Immigration Appeals*, published by TSO. Also available from TSO are the *Value Added Tax and Duties Tribunals Reports*.

Many Lands Tribunal cases appear in the *Property, Planning and Compensation Reports* and in the *Estates Gazette* and the *Estates Gazette Law Reports*. The latter series also covers leasehold valuation tribunals. Barry Rose published a series of volumes entitled *Lands Tribunal Cases*.

Most reported cases, in subjects other than welfare law, appear in standard series of law reports and are conventionally cited. *Current Law* contains references to many tribunal decisions, under appropriate subject headings, and provides a summary for each one. Looseleaf encyclopedias frequently refer to both published and unpublished decisions in the appropriate subject.

The *Industrial Tribunal Reports*, published until 1978, now form part of the *Industrial Cases Reports*. These contain many cases heard by the Employment Appeal Tribunal and many E.A.T. decisions also appear in the *Industrial Relations Law Reports*.

4 | Legislation

INTRODUCTION

When a Bill (**6–5**) has been approved by both Houses of Parliament and has received the Royal Assent, it becomes an Act of Parliament. The Act is made available on the HMSO website (at www.legislation.hmso.gov.uk) and the first printed version is published by TSO, usually within a few days of receiving the Royal Assent.

There are two types of Acts. Public General Acts deal with public policy and apply to the whole population, or a substantial part of it. Local and Personal Acts, on the other hand, affect only a particular area of the country, or a named organisation or group of individuals. This chapter will concentrate on Public General Acts, which you are more likely to use regularly. Local and Personal Acts will, however, be examined in **4–25**.

THE STRUCTURE OF AN ACT

A copy of the Forestry Act 1991 is reproduced below. This is an unusually short Act, as most Acts are many pages in length. All Acts are structured in the same way, although some of the parts described below are not included in every Act.

The parts of an Act (see the illustration) are:

1. *Short title*;
2. *Official citation* (see **4–3**);
3. *Long title*. This may give some indication of the purpose and content of the Act;
4. *Date of Royal Assent*;
5. *Enacting formula*. This is a standard form of words indicating that the Act has been approved by Parliament;
6. *Main body of the Act*. This is divided into sections, which are further divided into subsections and paragraphs. When referring to a section, it is usual to abbreviate it to "s." whilst subsections are written in round brackets. You would therefore write section 2, subsection 1 as s.2(1);

The Structure of an Act

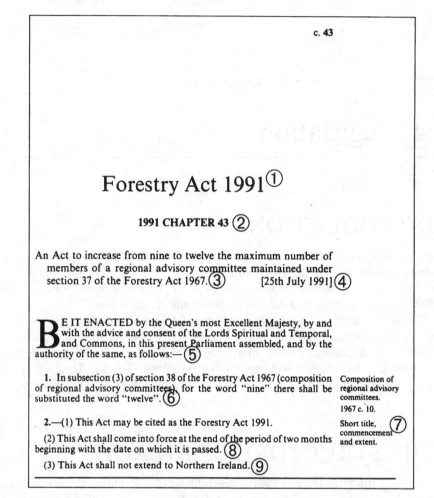

c. 43

Forestry Act 1991①

1991 CHAPTER 43 ②

An Act to increase from nine to twelve the maximum number of members of a regional advisory committee maintained under section 37 of the Forestry Act 1967.③ [25th July 1991]④

BE IT ENACTED by the Queen's most Excellent Majesty, by and with the advice and consent of the Lords Spiritual and Temporal, and Commons, in this present Parliament assembled, and by the authority of the same, as follows:—⑤

1. In subsection (3) of section 38 of the Forestry Act 1967 (composition of regional advisory committees), for the word "nine" there shall be substituted the word "twelve".⑥

Composition of regional advisory committees. 1967 c. 10.

2.—(1) This Act may be cited as the Forestry Act 1991.

(2) This Act shall come into force at the end of the period of two months beginning with the date on which it is passed. ⑧

Short title, commencement and extent. ⑦

(3) This Act shall not extend to Northern Ireland.⑨

7. *Marginal note.* This gives a brief explanation of the contents of the section;
8. *Date of commencement.* A specific date may be set for the Act to come into force. Alternatively, the Act may give a Minister of the Crown the power to bring it into force at a later date. This will be done through a commencement order, which is a form of delegated legislation. If there is no commencement section at the end of an Act, it comes into force on the date of the Royal Assent;
9. *Extent.* Acts of Parliament usually apply to the whole of the United Kingdom, unless specified otherwise in an extent section.

Schedules and tables are sometimes included at the end of an Act. They may contain detailed provisions not included elsewhere in the Act or may summarise and clarify the effect of the Act. They help to prevent the main body of an Act becoming too cluttered with detail and are used in the same way as appendices in a book.

CITATION OF STATUTES

4–3

Statutes (or Acts) are commonly referred to by a shortened version of their title (the short title) and the year of publication, *e.g.* the Theft Act 1968. Every Act published in a year is given its own individual number and Acts may also be cited by the year in which they were passed and the Act (or chapter) number. Thus the Theft Act was the 60th Act passed in 1968 and is cited as 1968, c. 60. "Chapter" is abbreviated to "c." when written, but it is spoken in full.

The present system of citing statutes by their year and chapter number began in 1963. Before that date, the system was more complicated. Prior to 1963, statutes were referred to by the year of the monarch's reign (the "regnal year") and the chapter number. For example, a citation 3 Edw. 7, c. 36 is a reference to the Motor Car Act 1903, which was the 36th Act passed in the third year of the reign of Edward VII.

A session of Parliament normally commences in the autumn and continues through into the summer of the following year. A "regnal year" is reckoned from the date of the sovereign's accession to the throne and a session of Parliament may therefore cover more than one regnal year. In the case of Queen Elizabeth II, who came to the throne in February, the first part of a Parliamentary session, from the autumn until February, falls into one regnal year, whilst the latter part of the session of Parliament falls into a different regnal year. Statutes passed before February bear a different regnal year to those passed after the anniversary of her accession to the throne. Two examples make this clearer:

1. The Children and Young Persons Act 1956 received the Royal Assent in March 1956, when the Queen had just entered the fifth year of her reign. It was the 24th Act to receive the Royal Assent during the Parliament which commenced sitting in the autumn of the fourth year of her reign, and which continued in session during the early part of the fifth year of her reign. The Act is therefore cited as 4 & 5 Eliz. 2, c. 24.
2. By contrast, the Air Corporations Act 1956 was passed during the following session of Parliament and it received the Royal Assent in December 1956, when the Queen was still in the fifth year of her reign. Since, at that time, there could be no certainty that the Queen would still be on the throne in two months' time or that Parliament would still be in session in February, when she would be entering the sixth year of her reign, the statute was cited as 5 Eliz. 2, c. 3 (*i.e.* the third Act passed in the Parliament held in the fifth year of the reign). When the Queen subsequently survived to enter her sixth year, the statute would henceforth be referred to as 5 & 6 Eliz. 2, c. 3.

Both these Acts are to be found in the 1956 volumes of the statutes, which contain all the Acts passed during that year, regardless of the session of Parliament in which they were passed.

Until 1939, the volumes of the statutes contained all the Acts passed in a particular session of Parliament. After that date, the annual volumes contain all the statutes passed in a calendar year. This can give rise to some confusion. For instance, the volume for 1937 contains the statutes passed in the parliamentary session which extended from November 1936 to October 1937. Thus, some Acts which actually bear the date 1936 are included in the 1937 volume. The volume for 1938 includes some statutes passed in December 1937 (which one might normally expect to find in the 1937 volume). The simple rule with older Acts is: if it is not in the volume you expect to find it in, look in the two volumes on either side of it!

4–4 Citation of the Names of Monarchs and their Regnal Years

The names of the monarchs are abbreviated as follows:

Anne	Ann.
Charles	Car., Chas. *or* Cha.
Edward	Edw. *or* Ed.
Elizabeth	Eliz.
George	Geo.
Henry	Hen.
James	Ja., Jac. *or* Jas.
Mary	Mar. *or* M.
Philip and Mary	Ph. & M. *or* Phil. & Mar.
Richard	Ric. *or* Rich.
Victoria	Vict.
William	Will., Wm. *or* Gul.
William and Mary	Wm. & M., Will. & Mar. *or* Gul. & Mar.

A list of the regnal year of monarchs showing the equivalent calendar year is found in *Sweet & Maxwell's Guide to Law Reports and Statutes* (4th ed.), pp. 21–33; in J. E. Pemberton, *British Official Publications* (2nd ed.), pp. 120–125 and at the back of *Osborn's Concise Law Dictionary*.

4–5 MODERN STATUTES

Acts are available on the HMSO website from 1988 and in print as *Public General Acts and Measures*. Publication details are available in the TSO *Daily Lists* and the TSO catalogue (at **www.clicktso.com**).

It is important to bear in mind that the HMSO website and the *Public General Acts and Measures* give you the text of an Act as it was when first published, *i.e.* without subsequent repeals and amendments. The same is true of three print series which reprint the Acts: the *Law Reports: Statutes,* published by the Incorporated Council of Law Reporting, *Current Law Statutes Annotated*, and *Butterworths Annotated Legislation Service*. Most of the electronic sources offer a statement of legislation as currently in force, following subsequent repeals and amendments (**4–8**). *Halsbury's Statutes of England* provides the only print source of legislation in force (**4–17**).

The presence of non-official reprints of legislation in law libraries might seem puzzling. All law libraries will have copies of the *Public General Acts*, statutes are available free from HMSO and most libraries offer access to an online source of legislation in force. However the value of the reprint series should not be discounted. Whether they print the text of legislation as first enacted, or, like *Halsbury's Statutes*, as currently in force, they carry useful annotations. These annotations are unavailable in the electronic sources of legislation. Although they do not have official status, they will help you to appreciate the text of an Act.

Print sources, of whatever kind, are also particularly useful if you are dealing with an important piece of primary legislation, as the text is likely to be extensive. The Education Act 1997, for example, runs to 58 sections and takes up 76 pages of *Current Law Statutes*

Annotated. A printed text of this length can be much more easily scanned than its electronic equivalent. A further advantage of *Halsbury's Statutes* is that it offers the only subject organisation of statutes. The legislation in general subject areas, such as civil liberties or road traffic for example, is brought together in a single volume.

Public General Acts and Measures   4–6

Electronic
The HMSO website (at **www.hmso.gov.uk**) lists Public General Acts on its legislation page (at **www.legislation.hmso.gov.uk/acts.htm**), first by year and then, for the more recent years, alphabetically by title within each year. If you are using the HMSO site it helps to know the year and full title of the Act you are seeking. Earlier years are arranged by year and chapter number. A search engine is available, which searches for legislation on the entire HMSO site and lists search results according to a "relevance ranking". This highlights the legislation in which your search words are prominent. There are also links to the listings of Northern Ireland, Scotland and Wales legislation. These can be found most conveniently from the legislation home page (at **www.hmso.gov.uk/legis.htm**).

The legislation on the HMSO pages can also be found on the BAILII web site (at **www.bailii.org**). Statutes are organised alphabetically by title on the United Kingdom Legislation page.

Print
At the end of the year, the Acts which have been printed individually during the year by TSO are published in annual volumes as the official *Public General Acts and Measures* of 2000, 2001, etc. This series of red volumes has been published since 1831 (originally under the title *Public General Acts*). At the front of the annual volumes will be found a list of all the Acts passed during the year, in alphabetical order, showing where they are to be found in the bound volumes. There is also a chronological list (*i.e.* a list in chapter number order), giving the same information. The General Synod Measures of the Church of England are also printed in full at the back of the annual volumes of the *Public General Acts*. A list of Local and Personal Acts published during the year is printed in the annual volumes, although the texts are not included.

The Statute Law Database   4–7

Another official source of legislation is the Statute Law Database, though at the time of writing the database is incomplete. The database is being developed by the Statutory Publications Office, an office within the Lord Chancellor's Department. The aim is to construct a database of legislation in force. A unique feature of the database will be its capacity to provide the text of primary legislation as in force on any day from February 1, 1991.

Current plans suggest that the database may not be directly available on the internet. Government users are to be given access and the intention is to sell on the data to online publishers in order that they might merge it with their existing products. Details of plans for the database should continue to be available from the Lord Chancellor's Department website (at **www.open.gov.uk/lcd**). You are advised to update this section by checking on developments on this website.

Should current plans change and the database become publicly and directly available, the Statute Law Database would become the first source for anyone looking for the text of legislation in force. It would provide an electronic successor to *Statutes in Force*, a looseleaf official publication which in its time was intended to provide the full text of primary legislation in force. In practice, *Statutes in Force* was often badly out of date and its publication has ceased.

4–8 Other Electronic Sources of Statutes

All the major legal database providers offer electronic access to the full text of Public General Acts. Of these, the Butterworths *Legislation Direct* service (at **www.butterworths.co.uk**), Lexis-Nexis Professsional (at **www.lexis-nexis.co.uk**) and Westlaw UK (at **www.westlaw.co.uk**) all provide the full text of legislation in force. The *UK Statutes* database from Context is different. It provides the text of Acts as first published along with a note of repeals and links to amending legislation. Your library or law school will probably have access to at least one of these databases, and in the absence of the Statute Law Database, they provide the only comprehensive sources for primary legislation for the U.K.

Let us look at an example to show the difference between a database which contains legislation as amended and one which contains the text of statutes as first published. If you use any of the services that provide access to current amended legislation, and search under title for the "Dangerous Dogs Act", ideally specifying 1991 as the year of the Act, you find on each of the services a results screen which lists all of the sections of the Act currently in force. Among those sections you will see section 4B, Contingent destruction orders, which has a date in force noted as June 8, 1997. In other words it was not part of the Act as it received the Royal Assent in 1991. After the text of the section you find an annotation stating that the section was "added by the Dangerous Dogs (Amendment) Act 1997, s.2". You will see that subsection 4 of section 5 is no longer present in the Act, and this will be noted in turn as having been repealed by the Dangerous Dogs (Amendment) Act 1997, s.2. The text you see for the Dangerous Dogs Act 1991 is, as a result of these incorporations and deletions, the amended text as currently in force. In other words, the law as it exists now. The amending text is usually contained within square brackets.

The *Justis UK Statutes* database from Context (at **www.justis.com**), is, in contrast, the only complete electronic source for the full text of statutes as originally published. If you search for the Dangerous Dogs Act 1991 using *UK Statutes*, you will again find a results list which is organised section by section, but this time the text will be unamended. This is helpful if you want to know how the Act was originally formulated, but also remember the Act might have been subsequently changed. It is possible to trace amendments by using the "cross ref" icon at the top of the screen which provides a link to the amending legislation for each section of the Act. The strength of the database lies in its ability to give the full text of older legislation that has been completely repealed. For example, *UK Statutes* is the only electronic source for the Treason Act 1790. (The databases providing access to legislation in force will note the last piece of amending legislation for statutes which are no longer in force. The Treason Act 1790 is noted as being repealed by the Crime and Disorder Act 1998, sections 36(3)(a), 120(2), Schedule 10.)

Further details for these electronic sources of statutes are noted below. These are subscription databases, and your library or law school is likely to have subscriptions to at least one of them. You will need to confirm first which of the databases is available to you.

Usernames and passwords will usually need to be issued to you by a librarian for access purposes (see **2–6**).

Butterworths Legislation Direct   **4–9**
Legislation Direct enables you to make a title search which will find the full, amended and annotated text of Acts of Parliament, along with statutory instruments of general application, in force in England and Wales. Acts of the Scottish Parliament and statutory instruments in the new series of Scottish statutory instruments are also included along with some local Acts. If your library also subscribes to the web versions of any of the Butterworths law reports, the legislation links found within law reports will also link you to *Legislation Direct*. *Legislation Direct* can be found on the Butterworths website (at **www.butterworths.co.uk**).

Justis UK Statutes   **4–10**
The *Justis UK Statutes* database may be available to you either on CD-ROM, or as part of the Justis.com web service. In either case, once you have selected *UK Statutes* from the available Justis databases, a search using the database "title" box is possible. *UK Statutes* contains the full text of the Acts of the Westminster Parliament from 1235 and Acts of the Scottish Parliament from 1999 and of the Northern Ireland Assembly from 2000. If your library subscribes to the web versions of law reports available from Justis.com, you will also find that the legislation links found within those reports link you to the text of *UK Statutes*. Statutory instruments are not included as they are to be found on a separate database, *UK Statutory Instruments*. Links to Justis.com and details of the CD-ROM can be found on the Context website (at **www.context.co.uk**).

Lexis-Nexis Professional   **4–11**
If you have access to Lexis-Nexis Professional, the web-based interface for Lexis-Nexis, you can search for statutes by clicking "UK legislation" under "Assisted searches". Your search results will then come from the database group file, Statutes and Statutory Instruments of England & Wales. It is also possible to search the Statutes of England & Wales file on its own. The full amended text of statutes in force is included. There are no local Acts, and Scottish and Northern Ireland legislation is not included. A link to Lexis-Nexis Professional can be found on the Lexis-Nexis site (at **www.lexis-nexis.co.uk**). There is also a link from the Butterworths website (at **www.butterworths.co.uk**).

Westlaw UK   **4–12**
If you are using Westlaw UK, a title search for an Act is possible using the U.K. legislation search box on the home page. You will then be presented with results from the Westlaw UK's *United Kingdom Law In Force* database. The sections of the act will then be listed on a results screen with links to the full text as currently in force. All Acts of the Westminster Parliament from 1267 are covered in this way. If the Act you have searched dates from 1992 onwards an "Analysis" tab can be clicked which will link to the original text of any amended legislation. It is, for example, possible to find in this way the original text of section 8 of the Education Act 1997, which has been repealed by subsequent legislation, and so is not given in the initial search. The *United Kingdom Law In Force* database includes statutory instruments from 1945. Acts of the Scottish Parliament and the Northern Ireland Assembly are not currently included. Legislation can be searched for from the Westlaw UK website (at **www.westlaw.co.uk**).

4–13 Other Print Sources of Statutes

Your library is likely to have a subscription to at least one of the non-official sources of statutes. As noted in **4–4**, the *Law Reports: Statutes* (**4–14**), *Current Law Statutes Annotated* (**4–15**) and *Butterworths Annotated Legislation Service* (**4–15**) all reprint the text of legislation as originally enacted. *Halsbury's Statutes of England* (**4–17**) prints the text of legislation in force.

4–14 Law Reports: Statutes

The Incorporated Council of Law Reporting publishes, as part of the *Law Reports*, a series entitled *Law Reports: Statutes*. These are issued in several parts each year, each part containing the text of one or more Acts. At the end of the year, the loose parts are replaced by an annual volume or volumes. Unfortunately, the loose parts are often not published until many months after the Act receives the Royal Assent. For the text of recent Acts, you will need to look in other sources, such as *Current Law Statutes Annotated* or the Queen's Printer version of the Act.

4–15 Current Law Statutes Annotated

Current Law Statutes Annotated reprints the full text of all Public General Acts soon after they receive the Royal Assent. They are printed in booklet form on grey paper and are filed into a looseleaf *Service File* in chapter number order. The grey paper denotes that the Act is simply a reprint of the Queen's Printer copy. Some months later, the Act printed on grey paper is replaced by the annotated version which is printed on white paper. At the front of the *Service File* are alphabetical and chronological lists of all the Acts included. If the Act you want to look at is in *italic* type in the contents list, it means that it has not yet been published in this series.

The annotations give a detailed account of the background to the Act, including references to discussions on the Bill in the Houses of Parliament as reported in *Hansard*. The annotations also include a summary of the contents of the Act, as well as definitions and explanations of the meaning of individual sections of the Act. The annotations are in smaller print to avoid confusion with the Act itself. Although the annotations have no official standing, they are extremely useful. The author is often a leading authority on the subject matter and some Acts are later reprinted as books by the publisher, Sweet & Maxwell.

The information in the *Service File* is reissued during the year in bound volumes. *Current Law Statutes Annotated* covers all Public General Acts since 1948, when the series commenced publication. You may find that your library has subscribed to *Scottish Current Law Statutes Annotated*. Despite the name, this contains information on English as well as Scottish legislation and the arrangement is the same as *Current Law Statutes Annotated*.

4–16 Butterworth's Annotated Legislation Service

Butterworth's Annotated Legislation Service was formerly called *Butterworth's Emergency Legislation Service*. It reprints the text of selected Acts, with notes. Many of the volumes cover only one Act, with detailed annotations. Every two years, a *Cumulative Index* volume is published, which lists all the Acts passed since 1939 when the service began, along with a list of Ecclesiastical Measures and certain private Acts. The index indicates where in the volumes to find each Act included in the series. A number of the titles in this series have also been published individually as books. The emphasis is on statutes which will be of use to the practitioner.

Halsbury's Statutes of England

Halsbury's Statutes differs from the other annotated series of statutes. The series outlined above provide annotations to the Acts as they were originally printed. The purpose of *Halsbury's Statutes* is to provide the correct and amended text of all legislation in force, whatever the date of Royal Assent. It includes all Public General Acts in force in England and Wales, although the texts of some Acts of limited importance are not printed. The text of each Act is accompanied by notes which provide, for example, judicial interpretation of words and phrases, details of statutory instruments made under the Act, case law and cross-references to other sections.

Halsbury's Statutes is in its fourth edition. The main work consists of 50 volumes, which are arranged alphabetically by subject. Hence, Volume 1 contains the Acts dealing with admiralty, agency and agriculture, whilst Volume 2 contains the law of allotments and smallholdings, animals, arbitration and so on. Legislation post-dating the volumes appears in the *Current Statutes Service* binders. The annual *Cumulative Supplement* summarises and explains the effect of new Acts, statutory instruments and case law on existing legislation and this in turn is kept up to date by a looseleaf *Noter-Up* service.

If you know the name of an Act, the easiest way to find it in *Halsbury's Statutes* is by looking in the Alphabetical List of Statutes in the front of the annual paper-covered *Tables of Statutes and General Index* volume. An example page from the Alphabetical Index is shown on page 66. The entry tells you the volume number (in bold type) and the page number in *Halsbury's Statutes* where you will find the full text of the Act. If the volume number in the Alphabetical List of Statutes is followed by (S), you will find the Act printed in the looseleaf *Current Statutes Service* under the volume and page number given. Some Acts are not printed in full in one place, but are divided up, each portion of the Act being printed under the most appropriate subject title. If you want to look at the complete text of an Act which has been split up this way, it may be easier to find the Act in one of the other publications outlined above.

If you want to find the text of a very recent Act, look in the Alphabetical List of Statutes which appears in the first volume of the *Current Statutes Service* under the heading "Contents". The entries give the volume number and page where the text of the Act will be found in the *Current Statutes Service* binders.

Once you have located your Act, either in the main volumes or in the *Current Statutes Service* binders, you will find the official text of the Act. Following each section there are notes, in smaller type, giving the meaning of words or phrases used, referring to cases on the interpretation of that section and providing details of any amendments which have been made to the text of the Act since it was first passed. You will also find references to statutory instruments which have been passed under the authority granted by that Act. At the beginning of each Act, you are informed when it became law and provided with a summary of the main provisions of the Act. An example page from Volume 48 of *Halsbury's Statutes* is shown on page 67.

It is important to check that the information on the Act is still up to date (*i.e.* it has not been amended or repealed). To do this, you will need to consult both the *Cumulative Supplement* and the looseleaf *Noter-up* service.

Let us take an example to see how this works. Suppose you want to know whether there have been changes to the Trade Marks Act 1994 since it was passed. You have looked in the Alphabetical List of Statutes (see p. 66) and found the relevant part of the text of the Act in Volume 48 (see p. 67). To find out if this Act has been amended since Volume 48 was published, turn first to the *Cumulative Supplement* and look at the entries for Volume 48. The *Cumulative Supplement* lists, volume by volume and page by page, changes which have

Example Page from the Alphabetical List of Statutes in Halsbury's Statutes Tables of Statutes and General Index

Example Page from Halsbury's Statutes, Volume 48

Persons. See the note "Person" to s 5 ante.

Sub-s (5): Statutory instrument. For provisions as to statutory instruments generally, see the Statutory Instruments Act 1946, Vol 41, title Statutes.

Laid before . . . Parliament. For meaning, see the Laying of Documents before Parliament (Interpretation) Act 1948, s 1(1), Vol 41, title Statutes.

Disapplication of s 7. S 7 ante does not apply when there is an order in force under this section; see s 7(5) ante.

Orders under this section. Up to 1 January 2001 no order had been made under this section and none may be made before the expiry of the period mentioned in sub-s (5) above.

Definitions.

"Community trade mark": s 51
"the Community Trade Mark Regulation": s 51
"earlier right": s 5(4)
"earlier trade mark": s 6

"the registrar": s 62
"registration": s 63(1)
"trade mark": s 1.

Effects of registered trade mark

9 Rights conferred by registered trade mark

(1) The proprietor of a registered trade mark has exclusive rights in the trade mark which are infringed by use of the trade mark in the United Kingdom without his consent.

The acts amounting to infringement, if done without the consent of the proprietor, are specified in section 10.

(2) References in this Act to the infringement of a registered trade mark are to any such infringement of the rights of the proprietor.

(3) The rights of the proprietor have effect from the date of registration (which in accordance with section 40(3) is the date of filing of the application for registration):

Provided that—

(a) no infringement proceedings may be begun before the date on which the trade mark is in fact registered; and

(b) no offence under section 92 (unauthorised use of trade mark, &c in relation to goods) is committed by anything done before the date of publication of the registration.

NOTES

General Note. This section and s 10 post implement Art 5 of EEC Council Directive 89/104.

Proprietor of a registered trade mark. As to the construction of references to the proprietor of a registered trade mark in the provisions of this Act relating to infringement, see s 31(1), (2) post.

Use of the trade mark. As to the burden of proving the use to which a registered trade mark has been put in any civil proceedings under this Act, see s 100 post.

United Kingdom. See the note to s 3 ante.

Without his consent. As to the construction of references to the consent of the proprietor of a registered trade mark, see s 28(3) post (and see also s 82 post (acts done by authorised agents)).

Infringement proceedings. As to infringement proceedings under this Act, see ss 14–21 post.

Trade mark is in fact registered. See s 40 post.

Restriction of rights, etc. The rights conferred by this section in relation to a registered trade mark are restricted if the registration is subject to a disclaimer or limitation; see s 13 post. See also, as to the power of the registrar to suspend the rights given by the registered trade mark where the proprietor of the registered trade mark is an enemy or enemy subject, the Patents, Designs, Copyright and Trade Marks (Emergency) Act 1939, ss 3, 10(1), Vol 50, title War and Emergency.

Transitional provisions. See s 105, Sch 3, para 4 post.

Definitions.

"consent": s 28(3)
"date of filing of an application for registration of a trade mark": s 33(1)
"infringement proceedings": s 103(1)
"proprietor": s 31(2)
"publication": s 103(1)
"registered": s 63(1)

Example Page from Halsbury's Statutes Cumulative Supplement

PAGE

Business Names Act 1985 (c 7)

103   Section 2

In sub-s (1)(a), after the words "Her Majesty's Government" there are inserted the words ", with any part of the Scottish Administration," by the Scotland Act 1999 (Consequential Modifications) (No 2) Order 1999, SI 1999/1820, art 4, Sch 2, Pt I, para 79.

Secretary of State. Any function of the Secretary of State conferred by or under this section may be exercised by, or by employees of, such person as may be authorised in that behalf by the Secretary of State; see the Contracting Out (Functions in relation to the Registration of Companies) Order 1995, SI 1995/1013, art 5, Sch 3, paras 2, 3.

Modification in relation to Scotland. This section is modified in relation to Scotland, by virtue of the Scotland Act 1998 (Modification of Functions) Order 1999, SI 1999/1756, arts 2, 8(1), Schedule, para 9, subject to a saving.

104   Section 3

General Note. By the Company and Business Names (Chamber of Commerce, etc) Act 1999, s 1, Vol 48, title Trade Marks, the Secretary of State is required to include the title "chamber of commerce" (and its Welsh equivalent) in the list of controlled titles maintained in accordance with regulations made under sub-s (1)(a) of this section.

Regulations under this section. The Company and Business Names Regulations 1981, SI 1981/1685, are further amended by SI 1995/3022.

Patents, Designs and Marks Act 1986 (c 39)

109   *No change*

Copyright, Designs and Patents Act 1988 (c 48)

112   Section 302

Trade marks. As to the construction of references to trade marks, cf the Trade Marks Act 1994, ss 1, 106(1), Sch 4, para 1(1), Vol 48, title Trade Marks and Trade Names.

→ Trade Marks Act 1994 (c 26)

117   *Rules of court.* For rules of court relating to proceedings under this Act, see the Rules of the Supreme Court 1965, SI 1965/1776, Ord 100, as substituted by SI 1995/3316, r 3.

121   Section 4

Sub-s (5) is added by the Olympic Symbol etc (Protection) Act 1995, s 13(2), (3), Vol 48, title Trade Marks and Trade Names, with effect in relation to applications for registration made on or after 20 September 1995.

125   Section 6

In sub-s (1)(c), after the words "protection under the Paris Convention" there are inserted the words "or the WTO agreement" by the Patents and Trade Marks (World Trade Organisation) Regulations 1999, SI 1999/1899, reg 13(1).

Example Page from Halsbury's Statutes Noter-Up Service

PAGE

VOLUME 46(S)

Regional Development Agencies Act 1999 (c 45)

31 **Section 35**
Orders under this section. The Development Commission (Transfer of Functions and Miscellaneous Provisions) Order 1999, SI 1999/416.

33 **Section 37**
Orders under this section. The Development Commission (Transfer of Functions and Miscellaneous Provisions) Order 1999, SI 1999/416.

TRADE AND INDUSTRY

VOLUME 47 (1998 Reissue)

Part 1
Trade and Industry in General

Industrial Development Act 1982 (c 52)

482 **Section 8**
Transfer of functions. By the National Assembly for Wales (Transfer of Functions) Order 1999, SI 1999/672, art 5(1), Sch 2, the functions of the Secretary of State under sub-ss (5), (7) of this section are, so far exercisable in relation to Wales, exercisable by the Secretary of State only after consultation with the Assembly. Any orders amending SI 1999/672 are noted to the Government of Wales Act 1998, s 22, Vol 10(S), title Constitutional Law (the principal order-making power).

489 **Section 15**
Transfer of functions. By the National Assembly for Wales (Transfer of Functions) Order 1999, SI 1999/672, art 5(1), Sch 2, certain functions of the Secretary of State under this section are, so far exercisable in relation to Wales, exercisable by the Secretary of State only with the agreement of the Assembly. Any orders amending SI 1999/672 are noted to the Government of Wales Act 1998, s 22, Vol 10(S), title Constitutional Law (the principal order-making power).

Deregulation and Contracting Out Act 1994 (c 40)

550 **Section 1**
Orders under this section. Add: the Deregulation (Weights and Measures) Order 1999, SI 1999/503.

TRADE MARKS AND TRADE NAMES

VOLUME 48 (1995 Reissue)

Trade Marks Act 1994 (c 26)

129 **Section 10**
Sub-s (3): Infringes a registered trade mark. British Telecommunications plc v One In A Million Ltd, cited, also reported at [1999] 1 WLR 903.
In the course of trade, etc. British Telecommunications plc v One In A Million Ltd, cited, also reported at [1999] 1 WLR 903.

occurred in the law since each of the main volumes was published. There are a number of entries showing changes to the Trade Marks Act 1994 and references are provided to Statutory instruments issued under authority granted by the Act (see p. 68).

The information in the *Cumulative Supplement* is up to date to the end of the preceding year. For more recent changes to the Act, you should consult the looseleaf *Noter-up* service under the appropriate volume and page number (see p. 69). This will tell you of any changes in the law in the last few months.

SUMMARY: FINDING UP-TO-DATE INFORMATION ON AN ACT USING HALSBURY'S STATUTES

1. Look for the name of the Act in the Alphabetical List of Statutes in the paper-covered *Table of Statutes and General Index* volume. This will refer you to the appropriate volume (in **bold** type) and page number. An (S) following the volume number refers you to the *Current Statutes Service*.
2. If the Act is more recent than the *Table of Statutes* volume, consult the Alphabetical List of Statutes at the front of Volume 1 of the *Current Statutes Service*.
3. Look up the Act in the appropriate volume, or the *Current Statutes Service*, and note the volume number and the page which contains the relevant information.
4. Look to see if there is an entry for your volume and page number in the *Cumulative Supplement*. If there is an entry, there has been a change in the law. Whether or not there is a relevant entry in the *Cumulative Supplement*, you should now turn to the *Noter-up* service (see below).
5. Finally, look for any entries for your volume and page number in the *Noter-up* service. Read this information (if there is any) in conjunction with the information in the main volume and the *Cumulative Supplement*.

Remember the stages:

main volume;
Cumulative Supplement;
Noter-up service;

and consult them in that order.

4-18 CHECKING WHETHER LEGISLATION IS IN FORCE OR HAS BEEN AMENDED

It is important to know the status of legislation. Has the Act been changed, if so when and in what manner? Is the Act in force and are all or only some of the sections of the Act operational? Fortunately, this essential but complex process has been tackled for you.

Electronic

If you are using *Butterworths Legislation Direct* (at **www.butterworths.co.uk**), Lexis-Nexis Professional (at **www.lexis-nexis.co.uk**) or Westlaw UK (at **www.westlaw.co.uk**), the legislation shown on your screen is as amended and currently in force (see **4–8**). Remember, there is a delay between the publication of a statute and its incorporation into one of these databases, though the delay may be brief. Butterworths claim that their *Legislation Direct* service is up to date within four to five working days.

If you wish to check the commencement date of legislation (the day it comes into force), there are two further possibilities using online sources. Lawtel (at **www.lawtel.co.uk**) carries commencement dates for all Acts along with details of repeals and amendments. If you search for an Act by title in the Lawtel statutory law database, a link is provided under the Act's title to a "Statutory Status Table". The table lays out, section by section, the amended sections and those repealed or partially repealed. Consider the Dangerous Dogs Act 1991, for example (**4–8**). Under section 4A there is a link which leads you to the amending legislation. Summaries of Acts are available from 1984 onwards, including full text from 1990.

Butterworths Legislation Direct (at **www.butterworths.co.uk**) also includes *Is It In Force?* This allows you to search for commencement dates. Information on repeals and amendments is included in this database, but partial repeals and amendments are not always listed.

Significantly, in 2000, the *Is It In Force?* database was made available free as part of the *Butterworths Law Direct* service (at **butterworths.co.uk**). This is the only non-subscription source for checking whether legislation is in force. If you follow the *Is It In Force?* link from the *Law Direct* website and search the title and year of a statute, the web results page shows the date of Royal Assent and gives the number and commencement date that brought the Act into force. The entire Act may not come into force on a single day. Thus, commencement dates are also listed for individual sections of an Act. If a search is made for the Dangerous Dogs Act 1991, a commencement date of August 12, 1991 appears for most sections, along with a note citing the Dangerous Dogs Amendment Act 1997 as the source for the inserted sections 4A and 4B. Commencement dates for those sections can be traced by searching under the Dangerous Dogs Amendment Act 1997.

Print

The *Cumulative Supplement* and the *Noter-up* service in *Halsbury's Statutes* enable you to find out whether a statute has been repealed or amended (**4–17**). In addition, *Halsbury's Statutes* also includes *Is It In Force?*. This provides a quick alternative method of checking the current status of any Act passed since 1961.To find out if an Act has recently come into force, consult the *Is It In Force?* update in the *Noter-Up* service binder in *Halsbury's Statutes*.

In addition to *Halsbury's Statutes*, there are other publications which provide information on whether legislation has been amended or repealed. The *Chronological Table of the Statutes* (described in **4–20**) is the easiest place to look if you wish to check whether a very old statute is still in force. For up-to-date information, however, the most useful alternative to *Halsbury's Statutes* is the *Current Law Statute Citator*, described in **4–19**.

Both *Halsbury's Statutes* and *Current Law* are updated monthly. You can update the information found in *Current Law* or *Halsbury's Statutes* by consulting the weekly practitioners' journals, such as the *New Law Journal* and the *Solicitors Journal*, or glance through the latest issues of the *TSO Daily List*.

Example Page from the Current Law Legislation Citator 1989–1995

1991—cont.

57. Water Resources Act 1991—*cont.*
s. 209, see *Att.-Gen's Reference (No. 2 of 1994), The Times,* August 4, 1994, C.A.
ss. 213–215, repealed: 1995, c.25, schs. 22, 24.
s. 218, repealed: 1995, c. 25, sch.22.
ss. 219, repealed: 1995, c.25, sch.22.
s. 219, regs. 92/337; 94/1057.
s. 221, amended: 1994, c. 19, sch.11; 1995, c.25, sch.22.
s. 222, substituted: 1995, c.25, sch.21.
s. 224, substituted: 1995, c.25, s.118.
sch. 1, repealed: 1995, c.25, schs. 22, 24.
schs. 3–4, repealed: 1995, c.25, schs. 22, 24.
sch. 3, order 94/245.
sch. 5, amended: 1995, c.25, sch.22.
schs. 8, 14, amended: 1994, c.19, sch.11.
sch. 10, substituted: 1995, c.25, sch.22.
sch. 15, amended: 1992, c.14, sch.13; 1994, c.19, sch.11.
schs. 16, 19, amended: *ibid.*
sch. 22, amended: 1994, c.21, sch.9.
sch. 24, amended: 1993, c.43, sch.12; 1994, c.21, sch.9.
sch. 25, amended: 1995, c.25, sch.15.
58. Statutory Water Companies Act 1991.
Royal Assent, July 25, 1991.
ss. 12, 14, orders 92/424, 1988, 1993; 94/2205; 95/79.
59. Land Drainage Act 1991.
Royal Assent, July 25, 1991.
amended: 1995, c.25, sch.22.
s. 3, orders 92/2287; 93/33–55, 451–454, 815–817, 824, 825, 829, 910, 1041, 1174, 1175, 1570, 1640, 1738, 2712; 94/310, 723, 1411; 95/1325, 2851.
s. 10, amended: 1994, c.19, sch.11.
s. 12, amended: 1995, c.21, sch.13.
ss. 12, 13, repealed: 1994, c.25, s.2.
ss. 14–16, 18, 20, amended: 1994, c.19, sch.11.
s. 23, amended: 1995, c.25, sch.22.
s. 32, order 93/1590.
s. 37, amended: regs. 92/3079.
ss. 45, 46, amended: 1992, c.14, sch.13.
ss. 48, 49, regs. 93/223.
ss. 55, 57, 58, amended: 1994, c.19, sch.11.
s. 59, amended: 1995, c.25, s.101.
ss. 61A–61E, added: 1994, c.25, s.1.
s. 61C, repealed in pt.: 1995, c.25, sch.24.
s.61C, amended: 1995, c.25, sch.10.
s. 61F, added: 1995, c.25, sch.22.
s. 62, amended: 1994, c.19, sch.11.
s. 65, regs. 93/223.
ss. 66, 72, amended: 1994, c.19, sch.11.
s. 72, regs. 93/223.
s. 72, repealed in pt.: 1995, c.25, sch.24.
s. 72, amended: 1995, c.21, sch.13.
s. 74, amended: 1995, c.21, sch.21.
s. 75, substituted: 1995, c.25, s.118.
sch. 1, amended: regs. 92/3079.
schs. 2–4, amended: 1994, c.19, sch.11.
sch. 6, amended: 1994, c.21, sch.9.
60. Water Consolidation (Consequential Provisions) Act 1991.
Royal Assent, July 25, 1991.
sch. 1, repealed in pt.: 1993, c.12, sch.6; 1995, c.25, sch.24.
sch. 1, C, in pt.: 1993, c.12, s.40, sch.3.
61. Statute Law Revision (Isle of Man) Act 1991.
Royal Assent, July 25, 1991.
62. Armed Forces Act 1991.
Royal Assent, July 25, 1991.

1991—cont.

62. Armed Forces Act 1991—*cont.*
s. 1, orders 92/1712; 93/1804; 94/1903; 95/1964.
s. 16, see *Legrove* v. *Legrove* [1994] 2 F.L.R. 119, C.A.
s. 17, amended: 1995, c.36, sch.4(S); order 95/756.
s. 18, amended: 1995, c.36, sch.4(S); order 95/756.
s. 20, amended: order 95/756.
s. 21, amended: 1995, c.36, sch.4(S); order 95/756.
s. 23, amended: 1995, c.36, sch.4(S); order 95/756.
s. 27, order 91/2719.
sch. 2, repealed in pt.: 1991, c.53, sch.13; 1995, c.40, sch.5(S).
sch. 2, C.: 1995, c.46, s.253.
schs. 3, 5, repealed in pt.: 1991, c.53, sch.13.
63. British Railways Board (Finance) Act 1991.
Royal Assent, July 25, 1991.
s. 2, repealed: 1993, c.43, sch.14.
64. Breeding of Dogs Act 1991.
Royal Assent, July 25, 1991.
65. Dangerous Dogs Act 1991. ←
Royal Assent, July 25, 1991.
Commencement Order, 91/1742.
see *D.P.P.* v. *Kellett, The Times,* July 14, 1994, D.C.; *R.* v. *Metropolitan Police and the Index of Exempted Dogs, ex p. Wheeler* [1993] Crim.L.R. 942, D.C.; *R.* v. *Secretary of State for the Home Office, ex p. James (Nicola)* [1994] C.O.D. 167, D.C.
s. 1, see *R.* v. *Knightsbridge Crown Court, ex p. Dunne; Brock* v. *D.P.P.* [1993] 4 All E.R. 491, D.C.; *Normand* v. *Freeman,* 1992, S.L.T. 598; *Parker* v. *Annan,* 1993 S.C.C.R. 185; *Annan* v. *Troup,* 1993 S.C.C.R. 192; *Bates* v. *D.P.P.* (1993) 157 J.P. 1004, D.C.
s. 1, orders 91/1742–1744, 2297, 2636.
s. 3, see *R.* v. *Bezzina; R.* v. *Codling; R.* v. *Elvin, The Times,* December 7, 1993, C.A.; *W.* v. *C.I.C.B.,* August 10, 1993; C.I.C.B.; Plymouth; *Swinlay,* v. *Crowe,* 1995 S.L.T. 34; *Tierney* v. *Valentine,* 1994 S.C.C.R. 697; *R.* v. *Rawlings* [1994] Crim.L.R. 433, C.A.; *R.* v. *Trafford Magistrates Court, ex p. Riley (Robertina)* (CO/1603/95), March 16, 1995, Balcombe L.J.; *Stewart* v. *Donnelly,* 1994 S.C.C.R. 545; *McGeachy* v. *Normand,* 1993 S.C.C.R. 951; *D.P.P.* v. *Fellowes* [1993] Crim.L.R. 523, D.C.
s. 4, see *Normand* v. *Freeman,* 1992 S.L.T. 598; *Stewart* v. *Donnelly,* 1994 S.C.C.R. 545.
s. 4, amended: 1995, c.40, sch.4(S.).
s. 5, see *R.* v. *Walton Street Justices, ex p. Grothers, The Times,* June 30, 1992, D.C.; *R.* v. *Bezzina; Same* v. *Codling; Same* v. *Elvin* [1994] 1 W.L.R. 1057, C.A.; *Parker* v. *Annan,* 1993 S.C.C.R. 185; *Annan* v. *Troup,* 1993 S.C.C.R. 192.
s. 10, order 91/1742.
s. 10, see *Tierney* v. *Valentine,* 1994 S.C.C.R. 697; *Bates* v. *D.P.P.* (1993) 157 J.P. 1004, D.C.; *McGeachy* v. *Normand,* 1993 S.C.C.R. 851; *D.P.P.* v. *Fellowes* [1993] Crim.L.R. 523, D.C.
s. 35, see *R.* v. *Bezzina; Same* v. *Codling; Same* v. *Elvin* [1994] 1 W.L.R. 1057, C.A.
66. British Technology Group Act 1991.
Royal Assent, October 22, 1991.
Commencement order, 91/2721.
s. 1, orders 91/2721, 2722.

Current Law Statute Citator

The printed *Current Law Statute Citator* enables you to check whether any statute has been repealed or amended since 1947. An additional, unique feature of the *Statute Citator* is the inclusion of references to cases in which a statute or section of a statute has been interpreted. These cases will show how the judiciary have interpreted words, sentences and sections of the Act. You will also find listings of Statutory Instruments passed under a particular Act. Since 1972 the printed *Statute Citator* is combined with the *Statutory Instrument Citator* in the *Current Law Legislation Citators*. Joined in this way, the *Legislation Citators* form the content of the *Current Law Legislation Citator* database available either directly from Sweet & Maxwell as part of the *Current Legal Information* service, or from Westlaw UK in the form of its UK Legislative Locator database.

Electronic

If your library or law school has a subscription to the *Current Law Legislation Citator* database as part of Sweet & Maxwell's *Current Legal Information*, you will find that it is available either on the internet (at **www.smlawpub.jhc.net**) or on CD-ROM. In either case *Current Legal Information* is the service you will be using.

Another database carrying the same information is available through Westlaw UK. Choose the UK Legislative Locator using the Quick search link on the Welcome page (at **www.westlaw.co.uk**).

Whichever search access route you select you must enter the title of the statute in the search box. Following your search, a results list displays entries for the Act section by section. Under the entry for each section you see details of repeals and amendments. If, as in **4–8**, the legislation you are interested in is the Dangerous Dogs Act 1991, you can follow the database link for section 5 and discover a reference to the Dangerous Dogs (Amendment) Act 1997 c. 53, s. 3 (2) – this tells you that subsection 4 is superseded by amending legislation. Likewise, you will also find links for the added sections 4A and 4B, again with a reference to the Dangerous Dogs (Amendment) Act 1997 which carried it.

The entries for each section of the Act list the cases in which a particular section of a statute has been judicially interpreted. If you are using Westlaw UK, you can follow a link from the case name to the *Current Law Cases* summary. Westlaw UK also has hyperlink references to the text of statutory instruments made under an Act.

Print

If you are using the print version of the *Citator*, you will find that it is divided into several volumes, entitled either *Statute Citator* or *Legislation Citator*. The oldest volume details changes to Acts (of whatever age) that took place between 1947 and 1971. Subsequent volumes detail changes to Acts for the periods 1972–1988, 1989–1995 and 1996–1999. Changes since 1999 are covered by annual paper-covered volumes. For the most recent developments, you will need to look in the Statute Citator section of the most recent issue of the *Current Law Monthly Digest*.

Entries in the *Citators* are arranged by year and chapter number of the legislation and cover Acts which have been altered or amended between the dates mentioned in the title of the Citator. The *Statute Citator 1947–1971*, for example, includes Acts as far back as the thirteenth century, provided they were amended or cited in court during the years 1947–1971. The entries indicate which statutes have amended the Act, any statutory instruments that have been made under the Act and any judgments which have interpreted the meaning of the Act. At the front of the bound volumes from 1972–1988 onwards, there is an Alphabetical List of Statutes. This is very useful if you are unsure of the year or chapter of an Act, and wish to locate it in the *Citator*. For any Act you are interested in, you need to begin with the volume which covers the year of the Act and then continue on, checking the Act in subsequent volumes of the *Citator*.

To continue with the example used in **4–8**, the entry from the *Legislation Citator* on page 72 shows that the Dangerous Dogs Act 1991, which was chapter 65 in the Statute Book, received the Royal Assent in July 1995. Section 4 of the Act was amended by the 1995 Act numbered chapter 40. (To find the name of this Act, move forward in the *Citator* to the entries for 1995, and locate chapter number 40 within that year.) The meaning of various sections of the Dangerous Dogs Act 1991 was interpreted by a number of cases. The cases are listed against the Act as a whole and then against each relevant section. Statutory instruments passed under the Act are listed for sections 1 and 10. The statutory instrument number is given, preceded by the word "order" or "orders".

To find the amendments that were made to section 4 of the Act in 1997, you need to look in the next volume of the *Legislation Citator*, covering 1996–1999. Here you will find references to the Act which is chapter 53 for 1997, the Dangerous Dogs (Amendment) Act 1997.

Finally, you may need to find the latest changes to the Act. Look in the Statute Citator section of the latest issue of the *Current Law Monthly Digest* for changes which have taken place in the current year.

If you wish to check amendments or repeals made to Acts prior to 1947, the *Chronological Table of Statutes* (**4–20**) provides the most comprehensive route.

4–20 Chronological Table of the Statutes

The *Chronological Table of the Statutes* is an official publication which lists every statute which has been passed since 1235, and shows, for each one, whether it is still law. This is done by the use of different type faces—an entry in *italic* type indicates that the statute in question is no longer law, whilst entries in **bold** type represent Acts which are still wholly or partly in force. The use of a number of abbreviations can make the entries appear a little confusing.

The entries are arranged in date order in the two volumes. Let us suppose that you wish to discover if any part of the Children and Young Persons Act 1956 is still law. Turn to the entries for 1956, and locate the relevant entry (4 & 5 Eliz. 2, c. 24). The entry, which is reproduced on page 75, is printed in *italic* type. This is an indication that the Act is *not* in force. The entry tells us that the statute was repealed (r.) in respect of Scotland (S.) by the Social Work (Scotland) Act 1968 (c. 49), s.95(2) and Schedule 9, Part I; and in England (E.) the Act was repealed by the Children and Young Persons Act 1969, s.72(4).

The entry for the Agricultural Research Act (4 & 5 Eliz. 2, c. 28) is printed in **bold** type. This indicates that part of this Act is still law, although the entry tells you that most of section 1 was repealed by the Science and Technology Act 1965. A list of the abbreviations used will be found at the front of the volume.

The *Chronological Table* also includes a list of Acts of the Parliament of Scotland 1424–1707, and of Church Assembly Measures, showing if they are still law.

Unfortunately, the *Chronological Table* is usually two or three years out of date. It is updated by the annual publication entitled *The Public General Acts and General Synod Measures: 20 . . .: Tables and Index*, under the heading "Effect of legislation". This shows whether the Acts passed during that year have amended or repealed any previous legislation. As in the *Chronological Table*, the entries in this index are arranged by the date

Example Page from the Chronological Table of the Statutes, Part II 1951–1990

CHRONOLOGICAL TABLE OF THE STATUTES   929

1955 (4 & 5 Eliz. 2).
 c. 20 .. *Agriculture (Improvement of Roads).*—r. S.L. (Reps.), 1986 (c. 12), s. 1 (1), sch. 1
        pt. II.
 c. 21 .. *Diplomatic Immunities Restriction.*—r., Diplomatic Privileges, 1964 (c. 81) s. 8 (4),
        sch. 2.
 c. 22 .. *E.L.C.*—r., S.L.R., 1963.

1956 (4 & 5 Eliz. 2).
 c. 23 .. *Leeward Islands.*—r., S.L. (Reps.), 1986 (c. 12), s. 1 (1), sch. 1. pt. IX.
➤ c. 24 .. *Children and Young Persons.*—r. (S.) Social Work (S.), 1968 (c. 49), s. 95 (2), sch. 9
        pt. I; (E.), Children and Young Persons, 1969 (c. 54), s. 72 (4), sch. 6.
 c. 25 .. **Therapeutic Substances.**
        r. (*prosp.*(exc. s. 1 pt., ss. 2, 8–15, pt. sch. 1)—Medicines, 1968 (c. 67), s. 135 (2),
          sch. 6.
        s. 1 r. in pt.—Medicines, 1968 (c. 67). s. 135 (2), sch. 6.
          4 am.—S.I.s 1968/1699; 1969/388; Biological Standards, 1975 (c. 4), s. 6 (1);
            S.I. 1988/1843.
          transfer of functions—Biological Standards, 1975 (c. 4), s. 6; S.I. 1988/1843.
          5 transfer of functions—S.I. 1988/1843.
          17 r.—N.I., 1962 (c. 30), ss. 7 (9), 30 (2), ss. 1, 4 pt. IV; N.I. Constitution,
            1973 (c. 36), s. 41 (1), sch. 6 pt. I.
        sch. 1 am.—S.I.s 1963/1456; 1966/501, 502, 505, 506; 1967/1195.
 c. 26 .. *Police (S.).*—r., Police (S.), 1967 (c. 77), ss. 52 (2), 53, sch. 5 pts. I, II.
 c. 27 .. *Charles Beattie Indemnity.*—r., Representation of the People, 1969 (c. 15), s. 24 (4),
        sch. 3 pt. I.
➤ c. 28 .. **Agricultural Research.**
        expld.—Science and Technology, 1965 (c. 4), s. 2 (5).
        s. 1 r. (exc. subs. (1))—Science and Technology, 1965 (c. 4), ss. 2 (4), 6 (3),
          sch. 4.
 c. 29 .. *Dentists.*—r., Dentists, 1983 (c. 38), s. 33 (2), sch. 3 pt. I.
 c. 30 .. **Food and Drugs (S.).**
        r. (1991)—Food Safety, 1990 (c.16), s.59(4), sch.5.
        saved—Trade Descriptions, 1968 (c. 29), s. 2 (5); Agriculture, 1970 (c. 40), s. 25
          (5).
        appl.—Weights and Measures, 1985 (c. 72), s. 94 (1).
        s. 1, 2 r. in pt.—Medicines, 1968 (c. 67), s. 135 (2), sch. 6.
          3 r. in pt.—Medicines, 1968 (c. 67), s. 135 (2), sch. 6; Finance, 1981 (c. 35),
            s. 139 (6), sch. 19 pt. III, Note I; S.I.1990/1196;
          am.—Alcoholic Liquor Duties, 1979 (c. 4), s. 92 (1), sch. 3 para. 2.
          4 am.—European Communities, 1972 (c. 68), s. 4, sch. 4 para. 3.
          6 am.—Agriculture, 1967 (c. 22), s. 7 (3).
          r. in pt.—Medicines, 1968 (c. 67), s. 135 (2), sch. 6.
          appl. (mod.)—Agriculture, 1970 (c. 40), s. 25 (4).
          7 r. in pt.—Weights and Measures, 1963 (c. 31), s. 63 (1), sch. 9 pt. II.
          9 ext.—S.I. 1979/1641.
          appl.(mods.)—S.I.1989/2157.
          11 am.—Transport, 1962 (c. 46), s. 32 sch. 2; Transport, 1968 (c. 73), s. 156
            (2), sch. 16 para. 7.
          12 am.—Slaughter of Animals (S.), 1980 (c. 13), s. 23, sch. 1 para. 1.
          16 r. in pt.—European Communities, 1972 (c. 68), s. 4, sch. 4 para. 3.
          17 am.—Food and Drugs (Milk), 1970 (c. 3), s. 1 (2).
          r. in pt.—European Communities, 1972 (c. 68), s. 4, sch. 4 para. 3;
            S.I. 1990/816.
          20 am.—Local Govt (S.), 1973 (c. 65), s. 214 (1), sch. 27, pt. II para. 121.
          21 am.—Local Govt. (S.), 1973 (c. 65), s. 214 (2), sch. 27 pt. II para. 122.
          r. in pt.—Local Govt. (S.), 1973 (c. 65), ss. 209 (1), 237 (1), sch. 25 para. 27,
            sch. 29.
          22 am.—Nat. Health Service (S.), 1972 (c. 58), s. 64 (1), sch. 6 para. 95; Nat.
            Health Service (S.), 1978 (c. 29), s. 109, sch. 15 para. 10.
          r. in pt.—Local Govt. (S.), 1973 (c. 65), ss. 209 (1), 237 (1), sch. 25 para. 28,
            sch. 29.
          24 am.—Nat. Health Service (S.), 1972 (c. 58), s. 64 (1), sch. 6 para. 96; Nat.
            Health Service (S.), 1978 (c. 29), sch. 15 para. 10.
          Pts. II, III (ss. 25–51) appl. (mod.)—Weights and Measures &c., 1976 (c. 77),
            s. 12, sch. 6 para. 3 (2).
          s. 25 r.—Local Govt. (Misc. Provns.) (S.), 1981 (c. 23), ss. 30, 41, sch. 4.

[See next page.]

of the original Act, so that it is possible to tell at a glance if there has been any change to a particular statute. The *Public General Acts: Table and Index* is published separately by TSO and it is also printed at the end of the annual volumes of the *Public General Acts and Measures*.

A quicker method of bringing the information in the *Chronological Table* up to date is to look in the latest *Current Law Statute Citator* (**4–19**).

4–21 OLDER STATUTES

Through the *Chronological Table of the Statutes*, you will be able to discover whether an Act is still in force. Acts, or sections of Acts, which are in force, whatever their date, can be found in *Halsbury's Statutes* (**4–17**). However, it will sometimes be necessary to look at an Act of Parliament which is no longer in force and dates back beyond 1831 when the *Public General Acts* series (**4–6**) was first published. These can be found in the collections described below.

The earliest statute which is still part of the law of the land was passed in 1267. The first parliamentary statute dates from 1235 (the Statute of Merton), although some collections of the statutes commence in 1225. Collections of the legislation prior to 1225 do exist (*e.g.* A. J. Robertson, *The Laws of the Kings of England from Edmund to Henry I*) but they are not regarded as forming part of the statutes of the realm.

4–22 Statutes of the Realm
Produced by the Record Commission, *Statutes of the Realm* is generally regarded as the most authoritative collection of the early statutes. It covers statutes from 1235 to 1713, including those no longer in force, and prints the text of all Private Acts before 1539. There are alphabetical and chronological indexes to all the Acts and there is a subject index to each volume, as well as an index to the complete work.

4–23 Statutes at Large
The title of *Statutes at Large* was given to various editions of the statutes, most of which were published during the eighteenth century. They normally cover statutes published between the thirteenth and the eighteenth or nineteenth centuries.

4–24 Acts and Ordinances of the Interregnum
Acts passed during the Commonwealth are excluded from the collections of the statutes mentioned above. They can be found in C. H. Firth and R. S. Rait, *Acts and Ordinances of the Interregnum 1642–1660*.

4–25 LOCAL AND PERSONAL ACTS

In addition to Public General Acts, which apply to the whole population or a substantial part of it, there are also passed each year a few Local and Personal Acts. These Acts affect only a particular area of the country or a particular individual or body, *e.g.* Railtrack (Waverley Station) Order Confirmation Act; Colchester Borough Council Act 2001.

The chapter number of a Local Act is printed in roman numerals, to distinguish it from the Public General Act of the same number. Thus the Railtrack (Waverley Station) Order Confirmation Act may be cited as 2000, c. vi (*i.e.* the sixth Local Act passed in 2000), whilst

2000, c. 6 is the citation for a Public General Act, the Powers of Criminal Courts (Sentencing) Act.

Personal Acts are cited in the same way as Public General Acts, but with the chapter number printed in italics, *e.g. c. 3*. The citation of Local and Personal Acts was amended in 1963. Prior to that date, they are cited by regnal years, in the same way as Public General Acts, *e.g.* 12 & 13 Geo. 5, c. xiv relates to a Local Act, whilst 12 & 13 Geo. 5, c. 14 is a Public General Act (**4–3**).

Local and Personal Acts are listed in alphabetical order in the annual *Local and Personal Acts 19 . . .: Tables and Index*, which can also be found in the bound volumes of the *Public General Acts and Measures*. From 1991 onwards, they are available on the HMSO legislation web pages (at **www.legislation.hmso.gov.uk**). In addition, HMSO published two cumulative indexes: the *Index to Local and Personal Acts 1801–1947* and the *Supplementary Index to the Local and Personal Acts 1948–1966*.

Although most libraries will possess copies of the Public General Acts in some form, printed copies of the Local and Personal Acts are not so widely available. Those which are published are listed in the *TSO Daily Lists*, which are cumulated in the *TSO Catalogues*. Local Acts since 1992 are printed in the final volume of *Current Law Statutes Annotated* each year. To obtain a copy of the text of an older Local Act or a Personal Act, you may need to contact the local library or the organisation affected by the legislation.

STATUTORY INSTRUMENTS   4–26

In order to reduce the length and complexity of statutes and increase flexibility in the light of changing circumstances Parliament may include in an Act an "enabling" section, which grants to some other authority (usually a Minister of the Crown) power to make detailed rules and regulations on a principle laid down in general terms by the Act. The various Road Traffic Acts, for example, give the Secretary of State for Transport power, amongst other things, to impose speed limits on particular stretches of road, to vary these limits at any time, to create experimental traffic schemes, to introduce new road signs, to control the construction and use of vehicles and to impose regulations concerning parking, pedestrian crossings, vehicle licences, insurance and numerous other aspects of the law relating to motor vehicles. An advantage of this power is that the rules can be readily changed, without the necessity for Parliamentary debate and approval of every amendment.

Statutory instruments, together with statutory codes of practice and byelaws, form what is called *secondary* or *subordinate* legislation, often also called *delegated* legislation, since Parliament has delegated the power to make this legislation to another authority.

The term *statutory instruments* is a generic one, and includes rules, regulations and orders. Commencement orders are a particularly important type of statutory instrument, since they set the date for the commencement of an Act or bring certain provisions of an Act into force (see point 8 of **4–2**). Like statutes, statutory instruments may be of general or of purely local interest. Local instruments are not always printed and published in the normal way. An Order of Council, made by the Queen and her Privy Council, is also a form of statutory instrument. These are printed as an appendix to the annual volumes of statutory instruments, together with Royal Proclamations and Letters Patent.

Citation of Statutory Instruments   4–27

Each statutory instrument published during the year is given its own number. The official citation is: S.I. year/number. For example, the Genetically Modified Organisms

(Contained Use) Regulations 1993 was the 15th statutory instrument to be passed in 1993 and its citation is therefore S.I. 1993/15.

Statutory instruments typically have a title which includes the word "Rules", "Regulations" or "Order", *e.g.* Rules of the Supreme Court, the Safety of Sports Grounds (Designation) Order, the Registration of Births and Deaths Regulations. If you are undecided whether the document you are seeking is a statutory instrument, check in the Alphabetical List of Statutory Instruments in *Halsbury's Statutory Instruments*.

4–28 Tracing Statutory Instruments

Electronic
Statutory instruments are listed on the HMSO website (at **www.hmso.gov.uk**). They can be found on the United Kingdom legislation page under "Statutory Instruments", arranged by year and then number. Coverage begins in 1987. The keyword search engine on the website can help if you do not know the number. It can be found under the "Search" link at the bottom of the legislation pages (see also **7–26** on subject searching for statutory instruments). Results are presented according to a relevance ranking and the search engine will search all legislation on the HMSO site, *i.e.* both statutes and statutory instruments.

Most of the subscription databases noted in **4–8** combine statutory instruments with statutes in their legislation searches. If you know the title of the statutory instrument you wish to find, enter the title in the database search box and continue as for statute searching (**4–8**). It helps to know the exact title, *e.g.* "Working Time Regulations 1998". Keyword searching on the text of statutory instruments is also possible. These databases present the text of legislation in force (**4–8**). If a statutory instrument has been amended, you see the text of the amended statutory instrument. If the statutory instrument is no longer in force, it will not be found in the database.

The *UK Statutory Instruments* database from Context, available on CD-ROM or online from Justis.com (at **www.justis.com**), provides the exception. It carries the text of statutory instruments as published. Coverage begins in 1987.

Print
The statutory instruments published each day are listed in the *TSO Daily Lists*. Every week, a summary of the most important new instruments is printed in the *New Law Journal*. The *Solicitors Journal*, many specialist journals and *Current Law* all note recent changes in the law which have been brought about by statutory instruments.

A monthly publication called the *List of Statutory Instruments* summarises the statutory instruments published during a particular month, along with alphabetical and numerical lists. A detailed subject index cumulates during the year and an annual *List of Statutory Instruments* replaces the monthly parts.

Individual statutory instruments can be bought from TSO. In many libraries, these are replaced at the end of the year by a number of bound volumes. The instruments are now printed in these volumes in numerical order, although, until 1961, they were arranged by subject. The last volume of each yearly set contains a subject index to all the instruments published during the year.

All the statutory instruments which were still in force at the end of 1948 were reprinted in a series of volumes entitled *Statutory Rules and Orders and Statutory Instruments Revised*. This was arranged in subject order, showing all the instruments which were then in force.

If your library does not possess a complete set of statutory instruments, you may be able to trace the text of the instrument in *Halsbury's Statutory Instruments* (see **4–29**) or in one of the many specialist looseleaf encyclopedias, *e.g.* the *Encyclopedia of Housing Law and Practice*. Failing this, a summary may often be found in the *Current Law Year Book* or the *Current Law Monthly Digest* under the appropriate subject heading. There are chronological, alphabetical and subject lists at the beginning of each *Year Book* showing where each instrument appears in the volume. An alphabetical list in the *Monthly Digest* covers statutory instruments digested during the year, with a reference to the relevant *Monthly Digest* issue and paragraph number. Statutory instruments enforcing European legislation are ordered chronologically in another list, which includes a reference to the legislation which the statutory instrument implements and where to find a summary of the instrument in *Current Law*. The annual *Current Law Statutory Instrument Citator* brings together a full list of statutory instruments enforcing European legislation.

Halsbury's Statutory Instruments   4–29
Halsbury's Statutory Instruments provides up-to-date information on every statutory instrument of general application in force in England and Wales. It reproduces the text of a selected number and provides summaries of others. The work consists of 22 volumes, in which the statutory instruments are arranged in broad subject categories. The service is kept up to date by two looseleaf *Service* binders containing, in Binder 1, notes of changes in the law and, in Binder 2, the text of selected new instruments.

If you know the year and number of a statutory instrument, the easiest way to locate it in *Halsbury's Statutory Instruments* is through the Chronological List of Instruments in Binder 1. Alternatively, if you know the name of a statutory instrument, look in the Alphabetical List in the back of the annual paper-covered volume of the *Consolidated Index and Alphabetical List of Statutory Instruments*. You may, for example, be looking for information on the Asylum Support Regulations 2000. The relevant page from the Alphabetical List is shown on page 80. The list tells us that the number of the statutory instrument is 704 and that it has been allocated the subject title "Nationality and Immigration" in *Halsbury's Statutory Instruments*. (Entries in the Chronological List in Binder 1 are displayed in the same way.)

On the inside front cover of each of the main volumes, there is a list of subject titles, indicating in which volume they are printed. "Nationality and Immigration" is located in Volume 14. Consult the Chronological List of Instruments at the beginning of the section headed "Nationality and Immigration" in Volume 14. At the time of the writing of this book, S.I. 2000/704 does not appear in this list, and by looking at the title page of the volume, we find that the volume contains only those statutory instruments which became available before February 1, 1999. To find information on instruments published after that date, look in the *Annual Supplement* in Binder 1. The arrangement is the same as in the main volumes. The entry under the heading "Nationality and Immigration", at the time of writing this book, is shown on page 81. The Chronological List of Instruments at the beginning of the section lists the statutory instrument we want and indicates on which page it can be found. If a line appears instead of a number in the "Page in Supp" column, the statutory instrument described cannot be found in *Halsbury's Statutory Instruments*. S.I. 2000/704 is summarised on the same page. The summary indicates the Act under which the instrument was made and the date the instrument came into force.

Changes subsequent to the *Annual Supplement* are recorded in the Monthly Survey— Key in Binder 1. The Monthly Survey is arranged by subject titles as in the main volumes. Look for the number of the instrument in the "Amendments and Revocations" section in

Example Page from the Consolidated Index and Alphabetical List of Statutory Instruments

Assured

Serial No	*Description*	*Title*
1525	Assured Tenancies (Approved Bodies) (No 4) Order 1987	Landlord and Tenant
2018	Assured Tenancies (Approved Bodies) (No 4) Order 1988	Landlord and Tenant
1481	Assured Tenancies (Approved Bodies) (No 5) Order 1982	Landlord and Tenant
840	Assured Tenancies (Approved Bodies) (No 5) Order 1983	Landlord and Tenant
1551	Assured Tenancies (Approved Bodies) (No 6) Order 1982	Landlord and Tenant
1079	Assured Tenancies (Approved Bodies) (No 6) Order 1983	Landlord and Tenant
1638	Assured Tenancies (Approved Bodies) (No 7) Order 1982	Landlord and Tenant
1375	Assured Tenancies (Approved Bodies) (No 7) Order 1983	Landlord and Tenant
1815	Assured Tenancies (Approved Bodies) (No 8) Order 1982	Landlord and Tenant
1537	Assured Tenancies (Approved Bodies) (No 8) Order 1983	Landlord and Tenant
1856	Assured Tenancies (Approved Bodies) (No 9) Order 1983	Landlord and Tenant
1694	Assured Tenancies (Approved Body) (No 1) Order 1980...............	Landlord and Tenant
590	Assured Tenancies (Approved Body) (No 1) Order 1981...............	Landlord and Tenant
1009	Assured Tenancies (Approved Body) (No 2) Order 1981..................	Landlord and Tenant
850	Assured Tenancies (Approved Body) (No 2) Order 1982..................	Landlord and Tenant
591	Assured Tenancies (Notice to Tenant) Regulations 1981..................	Landlord and Tenant
122	Assured Tenancies (Prescribed Amount) Order 1987	Landlord and Tenant
194	Assured Tenancies and Agricultural Occupancies (Forms) Regulations 1997	Landlord and Tenant
1474	Assured Tenancies and Agricultural Occupancies (Rent Information) (Amendment) Order 1990	Landlord and Tenant
657	Assured Tenancies and Agricultural Occupancies (Rent Information) (Amendment) Order 1993	Landlord and Tenant
2199	Assured Tenancies and Agricultural Occupancies (Rent Information) Order 1988..	Landlord and Tenant
2671	Asylum (Designated Countries of Destination and Designated Safe Third Countries) Order 1996	Nationality
2053	Asylum and Immigration Act 1996 (Commencement No 1) Order 1996...	Nationality
2127	Asylum and Immigration Act 1996 (Commencement No 2) Order 1996...	Nationality
2970	Asylum and Immigration Act 1996 (Commencement No 3 and Transitional Provisions) Order 1996....................................	Nationality
1264	Asylum and Immigration Act 1996 (Guernsey) Order 1998.............	Nationality
1070	Asylum and Immigration Act 1996 (Jersey) Order 1998	Nationality
1655	Asylum and Immigration Appeals Act 1993 (Commencement and Transitional Provisions) Order 1993	Nationality
2070	Asylum Appeals (Procedure) Rules 1996	Nationality
3056	Asylum Support (Interim Provisions) Regulations 1999....................	Nationality
541	Asylum Support Appeals (Procedure) Rules 2000	Nationality
→ 704	Asylum Support Regulations 2000	Nationality
100	Atomic Energy (Disclosure of Information) (No 1) Order 1947.........	Criminal Law
235	Atomic Energy (Mutual Assistance Convention) Order 1990............	Trade and Industry
1317	Atomic Energy Act 1989 (Commencement) Order 1989..................	Trade and Industry
832	Atomic Energy Authority (Appointed Day) Order 1954	Trade and Industry
436	Atomic Energy Authority (Weapons Group) Act 1973 (Appointed Day) Order 1973	Trade and Industry
478	Atomic Energy Authority Act 1971 (Appointed Day) Order 1971.....	Trade and Industry
2743	Atomic Weapons Establishment (Designation and Appointed Day) Order 1992...	Trade and Industry
1396	Atomic Weapons Establishment Act 1991 Amendment Order 1997 ..	Trade and Industry
3098	Attachment of Debts (Expenses) Order 1996.................................	Courts
356	Attachment of Earnings (Employer's Deduction) Order 1991............	Matrimonial Law
3281	Attendance Centre Rules 1995..	Prisons
526	Auditors (Financial Services Act 1986) Rules 1994	Money
449	Auditors (Insurance Companies Act 1982) Regulations 1994.............	Companies
828	Audley End Grounds Regulations 1950...	Open Spaces
345	Aujeszky's Disease (Compensation for Swine) Order 1983	Animals
344	Aujeszky's Disease Order 1983	Animals
319	Australia Act 1986 (Commencement) Order 1986	Commonwealth (Pt 1)

Example Page from the Annual Supplement in Binder 1 of Halsbury's Statutory Instruments

541   ASYLUM SUPPORT APPEALS (PROCUDURE) RULES 2000
Authority   Made by the Home Secretary under the Immigration and Asylum Act 1999, ss 104, 166(3).
Date made   2 March 2000.
Commencement   3 April 2000.
Summary   These rules prescribe the procedure to be followed in deciding appeals to adjudicators arising from claims made under the Immigration and Asylum Act 1999, s 103. (*Additional Text*)

685   CARRIERS' LIABILITY (CLANDESTINE ENTRANTS AND SALE OF TRANSPORTERS) REGULATIONS 2000
Authority   Made by the Home Secretary under the Immigration and Asylum Act 1999, ss 32(2), (3), (10), 35(7)–(9), 36(2), 166(3), 167, Sch 1, paras 2, 5.
Date made   8 March 2000.
Commencement   3 April 2000.
Summary   These regulations provide the penalties for carrying clandestine entrants established by the Immigration and Asylum Act 1999, s 32(2). The regulations prescribe: (a) £2000 as the penalty payable in respect of each clandestine entrant; (b) 60 days as the period of time within which a penalty must be paid; (c) Coquelles, France as the immigration control zone outside the United Kingdom; (d) 30 days as the period of time within which a notice of objection to a penalty must be given; and (e) the manner in which service of a penalty notice may be served in relation to detached trailers. The regulations also make provision relating to the sale of transporters under Sch 1 to the 1999 Act. The regulations prescribe: (a) the steps which the Secretary of State must take prior to applying to the court for leave to sell a detained transporter; and (b) how the proceeds of any such sale are to be applied.
Amendment   Amended as from 1 March 2001 by SI 2001/311 so as to extend certain provisions of the regulations, subject to a modification, to the carriage of clandestine entrants by rail freight.

704   ASYLUM SUPPORT REGULATIONS 2000
Authority   Made by the Home Secretary under the Immigration and Asylum Act 1999, ss 94, 95, 97, 114, 166, 167, Sch 8.
Date made   6 March 2000.
Commencement   3 April 2000.
Summary   These regulations require local authorities to provide support to asylum-seekers and their dependants who apply in accordance to these regulations and appear to be destitute or likely to be destitute within 14 days. Support is to be in the form of providing accommodation and/or essential living needs. The provision for essential living needs will be in the form of redeemable vouchers and a cash sum not exceeding £10 per week. The regulations enable the Secretary of State to require from a supported person contributions towards the cost of provisions of asylum support in some cases, and to recover sums. The regulations also make provision relating to the suspension or discontinuation of support and bringing tenancies to an end.
Amendment   Amended as from 4 December 2000 by SI 2000/3053.

705   IMMIGRATION (ELIGIBILITY FOR ASSISTANCE) (SCOTLAND AND NORTHERN IRELAND) REGULATIONS 2000
Authority   Made by the Home Secretary under the Immigration and Asylum Act 1999, ss 115(3), (4), 122(11), 166, 167.
Date made   6 March 2000.
Commencement   3 April 2000.
Summary   These regulations provide that s 115 of the Immigration and Asylum Act 1999 does not apply in Scotland and Northern Ireland, on or after 3 April 2000, to certain people who were not eligible for certain social security benefits but were eligible for assistance under the Social Work (Scotland) Act 1968, the Mental Health (Scotland) Act 1984 or the Health and Personal Social Services (Northern Ireland) Order 1972. These regulations preserve eligibility for support for children in Scotland and Northern Ireland to those receiving such assistance immediately before 3 April 2000.

912   IMMIGRATION (PASSENGER INFORMATION) ORDER 2000
Authority   Made by the Home Secretary under the Immigration Act 1971, Sch 2, para 27B(9), (10).
Date made   29 March 2000.
Commencement   28 April 2000.
Summary   This order specifies information relating to a passenger as given on or shown by the passenger's passport or other travel document and other information relating to a passenger for the purposes of the Immigration Act 1971, Sch 2, para 27B(9).

1161   IMMIGRATION (LEAVE TO ENTER AND REMAIN) ORDER 2000
Authority   Made by the Home Secretary under the Immigration Act 1971, ss 3A(1), (2), (3), (4), (6), (10), 3B(2)(a), (c), (3)(a).
Date made   19 April 2000.
Commencement   Partly on 28 April 2000; fully on 30 July 2000.

"Nationality and Immigration". This will tell you if the instrument has been revoked, superseded or amended. The Monthly Survey—Summaries pages in Binder 1 give summaries of the new statutory instruments mentioned in the Key.

An explanation of how to use *Halsbury's Statutory Instruments* to find statutory instruments on a subject is given in **7–27**.

4–30 Finding Out whether a Statutory Instrument is Still in Force

Electronic

The online databases carrying current legislation in force, noted in **4–8**, include statutory instruments along with statutes. If you are using *Butterworths Legislation Direct*, Lexis-Nexis Professional or Westlaw UK, and search for a statutory instrument by title, the text you see is that of the statutory instrument as amended and currently in force (see **4–8**).

You can also check whether a statutory instrument is still in force by looking at the *Current Law Legislation Citators*. These are available either directly from Sweet & Maxwell as part of the *Current Legal Information* service, or from Westlaw UK through the UK Legislative Locator database (see **4–19**). For example, use *Current Legal Information* or Westlaw UK's UK Legislative locator database to search for the Working Time Regulations 1998. You find the enabling legislation is listed (in this case the European Communities Act 1972), along with related legislation. This includes a reference to the Working Time Regulations 1999/3372 which can be read with the Working Time Regulations 1998 in order to build up a picture of the current legislative position. You also find for some statutory instruments, as in this example, a list of cases that have cited the statutory instrument and a reference to a journal article, in this case "EC law; Exemptions; Hours of employment. Derogations in the Working Time Regulations 1998", *Comparative Law*, 2000 21(6), 166–172. This provides you with a comprehensive review of the statutory instrument as in force. The *Is It In Force?* database noted in **4–18** does not include statutory instruments.

Print

Halsbury's Statutory Instruments collects together all the statutory instruments which are still in force. The information in *Halsbury's* is likely to be more up to date than information provided in other printed sources. Using *Halsbury's Statutory Instruments* to find out if an instrument is in force is described in **4–29.**

4–31 Tracing statutory instruments made under a particular Act

Electronic

The *Current Law Legislation Citators*, available either directly from Sweet & Maxwell as part of the *Current Legal Information* service, or Westlaw UK in the form of its UK Legislative Locator database, provide a relatively effective and direct way of tracing statutory instruments made under a particular Act (see **4–19**). If we return to the example used in **4–8**, a search for the Dangerous Dogs Act 1991 presents, section by section, database links which list statutory instruments made under the Act, along with citations for amending legislation. For section 1 of the Act for example, the Commencement Order is cited along with four other statutory instruments, including the Dangerous Dogs (Designated Types) Order 1991/1743.

Lawtel (see **4–18**) provides an alternative way of tracing statutory instruments made under an Act. For statutes passed since 1984, the database provides links to all statutory instruments which are enabled by the Act. Again, search by the title of the Act. Lawtel's "Statutory Status Table" provides a link to the four statutory instruments currently enabled by the statute.

Print
If you are using print sources, you should turn to *Halsbury's Statutes* (**4–17**).

Wales Legislation   4–32

Under the Government of Wales Act 1998, the National Assembly for Wales has taken over powers formerly exercised by the Secretary of State for Wales. This means in practice that the Assembly is able to debate and approve secondary or delegated legislation for Wales. Its legislation takes the form of statutory instruments which are cited in the same way as other statutory instruments, *e.g.* Children's Homes Amendment (Wales) Regulations 2001. This particular statutory instrument is numbered as No. 140 (W. 6), the "W. 6" denoting the sixth regulation made by the Assembly for 2001.

The Government of Wales Act 1998 does not lay out broad areas of legislative competence; instead the powers of the Assembly are defined in relation to some 300 Acts of Parliament. The Acts themselves are listed in the National Assembly for Wales (Transfer of Functions) Orders made in 1999 and 2000. Broadly speaking, the Assembly can make regulations in the areas of industrial and economic development, education and training, health, agriculture, local government, housing, social services, transport and the environment and arts and cultural heritage.

Statutory instruments made by the National Assembly can be found on the Wales Legislation page of the HMSO website (at **www.wales-legislation.hmso.gov.uk**). Draft statutory orders can be found on the National Assembly of Wales website (at **www.wales.gov.uk**), along with links to Assembly business and other information about the Assembly. Proceedings of the Assembly are not available in print form. The Wales Legislation online website (at **www.wales-legislation.org.uk**), managed by Cardiff Law School, contains a Digest of National Assembly Functions & Subordinate Legislation which lists the powers of the National Assembly for Wales and its subordinate legislation by subject area. Using the site it is possible to take a given Act, *e.g.* the Environment Act 1995, and find out which sections list functions that are exercised solely by the Assembly, which list functions that are shared between the Assembly and a Minister of the Crown, and which list functions which have not been devolved to the Assembly. Legislation made by the Assembly is to be added to the entries for each Act where relevant.

5 Journals

TYPES OF JOURNALS

Journals (or periodicals) are important to lawyers: they keep you up to date with the latest developments in the law, and provide comments and criticisms of the law. In your preparations for seminars, essays and moots, it is essential to show that you are aware of what has been written in journals. You cannot rely exclusively on textbooks which are always, to some degree, out of date, and which may provide inadequate information on some topics. You should develop the habit of glancing at the title pages of recently published journals, which are normally kept on a separate display shelf. This will help to keep you up to date with recent cases, statutes, official publications, comments and scholarly articles.

For convenience, we can divide journals into four different types, although there is some overlap between them. However, they are treated similarly in libraries. There are a number of weekly publications, such as the *New Law Journal, Justice of the Peace*, the *Solicitors Journal* and the *Law Society Gazette*, which aim to keep practitioners and students up to date. They provide reports and comments on recent cases, statutes, statutory instruments and the latest trends and developments in the law, together with some longer articles, usually on topical or practical subjects. In contrast are the academic journals, which are published less frequently. They contain lengthy articles on a variety of topics, comments on recent cases, statutes and government publications, and book reviews. Some examples are the *Law Quarterly Review*, the *Modern Law Review* (six issues a year) and the *Journal of Law and Society* (four issues a year). The third category is the specialist journal dealing with particular aspects of the law. Some specialist journals combine notes of recent developments with longer articles on aspects of that area of the law. Examples of these journals include the *Criminal Law Review* (monthly), *Legal Action* (monthly) and *Family Law* (ten issues a year). Other specialist journals are more like newsletters and are designed as current awareness bulletins for practitioners. These journals (*e.g.* the *Property Law Bulletin, Simon's Tax Intelligence*) are only a few pages in length and summarise and briefly comment on the latest developments. The final category is foreign journals. English-language publications, particularly from common law jurisdictions, are of assistance in providing a comparative view of similar United Kingdom issues. Examples of this group are the *Yale Law Journal* (eight issues a year), the *Harvard Law Review* (eight issues a year), the *Canadian Bar Review* (four issues a year) and the *Australian Law Journal* (monthly).

5-2 ONLINE JOURNALS

An increasing number of journals offer a full-text version online. This trend is likely to grow. Currently law publishers are behind the major medicine, science and social science publishers, in making their journals available in full text. Among those available online are the *Journal of Law and* Society, *Statute Law Review*, the *Oxford Journal of Legal Studies*, the *European Law Review* and the *Netherlands Quarterly of Human Rights*. Access to the full text of these and other journals online requires your library to have an appropriate subscription. There are either password or site restrictions covering access. In general, journal articles are available in full text from the late 1990s onwards. The largest single group of law journals available online consists of the 25 Sweet & Maxwell journals made available in full text as part of the Westlaw UK service (at **www.westlaw.co.uk**). These include the *European Human Rights Law Review*, *Intellectual Property Quarterly* and the *Journal of Planning & Environment Law*.

Aside from the law journals available from Westlaw UK, the vast majority of the other, largely non-law journals available online, are found through the websites which act as agents for the journal publishers. Swetsnet*Navigator* (at **www.swetsnet.nl**) and IngentaJournals (at **www.ingenta.com**) are the most important websites for social science and—to a limited extent—law publishers. You have access to contents listings for the journals listed on these websites, while the full text of journals is available to you only if your own library subscribes to the journal, and has made use of the agent's journal service. Increasingly libraries are adding links to electronic journals from the web-based versions of their library catalogues.

If you are simply interested in seeing the contents listing of journals online, in addition to Swetsnet*Navigator* and IngentaJournals, a more comprehensive service is provided by the British Library's ZETOC service (at **zetoc.mimas.ac.uk**) which is available free to academic institutions in the United Kingdom.

The final category is the journal which is available only online in its electronic form. UK law journals of this type include the *Journal of Information, Law and Technology, (JILT)* (at **elj.warwick.ac.uk**) and the *Web Journal of Current Legal Issues* (at **webjcli.ncl.ac.uk**). The text of the articles found in these journals is available free from the journal website

5-3 TRACING ARTICLES IN LEGAL JOURNALS

There are several indexes you can use to find journal articles on a subject or on a particular case, statute or other document. The most relevant indexes are described below. Although you would not need or wish to consult every index every time you require articles on a topic, you should remember that the information given and the journals covered vary and by using only one index you may miss helpful material.

As an alternative to looking in indexes, you could rely on footnotes in recent books or journal articles which discuss your topic. If the article is well researched, it may give you numerous citations to read. You are likely, however, only to get coverage of those articles which support the view of the author. Using footnotes from key texts is a good way to widen your search for documents on a subject but for the most comprehensive and recent coverage, you must also look in the indexes of journal articles.

Legal Journals Index   5–4

The printed *Legal Journals Index* began publication in 1986 and is the most useful source for tracing law articles in journals published in the United Kingdom. It is available online and on CD-ROM as part of the *Current Legal Information* service from Sweet & Maxwell (at **www.smlawpub.jhc.net**) and also as part of Westlaw UK (at **www.westlaw.co.uk**). It covers articles from approximately 260 legal journals and is more comprehensive than the journal index that forms part of the Lawtel service, the *Index to Legal Periodicals*, or other titles mentioned later in this chapter. The online versions of the *Index* includes entries from the print *European Legal Index* which has carried references to articles on E.U. law since 1993.

Each entry in the *Legal Journals Index* database gives you the title and author or authors of the journal article, along with details of the journal in which the article is published, and the volume, issue and page numbers (see illustration on page 88). Where the title does not clearly describe its content, an abstract is added in parentheses. Brief abstracts are added for all recent article references. In addition there is a string of subject words which correspond to the headings used in the subject index of the printed volumes. The illustration on page 88 for example, carries the string of keywords "Causes of Action; Freedom of expression; Injunctions; Photographs; Privacy; Publishing". It is important to bear mind that when you use keywords to search the database, you will only find references to articles if the keywords you have used are to be found either in these subject strings or the title words, descriptors or brief abstracts found in the database entry. There is no full summary of the article which can be searched as is the case with some indexes. It therefore makes sense to pay particular attention to the subject headings which you find following your initial search. You will often be able to find more relevant articles by searching again using the subject strings which seem to offer the closest match to your interests. Once you have found that an article you are interested in has the heading "Causes of Action; Freedom of expression; Injunctions; Photographs; Privacy; Publishing", for example, then searching again using some or all of these terms will produce a highly relevant list of journal articles. These are references to journal articles which will be listed even if only some of the terms appear in the titles of the articles. As you will need to use "Boolean" searching to link you search words (see **2–14**), your new search might, for example, be "Freedom of expression AND privacy".

The only additional information found in the database entries are the names of cases where the article is a comment on a case, or contains substantial discussion of a piece of legislation. Keyword searches using the names of the parties in cases, or the title of a statute identify journal articles discussing the case or statute. The article on page 88 could also be located using the name "Zeta-Jones", taken from one of the parties in the case discussed, or "European Convention on Human Rights 1950 Art. 10".

The printed versions of the *Legal Journals Index* and the *European Legal Journals Index* are published monthly, with quarterly and annual cumulative volumes.

Current Law   5–5

Current Law commenced in 1947 and entries are arranged by subject (see **7–1**). It is a useful print source of references. At the end of each subject heading in the *Monthly Digest* is a list of recent books and journal articles which have been published on that subject. All the books listed separately under the relevant subject headings are brought together in the list of new books at the back of the issue.

Sample entry from Legal Journals Index

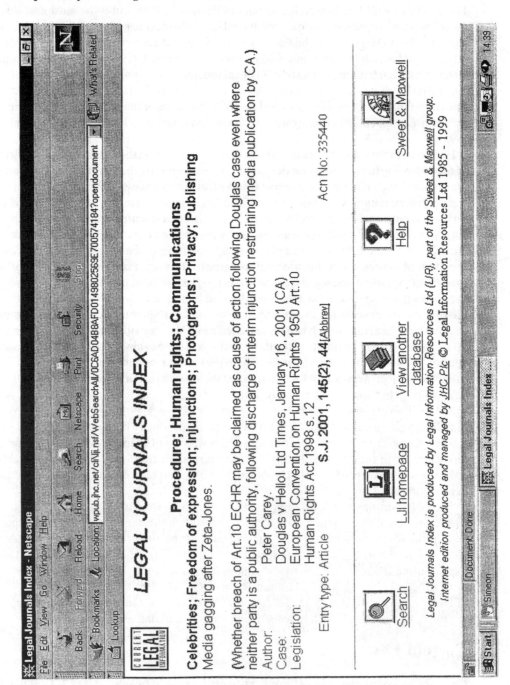

When the *Current Law Year Book* is published, the index to articles is found at the back of the volume. (Before 1956, journal articles were listed at the end of each subject heading.) The *Current Law Year Books* are useful for tracing older articles, but for a full list of recent articles written in British journals it is advisable to consult the *Legal Journals Index* (**5–4**).

Index to Legal Periodicals & Books 5–6

The *Index to Legal Periodicals & Books*, which commenced in 1908, is published in the United States. Most of its coverage is of American journals, but it includes some journals from the United Kingdom, Canada, Ireland, Australia and New Zealand. The index is available in electronic form as part of the OCLC FirstSearch service (at **firstsearch.uk.oclc.org**) and also as the *Wilson Index to Legal Periodicals & Books*, available either on CD-ROM or as an Internet service. Internet access to the *Wilson Index to Legal Periodicals & Books* is provided in the United Kingdom by Silverplatter (at **www.silverplatter.com**). If you are using the OCLC FirstSearch service you will find that the *Index to Legal Periodicals & Books* is one of a number of databases made available by OCLC. You must select the database from a database list. The link to the *Index* is abbreviated as LegalPeriodical. Whichever form of electronic access you use, the entries in the database go back only to 1981. If you wish to trace articles prior to this date you should use the printed version of the *Index*.

Each entry in the database and the printed version of the *Index* contains the title of the article, along with the author name(s) and details of the source of publication: journal title, issue and/or volume number and page numbers. There is also a "subject descriptor", or subject heading added to the article. If your keyword search used the terms "inherent jurisdiction AND Great Britain", you are shown a database entry as follows:

> Author(s): Dockray, M. S.
> Title: The inherent jurisdiction to regulate civil proceedings.
> Source: The Law Quarterly Review v. 113 (Jan. '97) pp. 120–132
> Descriptor: Jurisdiction—Great Britain.

The descriptor entry "Jurisdiction—Great Britain" is also a hyperlink which enables you to list references to all the articles that are indexed using the terms "Jurisdiction—Great Britain". As with any index it makes sense to take full note of these descriptor terms or subject headings, as they provide a means of improving the accuracy and relevance of your search results. The headings use American terminology and spelling which may occasionally cause difficulties.

The printed version of the *Index to Legal Periodicals & Books* is published 11 times a year. There is a quarterly cumulative edition. These are replaced by an annual volume containing all the periodical articles for that year. A list of the subject headings used, along with a list of all the abbreviations, is found at the beginning of each volume.

Lawtel 5–7

The Lawtel service (at **www.lawtel.co.uk**) includes an articles index which contains references to the contents of 57 U.K. publications. The emphasis is on publications that are likely to be of interest to legal practitioners. *Corporate Briefing, Counsel* and *Pensions World* are included, for example, along with academic law journals such as the *New Law*

Journal and *Modern Law Review*. References to the legal sections of *The Times*, *The Guardian* and *The Independent* are included. Most of the publications are indexed from 1998 onwards, a few from 1995.

Each entry for the article index has a paragraph summarising the contents of the article along with references to any case law or legislation cited in the article. As with other indexes it is possible to search for articles using a case name or the name and section of a statute. You can also search using subject headings.

5–8 Index to Foreign Legal Periodicals

The *Index to Foreign Legal Periodicals* commenced in 1960. It indexes articles on international and comparative law and the municipal law of countries other than the United States, the United Kingdom and the common law of Commonwealth countries. Close to 500 legal journals are indexed. The *Index* is available electronically from 1985 onwards as a CD-ROM or internet subscription from Silverplatter (at **www.silverplatter.com**).

5–9 Legal Resource Index (LegalTrac)

The *Legal Resource Index* indexes over 800 legal publications, most of which are American, although a few U.K. journals are included. The index is made available online as the LegalTrac database from the Gale Group (at **www.galegroup.com**). U.K. access is possible through the company's InfoTrac service (at **www.infotrac.london.galegroup.com**).

5–10 Halsbury's Laws

Halsbury's Laws of England is available from Butterworths (at **www.butterworths.co.uk**) and references to journal articles are included. Only a small range of journals is covered. The print version of *Halsbury's Laws* includes a Table of Articles in Binder 2. References to articles are arranged alphabetically by title within broad subject areas. As a result, this is not the easiest way to locate specific articles.

The Table of Articles in Binder 2 is updated by the latest copy of the Monthly Review in Binder 1. The *Monthly Review* summarises changes in the law by broad subject area and new articles are listed at the beginning of each section.

The *Annual Abridgement* to *Halsbury's Laws* includes a Table of Articles. This gives a selection of the journal articles written on a subject during that year. The *Annual Abridgement* replaces the information in the Table of Articles in Binder 2. *Halsbury's Laws* is described in more detail in **7–3**.

5–11 TRACING LAW-RELATED JOURNAL ARTICLES

The effective study of law will of necessity take you into other disciplines. Articles on subjects such as housing, delinquency, sentencing, families and town and country planning are found in a wide range of journals, many of which are not solely concerned with law and which as a consequence are not usually found in a law collection. You may wish to consult journals which carry articles by sociologists, economists, criminologists, social administrators or historians. To trace social science and arts material on law-related topics, you will need to use a different selection of indexes. Web-based and CD-ROM versions of these indexes, where available, are noted in the following paragraphs. Some of the indexes can also be searched using "pay as you go" services such as DIALOG, Datastar, DIMD and STN. You will not have direct access to these services, but a librarian can search them on your behalf.

Index to Periodical Articles Related to Law
5–12

This index commenced in 1958. It contains a selective coverage of English-language articles not included in the *Legal Journals Index*, or the *Index to Legal Periodicals & Books*. It is not available in electronic form. There is an index to articles by subject, a list of journals indexed and an author index. All the entries from 1958 to 1988 have been published in one cumulative volume. Thereafter, the index appears quarterly, with the last issue of the year being an annual cumulation.

Applied Social Sciences Index and Abstracts (ASSIA)
5–13

ASSIA is aimed at those in practice in social services, prison services, employment, race relations, etc., and includes articles on many aspects of the law. Articles from approximately 650 journals are indexed. Although produced in Britain, the index covers English-language journals from 16 countries. The ASSIA *PLUS* CD-ROM is available from the publishers Bowker-Saur (at **www.bowker-saur.com**), who also provide access via ASSIAnet (at **www.assianet.com**). ASSIA is also available in print form.

British Humanities Index
5–14

This covers a broad range of subjects and includes articles from British newspapers and popular weekly journals, as well as more scholarly periodicals. The BHI *PLUS* CD-ROM is available from Bowker-Saur (at **www.bowker-saur.co.uk**) and contains references from 1985 to the present. The BHI is also available in print form.

Social Sciences Index
5–15

This index, which took over from the *Social Sciences and Humanities Index*, includes articles on law, criminology, sociology, political science, sociological aspects of medicine and other socio-legal topics. The index is available in CD-ROM form and online from the publishers H. W. Wilson (at **www.hwwilson.com**) from 1983 onwards. Silverplatter (at **www.silverplatter.com**) also provides CD-ROM and internet access to the index. This index is also available in print form.

Criminology and Penology Abstracts
5–16

These abstracts are only available in print. Detailed subject and author indexes refer to individually numbered entries. The entries themselves are arranged by subject, and include abstracts (*i.e.* summaries) of the articles.

5–17   Psychological Abstracts (PsycINFO)

The scope of this is far wider than the title suggests, covering abortion, drug use, alcoholism, etc. Over 1,300 journals are indexed and dissertations, books and book chapters are included. Coverage of the PsycINFO CD-ROM and online database begins as early as 1887. Access is provided both by Silverplatter (at **www.silverplatter.com**) and Ovid (at **www.ovid.com**) in the United Kingdom. PsycINFO is also available from OCLC FirstSearch (at **firstsearch.uk.oclc.org**). The abstracts are also available in print form.

5–18   Current Contents

Current Contents provides access to tables of contents from over 7,000 journals, including many social science titles. The Current Contents database is available directly from the Institute for Scientific Information, which produces *Current Contents*, as Current Contents Connect (at **www.isihost.com**). Ovid (at **www.ovid.com**) and Silverplatter (at **www.silverplatter.com**) also provide online access to the database. *Current Contents* is also available in print form. The contents pages of recent journals are published weekly with social science and law titles appearing in the *Social and Behavioral Sciences* series.

5–19   The Philosopher's Index

This index contains references (with abstracts) to articles found in almost 500 philosophy journals from a wide range of countries. Records of books and contributions to anthologies are included. Coverage is from 1940 and the index is available on CD-ROM and as an internet subscription from Silverplatter (at **www.silverplatter.com**). This index is also available in print form.

5–20   Sociological Abstracts

Sociological Abstracts includes coverage of law, penology and the police and is available from a variety on online sources. The producers themselves, Cambridge Scientific Abstracts, make the database available as part of their internet database service (at **www.csa.com**). The database is also available online from Ovid (at **www.ovid.com**), Edina (at **edina.ed.ac.uk),** OCLC Firstsearch (at **firstsearch.uk.oclc.org**) and Silverplatter (at **www.silverplatter.com**). Silverplatter also produces a CD-ROM version of the database. Coverage is from 1963 and abstracts are added to records from 1974 onwards. *Sociological Abstracts* is also available in print form.

5–21   Social Sciences Citation Index

The *Citation Index* is so called because, in addition to the usual bibliographic details, every entry in the index database carries a list of the articles referred to (or "cited") by the article in question. It is possible, using the index, to begin with a particular article, found perhaps after a subject search, and then trace details of the articles which have in turn discussed or used the article you started with. This is particularly useful if you already know of a key article and wish to find the latest articles in a long-running debate in the literature. In addition to the *Social Sciences Citation Index*, there is also an *Arts and Humanities Citation*

Index and a *Sciences Citation Index,* all of which are available on CD-ROM from the database producers, the Insititute of Scientific Information (at **www.isinet.com**). The indexes are also available online as part of the Web of Science service (at **wos.mimas.uk**). The index is available in print form.

These are by no means the only subject indexes to the contents of journals. Indexes exist covering many different subjects. The library staff will help you find out which indexing or abstracting services are available to cover the subjects that interest you.

NEWSPAPER ARTICLES

5–22

In addition to factual reporting, newspapers often contain commentary, analysis and background information on recent legal developments and controversial topics. Many libraries keep back copies of newspapers or have them on microfilm. Current news and comment is also available from the websites of the broadsheet newspapers. *The Times* (at **www.thetimes.co.uk**) includes content from its "Law" section, published on Tuesdays, on the newspaper's website (under "Specials"). The news and comment available on newspaper websites does not always correspond to that found in the printed editions of the newspaper.

The broadsheet newspapers are available in full-text on CD-ROM, although advertisements and crosswords are usually excluded. Here, you see the text of the printed editions of the newspaper. A number of years will usually be available for full-text searching. However monthly or quarterly updating means that you do not see current issues of the newspaper. The full text of the *Financial Times* and other newspapers can also be searched from 1980 onwards using the FT Profile database available from Lexis-Nexis (at **www.lexis-nexis.co.uk**).

Newspapers such as *The Times* and *The Guardian* publish printed indexes. The *Clover Newspaper Index* goes back to 1987 and covers a range of papers. It is updated on the Clover website (at **www.cloverweb.co.uk**). Entries for the previous week's news are available free, arranged by subject heading. Your library may subscribe to the full *Clover* index online (at **clover.niss.ac.uk**). Full keyword searching is available for the database.

The BADGER index, available as part of *Current Legal Information* (at **www.smlawpub.jhc.net** and on CD-ROM) contains brief summaries of items of legal interest from the broadsheet newspapers.

LOCATING JOURNALS IN YOUR LIBRARY

5–23

Having traced a reference to an article, how do you locate the relevant copy of the journal? The first problem may be to decipher the abbreviation which has been used for the name of the journal. If you obtained your information from a periodical index or from the *Current Law Case Citators*, a list of the abbreviations will be found at the front of the volume. If the information was obtained from elsewhere, *e.g.* from a footnote in a textbook, look up the abbreviation in the *Legal Journals Index*, or D. Raistrick, *Index to Legal Citations and Abbreviations*.

Once the full title of the journal is known, look up the name of the journal in the library's periodicals catalogue. The catalogue entry will guide you to the part of the library in which the journal is to be found, and will indicate which volumes of the journal are available in your library. Law journals are often arranged in alphabetical order (see **1–9**).

5-24 LOCATING JOURNALS FROM OTHER LIBRARIES

If the journal is not available in your library, you may wish to obtain it from elsewhere. One approach would be to use the online catalogues of other libraries, which contain details of the journal titles held by the library (see **7–29**). Most online catalogues allow you to limit your title search to a "journals only" section of the catalogue. If you are searching for older journal titles, the *Union List of Legal Periodicals*, published by the Institute of Advanced Legal Studies, may be of use. It lists the locations of journals throughout the United Kingdom, though it is now somewhat dated. The second edition was published in 1978 (although take comfort from the knowledge that libraries are unlikely to discard journal collections).

If you wish to consult a large number of journals or reports, it may be more convenient to go to another library and use the material there. If only a few articles are required, it may be easier to obtain them through the inter-library loan service. Details of this service are available from your librarian. If you wish to use this service, plan ahead and allow time for your request to be processed and for the material to arrive. The process can take several weeks, but usually around two to three weeks.

Copies of journal articles can be obtained directly from a wide range of organisations offering a document supply service. Even if you have to pay for copies from your own library, copies supplied by these services are likely to be more expensive, as a copyright fee is usually charged by publishers. This fee is added to the cost of supply. A university or other educational or public library does not charge this copyright fee. Two service providers particularly worth noting are Legal Information Resources Ltd, which produces the *Legal Journals Index* and the British Library (at **www.bl.uk**). The British Library has an Articles Direct service for one-off orders using a web page order form which exists alongside its "inside" service, designed to provide document delivery to subscribing organisations.

6 | Government Publications

INTRODUCTION

Government publications were notoriously difficult to trace. This is changing as more official publishing takes place on the internet. Much of the print publication is the responsibility of *The Stationery Office* (*TSO*) which became the U.K. government publisher following the privatisation of HMSO (Her Majesty's Stationery Office) in 1996. TSO publishes on behalf of a residual HMSO which exists as a division of the Cabinet Office. It is this residual HMSO body which controls Crown copyright. For this reason, legislation is found on HMSO, not TSO, web pages on the internet. TSO is also responsible for putting a significant amount of government publishing on to the internet. However, a great deal of publishing by government departments is undertaken directly by the department, whether in print or on the internet. Consequently TSO cannot be regarded as the only source for government publications.

In this chapter, we look at those government publications most likely to be encountered by law students, *e.g.*:

Command Papers;
Bills;
House of Commons and House of Lords Papers;
Official Reports of Parliamentary Debates (*Hansard*).

Acts of Parliament, which are government publications, are covered in Chapter 4.

TSO publishes approximately 11,000 items a year. This represents less than half the vast number of parliamentary and non-parliamentary publications.

Parliamentary publications are those documents which are required by Parliament in the course of its work, *e.g.* Bills, records of proceedings in the House and information papers on a wide variety of topics. All parliamentary publications are published by TSO. Documents other than parliamentary publications published on behalf of government departments or other official bodies are called non-parliamentary publications. These items vary considerably and include, for example, public information pamphlets such as the *Highway Code* and directories such as the *Civil Service Yearbook* which lists civil service departments, telephone numbers and names of senior civil servants. Some non-parliamentary publications are published by TSO, but many are published by the responsible department or organisation.

This is a field in which you should not hesitate to seek the advice of library staff whenever you are in difficulty. Most libraries which have a collection of government publications have at least one person who is responsible for helping readers to use this material. For more detailed information on government publications, refer to D. Butcher, *Official Publications in Britain* (2nd ed.).

6–2 PARLIAMENTARY PUBLICATIONS

If your library has a complete collection of parliamentary publications, they may be bound together in volumes containing all the material produced during a particular session of Parliament. These volumes are known as *sessional papers* or *sessional sets*. A Sessional Index provides a subject approach to the material. The sessional papers are also available on microfiche. These are arranged by type of material (Bills, Command Papers, etc.) and then in numerical order within each session.

Libraries with large collections of government publications do not usually enter parliamentary publications in the library catalogues, relying instead on the indexes produced by TSO and others (**6–14**) to trace relevant material. If, however, your library has only a small collection of parliamentary publications, they may be catalogued individually.

In many libraries, recent parliamentary publications are gathered together in boxes. Every parliamentary paper has its own individual number and the papers will usually be arranged by these numbers in boxes comprising:

House of Commons Papers;
House of Commons Bills;
House of Lords Papers and Bills;
Command Papers.

These recent publications can also be traced through various indexes (**6–14**). You will probably find that all the parliamentary publications have been housed in an official publications collection, in a separate area of the library (which may not form part of the law library). In some libraries, government publications collections may be held on microfiche or microfilm. Therefore, you should ask the librarians whether there is a collection of government publications available and get them to show you where they are located and how they are arranged.

Older parliamentary papers may only be available in your library on microfiche or microfilm (**6–18**) or in the form of reprints published by bodies such as the Irish University Press. (These reprints are arranged in subject order.) If your library does not have a complete collection of older material, it may be possible to trace a summary of a report in the *Breviates of Parliamentary Papers*, produced by P. & G. Ford by using the BOPCRIS database (**6–18**). Material which is still in print may be purchased from any branch of TSO (addresses appear on the *Daily Lists* and in the monthly and annual *TSO Catalogues*) or through any bookseller. Photocopies of out of print publications can be purchased from TSO. Publications may also be available on loan through the inter-library loan service.

We shall now look in more detail at some of the most important types of parliamentary publications and how they are arranged in the library.

Command Papers

This is a very important category of parliamentary papers and one to which you may frequently be referred. It includes many major government reports, *e.g. Criminal Justice: the Way Ahead* (2001), some, but not all, of the reports of the Law Commission and the reports of all Royal Commissions. A Command Paper is, as it states on the front cover, presented to Parliament "By Command of Her Majesty." In practice, this means that it is presented to Parliament by a Minister of the Crown on his or her own initiative; its preparation has not been requested by Parliament. Command Papers are often statements of government policy, which are likely to be the subject of future legislation, or they are presented for the information of the Members of Parliament. Command Papers include:

statements of government policy (often referred to as *White Papers*);

some annual statistics and annual reports (many more are issued as non-parliamentary publications);

reports of Royal Commissions;

reports of some committees (other committee reports may be issued as non-parliamentary publications);

reports of tribunals of inquiry, *e.g. Report of the tribunal appointed to inquire into the Vassall Case* (Cmnd. 2009);

state papers (including the Treaty Series—**12–8**).

Citation and location of Command Papers

Command Papers are each given an individual number, prefaced by an abbreviation for the word "command". This abbreviation and the number are printed at the bottom left-hand corner of the cover of the report. The numbers run on continuously from one session of Parliament to another. The present abbreviation "Cm." has been used for publications issued since 1986. Prior to 1986, different abbreviations of the word "command" were used. They are:

1st series 1833–1869	[1]–[4222] (the abbreviation for "Command" was omitted in the first series)
2nd series 1870–1899	[C. 1]–[C. 9550]
3rd series 1900–1918	[Cd. 1]–[Cd. 9239]
4th series 1919–1956	[Cmd. 1]–Cmd. 9889
5th series 1956–1986	Cmnd. 1–Cmnd. 9927
6th series 1986–	Cm. 1–

(The use of square brackets was abandoned in 1922.) It is important to note exactly the form of the abbreviation so that you have some idea of the date of the report. For instance, Cmd. 6404, which relates to social insurance and allied services (the Beveridge Report), is a different item from Cmnd. 6404, which is an international agreement relating to pensions. One was published in 1942 and the other in 1976.

If your library keeps all the Command Papers together in boxes arranged by command numbers, you will have no difficulty in tracing the report you want. However, if the publications are arranged by sessions or are bound into sessional sets (see **6–2**), it will be necessary to have some idea of the date of the Command Paper. You may find the *Concordance of Command Papers 1833–1972*, which is in J. E. Pemberton, *British Official*

Publications (2nd ed.), pp. 66–66, of help. Occasionally, a report is published later than the Command Papers with adjoining numbers, with the result that it appears in a different session of Parliament (and is therefore in a different sessional set (**6–2**)). If you know the Command Paper number of a publication issued before 1979–80 and wish to locate it in the bound sessional sets, first ascertain the correct session by consulting Pemberton's list or the *HMSO Annual Catalogues* (see **6–14**). Until the 1979–80 session, Command Papers were not arranged in number order in the sessional sets. They were arranged alphabetically by subject in a sequence with all reports, accounts and papers. To find a Command Paper in the sessional sets before 1979–80 therefore, you need to consult the Sessional Index at the back of the last volume of the session. There you will find a list of Command Paper numbers indicating, for each one, the volume and page within the sessional set where it can be found. Command Papers bound in the sessional sets since 1979–80 can be readily traced under the Command Paper number.

Some Command Papers also form part of another series. For instance, some of the reports of the Law Commission (but not all) are Command Papers: but each Law Commission report also bears its own running number. For convenience, law libraries may keep all Law Commission reports together, regardless of whether they are issued as Command Papers, House of Commons Papers, or non-parliamentary papers (and some of the series have been issued in all these categories). Another major series within the Command Papers are the state papers known as the Treaty Series (**12–8**). These are Command Papers and each has a number, but, in addition, each has its own Treaty Series number. If they are not bound into the sessional sets, the library may keep all the Treaty Series together. There are separate annual and three- or four-yearly consolidated indexes to the series; in addition, they also appear in the monthly and annual *TSO Catalogues*. Both the Treaty Series number and the Command Paper numbers are given. In 1970, TSO published an *Index of British Treaties 1101–1968* (compiled by Clive Parry and Charity Hopkins) (see **12–16**). There are entries under subjects (Volume 1) and by the date of the treaties (Volumes 2 and 3).

6–5 Bills

Bills are the draft versions of Acts, laid before Parliament for its consideration and approval. If your library has a complete collection of parliamentary papers, the Bills will be shelved with this collection; if not, they may be available in the law library. If the library's parliamentary papers are bound up into sessional sets, the Bills will form the first volumes of each set. The most recent Bills are likely to be shelved separately in boxes.

A Bill may be introduced into Parliament by a Member of Parliament (or by a peer) as an independent action (called a Private Member's Bill), or it may be introduced by a Minister as a Government Bill. Ultimately, however, if it is passed, it becomes a Public General Act whoever introduces it. Private Members' Bills are not always published by TSO: if not otherwise available, they can usually be obtained by writing directly to the Member of Parliament concerned.

6–6 Stages in the passage of a Bill

Before a Bill can become law, it passes through a number of stages. The exact stage which any Bill has reached on its passage through Parliament can be discovered by consulting the *House of Commons Weekly Information Bulletin* (**6–7**). A Bill may be introduced into the House of Lords or the Commons. If they commence in the House of Commons, Bills progress through the following stages. Bills fail if they do not pass through all these stages before the end of the parliamentary session.

(i) *First Reading*—a purely formal reading of the Bill's title by the Clerk of the House; after this, the Bill is printed, a day is fixed for its Second Reading and it becomes available to the public.

(ii) *Second Reading*—the principles of the Bill are debated. If the Bill fails to gain the approval of the House at this stage, it cannot proceed. The debate is reported in *Hansard* (see **6–11**).

(iii) *Committee stage*—the whole House may sit in committee to examine the clauses of a Bill. More usually, the Bill is discussed in a Standing Committee consisting of approximately 20 Members of Parliament. The Standing Committee debates are found on the Parliament website (at **www.parliament.uk**), specifically on the House of Commons "publications on the internet" page. The link to the debates is under the main Hansard heading, where they are arranged by session (chronologically), and then alphabetically by the name of the Bill under discussion. TSO also prints the text of the debate on the particular Bill as an individual item. Bound volumes are issued as *Parliamentary Debates. House of Commons Official Report. Standing Committees.* Six volumes are published for each session and their publication lags well behind that of the individual items. The volumes for the 1997–98 session appeared in 2001.

If you are using the print copies of the debates you will need to find out which committee discussed the Bill you are interested in. This can be done by looking in the *House of Commons Information Bulletin* (**6–7**). Standing Committees can also be traced using the TSO's **clicktso.com** website (**6–14**) or the UKOP catalogue (**6–18**). If you are searching using UKOP you will find that the name of the committee appears in the title area of the records used. Particular debates can be found by combining the Bill's title with "standing committee" or "grand committee".

(iv) *Report stage*—if the Bill has been amended by the Standing Committee, this stage gives the House an opportunity to consider the changes. If necessary, the Bill may be referred back to the committee. (If the Bill was debated and approved without amendment in a Committee of the whole House, then this stage is a formality.)

(v) *Third Reading*—a general discussion of the Bill as amended, after which it is passed to the House of Lords for its approval.

(vi) *Lords' stages*—The Bill is reprinted when it is passed to the Lords for their consideration and approval. If the Lords make any amendments, these are referred back to the Commons for their approval. Normally, both Houses must be in agreement on the text before the Bill can receive the Royal Assent. The Parliament Acts 1911 and 1949 provide for certain exceptions to this rule. Finance Bills are the standard exception.

The citation of Bills   6–7

Bills before Parliament are found on the Parliament website (at **www.parliament.uk**). Public Bills are arranged in an alphabetical sequence on the "Public Bills before Parliament" page, which is reached either from the House of Commons or the House of Lords "publications on the internet" link. Bills which originated in the House of Lords have [H.L.] after the title. The Bills are available in the form in which they are currently being considered by Parliament and carry a note explaining their status, as, *e.g.,* a Bill passed by the House of Commons and introduced in the House of Lords, or "under consideration by Standing Committee F". If you are looking at the text of a Bill which has already passed through the House of Commons, this means you will see the Bill on the Parliament website as a House of Lords Bill. Because of the amendments made in the Commons, the text of the Bill will also not be that of the original House of Commons Bill. If you want to go back to the text of the Bill as introduced to the Commons, you need to find the printed copy of the Bill published at first reading in the House of Commons. Consequently, the exact citation of a Bill becomes crucial.

The paper versions of a Bill can be printed more than once within each House as its content is changed. Thus, it is important to distinguish one printing of a Bill from another. There can be multiple printed versions of a Bill as a House of Commons Bill for example, as well as multiple versions of a Bill as it proceeds through the House of Lords. Most Bills are printed and placed on sale to the public by TSO as soon as they are given their first reading and the first number a Bill will carry is allocated at this point. This will be its number as a Bill introduced in either the Commons or the Lords. The Health and Social Care Bill for example was allocated the number 9 for its first printing as a House of Commons Bill. As it received its first reading in the 2000–01 session, the full citation of the Bill at this point is therefore Health and Social Care Bill [H.C.] [2000–01] 9.

When Parliament discusses the Bill, some amendments may be incorporated. If these are only minor amendments, this is done by issuing a sheet of paper carrying the amended text. This bears the same number as the original Bill but with the addition of a lower case letter, *e.g.* 38a. If a major alteration is made, the complete text is reprinted, and this reprinted version is given a completely new number. The Health and Social Care Bill was for example reprinted and renumbered 42 for the House of Commons, and the full citation for this version of the Bill is the Health and Social Care Bill [H.C.] [2000–01] 42. If a significant number of amendments have been made to a Bill then a marshalled list of amendments may be published which bears the same number as the original Bill, but with the addition of a roman number, *e.g.* 123 II.

As most Bills require the approval of both Houses of Parliament, a House of Commons Bill will be renumbered when it passes to the House of Lords and becomes a House of Lords Bill. When it became a House of Lords Bill, the Health and Social Care Bill for example became the Health and Social Care Bill [H.L.] [2000–01] 27. HMSO catalogues also marked the transition of a Bill from Commons to Lords by placing Commons Bill numbers in square brackets and Lords Bill numbers in round brackets. However, this is not current practice.

If you wish to trace the various printed copies of a Bill, the *House of Commons Weekly Information Bulletin* can act as your guide. The entry on page 101 from the *Bulletin* for November 25, 2000 relates to the Child Support, Pensions and Social Security Bill which was introduced into the House of Commons by Mr Alistair Darling. The Bill was printed three times during its passage through the Commons as H.C. Bills 9, 83 and 167, all printed in the 1999–2000 Parliamentary Session. The first version of the Bill to be considered by the House of Lords was H.L. Bill 54; there were later printings as H.L. Bills 70, 92 and 110 incorporating subsequent amendments. The Bill received its first reading in the House of Commons (1R) on December 1, 1999; after the Second Reading (2R), it was referred to Standing Committee F (Comm(SC F)) which discussed it between January and early March 2000. The Report Stage took place on April 3. After the Commons had considered the Lords amendments (LA) on July 24, the Bill received the Royal Assent on July 28, 2000 and became law as the Child Support, Pensions and Social Security Act 2000 (c. 19). A full list of abbreviations can be found in the *Weekly Information Bulletin* under "Public Legislation—General Notes". The debates on the Bill are found in Hansard (**6–11, 6–17**) on the appropriate dates. However, the *Bulletin* does not contain a record of individual

Example Page from the House of Commons Weekly Information Bulletin for November 25, 2000

CENSUS (AMENDMENT) [HL] (L)   Lord Weatherill / Mr Jonathan Sayeed

Lords: (15,29)   1R: 16.12.99   2R: 27.1.2000   Comm: 3.2.2000   Rep: 3.3.2000   3R: 14.3.2000

Commons: (92)   1R: 20.3.2000   Order for 2nd Reading discharged; returned to the Lords due to an error in the Bill

Lords: 3R: 28.3.2000   CA: 27.7.2000

Commons: (100)   1R: 28.3.2000   2R: 20.6.2000   MR: 26.6.2000   Comm (SC D): 5.7.2000   RS 26.7.2000

Royal Assent: 28.7.2000 (Ch 24, 2000) **CENSUS (AMENDMENT) ACT 2000**

CHEQUES (SCOTLAND) [HL] (L)   Viscount Younger of Leckie

Lords: (27)   1R: 1.2.2000   2R: 8.3.2000   OCD: 17.7.2000   3R: 19.7.2000*

CHILD CURFEW (SPECIFIED AGE) (T)   Vernon Coaker

Commons: (94)   1R: 22.3.2000 (not printed)   Order for 2nd Reading lapsed

➡ CHILD SUPPORT, PENSIONS AND SOCIAL SECURITY (G)   Mr Alistair Darling/Baroness Hollis of Heigham

Commons: (9,83,167)   1R: 1.12.99   2R: 11.1.2000   Comm(SC F): 18.1-7.3.2000   Rep: 29.3.2000   RS: 3.4.2000   LA: 24.7.2000

Lords: (54,70,92,110)   1R: 5.4.2000   2R: 17.4.2000   Comm: 8,15&22.5.2000   Rep: 22&27.6.2000

3R: 19.7.2000   CA: 26.7.2000

Royal Assent: 28.7.2000 (Ch 19, 2000) **CHILD SUPPORT, PENSIONS AND SOCIAL SECURITY ACT 2000**

CHILDREN (LEAVING CARE) [HL] (G)   Lord Hunt of Kings Heath / Mr Alan Milburn

Lords: (2,33,123)   1R: 18.11.99   2R: 7.12.99   Comm**:10.2.2000   Rep: 9.3.2000   3R: 22.5.2000   PCA: 28.11.2000

Commons: (134)   1R: 23.5.2000   2R: 21.6.2000   Comm (SC A): 6,11&13.7.2000   RS: 31.10.2000

CHILDREN'S RIGHTS COMMISSIONER (T)   Mr Hilton Dawson

Commons: (119)   1R:3.5.2000   Dropped

COMMUNITY AND AMATEUR SPORTS CLUBS (NATIONAL STANDARDS) (T)   Mr Andrew Reed

Common: (146)   1R: 21.6.2000 (not printed)   Order for 2nd Reading lapsed

COMMUNITY FINANCE TAX CREDIT (T)   Mr Tony Colman

Commons: (44)   1R: 11.1.2000 (not printed)   Order for 2nd Reading lapsed printings of single amendments. These can be traced using the TSO website (**6–14**). A House of Lords amendment moved on the 3rd reading of the Child Support, Pensions and Social Security Bill for example was printed as [H.L.] [1999–00] 92h.

In summary, the Parliament website shows you the current state of a Bill, but if you want a series of snapshots of the passage of a Bill through Parliament, this can only be obtained by tracing the various printings of a Bill. This can be complex and you require the exact citations of the Bill as it progresses and changes through its Parliamentary life.

6–8   Tracing recent Bills

As described in **6–7**, the *House of Commons Weekly Information Bulletin* provides one way of tracing the passage of a Bill through Parliament. A list of current Bills can be seen and the various re-printings of the paper copies traced. The publication of a recent Bill can also be traced by looking at recent issues of the TSO *Daily List* (**6–14**). TSO's **clicktso.com** site (**6–14**) and the UKOP catalogue (**6–18**) provide alternatives which allow for keyword searching.

If your Library has a subscription to Parlianet from Context (**6–11**), formerly Justis Parliament, you will find that this service provides perhaps the most effective way of tracing the full story of a Bill's passage through Parliament. Restrict your database search to Commons and Lords Bills. A keyword search on the title of a Bill will display a list of the various printings of a Bill, with a note explaining the point the Bill had reached when printed, *e.g.* "as amended on report (HL)", or "Amended in Special Standing Committee".

Should you be interested in tracing the stage a Bill has reached in the current session of Parliament, the free Bill Tracker service from Butterworths Direct (at **www.butterworths.co.uk**) provides a list of the Bills and a note of the date at which they received their first, second reading, etc.

The current version of a Bill is on the Parliament website (at **www.parliament.uk**) at the "Public Bills before Parliament" page, but only Bills currently under consideration are there. If your library holds a set of the printed copies of Bills, then *all* the various printings of a Bill are included (see **6–7**). The House of Commons Bills are shelved together, but House of Lords Bills may be interfiled with House of Lords papers. This is because both the Bills and the papers shared the same sequence until 1987/88, after which they are separately numbered.

The debates on a Bill that take place at the committee stage are in the *Official Reports of Standing Committees* (**6–6**). Debates in the House of Commons are reported in Hansard (**6–11** and **6–17**). When a Bill receives the Royal Assent, this is noted in the *House of Commons Weekly Information Bulletin*, as well as in publications such as the *New Law Journal* and *Current Law*. When the Royal Assent is given, a copy of the Act is printed, and an entry for the Act appears in the TSO *Daily List*. It also appears on the HMSO website (at **www.legislation.hmso.gov.uk**).

6–9   Tracing older Bills

It is not often that you will need to refer to Bills from earlier sessions, for either they will have become law (in which case you should consult the resultant Act) or they will have lapsed. However, when you do need to consult older Bills, if your library has the bound sessional sets available, the text of all the versions of the Bill, together with all amendments, will be found in alphabetical order in the volumes entitled *Bills* at the beginning of the sessional set. If the bound sets are not available, details of all the published versions of the Bill will be found at the beginning of the *TSO or HMSO Annual Catalogue* and in the *House of Commons Weekly Information Bulletins* during that session.

Publication details for Bills from the 1970s onwards can also be found using TSO's website (**16–14**) or the UKOP catalogue (**6–18**).

Papers of the House of Lords and House of Commons   6–10

Until 1988, the House of Lords Papers and Bills were issued in a common numerical sequence, so the Papers and Bills were integrated. Since then, they have been issued in separate numerical sequences in the same way as the House of Commons Papers are numbered separately from the Commons Bills.

The number of each House of Lords Paper is printed in round brackets at the foot of the front cover. The citation is: H.L. session (paper number), *e.g.* H.L. 1993–94 (7) 1st Report [Session 1993–94]: Enforcement of Community Competition Rules: Report with Evidence—Select Committee on the European Communities.

The Papers of the House of Commons include reports of some committees, together with accounts, statistics and some annual reports which are required by Parliament for its work. The citation of a House of Commons Paper contains the initials H.C., the session and the paper number, *e.g.* H.C. 1992–93 371 is a report by the National Audit Office, *The Administration of Student Loans*.

Parliamentary Debates   6–11

The first semi-official reports of Parliament's debates were published in 1803 by William Cobbett. The man whose name is so closely linked with the publication, *Hansard*, was a subsequent printer of the reports. There have been six series of *Parliamentary Debates, i.e.* first series, 1803–20; second series, 1820–30; third series, 1830–91; fourth series, 1892–1908; fifth series, 1909–1981; sixth series, 1981–present. Since 1909, the *Official Reports of Parliamentary Debates* have been published by the House of Commons itself. The House of Lords Debates have been published separately since 1909; previously, Lords and Commons Debates were published together.

The Official Report of Debates (*Hansard*) is published daily, both on the internet and in print. If you are looking for parliamentary debates that have taken place from the 1988/89 session onwards, the full text of the Hansard reports is available in electronic form, and may well be your first choice for convenience of access. However, long debates remain easier to follow in print, and you will need to use print sources for sessions before 1988/89. Electronic and print versions of Hansard are described below.

Electronic
Hansard is available on the web from the United Kingdom Parliament website (at **www.parliament.uk**) where it is found by first selecting the link to the House of Commons (or Lords) and then selecting "Publications on the internet". An alternative route is provided by the TSO's Official Document website (at **www.official-publications.co.uk**). Selecting "Official Publications on the internet by category" brings you back to the Hansard debates. The debates are organised by session and date. If you do not know the date of a particular debate the search engine available on the Parliament website allows you to restrict your search to the Hansard pages. Try keyword searching using speakers' names and subject terms. The *Fortnightly Index* to the debates is also available on the website, as are the indexes to the bound volumes.

The Hansard debates are available on CD-ROM from Chadwyck-Healey, and you may

Example Page from the House of Commons Parliamentary Dabates (Hansard)

Previous Section   Index   Home Page

LORD CHANCELLOR'S DEPARTMENT

Human Rights Act

Mr. Gareth Thomas: To ask the Parliamentary Secretary, Lord Chancellor's Department what assessment he has made of the impact of the Human Rights Act 1998 on the eligibility criteria for the determination of the public funding by the Legal Services Commission of cases before employment tribunals. [142382]

Mr. Lock: Sir Andrew Leggatt is conducting a review of all tribunals. He will, among other things, assess the extent to which current procedures and other arrangements, including representation, comply with our ECHR and EU obligations; and to identify the options for

14 Dec 2000 : Column: 240W

ensuring compliance in the future. It would be premature to make any decisions on extending publicly funded representation in employment tribunals until Sir Andrew's review has been completed.

Mr. Gareth Thomas: To ask the Parliamentary Secretary, Lord Chancellor's Department what assessment he has made of the impact of the Human Rights Act 1998 on the work of his Department. [142381]

Jane Kennedy: The Lord Chancellor's Department prepared at all levels for the implementation of the Human Rights Act 1998; for example, ensuring that all judges and magistrates and the Department's staff were trained; that judges have speedy access to ECHR case law, and that the High Court has sufficient judges, if needed, to deal with any additional workload. Guidance was issued to clarify best practice in certain areas and necessary changes to procedure were made.

It is too early to make an assessment of the impact of the Act on court workload but so far there has been no turbulence in the courts.

Enforcement Review

Mr. Chope: To ask the Parliamentary Secretary, Lord Chancellor's Department what action has been taken to implement the recommendations of the report of the First Phase of the Enforcement Review; and if he will make a statement. [142269]

Mr. Lock: Those proposals not requiring primary legislation and not likely to be affected by Phase 2 of the Review will be considered by the Civil Procedure Rule Committee in the New Year. Phase 2 of the Enforcement Review is itself continuing.

Commonhold and Leasehold

Mr. Waterson: To ask the Parliamentary Secretary, Lord Chancellor's Department when he plans to introduce his bill on commonhold and leasehold. [142149]

Mr. Lock: Following this Government's policy of exposing their legislation to maximum expert

Example Page from the Fortnightly Index to the House of Commons Parliamentary Debates (Hansard)

84-7w, 300-1w, (15.12.00) 878-939

Human Fertilisation and Embryology Authority

Annual reports 1w

Human rights

China 120-1w, 148-9w

East Timor 135w

EC action 471-2

Human Rights Act 1998

Questions

104-5w, 241-2w

→ Lord Chancellor's Dept 242w

Hunting

Church Commissioners 347-8

Dogs 307-8w

Wales 174w

Hunting Bill 2000/01

Debates etc.

1R (07.12.00) 134

Questions

181w, 307-10w

Hurst, Mr Alan

Debates etc.

Waste disposal, Essex (12.12.00) 613-6

Hutton, Mr John, Minister of State, Dept of Health

Debates etc.

Queen's speech, Health services (07.12.00) 214

Questions

Autism 87-8w

Child protection registers 88w

find that although the debates are available free on the internet, your library has a subscription. The House of Commons Hansard on CD-ROM contains the text of debates from 1988/89 and offers full keyword searching. The CD-ROM is updated quarterly and includes a separate database of MPs' personal details, constituency details and political careers. The House of Lords Hansard on CD-ROM covers sessions from 1992/93 onwards.

Print
The daily issues of the print version of Hansard are replaced by volumes containing reports of the debates during a parliamentary session, with a sessional index. There are also indexes at the back of each individual bound volume. A *Weekly Hansard* (containing all the daily reports, in one issue) is also published, and a fortnightly index to the debates is available.

6-12   NON-PARLIAMENTARY PUBLICATIONS

These are publications which are not presented to Parliament. The term covers a vast range of government publications, including statutory instruments (**4–26**). In most libraries, these publications (other than statutory instruments) are entered in the library catalogue, so you should start your search for them in the catalogue. Checking the catalogue is particularly important in those libraries where non-parliamentary publications are scattered among the book collections according to the subject matter of their content, rather than being kept in a single central location. If a central collection exists, additional copies may also be kept in subject collections.

Non-parliamentary publications are increasingly available on the internet, usually on the website of the body responsible for their publication. As there are many official bodies, a useful starting point is the UKonline website (at **www.ukonline.gov.uk**), as this features an alphabetical list of government, or government funded or controlled bodies under the "Quick Find" link. This allows you to trace relevant or potentially relevant home pages. Home pages of public bodies as diverse as the Child Support Agency, the Commission for Racial Equality and the Employment Appeal Tribunal can be found using the UKonline site. Your next step is to explore the site, looking for a publications link, a site map or a search engine.

Previously, much of the non-parliamentary publishing was undertaken by HMSO, but this is no longer the case, so the current TSO catalogues (**6–14**) are only of limited use. If you wish to trace non-parliamentary papers, the UKOP catalogue, available online and on CD-ROM, is of more use, as it includes publications found in Chadwyck-Healey's *British Official Publications not Published by the Stationery Office* (see **6–18**). The UKOP database also includes links to non-parliamentary publications found on departmental sites, along with archived copies of some publications from 2000 onwards.

6-13   TRACING GOVERNMENT PUBLICATIONS

6-14   Stationery Office Catalogues and Indexes

The *TSO Daily Lists* (see illustration on p. 108) are useful for tracing very recent Acts and other recent government publications. The lists appear both in print and on the TSO websites. The current list is at the clicktso.com website (at **www.clicktso.com**). The site also features links to previous lists by month and year. Whether you are using the online or print version of the *Daily List*, you can find publication details of House of Lords and Commons Papers and Bills, Command Papers, Acts and Debates at the beginning of the list in the parliamentary section. Non-parliamentary publications appear in the official publications section. Other sections are devoted to Scottish Parliament publications, Northern Ireland Assembly publications and Northern Ireland official publications and a final section is devoted to agency publications. Agency publications, by bodies such as the E.U., the U.N. and the WHO, are those that are sold, but not published, by TSO.

If your required publication is more than a few days old, it is easier to use the search facilities on the **clicktso.com** site (other sources for keyword searching are covered in **6–18**). The **clicktso.com** site includes details of all publications sold by TSO and it is possible to keyword search for any TSO publication, along with HMSO publications from 1972 onwards, using the Search feature on the site. Click the link for the "Advanced Search" and you can limit your search to Bills, Acts, House of Commons Papers, etc. The author search allows searches by the names of chairmen of committees and date limits can also be set. The **clicktso.com** site is designed to act for the Stationery Office as an internet bookshop, so along with pricing information, the site provides the ability to order online. If the item you are interested in is out of print, a price is given for TSO's "print on demand" facility.

If you wish to trace HMSO titles published before 1972, or do not have internet access, you should use the printed TSO and HMSO catalogues. These catalogues have numerical and subject listings of publications which, for later publications, provide an alternative approach to keyword searching the **clicktso.com** site.

Should you want to trace relatively recent publications using print sources, you will find that many libraries hold the printed *TSO Weekly List*. This contains the contents of the week's *Daily Lists* and these are in turn replaced (some months later), by the *Stationery Office Monthly Catalogue*. This has lists of House of Lords and House of Commons Papers arranged in numerical order, a list of Command Papers in numerical order and a list of Acts produced during that month. The list of Command Papers can be used to trace the title of publications, if you have only the Command Paper number. Scottish Parliament and Northern Ireland Assembly publications are also included using a numerical sequence. Non-parliamentary and agency publications are listed as indeed they are in the *Daily* and *Weekly Lists*. Finally, a cumulative alphabetical index is included for the year which has entries for subject terms, authors, chairmen and editors. Statutory instruments are not included, as they are included in a separate monthly index (see **4–28**). The current *Stationery Office Annual Catalogue* is structured in the same way as the monthly lists, though its publication lags well behind the year covered. The 1998 catalogue appeared, for example, some way into 2000.

If you are looking for earlier material, you should use the annual catalogues which appeared as either the *HMSO Annual Catalogue 19 …,* or before that, *Government Publications 19 …*. As you go back through the catalogues you see that where the name of the Ministry began with the word "Ministry" or "Department", the entry was inverted, as, for example, Environment, Department of. Otherwise the structure and layout of the catalogues remains essentially unaltered.

Every five years a Consolidated Index was produced for the older catalogues, *e.g.* for 1961–65, 1966–70, 1971–75, 1976–80 and in many libraries, the catalogues for these years are bound together. To allow for this, the pagination of the catalogues was continuous over the five year period.

Example TSO Daily List on the clicktso.com Website

| Category | Quick Search | Go | Advanced Search | | |

Browse

clicktso.com - HOME

Daily List
  Full Daily List
  Today's Highlights
Acts
Parliamentary
Publications
Statutory Instruments
Official Publications
Stationery Office
Scottish Acts
Scottish Parliament
Publications
Scottish Statutory
Instruments
Scottish Official
Publications
Northern Ireland Acts
Northern Ireland
Assembly Publications
Northern Ireland
Statutory Rules
Northern Ireland
Official Publications
Agency Publications
Previous Lists

Services

Register your details
Customer Charter
Terms & Conditions
Your subscriptions
& Standing Orders

clicktso
Affiliate Programme

Current TSO
Promotions

Links to more
TSO websites

s cure
site
Click to Verify
TrustWise

3 April 2001   Published by The Stationery Office

TSO Daily List   No. 066

Today's Highlights - Tuesday 3 April 2001

Environment

Annual report 2001. the Government's expenditure plans 2001-02 to 2003-04. , Department of the Environment, Transport and the Regions; Office of the Rail Regulator; Office of Water Services; Ordnance Survey.

Cm. 5105.

This annual report summarises the main achievements of the DETR in 2000-01, as well as the Office of the Rail Regulator (ORR), The Office of Water Services (Ofwat) and Ordnance Survey. One of a series of departmental reports which, accompanied by the document 'Public expenditure: statistical analyses 200-02', present the Government's expenditure plans for 2001-04. The plans were published in summary form in the Budget documentation. The complete set is available at a discount price. Information is also available on the internet at: http://www.detr.gov.uk.

Corporate Author: Department of the Environment, Transport and the Regions. H.M. Treasury.

Buy Now Price: £30.00 ISBN 0101510527

Food

Food Standards Agency departmental report. the Government's expenditure plans 2001-02 to 2003-04 and main estimates 2001-02.

Cm. 5104.

The UK Food Standards Agency (FSA) was established on 1 April 2000. It is a non ministerial department and the staff, although they are civil servants, are accountable to the Board rather than to a minister. Its remit is to protect public health from risks that may arise in connection with the consumption of food. Its areas of responsibility include: food contaminants; food additives; microbiological safety; inspection and enforcement; food labelling; the effect of pesticides and veterinary medicines; nutritional advice. This is the first annual report with expenditure plans.

Corporate Author: Food Standards Agency
Author: Sir John Krebs (chairman)

Buy Now Price: £17.20 ISBN 010151042X

Government

Programming of legislation. report and appendix, together with the proceedings of the Committee relating to the report. , first report, session 2000-01.

House of Commons papers (2000-01) - 382.

The experimental Sessional Orders relating to the programming of legislation will expire at the end of the current Session. The House has to decide whether to renew the current arrangements or make modifications

Corporate Author: Select Committee on Modernisation of the House of Commons

Example Search Results Page from clicktso.com

Buy Now Price: £9.60ISBN 0339200103

Child Support, Pensions and Social Security Bill Commons reasons:
House of Lords bills 1999-00 110

Corporate Author: Great Britain Parliament House of Lords

Publication Date: 26th July 2000

Publisher: Stationery Office

MORE...

Buy Now Price: £1.10ISBN 0108391108

Lords amendments to the Child Support, Pensions and Social Security Bill:
House of Commons bills 1999-00 167

Corporate Author: Great Britain Parliament House of Commons

Publication Date: 20th July 2000

Publisher: Stationery Office

MORE...

Buy Now Price: £2.90ISBN 0103167005

Child Support, Pensions and Social Security Bill marshalled list of amendments to be moved on 3rd reading:
House of Lords bills 1999-00 92-I

Corporate Author: Great Britain Parliament House of Lords

Publication Date: 19th July 2000

Publisher: Stationery Office

MORE...

Buy Now Price: £2.10ISBN 0108397335

Child Support, Pensions and Social Security Bill amendment to be moved on 3rd reading:
House of Lords bills 1999-00 92h

Corporate Author: Great Britain Parliament House of Lords

Publication Date: 18th July 2000

Publisher: Stationery Office

MORE...

Buy Now Price: £0.65ISBN 0108397289

Child Support, Pensions and Social Security Bill amendments to be moved on 3rd reading:
House of Lords bills 1999-00 92f

Corporate Author: Great Britain Parliament House of Lords

Publication Date: 13th July 2000

Publisher: Stationery Office

Indexes covering longer periods have also been published by HMSO. The last published (in 1995) was the *General alphabetical index to the bills, reports and papers printed by Order of the House of Commons and to the reports and papers presented by Command 1969–70 to 1978–79* (HC 624 1994–95). Similar indexes, usually covering 10-year periods, were published for parliamentary sessions from 1852 onwards. Other indexes and catalogues, both online and in print, are noted in **6–18**.

6–15   Tracing Lords and Commons Papers

If you have the Paper number, the citation (**6–10**) should include the session, the Paper number, and whether it relates to the Lords or the Commons. If the library has bound the papers into sessional sets the appropriate volume and page can be traced from the Sessional Index. In more recent sessions, the Papers have been arranged in the sessional sets in numerical order.

6–16   Tracing Reports if You Know the Chairman

If you know the name of the chairman of the report but lack further details (except possibly some idea of the subject matter), you should use TSO's website (**6–14**) or the UKOP catalogue (**16–18**) if you believe the report to be relatively recent. Otherwise consult:

S. Richard, *British Government Publications: an Index to Chairmen of Committees and Commissions of Enquiry, Vol. I 1800–1899*;
S. Richard, *British Government Publications: an Index to Chairmen and Authors, Vol. II 1900–1940*;
S. Richard, *British Government Publications: an Index to Chairmen and Authors, Vol. III 1941–1978, Vol. IV 1979–1982*.

More recent reports can be traced in the *Index to Chairmen of Committees*, now renamed as *Committee Reports published by the Stationery Office, Indexed by Chairman*.

6–17   Tracing Parliamentary Debates

Recent parliamentary debates can be traced by making use of the United Kingdom Parliament website (at **www.parliament.uk**) as noted in **6–11**. First select the link for the House of Commons (or Lords) and look for the link to "Publications on the Internet". If the debate took place in the last few days, you might want to scan the debates directly. If you wish to go directly to a statement by a particular speaker, or are unsure of the date of the debate, a more effective method of tracing the debate would be to make access to the search engine on the Parliament site. To make use of the search engine, click the "Search" link and modify the search form so that you are only searching Hansard. Then add keywords relevant to the debate or the names of speakers. This enables you to retrieve a results list organised by relevance ranking, which places (hopefully near the top of the page) a link to the debate you are interested in.

A more systematic approach to tracing slightly older debates is possible using the fortnightly indexes to debates and the indexes to the bound volumes of Hansard which are available on the U.K. Parliament website, again under the link for "Publications on the Internet" (they also continue to be available in print). These indexes are useful if the debate is at least three months old in the case of the fortnightly index, or at least six months in the case of the indexes to the bound volumes, as the indexes take time to prepare. The indexes are arranged using standard subject headings, though you may find these do not always correspond to your expected terms. For example, debates on asylum seekers are listed under the "Refugees" heading. There are also entries under the names of Members of Parliament. The references in the indexes give the column number of the printed Hansard and those ending in a 'w' indicate written questions. If you are using the internet version of the indexes the reference links you directly to the relevant part of the Hansard debate.

The Sessional Information Digest is a particularly useful source for tracing the full history of a Bill in a particular session of parliament. The Digest can also be found under the "Publications on the Internet" link on the U.K. Parliament website and under the section on legislation. There is a complete list of public Bills and their stages in both houses. The discussions on a Bill are entered under the name of the Bill and the abbreviations 1R, 2R and 3R indicate the first, second and third readings. The dates of the readings are given. The Sessional Information Digest is available on the U.K. Parliament website from the 1995–96 session onwards. The last bound volume of the print *Parliamentary Debates* for each session contains the print sessional index.

The Hansard debates on CD-ROM from Chadwyck-Healey provide an alternative way of tracing debates from 1988/89. Debates from 1980 onwards can also be traced online if your library has a subscription to the Parlianet service (**6–18**). Parlianet does not give you direct access to the text of the debates.

Tracing Publications on a Subject 6–18

A number of online and CD-ROM sources make it relatively easy to trace recent government publications by subject: several catalogues carry details of both parliamentary and non-parliamentary publications published since 1979, and entries in the TSO catalogue date from 1972 (see **6–14**). A substantial body of earlier parliamentary material can also be traced, though the available electronic sources are less comprehensive. For earlier material you may need to use either the indexes to the annual HMSO print catalogues or the general indexes produced by HMSO (**6–14**). Other print indexes are noted at the end of this section.

Although parliamentary and non-parliamentary material can be traced using the TSO catalogue (at **www.clicktso.com**), your library may subscribe to the UKOP catalogue, available either online (at **www.ukop.co.uk**) or as a CD-ROM from Chadwyck-Healey. The UKOP catalogue combines the TSO catalogue with Chadwyck-Healey's *Catalogue of Official Publications Not Published by the Stationery Office* to provide coverage of both parliamentary and a great deal of non-parliamentary material from 1980 onwards. UKOP's "Advanced search" option offers the ability to search using either a "Boolean search" (see **2–14**) or a "Flexible Search". The "Flexible Search" option adds related words from the UKOP thesaurus to your search, so that if you search for "asylum seekers", publications with titles featuring the words "immigration" and "refugees" will also be found. At the beginning of 2001 a Boolean search for "asylum AND seekers" found 31 references, whereas a "Flexible Search" for "asylum seekers" found 818 records. Fortunately, in the latter case, the relevance ranking of the search results places titles with the words "asylum seekers" in the title at the top of the list. From January 2000 onwards, links to 12,000 or so full-text documents have been added to the UKOP catalogue, some linking to digital copies only available from UKOP. The search for publications relating to asylum seekers for example found the digital full text of *Full and equal citizens: a strategy for the integration of refugees into the United Kingdom*, published by the Home Office Communication Directorate [Nov 2000].

Your library may subscribe to the BOPCAS service from the University of Southampton (at **www.bopcas.ac.uk**) which has catalogued parliamentary publications, along with non-parliamentary publications taken by the university's Ford Collection, since 1996. There are also email current awareness services linked to the BOPCAS database.

Another approach to tracing parliamentary publications is via the Parlianet service (**6–17**) from Context (at **www.context.co.uk**), which, like BOPCAS, is a subscription service. It superseded the JUSTIS Parliament series of CD-ROMS in 2001. The Parlianet service is based on the POLIS database prepared by the House of Commons Library. References to parliamentary papers are included from 1980 onwards along with some non-parliamentary publications. You will find it helpful to restrict the database search by type of publication as the database contains a large number of references to parliamentary debates.

If you want references to older parliamentary papers the *Index to the House of Commons Parliamentary Papers on CD-ROM*, available from Chadwyck-Healey, contains references to Bills, Command Papers and House of Commons Papers. The latest edition covers 1801–1999. The nineteenth-century references are taken from Chadwyck-Healey's *Subject Catalogue of the House of Commons Parliamentary Papers, 1901–1900*, by Peter Cockton, and later references are taken from HMSO indexes and the POLIS database. Broad subject headings are provided, though for most searches you should rely on keyword searching for words appearing in the titles of the papers.

Another significant database, if you are searching for older material, is the BOPCRIS database (at **www.bopcris.ac.uk**), which is available free. Although the coverage is not comprehensive, abstracts in the database cover 23,000 key documents, between 1688 and 1995. Most of the documents are parliamentary papers, though some non-parliamentary papers are included. From 2001 onwards, scanned copies of some of the documents are available as full-text links. Much of the content of the database comes from the Ford lists and breviates (see below) and it is possible to search the database using the broad subject headings used in the Ford lists. More detailed subject indexing is planned for the database and currently it is possible to keyword search both document titles and abstracts.

A comprehensive approach to finding older material requires the use of printed indexes. Along with the indexes published by HMSO (**6–14**), the general indexes printed for the House of Commons covering the nineteenth century should be examined. These provide a detailed alphabetical approach to finding parliamentary papers and were published as the *General Index to the Accounts and papers... Printed by Order of the House of Commons or Presented by Command* for 1801–1852, 1852/53 to 1868/69 and 1869–1878/79. The Ford lists and breviates, already mentioned, were published as *Select list of British parliamentary papers for 1833–99*; *A breviate of parliamentary papers*, with volumes covering the period from 1900 to 1954; *Select list of British parliamentary papers, 1955–1964*; and *Ford list of British parliamentary papers*, with volumes covering 1965–83.

6–19 Tracing Law Commission Reports and Working Papers

Some of the Law Commission reports are published as Command Papers and others are House of Commons Papers, whilst many more are non-parliamentary papers. As a result you may find that in your library they are not all shelved as one collection. Every report and working paper has its own individual number. A complete list of all the reports and working papers which have been published is given in the latest copy of the *Law Commission's Annual Report* (issued as a House of Commons Paper). The list gives the Command Paper number or Paper numbers, where relevant, and indicates, for each report, whether the Commission's proposals for reform have been implemented. Law Commission papers can also be traced using TSO's website for recent publications and the HMSO catalogues for older reports and publications.

Tracing Press Releases

6–20

The press releases of government departments are relatively easy to trace thanks to the UK online website (at **www.ukonline.gov.uk**). This provides a means of tracing the departmental websites and the press releases they carry. The BADGER database, available as part of *Current Legal Information* (at **www.smlawpub.jhc.net** and on CD-ROM), also contains the text of press releases. BADGER abstracts and indexes selected press releases and consultative documents along with other official publications.

Some libraries may continue to keep paper archives of press releases from key departments.

Tracing Statistics

6–21

The National Statistics website (at **www.statistics.gov.uk**) provides a particularly useful starting point for official statistics. The site includes a link to the StatBase database, which provides a detailed description of the U.K. Government Statistical Service's data sources, products and services. It provides an authoritative route into the available statistical sources. In some cases statistical data are provided directly, and in others you are given details of a print source or a relevant government department. It is possible to search StatBase by theme (*e.g.* crime and justice), subject (*e.g.* court and judicial procedings) and then topic (*e.g.* children's procedings). A good departmental site for lawyers is the Home Office site, and in particular the Home Office Research Development statistics (at **www.homeoffice.gov.uk/rds**).

TSO publishes the printed *Guide to Official Statistics*, revised annually, which again provides a valuable starting point. It is produced by the Office for National Statistics, now incorporated into National Statistics.

7 How to Find Information on a Subject

INTRODUCTION

It is probable that you will frequently be asked to discover the law relating to a particular topic. Your essays, moots and seminar preparation will often require you to know not simply the present state of the law but also its development and such criticisms and suggestions for reform as have been made.

To find information on a subject you will need to consult some or all of the following sources:

Acts of Parliament;
Delegated legislation;
European Communities legislation, and international Treaties and Conventions;
Cases;
Textbooks;
Journal articles;
Relevant government publications, including Law Commission Reports (especially those which have made suggestions for reform of the law);
Reports and comments in newspapers;
Bills and Parliamentary Debates.

In order to tackle a legal problem, you may need to ask yourself the following questions:

QUESTION: Where can I find a general statement of the law on this subject?
ANSWER: In encyclopedias, such as *Halsbury's Laws* (**7–3**) and in textbooks (**7–29**).

QUESTION: What books are there on this subject?
ANSWER: Consult library catalogues (**7–29**) and bibliographies (**7–30**).

QUESTION: What journal articles have been written on this subject?
ANSWER: Consult indexes to journals (**5–3**).

QUESTION: What cases have there been on this topic?
ANSWER: Use either electronic databases or print indexes (**7–7**).

QUESTION: What judicial interpretation has been placed on particular words?

ANSWER: Look in *Words and Phrases Legally Defined* and similar works (**7–18**).

QUESTION: Which Acts of Parliament deal with this subject and are in force?
ANSWER: Use electronic databases (**7–20** and **7–21**), *Halsbury's Statutes* (**7–23**) or the *Index to the Statutes* (**7–22**).

QUESTION: Are there any relevant statutory instruments?
ANSWER: Use electronic databases (**7–26**) or *Halsbury's Statutory Instruments* (**7–27**).

QUESTION: Have there been any government reports or Law Commission reports on this topic?
ANSWER: Use the TSO or UKOP databases (**6–14** and **6–18**) and the *Annual Reports* of the Law Commission (**6–19**).

QUESTION: Are there any Bills before Parliament which would change the law on this subject? Has the issue been discussed in Parliament?
ANSWER: Consult the *House of Commons Weekly Information Bulletin* (**6–7**) and *Parliamentary Debates* (**6–11** and **6–17**).

Having mapped out the ground, you can now proceed to tackle these questions. If you encounter any difficulties in carrying out a search on a legal subject, never be afraid to ask the library staff or your lecturer for help. Remember that other students may also be working on the same subject—start work well within the time limits set, otherwise you may discover that the material is unavailable because of high demand.

7-2 LEGAL ENCYCLOPEDIAS

These contain a detailed up-to-date statement of the law on a particular subject. The major general legal encyclopedia is *Halsbury's Laws of England*, which is now in its fourth edition. It is a most useful source of information on a wide variety of topics. In addition, there are a number of more specialised encyclopedias, many of them issued in looseleaf form or on CD-ROM, so that the information can be kept up to date.

7-3 Halsbury's Laws of England

This is the major legal encyclopedia. It covers all areas of English law and is a useful starting point for research on any legal topic. Because it is kept up to date, it has the advantage over textbooks of including recent information.

The encyclopedia is available either online from Butterworths (at **www.butterworths.co.uk**) as *Halsburys Laws Direct*, or as 60 print volumes. The fourth edition was completed in 1987 and forms the basis of both the online and print versions. There is an ongoing programme to update the encyclopedia. The online version features links to updating text, and the print volumes which have been most affected by changes in the law are reissued.

Whether online or in print, *Halsbury's Laws* provides an effective statement of the whole of the law of England and Wales. The print volumes are arranged alphabetically by subject, from "Administrative Law" to "Wills" and these divisions are also present in the *Halsburys Laws Direct* database. Each print volume covers between one and seven subjects. The subjects are in turn divided into numbered paragraphs and each paragraph gives a description of the law relating to a particular topic, together with copious footnote references to relevant statutes and cases. Remember that *Halsbury's Laws* gives a useful summary of the law: you will need to go to other works to find the actual text of an Act of Parliament or law report.

How to use Halsbury's Laws 7–4

Electronic

Halsbury's Laws Direct can be accessed from the Butterworths home pages (at **www.butterworths.co.uk**), as one of the Butterworths online services. This is a subscription database, so you need to confirm that your library or law school has a current subscription. Once you have entered the username and password, select the "search Halsbury's Laws" link on the *Halsbury's Laws Direct* home page. There are two kinds of search under the main "search" link, a "normal search", and one using Butterworths' "Eureka!" software. The "Eureka!" search caters for searches using natural language (see below).

To use the "normal" search, enter a word or phrase to find in the text box on the search page. If you want to find entries on the law relating to "bomb hoaxes", enter the phrase and click to search. The phrase occurs five times in the database and the results page provides links to the relevant paragraphs in the encyclopedia. Two of the links for "bomb hoaxes" are to paragraph 484 and the text displayed is identical to that found in the print version of the encyclopedia. There is also an update screen which displays changes and additions to the law described in the main text. This update screen is the equivalent of the *Cumulative Supplement* and *Noter-Up* binder in the printed version. It tells you the maximum term of imprisonment relating to bomb hoaxes has been increased by the Criminal Justice Act 1991, s.26(4). The initial search can be changed so that words do not have to be adjacent to produce a matching paragraph.

The phrase "bomb hoaxes" can be found in the printed indexes for *Halsbury's Laws* and is the title of one of the encyclopedia paragraphs. However, a keyword search can find relevant paragraphs containing phrases which do not occur in the index or paragraph titles. A search for the law relating to "hoax telephone calls" for example finds an entry on "Criminal liability for public nuisance" (paragraph 6) which contains the statement, refering to *R. v. Madden* [1975] 3 All ER 155, that "a hoax telephone call about the planting of a bomb was held not to be a public nuisance". As with all keyword searches, you need to think about the different ways in which your search interest could be expressed.

The Eureka! search software is designed to allow searching using a naturally phrased question. You are encouraged to ask a question as you would of a librarian. The operation of the search software is not explained, but it can be effective if your question is sufficiently specific. However, be prepared to look at a number of potential matches, in order to find a relevant encyclopedia entry. A search using the question "Is there such a thing as a right to light?" produces an 89 per cent relevance ranking for a paragraph on Boundaries and party walls, but also an 89 per cent relevance ranking for a paragraph on human rights and freedoms (the result of the prominence of the word "right" in the question).

Print

Start by looking up the subject that interests you in the *Consolidated Index* (Volumes 55 and 56). The entry refers you to the appropriate *volume* number (in **bold** type) and *paragraph* number (not page number). The presence of "n" followed by a small number indicates that you are being referred to one of the footnotes at the end of the appropriate paragraph number. Thus the entries for "Body corporate—*meaning*" reproduced on page

119, refer you to Volume 4(2), paragraph 916 for details of the "type A" meaning of "body corporate" and to Volume 4(2), paragraph 920, footnote 1 for details of the "type B" meaning.". For information on the law related to bomb hoaxes, you would turn to Volume 11(1), paragraph 484. The relevant page from Volume 11(1) is reproduced on page 120. Paragraph 484 gives a statement of the law relating to bomb hoaxes, together with footnotes which refer you to relevant statutes. *Halsbury's Laws* also refers you to cases and other sources of information, as appropriate.

Remember that it is possible that the information in the volumes is out of date. New legislation, or other changes in the law, could have made the information incomplete or inaccurate. To find out if there have been any changes in the law since the volumes were published, make a note of the relevant volume and paragraph numbers, and turn to the *Cumulative Supplement*. For example, the information on bomb hoaxes was contained in Volume 11(1), paragraph 484. If you turn to the latest *Cumulative Supplement* (only the latest Supplement should be used) and look up the entry for Volume 11(1), paragraph 484, you will find that there have been changes in the law since Volume 11(1) was written. (See figure on p. 121.) It is therefore important to read the information in the *Cumulative Supplement* in conjunction with that found in the main volume.

These two volumes bring the information up to date to the end of last year. But have there been changes in the law since then? To find out, turn to the looseleaf *Noter-Up* in Binder 2. The *Noter-Up* is arranged in the same way as the *Cumulative Supplement*, in volume and paragraph number.

Summary: How to use Halsbury's Laws, in Print

1. Look up the subject in the *Consolidated Index*. This tells you the number of the *volume* and *paragraph* which contains the information.
2. Find the relevant volume and paragraph number in the main work.
3. To make sure the information is up to date, consult:
   (a) the *Cumulative Supplement*, and
   (b) the *Noter-Up* in Binder 2, under the relevant volume and paragraph number.

Remember there are four steps in using *Halsbury's Laws*:

Consolidated Index;
Main Work;
Cumulative Supplement;
Noter-Up.

At the back of each volume of the main work, there are separate indexes to each of the subject areas dealt with in the volume.

The last two volumes of *Halsbury's Laws* (Volumes 51 and 52) are devoted to the law of the European Communities, and its effect upon United Kingdom law. A similar but more sophisticated system of paragraph numbers is used in these two volumes and footnote references refer you to the relevant Directives, Decisions and Regulations of the European Communities. Volume 52 contains a useful glossary of technical terms, as well as a detailed index to both volumes. The information is kept up to date by the information in the *Cumulative Supplement* and *Noter-Up*.

The *Monthly Reviews* (published as booklets and filed in Binder 1) can be used as a

Example Page from Halsbury's Laws, Volume 55 Consolidated Index

Example Page from Halsbury's Laws Volume 11(1) Reissue

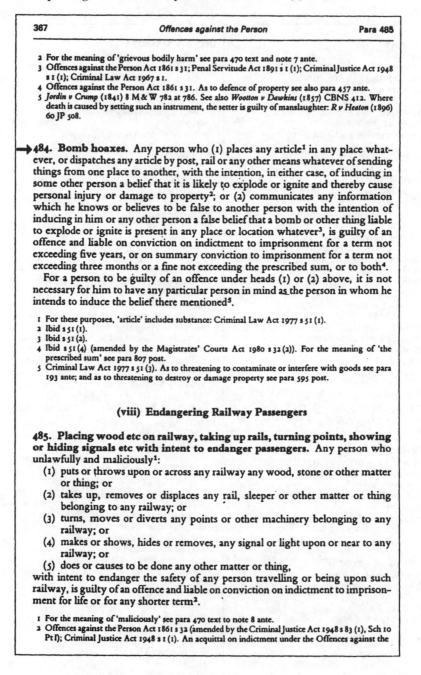

2 For the meaning of 'grievous bodily harm' see para 470 text and note 7 ante.
3 Offences against the Person Act 1861 s 31; Penal Servitude Act 1891 s 1 (1); Criminal Justice Act 1948 s 1 (1); Criminal Law Act 1967 s 1.
4 Offences against the Person Act 1861 s 31. As to defence of property see also para 457 ante.
5 *Jordin v Crump* (1841) 8 M & W 782 at 786. See also *Wootton v Dawkins* (1857) CBNS 412. Where death is caused by setting such an instrument, the setter is guilty of manslaughter: *R v Heaton* (1896) 60 JP 508.

484. Bomb hoaxes. Any person who (1) places any article[1] in any place what-ever, or dispatches any article by post, rail or any other means whatever of sending things from one place to another, with the intention, in either case, of inducing in some other person a belief that it is likely to explode or ignite and thereby cause personal injury or damage to property[2]; or (2) communicates any information which he knows or believes to be false to another person with the intention of inducing in him or any other person a false belief that a bomb or other thing liable to explode or ignite is present in any place or location whatever[3], is guilty of an offence and liable on conviction on indictment to imprisonment for a term not exceeding five years, or on summary conviction to imprisonment for a term not exceeding three months or a fine not exceeding the prescribed sum, or to both[4].

For a person to be guilty of an offence under heads (1) or (2) above, it is not necessary for him to have any particular person in mind as the person in whom he intends to induce the belief there mentioned[5].

1 For these purposes, 'article' includes substance: Criminal Law Act 1977 s 51 (1).
2 Ibid s 51 (1).
3 Ibid s 51 (2).
4 Ibid s 51 (4) (amended by the Magistrates' Courts Act 1980 s 32 (2)). For the meaning of 'the prescribed sum' see para 807 post.
5 Criminal Law Act 1977 s 51 (3). As to threatening to contaminate or interfere with goods see para 193 ante; and as to threatening to destroy or damage property see para 595 post.

(viii) Endangering Railway Passengers

485. Placing wood etc on railway, taking up rails, turning points, showing or hiding signals etc with intent to endanger passengers. Any person who unlawfully and maliciously[1]:

(1) puts or throws upon or across any railway any wood, stone or other matter or thing; or

(2) takes up, removes or displaces any rail, sleeper or other matter or thing belonging to any railway; or

(3) turns, moves or diverts any points or other machinery belonging to any railway; or

(4) makes or shows, hides or removes, any signal or light upon or near to any railway; or

(5) does or causes to be done any other matter or thing,

with intent to endanger the safety of any person travelling or being upon such railway, is guilty of an offence and liable on conviction on indictment to imprison-ment for life or for any shorter term[2].

1 For the meaning of 'maliciously' see para 470 text to note 8 ante.
2 Offences against the Person Act 1861 s 32 (amended by the Criminal Justice Act 1948 s 83 (1), Sch 10 Pt I); Criminal Justice Act 1948 s 1 (1). An acquittal on indictment under the Offences against the

Example Page from Halsbury's Laws Cumulative Supplement

Vol 11(1) (reissue), para 471   *Laws of England (4th Edn) Supp*

471   Unlawful wounding
NOTES—For extended territorial scope of unlawful wounding in connection with acts in relation to or by means of Nuclear Material, see Nuclear Material (Offences) Act 1983, Vol 16, Supp para 415A post.
NOTE 1—As to the direction to be given, see also *R v Rushworth* (1992) 95 Cr App Rep 252, CA.
NOTE 6—*R v Durkin*, cited, reported at (1989) 11 Cr App Rep (S) 313.

475   Administering poison etc
NOTE 4—As to appropriate sentence, see *R v Jones* (1990) 12 Cr App Rep (S) 233, CA (equation of offence with either offence under s 20 (para 471) or serious assault occasioning actual bodily harm (para 490)).

479   Attempting to cause explosion
NOTE 7—See *R v Ellis* (1992) 95 Cr App Rep 52 ("who in the United Kingdom" in the Explosive Substances Act 1883, s 3(1) governs the acts rather than the person and in doing so it creates a geographical limitation on the place where the relevant acts complained of take place).

484   Bomb hoaxes
TEXT and NOTE 4—Maximum terms of imprisonment increased to seven years and six months respectively: Criminal Justice Act 1991, s 26(4).

488   Assault and battery
NOTE 6—See *DPP v Taylor; DPP v Little* [1992] 1 ALL ER 299, DC (assault and battery separate statutory offences; information alleging assault and battery contrary to Criminal Justice Act 1988, s 39 therefore bad for duplicity).
NOTE 10—*DPP v K (a minor)*, cited, overruled in *R v Spratt* [1990] 1 WLR 1073, CA, itself disapproved in *R v Savage; R v Parmenter* [1991] 4 All ER 698, HL, para 490 post.

490   Assault occasioning actual bodily harm
NOTE 1—In order to establish the offence of assault occasioning actual bodily harm, it is sufficient to prove that the defendant committed an assault and that actual bodily harm was occasioned by the assault; it is not necessary to prove that the defendant intended to cause some actual bodily harm or was reckless as to whether such harm would be caused: *R v Savage; R v Parmenter* [1991] 4 All ER 698, HL.

493   Kidnapping
TEXT and NOTES 9, 10—Where a count alleging abduction contrary to 1984 Act, s 1 encompasses the allegation against the defendant, inclusion on the indictment of a count alleging kidnapping is to be deprecated: *R v C (Kidnapping: Abduction)* [1991] 2 FLR 252, CA.

494   Consent to assault
NOTES 2, 3—See also *R v Brown* [1992] 2 All ER 552, CA (consent no defence to charge of assault occasioning actual bodily harm where defendants participating in sado-masochistic acts of violence against each other).

495   Marital rights
TEXT and NOTE 2—Marital exemption in respect of rape no longer applies: *R v R (rape: marital exemption)* [1991] 4 All ER 481, HL.

501   Alternative verdicts
NOTE 1—See also *R v Savage; R v Parmenter* [1991] 4 All ER 698, HL (offence of assault occasioning actual bodily harm may be substituted for offence of wounding or causing grievous bodily harm).

502   Effect of summary conviction or dismissal of information
NOTE 5—1973 Act, s 13(4)(a) now ibid, s 1C(1): Criminal Justice Act 1991, Sch 1.

513   Guardianship of victim of incest
TEXT and NOTES—Repealed: Children Act 1989, Sch 12, para 15, Sch 15.

514   Rape
NOTE 4—*R v Khan, R v Dhokia, R v Banga, R v Faiz*, cited, reported: [1990] 2 All ER 783, CA.

515   Husband and wife
TEXT and NOTES 1–4—A husband can now be convicted of raping his wife: *R v R (rape: marital exemption)* [1991] 4 All ER 481, HL.

520   Restrictions on reporting; anonymity of victim of a rape offence
TEXT and NOTES 2–10—In heads (1)(b), (2)(b) for "broadcast or included in a cable programme" read "included in a relevant programme for reception" and for "broadcasting or inclusion in a cable programme" read "inclusion in a relevant programme": 1976 Act, s 4(1); Broadcasting Act 1990, Sch 20, para 26(1)(a). "Relevant programme" means a programme included in a programme service (within the meaning of the 1990 Act; see s 201 and TELECOMMUNICATIONS AND BROADCASTING): 1976 Act, s 4(6); 1990 Act, Sch 20, para 26(1)(d).
As to anonymity of victim of other sexual offences, see paras 520A, 520B post.
NOTE 10—Head (1) omitted: Criminal Justice Act 1988, Sch 16. In head (2) for "broadcast or inclusion in

general means of keeping up with new developments in subjects you are studying since they give, under subject headings, recent changes in the law with summaries of cases, statutes, statutory instruments and other materials. The *Monthly Reviews* are not arranged in the same volume and paragraph order as the main volumes, so in order to find relevant information you will need to look up the subject again in the Cumulative Index to the Reviews at the back of the Binder. The *Monthly Reviews* are replaced by an *Annual Abridgment*, which summarises all the changes in the law during a particular year (commencing in 1974 when the first *Abridgment* appeared). At the beginning of the volume, a section headed "In brief" summarises the major development in the law of each subject during the year. At the beginning of each subject, there is a reference to the main volume of *Halsbury's Laws* which deals with that subject and there is a highly selective list of journal articles written on the subject during the year.

7–5 Specialised Encyclopedias

There are a number of specialised encyclopedias which can provide you with an up-to-date statement of the law in particular subject areas. Many of these are issued in looseleaf format, so that the information can be updated by the insertion of replacement pages whenever there is a change in the law. Most of them are also available on CD-ROM. The *Encyclopedia of Planning Law and Practice*, published by Sweet & Maxwell, is an example. It is part of the series called "The Local Government Library", which also includes works on topics such as housing, environmental law and health and safety at work. The CD-ROM is called *Sweet & Maxwell's Planning Law Service*. A number of other publishers have issued similar works covering, for example, social welfare law (Longmans) and landlord and tenant (Butterworths). Specialised encyclopedias are particularly useful in subjects such as taxation, where the law changes very rapidly. When using the looseleaf version of a specialised encyclopedia, you should check the pages near the beginning of the volume which tell you how recent the information is. This will enable you to be certain that the latest supplementary pages have all been inserted. Specialised encyclopedias usually contain an explanation of the law, together with the up-to-date versions of the relevant statutes, statutory instruments and government circulars, and notes of relevant cases. Publishers are now issuing some books for practitioners, such as *Ruoff & Roper: Registered Conveyancing*, in looseleaf format, so that the text can be kept up to date. This is a development of the long-established practice of issuing cumulative supplements in between editions, to update the last edition.

7–6 Precedent Books and Rule Books

These are principally intended for the practitioner. The basic object of precedent books is to provide specimens of wills, conveyances, tenancy agreements or other forms of legal documents which solicitors are called upon to draw up. In addition, there are some precedent books which provide specimens of the types of forms that will be required whenever a case is taken to court. Rule books contain the rules that govern procedure in court, and specimen copies of the various orders and forms used by the courts and by the parties to litigation.

The multi-volume *Encyclopaedia of Forms and Precedents* aims to provide a form for every transaction likely to be encountered by practitioners, except for court forms. The Encyclopedia is also available on CD-ROM. The entries are arranged by subject, *e.g.*

"Animals", "Mortgages". Some idea of the wide scope of the work can be obtained by glancing through the subject headings. For instance, the section on animals covers such diverse topics as the sale and leasing of animals, applications for a licence to keep mink or to keep an animals' boarding establishment, a veterinary surgeon's certificate for the destruction of an animal and the relevant documents prohibiting movement of animals during an outbreak of disease. If you are using the print version, the looseleaf service volume keeps the information up to date. The *Cumulative Index* refers you to the *volume* (in **bold** type) and *paragraph* number that you require. Each individual volume also has its own index. References in the index to paragraph numbers in square brackets refer to precedents: paragraph numbers not enclosed in brackets refer to the preliminary notes. Checklists of procedures to be followed are provided under some subject headings.

Atkins Court Forms is a complementary publication, covering the procedure in civil courts and tribunals. Again, the volume is available on CD-ROM. The print volume on divorce, for instance, contains all the necessary documents needed during the court action, together with a detailed list of the steps to be taken and the forms required at each stage. The volumes are reissued from time to time to incorporate new material. An annual supplement keeps the information up to date. The *Consolidated Index* is also published yearly.

There are many precedent books dealing with specific areas of the law, *e.g.* the looseleaf *Jackson & Powell: Professional Liability Precedents*. In addition, some textbooks designed for practitioners will include precedents.

The rules and procedures governing various courts are set out in a number of places. *Civil Court Practice* (the *Green Book*) sets out the documents required for those appearing in the civil courts. It features the rules contained in the former *County Court Practice* (also the *Green Book*) and *The Supreme Court Practice* (the *White Book*), in so far as they still apply. *Archbold: Criminal Pleading, Evidence and Practice* is used by those engaged in criminal work. Both publications are available in print and on CD-ROM.

The coloured pages in each issue of the *Law Society Gazette* are of particular interest to practitioners. These often include specimen forms and precedents, and details of Home Office circulars and practice directions. Practice directions are also published in the major series of law reports, *e.g.* the *All England Law Reports* and the *Weekly Law Reports*.

TRACING CASES ON A SUBJECT   7–7

Cases on a particular subject can be traced by consulting the following sources.

Electronic
Full-text case law databases (**7–8**);
Current Law (**7–9**);
Other databases providing summaries of cases (**7–10**);
Halsbury's Laws Direct (**7–4**);
Legal Journals Index and the Lawtel articles index (**5–4** and **5–7**).

Print
Current Law (**7–11** and **7–12**);
The Digest (**7–13** and **7–14**);
Halsbury's Laws of England (**7–4**);
Daily Law Reports Index and *Legal Journals Index* (**7–15**);

Indexes to individual series of law reports (**7–16**);
Relevant textbooks (**7–29**).

7–8   How to Use Full-Text Databases

The legal database providers described in **2–9** to **2–13**, along with Lexis Nexis (**2–7**), provide access to the full text of law reports, and most include transcripts of unreported judgments. Because of the way these subscription databases are constructed, these sources are ideal for subject searching using keywords. Of the free Internet sources, the BAILII website provides effective database searching for judgment transcripts (see **3–12** for BAILII and other sources of transcripts). There are some important points to bear in mind.

You must understand the coverage of the database you are using. With Lexis-Nexis Professional for example, you can search the text of over 30 law reports. The Westlaw UK database has fewer report series, but is strong in some areas—for example intellectual property and human rights. The online versions of the *Law Reports* and *All England Law, Reports* on the other hand, will have stronger historical coverage. These are the versions available from Context (at **www.justis.com**) and Butterworths (at **www.butterworths.com**) respectively. Lexis-Nexis coverage starts (for the most part) in 1945. The extent of coverage means that you may obtain different results from your searches and you need to decide if you wish to repeat searches on different databases in order to obtain a more comprehensive result.

For all of these databases, the process of searching is straightforward. They have some form of free text search box in which you enter your search words and they accept the search syntax described in **2–14**, in particular the use of "AND", "OR" etc to combine search words.

The use of keyword searching on a full-text database has some important consequences. First, you must be as specific as possible in the keywords you enter. If you enter general terms such as "copyright" or even "copyright AND software", you will obtain as a search result a list of the many thousands of cases in which the word "copyright" appears or the many hundreds of cases in which both the word copyright and the word software appear, not necessarily in any proximity to each other. Most databases halt a search which would retrieve a very large number of cases. A corollary is that you need a good understanding of what it is you are researching in order to be able to home in on the important keywords. It makes sense to use full-text databases as the last stage in your subject searching. Try looking at likely textbooks before you make your search in order to select key terms to use. *Halsbury's Laws of England* (**7–3**) either online or in print might also help you in the initial stages of a subject search, clarifying terminology and listing key cases.

You should think of different ways your topic is likely to be discussed in a judgment. For the most part you are only searching the text of the words used in the judgment and you will need to think about the different ways the same basic issue can be expressed. If you wish to find cases that have discussed the way the word "charity" has been interpreted in English law, you need to look for judgments in which "charity" has been judicially interpreted. Because of the complexity of language your keywords might also include with "charity", "sense", "usage", or "definition" as they might have been used instead of "interpretation". All these terms could be included in your search (either by repeating searches or using "OR"). Different forms of the same word can also be used. You might want to search for "define", "defines" and "defining" along with "definition". Fortunately most databases allow a truncation symbol which can help, so that "defin*" could cover all of the forms mentioned. Less fortunately, "definite" would also be included in the search, so use truncation with care.

Having thought about your search terms, also make sure that you use the symbol or "search operator" for the database that specifies that your keywords must be found close to each other in the long text of a judgment. Many databases allow "NEAR" to specify a standard proximity, Lexis-Nexis uses "w/" so that "w/6" specifies within six words.

Putting these considerations together, a "good" search on a full-text database can become complex. The search for judgments on the interpretation of charity might lead to a search using the terms:

charit* w/6 (defin* OR sense OR usage)

and still other combinations are possible.

In many ways a more realistic approach to searching a case law database is to accept that no one search or even a combination of searches is likely to find all the relevant cases on a subject. Once you have considered various possibilities and tried different searches, the time will come to read the law reports you have found and see which cases they have cited.

Above all, be specific in your search terms, be aware of the coverage of the database you are using and don't be misled into thinking that any search is final or comprehensive.

How to Use the Current Law Databases   7–9

Access to *Current Legal Information* from Sweet & Maxwell, or Westlaw UK, means you can make a subject search for cases using the summaries or digests of cases that appear in print in the *Current Law Monthly Digest* and the *Current Law Yearbooks*. Because you are searching a relatively short case summary, you are more likely to find cases that are highly relevant to the subject terms you use. The ability to review quickly a series of case summaries is also a great help if you have a large number of cases listed.

Current Legal Information is available either online as a web-based service (at **www.smlawpub.jhc.net**) or on CD-ROM. In either case it is the *Current Law Cases* database that you will use. By using the "search for" box within *Current Legal Information* you can search for words in the digest summaries. Employ the keyword search technique discussed in the previous section (see also **2–14**). If you are interested in finding cases for example that involve significant discussion of the interpretation of recklessness outlined in *R. v. Caldwell* [1982] A.C. 341, a search using the words "Caldwell AND recklessness" finds summaries of relevant reported cases.

It is similar if you use Westlaw UK (at **www.westlaw.co.uk**). Select the *Case Locator* database to search the *Current Law* digests. The "Search for term(s)" box means you are again searching the full text of the summaries. Another option within the *Case Locator* database is to search only on the subject keywords and catchphrases added to the case summaries by *Current Law*, which is likely to restrict your search results to a small number of highly relevant cases. A search using "Caldwell AND recklessness" retrieves a list of 25 cases, when the "Search for term(s)" option was used. Restricting the search to "Subject, Keyword, Catchphrase" finds only one case.

Current Law Cases includes the *Daily Law Reports Index* which covers cases reported in the quality papers from 1988 onwards.

Example Page from Current Law Monthly Digest

MEDIA

---

537. **Confidential information – newspapers – variation of undertaking – publication of information already in public domain**

The Attorney General appealed against a decision to allow an application by TN and two of its journalists to vary their undertaking not to publish confidential information provided by RT, a former officer of the Special Intelligence Service, after he published a book in English which was available in Europe, the United States and on the internet. The variation allowed TN to republish previously published information which was considered to be in the public domain. The Attorney General submitted that the variation should contain a proviso that TN obtain clearance from the court or the Attorney General before publishing the information.

Held, dismissing the appeal, that it was not just to impose on TN the need to obtain confirmation from the Attorney General or the court that information it wanted to republish was in the public domain so that the cloak of confidentiality had been lifted. It was for the newspaper's editor to judge whether the information should be republished and the existing variation imposed a duty to comply with the law of confidentiality. Anything beyond that was a fetter on TN's freedom of expression.

ATTORNEY GENERAL v. TIMES NEWSPAPERS LTD; *sub nom*. ATTORNEY GENERAL v. KELSEY; ATTORNEY GENERAL v. LEPPARD [2001] EWCA Civ 97, *The Times*, January 31, 2001, Lord Phillips of Worth Matravers, M.R., CA.

538. **Films – cinematic co-production agreements – additional county – Cyprus**

EUROPEAN CONVENTION ON CINEMATOGRAPHIC CO-PRODUCTION (AMENDMENT) ORDER 2001, SI 2001 411; made under the Films Act 1985 Sch.1 para.4. In force: March 1, 2001; £1.50.

This Order amends the European Convention on Cinematographic Co-production Order 1994 (SI 1994 1065) by adding Cyprus to the list of countries set out in the Schedule.

539. **Articles**

BBC v TalkSport case tests the limits of exclusivity in sports media deals *(Daniel Harrington)*: S. & C.L. 2001, 13(Feb), 15-16. (Settlement of dispute between BBC and TalkSport on whether use of words live broadcast and simulated ambient crowd noise by TalkSport was infringement of BBC's goodwill and reputation as live sports broadcaster).

Deal week: telecoms/media *(Saira Zaki)*: Legal Week 2001, 3(5), 50-51. (How abundance of work in telecommunications and media market has benefited smaller riche firms even though most major deals are dealt with by top London firms, with table of largest deals and firms involved).

New media sports rights *(Nicholas Couchman and Daniel Harrington)*: S. & C.L. 2001, 13(Feb), 11-14. (Scope of media rights, definitions for contracts, elements making up sports content, ownership of sports data, statistics and real time scoring, value of Internet rights, strategies for brand management and online regulation).

Table of E.C. media related measures *(Freshfields Bruckhaus Deringer)* Ent. L.R. 2001, 12(2), N26-27. (Current status of EC measures on audio visual, copyright and information society).

Zooming in on news *(Linda Tsang)*: L.S.G. 2001, 98(4), 26-28. (Problems for law firms seeking media opportunities and those which become sudden subject of media interest, need for media training, crisis management plans and advisability of using external PR advisers).

How to Use Other Databases of Case Summaries   7–10

Alongside the *Current Law* databases, there are other databases that carry summaries of recent cases. Lawtel (at **www.lawtel.co.uk**) provides the major alternative subscription service and summaries are available from the (non-subscription) Butterworths *Law Direct* service (at **www.butterworths.co.uk**), the *Daily Law Notes* service from the Incorporated Council of Law Reporting (at **www.lawreports.co.uk**), and David Swarbrick's law-index (at **www.swarb.co.uk**). Unlike the *Current Law* databases, these sources provide summaries of very recent, as yet unreported cases, and so provide a very useful way to trace recent developments in case law by subject (see also **3–17**). Lawtel offers the widest service, as it summarises both recent unreported and reported cases. All these sources provide a means of searching under broad subject headings. *Lawtel* and *Law Direct* offer the possibility of keyword searching the summaries themselves. As with the *Current Law* databases, the fact that you are searching case summaries increases the likely relevance of your search results.

With Lawtel (at **www.lawtel.co.uk**), summaries of cases from a wide range of courts and law report series from 1980 onwards can be searched by selecting the "Case Law" link on the home page. Take the example used in the previous section. If you search Lawtel for "caldwell and recklessness" using the free text box, you are presented with a list of 14 cases in which the words "caldwell" and "recklessness" appear in the case summary. A search using general subject headings is also possible. This is achieved using the "Focused Search" tab which enables you to search general headings such as "Intellectual Property" or "Negligence". As the most recent cases are presented first, these general headings, combined with Lawtel's coverage, provide one of the most effective ways of reviewing the content of very recent cases. Additional words can be added to narrow the search.

Turning to the free sources of case summaries, if you follow the "Cases" link from the Butterworths *Law Direct* page (at **www.butterworths.co.uk**), you are able to search case summaries from 1995 onwards. Continuing with our existing example, a search using the "Search cases" box for "caldwell and recklessness", retrieves details of only one case (bear in mind the shorter time span covered by the database). Again searches by general subject area are possible.

The *Daily Law Notes* service from the Incorporated Council of Law Reporting (at **www.lawreports.co.uk**) is a more restricted service. You can only search for case summaries by court, week or month. Cases are arranged by general subject heading. As noted in 3–17, the cases summarised are those to be reported later in the *Weekly Law Reports*. Coverage began in May 2000.

David Swarbrick's law-index (at **www.swarb.co.uk**) in contrast dates back to 1992, and if you follow the "by Areas" link from the home page, you can search for cases using general subject headings. Again "Intellectual Property" and "Negligence" would be examples of the sort of heading you can search. As with the other databases, the most recent case summaries are presented first.

How to Use the Current Law Monthly Digest   7–11

Current Law is published monthly under the title *Current Law Monthly Digest*. It is an important publication and it is essential that you should learn how to use it.

The main part of each *Monthly Digest* is arranged by subject and under each subject heading is given a summary of recent cases on the subject, new statutes and statutory instruments, government reports and recent books and journal articles on that subject. Full details are given to enable you to trace the cases and other materials mentioned in your own library. A page from the *Monthly Digest* is shown on page 126. On this page alone, several articles are mentioned (item 539), a case is summarised (item 537) and a statutory instrument is outlined (item 538).

At the back of each issue is a Table of Cases which contains a list of all the cases which have been reported during the current year. It is therefore only necessary to look at the Table of Cases in the *latest* issue of the *Current Law Monthly Digest* to trace a case reported at any time during the year. (This list of cases brings the information in the *Current Law Case Citators* up to date (**3–14**).)

The *Current Law Monthly Digests* also contain a subject index. Again it is cumulative, so it is only necessary to consult the index in the latest month's issue. This enables you to trace any development in the law during the current year. The reference given, *e.g.* Feb 80, is to the appropriate monthly issue (in this example, the February issue) and the item number in the issue, *i.e.* item 80. If the reference is followed by an S (*e.g.* Jan 821S), the item contains Scottish material.

The Table of Cases provides a list of reports of cases. Suppose, however, that you know that there has been a recent case on the subject but you do not know the name of the parties. In this instance, you can trace the cases on the subject during the current year by looking in the cumulative Subject Index in the latest issue of the *Current Law Monthly Digest*. The Subject Index can also help when you have spelt the name of the parties incorrectly or have an incomplete reference.

7–12   How to Use the Current Law Year Books

The issues of the *Current Law Monthly Digest* are replaced by an annual volume, the *Current Law Year Book*.

The *Year Book* is arranged by subject, in the same way as the *Monthly Digest*, and contains a summary of all the cases, legislation and other developments in that subject during the year. Lists of journal articles and books written on a subject during the year are printed at the back of the volume. (The 1956 *Year Book* contains a list of journal articles published between 1947 and 1956.)

Since 1991, the *Current Law Year Book* contains Scottish material as well as that from England. Before then, there was a separate Scottish version, called the *Scottish Current Law Year Book*. Despite the name, this included all the English material, plus a separate section at the back of the volume containing Scottish developments during the year. The Scottish section remains separate from the English material in the *Current Law Year Book* and there are separate indexes to the two sections.

At the back of the 1976 *Year Book*, there is a Subject Index to all the entries in all the *Year Books* from 1947 to 1976. Entries give the last two digits of the year, and a reference to the individual item number within that year's volume, *e.g.* 69/3260 is a reference to item 3260 in the 1969 *Year Book*. Entries which have no year in front of them will be found in the *Current Law Consolidation 1947–1951*. Cumulative indexes were also published in the 1986 and 1989 *Year Books*. These indexes, together with the *Year Books* since 1989 and the latest *Current Law Monthly Digest*, provide complete coverage of any developments in the law of that subject since 1947.

Master Volumes were published in the 1956, 1961, 1966 and 1971 *Year Books*. These volumes contain, under the usual subject headings, detailed entries for all developments during the year in which they were published, together with a summary of the developments during the previous four years. References are given to enable you to trace the full details in the appropriate *Current Law Year Book*. Thus it is possible, by using the *Master Volumes* and the *Current Law Consolidation 1947–1951*, to see at a glance a summary of every entry that has appeared in *Current Law* on a particular subject over a five-year period.

Summary: How to Use Current Law in Print

(1) If you know the name of a case and want to find out where it has been reported and whether the case has subsequently been judicially considered, consult:
Current Law Case Citator 1947–1976;
Current Law Case Citator 1977–1997;
the *Current Law Case Citator* from 1998 to the end of last year; and
the Table of Cases in the latest *Current Law Monthly Digest*.

(2) To trace any developments (cases, statutes, etc.) on a particular subject, consult:
The Cumulative Index covering 1947–1976 at the back of the 1976 *Current Law Year Book*;
the Cumulative Index at the back of the 1986 *Year Book* covering the years 1972–1986;
the Cumulative Index at the back of the 1989 *Year Book* covering the years 1987–1989;
the Indexes in the back of the *Year Books* since 1989; and
the Subject Index in the latest issue of the *Current Law Monthly Digest*.

(3) To obtain a general view of developments in a topic over a number of years, consult:
the *Current Law Consolidation 1947–1951*;
the *Master Volumes* (1956, 1961, 1966, 1971 *Year Books*);
all the *Year Books* published since the last *Master Volume* was issued; and
all the issues of the *Current Law Monthly Digest* for this year.

(4) To trace books and journal articles on a subject, look in the back of the 1956 *Year Book* and each subsequent *Year Book* and in the *Current Law Monthly Digests* under the appropriate subject heading. There are, however, quicker and more comprehensive sources for tracing journals (**5–3**) and books (**7–29** *et seq.*).

Remember that *Current Law* only contains information on cases reported or mentioned in court since 1947 and other developments in the law since 1947. To trace earlier cases, use *The Digest*.

The Digest   7–13

The Digest (formerly known as the *English and Empire Digest*) contains summaries of cases that have appeared in law reports from the thirteenth century to the present day, arranged in subject order. It enables you to trace cases of any date that deal with your particular subject. In addition to English cases, reports of Irish, Scottish and many Commonwealth cases are included, together with cases on European Communities law. These are printed in smaller type to enable them to be easily distinguishable from English cases.

For each case, a summary of the decision is given, followed by the name of the case, and a list of places where the case is reported. The subsequent judicial history of the case is also shown, in the annotations section. A list of the abbreviations used for law reports will be found in the front of Volume 1 and also in the front of the *Cumulative Supplement*.

7–14   How to use The Digest to trace cases on a subject
To find cases on a particular subject, you start by looking in the three-volume *Consolidated Index*. The *Index*, however, is not always as simple as you might expect. To find cases on local authorities' duties to house the homeless, for example, you would need to look in the *Index* under "Local authority—housing accommodation powers—homeless persons", as shown on page 131. You would not have found the entry under "Homelessness", "Homeless persons", "Housing" or "Accommodation". The reference in the *Index* refers you to the volume number, the subject heading ("Housing") and the relevant case numbers (see page 132). In most volumes of *The Digest*, Scottish, Irish and Commonwealth cases are grouped together at the end of each section within the volume. In volumes that have not been reprinted for some time, all the cases, of whatever jurisdiction, are numbered consecutively: case 2040 may be an English case, while case 2041 is a Canadian case on the same subject.

In the back of each volume of *The Digest* is a Reference Adaptor. When a volume is reissued, the case numbers change as additional cases are inserted. Wherever you find a cross-reference to a volume which has been reissued more recently than the *Consolidated Index* or volume from which you have been referred, you will need to look in the volume's Reference Adaptor to convert the reference. The Reference Adaptor consists of a long list of all the case numbers from the old volume, alongside the number which replaces it in the reissued volume.

After finding the relevant cases on your subject in the main volumes, you should check to see if there have been more recent cases on the subject since the volume was written. To do this update, you must consult the *Cumulative Supplement*. Make a note of the volume number, subject heading and case number(s) in the main volumes which contain relevant information. Now turn to the *Cumulative Supplement* and look to see if there is an entry for that volume, subject heading and case number. If there is an entry, this will provide information on a later case, in which the case you were consulting in the main works has been referred to, considered, overruled, etc. (A full list of the abbreviations used and their meanings appears at the front of the *Cumulative Supplement*, under the heading "Meaning of the terms used in classifying annotating cases.") For example, the entry:

2542 **Expd** Awua v Brent London Borough Council [1995] 3 All ER 493

in the *Cumulative Supplement* means that case 2542 in the main volumes has subsequently been explained in the 1995 case of *Awua* v. *Brent London Borough Council* (see p. 134).

The *Cumulative Supplement* also includes references to new cases on the same subject matter. These new cases *either* provide a summary, followed by the name of the case (and a reference to where the case will be found in various series of law reports) *or* refer you to one of the *Continuation Volumes* where further details of the case, including a full-length summary, will be found. The system of numbering the new cases in the *Cumulative Supplement* corresponds to that in the main volumes. The small letter after the number shows that the case follows on naturally from the similarly numbered case in the volumes.

The *Cumulative Supplement* is revised annually; the front cover tells you how recent the information is. If you are looking for new cases on a particular subject, within the last few months, then *The Digest* is not sufficiently up to date and you should use electronic sources

Example Page from The Digest Consolidated Index

Example Page from The Digest, Volume 20

vided with "suitable alternative residential accommodation on reasonable terms". Applicant contended that s 39 required the authority to provide him with permanent accommodation on terms which gave him security of tenure equivalent to that which he had enjoyed by virtue of Rent Acts under his previous tenancy: *Held* applicant was not entitled to an order of *mandamus*. The duty imposed on the local authority to provide applicant with suitable accommodation on reasonable terms did not require them to give priority to applicant over other persons on the housing list; their duty was to act reasonably and do their best, as soon as practicable, to provide him with other accommodation. By providing for applicant until a council house was available and then offering the house to him on the terms normally offered to prospective tenants, the local authority were doing all that was required of them by s 39.

Per *Scarman LJ*: if there is evidence that a local authority is doing all it can to comply with its statutory obligation but has failed to do so because of circumstances over which it has no control, it would be improper for the court to make an order of *mandamus* compelling it to do that which it cannot do, or which it can only do at the expense of other persons not before the court.

R v Bristol Corporation, Ex p Hendy [1974] 1 All ER 1047; [1974] 1 WLR 498; 72 LGR 405; 27 P&CR 180; sub nom

Hendy v Bristol Corporation (1973) 117 Sol Jo 912, CA

iv ACCOMMODATION FOR HOME-LESS PERSONS

LAW See Halsbury's Laws (4th edn) vol 22 para 509 et seq, 1177

2541 Whether hostel a "house"

A council ordered certain works to be carried out on a building used as a hostel to provide accommodation for a thousand persons, and limited the number of occupants to be accommodated. The powers were exercisable under the Housing Act 1961 in respect of a "house" and the question was whether the hostel could be considered as such, within the meaning of the Act: *Held* there was nothing in the Act to suggest that the word "house" should be construed to include such buildings as hospitals, hotels, hostels or army barracks. However, the court was bound by *Reed v Hastings Corporation* (1964) (no 2816 post), in which it was held that a hostel providing accommodation for a large number of schoolchildren was a house for the purpose of the Housing Act 1957 s 90. Accordingly, there were grounds in the present case upon which the council

could correctly conclude in law that the hostel was a house for the purpose of the 1961 Act.

R v Camden London Borough Council, Ex p Rowton (Camden Town) Ltd (1983) 10 HLR 28; (1983) 82 LGR 614

2542 Definition of accommodation

A family occupied one room in a guest house with no cooking or washing facilities in the room. The local housing authority refused their application to be rehoused on the ground that they were neither homeless nor threatened with homelessness. The family applied for judicial review of the decision, submitting that the room allotted to them was not "accommodation" within the meaning of the Housing (Homeless Persons) Act 1977 s 1 and that a person was homeless if he occupied premises that were not large enough to accommodate the family unit or lacked the basic amenities of family life; such basic amenities should include not only sleeping, but also cooking, washing and eating facilities. Premises deficient in any of those respects were not accommodation. They contended that the authority had to take into account the size of the family and whether the premises were capable of being regarded as a home for that family, accommodation having to provide the ordinary facilities of a residence. At first instance, the authority's decision was quashed. The Court of Appeal reversed the decision on the ground that the applicants were not homeless. On appeal. *Held*, the Act of 1977 was an Act to assist persons who were homeless, not an Act to provide them with homes. There was no qualifying word before the word "accommodation" and none was to be implied; the word "appropriate" or "reasonable" was not to be imported; nor was accommodation not accommodation because it might in certain circumstances be unfit for human habitation for the purposes of the Housing Act 1957 or might involve overcrowding within the meaning of that Act. Those particular statutory criteria were not to be imported into the 1977 Act for any purpose. What was properly to be regarded as accommodation was a question of fact to be decided by the local authority. There were no rules.

In reaching a decision whether a person was homeless for the purposes of the 1977 Act, a local authority had to consider whether he had what could properly be described as accommodation within the ordinary meaning of that word in the English language. Accommodation had to be capable of accommodating. The authority in the present case had been entitled to find that the family was not homeless for the purposes of the 1977 Act because they had accommodation within the ordinary meaning of that expression.

(**7–7**) or print publications, such as *Current Law*, the latest *Pink Index* to the *Law Reports* or the *Monthly Reviews* in *Halsbury's Laws of England*.

Summary: Tracing Cases on a Subject in the Digest

1. Look up the subject in the *Consolidated Index*. This will refer you to the volume, subject heading and case numbers where cases on that subject can be found.
2. To see if there have been any more recent cases on the same subject, look in the *Cumulative Supplement* under the relevant volume, subject heading and case number. This will provide you with up-to-date information. You may be referred to one of the *Continuation Volumes* for further details. If so, look under the volume number, subject heading and case number in the *Continuation Volume*.

Daily Law Reports Index and Legal Journals Index 7–15

These two sources are very useful for finding recent cases which have not been reported by the major series of law reports but have been reported in the newspapers or discussed in journal articles. They are both published by Legal Information Resources Ltd. and therefore use the same indexing terms. The *Daily Law Reports Index* is included in the *Current Law Cases* database (**7–9**). The *Legal Journals Index* (**5–4**) is also available online.

The *Daily Law Reports Index* is published fortnightly in print and indexes the law reports from the daily newspapers. To find a case on a particular subject, look in the Keyword Index. Each case has an entry under several keywords (*i.e.* subject headings) to help make sure you find all the relevant cases. The entry in the Keyword Index gives the name of the case, as well as a full reference to the newspapers in which it was reported. A summary of each case is found in the Case Index. The quarterly and annual cumulations also contain a Case Report Index, which lists, with further citations, those newspaper law reports which have since been reported in one of the major law reports series.

The *Legal Journals Index* will enable you to find case notes, case summaries and other articles discussing cases on a particular subject published in British legal journals. Any cases discussed are clearly indicated after the title of the article. If there is no title other than the case name, the item will be a case note.

The *Daily Law Reports Index* and the *Legal Journals Index* are very useful for finding the most recent decisions, since they index the newspapers and journals, which are usually the first to report new cases. However, as the *Daily Law Reports Index* began publication in 1988 and the *Legal Journals Index* in 1986, you will need to use other sources to find older cases.

How to Use Individual Indexes to Series of Law Reports to Trace Cases on a Subject 7–16

If the facilities in your library are limited, you may need to use the indexes to individual series of law reports to trace relevant cases on a subject. The most useful is the *Law Reports Index* (**3–16**) because it covers a number of other important series in addition to the *Law Reports*. Indexes are available covering each 10-year period since 1951 and supplementary indexes (an annual *Red Index* and the latest *Pink Index*: **3–16**) bring the information up to date to within a few weeks. The *Law Reports Index* is easier to use than *The Digest*, but remember that it covers fewer series of English law reports and no foreign cases.

Example Page from the Digest Cumulative Supplement, Volume 26

Ali v Westminster City Council; Naime v Camden London Borough Council [1999] 1 All ER 450; [1999] 1 WLR 384; 31 HLR 349, CA

2539 Consd (dictum Lord Wilberforce) Wheeler and another v JJ Saunders Ltd and others [1995] 2 All ER 697

➤ **2542 Expld** Awua v Brent London Borough Council [1995] 3 All ER 493

2548a Homeless persons — Time at which duties arise — Whether authority required to take unborn child into account

Mr and Mrs D were evicted from their private rented home and applied to the local council for accommodation. The council's homeless persons unit was satisfied that the applicants were unintentionally homeless and had a priority need because they were expecting a child and offered them a seventh floor one-bedroom flat in line with its policy of offering one-bedroom accommodation to childless couples and two-bedroom accommodation (for which there was a longer waiting list) to applicants with one child. In its letter the council explained that it would make only one offer of reasonable accommodation and that if Mr and Mrs D refused it without good reason no further offer would be made. The council also stated that Mr and Mrs D could appeal against the offer provided they first signed the tenancy agreement and moved into the property offered and that if their appeal was successful another offer of accommodation would be made. Two days after the council's offer Mr and Mrs D visited the homeless persons unit and refused the offer, explaining that because Mrs D was eight months pregnant they did not consider the flat to be suitable. Two months later they purported to appeal against the offer, but because they had neither signed the tenancy agreement nor moved into the offered flat the council refused the appeal and made no further offer. Mrs D applied for judicial review of the council's refusal, contending (i) that the council was obliged under s 65 of the Housing Act 1985 to secure that accommodation became available for an applicant's occupation, availability being defined under s 75 of the Act as 'available for occupation both by him and by any other person who might reasonably be expected to reside with him', and that an unborn child was such a person, and (ii) that the council's appeals procedure was unlawful in that an appeal would not be entertained unless the applicant first took up the offer of, and started to occupy, the disputed dwelling. The deputy judge granted the application, holding that the council had not complied with its obligation under s 65. He further held that the council's appeals procedure was in fact lawful. The council appealed and the applicants cross-appealed for variation of the judgment on the second issue.

Held—(1) The ordinary and natural meaning of the word 'person' was a 'living person' and since there was nothing within the context of Pt III of the 1985 Act, which dealt with housing the homeless, to undermine that interpretation, there could be no doubt that the word 'person' in s 75 of the Act meant a person who was alive at the time the offer of accommodation was made. Accordingly, since an unborn child was not a 'person who might reasonably be expected to reside' with a pregnant homeless person for the purposes of s 75, the council was under no obligation to take an applicant's pregnancy into account in carrying out its duty under s 65 of the Act to 'secure that accommodation became available for his occupation'. The appeal would therefore be allowed.

(2) Although the council's appeals procedure stipulated that those wishing to appeal against an offer of unsuitable accommodation had first to enter into occupation of the property and sign the tenancy agreement, the fact that the appeals officer reviewed all offers made which had been unreasonably refused, to ensure that all relevant factors had been taken into consideration before a decision was made on appeal, introduced an element of discretion into the system sufficient to save it from being quashed on the ground of rigidity. The cross-appeal would accordingly be dismissed.

R v Newham London Borough Council, Ex p Dada [1995] 2 All ER 522; [1995] 3 WLR 540, CA

2552a Duty of housing authority to provide accommodation — Remedy for breach of duty — Whether civil action for damages available for breach of statutory duty

The plaintiff applied to the appellant local authority for accommodation under s 63(1) of the Housing Act 1985 when he had nowhere to go after leaving prison. Section 63(1) required a local authority to provide accommodation for those who were 'homeless and [had] a priority need', which included those who were 'vulnerable as a result of . . . physical disability or other special reason'. After an initial refusal, the local authority provided temporary accommodation but after 12 days the local authority evicted him and did not offer him any other accommodation. The plaintiff brought an action against the local authority claiming damages for, inter alia, wrongful eviction without providing alternative accommodation in breach of the local authority's duty under s 63(1) to provide him with accommodation. The county court judge struck out the claim as disclosing no cause of action on the grounds that the claim lay only in public   law and that the plaintiff's remedy was by way of judicial review. On appeal, the Court of Appeal held that breach of s 63 was a tort and rein-

Example First Page of the Entry under "Words and Phrases" in the Law Reports Cumulative Index—the "Pink Index"

The Weekly Law Reports   4 May 2001

Subject Matter   31

TRUSTS
Trustee
Breach of trust
Principal trust assets controlling shares in company — Alleged breaches causing losses for company — Whether beneficiaries having cause of action against trustees separate from company's — Whether entitled to bring action — Exemption clause in trust deed exonerating trustees for any action in professed exercise of trusts and powers save wilful fraud or dishonesty — Whether trustees liable for deliberate breaches — Solicitor-trustee believing alleged breaches in interests of beneficiaries — Whether acting dishonestly — Whether action to be struck out   **Walker v Stones**, CA [2001] 2 WLR 623

Pension scheme
Surplus fund
Occupational pension scheme providing for regular actuarial valuations — Scheme requiring employer to make arrangements to deal with actuarial surplus — Employer using part of surplus to offset existing accrued liabilities to make contributions — Whether permissible — Pensions Act 1995, s 37(1)
National Grid Co plc v Mayes, HL(E) [2001] 1 WLR 864

Resulting trust
School site
Conveyance of land for use as site for voluntary church school — Transfer to school board — Subsequent sale of land and buildings — Whether reverter to "estate" of original grantor on transfer — Whether reverter extinguished on sale of land — Whether reverter to successors of original grantor or to owners of neighbouring land from which site carved — Whether claim statute-barred — School Sites Act 1841, ss 2, 14 — Reverter of Sites Act 1987, s 1
Fraser v Canterbury Diocesan Board of Finance, CA [2001] 2 WLR 1103

WORDS AND PHRASES
"Action"—Trade Union and Labour Relations (Consolidation) Act 1992, s 146(1)
Southwark London Borough Council v Whillier, EAT [2001] ICR 142
"Aids"—Race Relations Act 1976, s 33(1)
Anyanwu v South Bank Student Union (Commission for Racial Equality intervening), HL(E) [2001] 1 WLR 638; [2001] ICR 391
"Any confession"—Police and Criminal Evidence Act 1984, s 76(2)(b)
In re Proulx, DC [2001] 1 All ER 57
"Any other bodily injury"—Carriage by Air (Application of Provisions) Order 1967, Sch 1, art 17
King v Bristow Helicopters Ltd, Ct of Sess [2001] 1 Lloyd's Rep 95
"Badger sett"—Protection of Badgers Act 1992, ss 3(a), 14
Director of Public Prosecutions v Green, DC [2001] 1 WLR 505
"Bankruptcy"—Civil Jurisdiction and Judgments Act 1982, Sch 1, art I (as substituted)
Ashurst v Pollard, CA [2001] 2 WLR 722
"Be commenced within 48 hours ... from the date on which oral notice of appeal is given"—Bail (Amendment) Act 1993, s 1(8)   **R v Middlesex Guildhall Crown Court, Ex p Okoli**, DC [2001] 1 Cr App R 1
"Blind eye knowledge"—Insurance contract
Manifest Shipping Co Ltd v Uni-Polaris Shipping Co Ltd, HL(E) [2001] 2 WLR 170
"Concerned with the advancement of religion, education or social welfare"—Copyright, Designs and Patents Act 1988, s 67(2)   **Phonographic Performance Ltd v South Tyneside Metropolitan Borough Council**, Neuberger J [2001] 1 WLR 400
"Consequential provision"—Insolvency Act 1986, s 18(3)
In re UCT (UK) Ltd, Arden J [2001] 1 WLR 436
"Criminal cause or matter"—Supreme Court Act 1981, s 18(1)(a)
Government of the United States of America v Montgomery, HL(E) [2001] 1 WLR 196
"Devolution issue"—Scotland Act 1998, Sch 6, para 1
Montgomery v HM Advocate, PC [2001] 2 WLR 779
Brown v Stott, PC [2001] 2 WLR 817
"Disposition of the company's property"—Insolvency Act 1986, s 127
Hollicourt (Contracts) Ltd v Bank of Ireland, CA [2001] 2 WLR 290
"Employed in the employment"—Equal Pay Act 1970, s 2(4) (as amended)
Young v National Power plc, CA [2001] ICR 328
"Estate"—School Sites Act 1841, ss 2, 14
Fraser v Canterbury Diocesan Board of Finance, CA [2001] 2 WLR 1103
"Extension period"—Crime and Disorder Act 1998, s 58(2)(b)
R v S (Graham), CA [2000] 2 Cr App R 111
"Failure by tribunal to deal with all the issues"—Arbitration Act 1996, s 68(2)(d)
Weldon Plant Ltd v The Commission for the New Towns, Judge Humphrey Lloyd QC [2001] 1 All ER (Comm) 264
"Imprisonment for a term"—Sex Offenders Act 1997, s 1(4)
R v S (Graham), CA [2001] 1 Cr App R 111
"In the course of his employment"—Race Relations Act 1976, s 32(1)
Sidhu v Aerospace Composite Technology Ltd, CA [2001] ICR 167
"Insurance transaction"—Council Directive 77/388/EEC, art 13(B)(a)
Card Protection Plan Ltd v Customs and Excise Comrs (No 2), HL(E) [2001] 2 WLR 329

Example Page from the Index of the Statutes 1235–1995

LONDON CITY

1297 (*Mag.Car.*) c.9 [Confirmation of liberties] (a) (106:1)	1964 c.48 Police (95)
1662 c.3 City of London Militia (b) (7:2)	1965 c.45 Backing of Warrants (Republic of Ireland) (48)
1751 c.30 Calendar (121)	1969 c.12 Genocide (39:4)
1820 c.100 Militia (City of London) (7:2)	1969 c.19 Decimal Currency (10)
1824 c.74 Weights and Measures	1969 c.57 Employers' Liability (Compulsory Insurance) (43:3)
1884 c.70 Municipal Elections (Corrupt and Illegal Practices) (c)	1971 c.23 Courts (37)
1888 c.41 Local Govt. (81:1)	1971 c.48 Criminal Damage (39:6)
1897 c.30 Police (Property) (95)	1972 c.70 Local Govt. (81:1)
1898 c.16 Canals Protection (London) (102)	1972 c.71 Criminal Justice (39:1)
1907 c.cxl City of London (Union of Parishes) (103:1)	1979 c.55 Justices of the Peace (82)
1921 c.37 Territorial Army and Militia	1980 c.9 Reserve Forces (7:2)
1925 c.49 Supreme Ct. of Judicature (Consolidation) (37)	1980 c.43 Magistrates' Courts
	1982 c.32 Local Govt. Finance (81:1)
1929 c.17 Local Govt. (81:1)	1982 c.48 Criminal Justice (39:1)
1936 c.49 Public Health (100:1)	1984 c.46 Cable and Broadcasting (96)
1945 c.42 Water (130)	1984 c.60 Police and Criminal Evidence
1960 c.67 Public Bodies (Admission to Meetings) (81:4)	1985 c.43 Local Govt. (Access to Information (81:1,2)
1963 c.33 London Govt. (81:1)	1985 c.51 Local Govt. (81:1)
1963 c.37 Children and Young Persons (20)	1985 c.61 Admin. of Justice (76:1)
1964 c.42 Admin. of Justice (82)	1985 c.68 Housing (61)
	1985 c.72 Weights and Measures (131)

1 *Constitution, etc.*
2 *Authorities*
3 *Administration of Justice*

4 *Finance*
5 *Miscellaneous*

1 Constitution, etc.

(a) POSITION OF CITY WITH REGARD TO GREATER LONDON OR OTHER AREAS

Inclusion in—
  Greater London: 1963 c.33 s.2(1)
  Metropolitan Traffic Area *See* ROAD TRAFFIC AND VEHICLES, 1*(b)*
Exclusion from—
  Metrop. Police District *See* METROP. POLICE DISTRICT, 1
  Tithe Commutation Acts *See* TITHES, E&W, 2*(l)*
A county borough for licensing purposes *See* LICENSING, E&W, 1
Separate county for purposes of lieutenancies and the militia: 1980 c.9 s.138(2)

(b) LIBERTIES, CUSTOMS, ETC.

City of London to have all its old liberties and customs: 1297 (*Mag. Car.*) c.9
Coroners for the City (including the Temples): 1972 c.70 s.220(1)-(3)(5)
                                1985 c.51 ss.13(1),102,sch.17
Saving of privileges of Lord Mayor, etc., as to—
  gauging of wines, oil, honey, and other liquors: 1824 c.74 s.25

(c) UNION OF PARISHES

Union of parishes in city of London into one parish: 1907 c.cxl s.5(1)-(3)
Common Council to be overseers: 1907 c.cxl s.11
Precepts to Common Council: 1907 c.cxl s.12
Transfer of powers of vestry: 1907 c.cxl s.13
Savings for wards and wardmotes: 1907 c.cxl s.27

2 Authorities

(a) CORPORATION

Application of Representation of the People Act 1983 c.2 to municipal elections in the City
  REPRESENTATION OF THE PEOPLE, 4*(b)*
Vacancy in office caused by decision of election ct.: 1884 c.70 s.35(5)

(a) 9 H. 3 in Ruffhead
(b) 13–4 c. 2 in Ruffhead
(c) Made permanent by Representation of the People Act 1948 (7–8 G. 5) c.64 s.35

In addition to the *Law Reports Index* (and the series of *Digests*, which preceded it, going back to 1865) there are indexes to other series, such as the *All England Law Reports*, which have a *Consolidated Tables and Index* in three volumes, covering 1937–1992. This is kept up to date by supplements (**3–16**). In addition, there is an *Index* volume to the *All England Law Reports Reprint*, which includes a subject index to selected cases from 1558–1935.

TRACING THE SUBSEQUENT JUDICIAL HISTORY OF A CASE

7–17

Judges often rely upon earlier cases to support the reasons which they have given for their decision, and from time to time a judge will review the case law in an attempt to explain the principles stated in earlier cases, or to use them as a springboard to create a new application of the principles. Occasionally a case will be distinguished in order that the judge will not feel obliged to follow it. Less frequently, a superior court will state that an earlier case was wrongly decided, and will overrule it, so that the principles laid down in the case will not be followed thereafter.

The treatment that a case receives when it is subsequently judicially considered has a direct bearing on its importance and reliability. For example, if in a moot or essay you cited as an authority the common law rules relating to compensation for war damage which were laid down in *Burmah Oil Co.* v. *Lord Advocate* [1965] A.C. 75, you would be embarrassed to discover that it was abolished by statute, the War Damages Act 1965. Similarly, you should be aware that the case of *Gillick* v. *West Norfolk Area Health Authority* [1985] 1 All E.R. 533 was reversed on appeal to the House of Lords. Consequently, you must be alert to the need to trace the full judicial history of a particular case.

The simplest way to do this is to use the *Current Law Case Citator*. As noted in **3–14** the citator is available as part of *Current Legal Information*, either as a web-based service (at **www.smlawpub.jhc.net**) or as a CD-ROM. It is also available as part of the Westlaw UK service (at **www.westlaw.uk**), where it is presented as the "Case Locator" database. The *Current Law Case Citator* gives the citation of any English case which has been judicially considered since 1947, and notes its treatment. For instance, the well-known old case *Carlill* v. *Carbolic Smoke Ball Co.* appears in the *Current Law Case Citator*, because it was considered in court several times since 1947. If you search the Citator for "Carlill" using *Current Legal Information*, for example, you will find that after the name of the case, and a reference to where the case is to be found in the *Law Reports*, the following entry appears:

> Applied, 57/592, 67/1745, 73/1529: Approved, 66/3146: Considered, 64/3479, 80/1888, 88/2020, 95/799: Distinguished, 52/2194, 73/3095

This means that if you turn to the print volumes of the *Current Law Year Book* for 1957, item 592 is a summary of a case in which the *Carlill* case was applied. Similarly the 1973 *Year Book* contains two reports of cases (items 1529 and 3095) in which the case was considered.

If you are using the print version of the *Current Law Case Citator* you will need to look up the *Carlill* case first in the volume covering 1947–76 and then in the subsequent volumes to pick up, for example, the cases considering *Carlill* in 1980, 1988 and 1995.

If you are using Westlaw UK's "Case locator" database, there is a full citation of all the cases which have considered *Carlill* and these are linked to the online text of the summary or digest that appears in the print *Current Law Year Book* volumes.

The *Law Reports Index* contains a list of cases judicially considered and the *Index* to the *All England Law Reports* also includes a list of cases reported and considered. *The Digest* (**7–14**) contains annotations to entries, showing the subsequent judicial history of a case. This is kept up to date by the information in the *Cumulative Supplement*.

7–18 HOW TO FIND WORDS AND PHRASES JUDICIALLY CONSIDERED

The meaning of words is of great importance to lawyers. The interpretation of statutes and documents may hinge upon the meaning of a single word. For example, does "day" in banking terms mean 24 hours, or does it end at the close of working hours? Can a mistress be considered part of a "family"?

Two specialised dictionaries record the courts' decisions on problems such as these. *Stroud's Judicial Dictionary* provides the meaning of words as defined in the case law and in statutes. *Words and Phrases Legally Defined* is a similar publication; both are kept up to date by supplements.

The *Law Reports Index* includes a heading "Words and Phrases", in which full details of cases defining a particular word or phrase are given (see the figure on p. 135).

The *Current Law Monthly Digests* and *Year Books* also include an entry "Words and Phrases" and the *Index* to the *All England Law Reports* and the *Consolidated Index* to *Halsbury's Laws* have a similar heading.

7–19 HOW TO TRACE STATUTES ON A SUBJECT

Electronic
Full-text databases (**7–20**);
Other sources (**7–21**);

Print
Index to the Statutes (**7–22**);
Halsbury's Statutes of England (**7–23**);
Current Law (**7–24**)

7–20 How to Use Full-Text Databases of Legislation

The full-text databases of legislation listed in 4–8, offer the possibility of subject searching for statutes using keywords. While these databases are ideal for retrieving the text of a statute when you know the title, they are of more limited use for subject searching. They work best when you already know the wording of a section of an Act, or of a phrase unique to a piece of legislation. There are no added keywords or subject links that might help guide you to a piece of legislation. As a result the advice given in section **7–8**, on keyword searching case law, remains valid when searching the legislation databases. It makes sense to turn to textbooks and other secondary searches first if you are taking a subject approach to legislation, in order to have a firm grasp of the key terms before you make use of the legislation databases.

Suppose for example you are reviewing the legislation in force on an aspect of insolvency law. Simply typing "insolvency" into the search box of a database will lead—if the database allows this—to pages and pages of "hits" being displayed on your results screen. Remember that these databases list their results section by section, so all the sections of Acts that feature the word "insolvency" will be displayed.

However, you may have clarified in advance that it is administration orders that interest you, and more specifically, how they are made. In this case, if you are using Lexis-Nexis Professional for example, put "insolvency" in the title search box and combine this with the words "administration order" in the "free text" search box. The search will result in 40 or so matching sections, most of which will be drawn from the Insolvency Act 1986. Scrolling down this list you come across Part II, section 9, "Application for an Order". You can view the full amended text of the section, incorporating, as it does, amendments from the Access to Justice Act 1999 and other legislation.

This kind of searching, combining title and free-text keywords, is also possible using Butterworths *Legislation Direct* (**4–9**) and Context's statute law database (**4–10**). Westlaw UK does not currently allow a free-text search on its legislation database, making this kind of searching very difficult. More flexible searching may become available in the future.

If you are using the text of statutes available free from the HMSO sebsite (**4–6**), remember that the database covers legislation from 1988 onwards, and the Acts appear in their original unamended form. Keyword searching of the HMSO pages is possible using the search engine available on the pages. This can by found by following the "Search" link that appears on the legislation pages (at **www.legislation.hmso.gov.uk**).

The nature of a websearch engine means you will be undertaking a somewhat different kind of search (see **2–15**). The HMSO search engine works by producing a relevance ranking of results which will be based on the number of times a word appears in a document. If you enter more than one word, proximity of words to each other in the original text becomes important. If you want to find legislation relevant to an application for an administration order, you might for example try entering the string of words "insolvency administration order application". The results pages will then place legislation in which the words are close together at the top of the list. Bear in mind that the search engine will search all legislation available on the HMSO pages, not just the Westminster Acts. In this particular case, your search results are dominated by references to the *Insolvency (Northern Ireland) Order 1989*. However, you will also find a reference to the Insolvency Act 2000, which contains amendments to the *Insolvency Act 1986*. The 1986 Act will not be included, as it predates the 1988 start date of the database.

The BAILII databases (at **www.bailii.org**) provide an alternative route to the legislation available on the HMSO pages. Like the HMSO pages, the databases use a search engine which produces a results page using relevance ranking. The search engine is found by selecting the "Full Search Form" from the home page, or "Database Search" from the UK Legislation pages. Much the same considerations apply as they do for the HMSO site, though BAILII offers the advantage of database selection, so you can restrict your search to U.K. statutes.

Other Electronic Sources for Tracing Legislation   7–21

Lawtel (at **www.lawtel.co.uk**) allows you to search for words appearing in the title of a statute or any of the sections. Though the database links to the full text of statutes for recent legislation, the database does not allow full text searching. A search on "insolvency" will retrieve a list of 20 or so matching statutes, where the word appears in the title of the Act or the title of one of the sections of the Act. The results are presented as a list of statutes (rather than sections of statutes). Unfortunately the database does not list the potentially relevant sections of the Acts, which makes the search results difficult to interpret. A search on "insolvency" retrieves the *Terrorism Act 2000*, but Lawtel does not tell you which of the 131 sections of the Act might be of interest.

The *Law Direct* service from Butterworths (at **www.butterworths.co.uk**) offers a similar, though somewhat more restricted service, as it contains brief digests of Acts of Parliament since the beginning of 1995. Find it via the "Statutes" link from the *Law Direct* home page. Although only recent legislation is covered, this service offers the possibility, currently unavailable elsewhere, of searching for legislation by general keyword. Searching using the "All acts relating to" box and selecting "Bankruptcy and Insolvency" leads to a brief note on the *Insolvency Act 2000*. Keyword searches on the titles and digests are also possible.

This is one area where the online versions of *Current Law Statute Citator* (see **4–19**) are less useful as they are designed on the assumption that you already have the details of the legislation that interests you, and that you wish to obtain further information on repeals, amendments and relevant case law.

7–22 Index to the Statutes

A detailed alphabetical index to the statute law on a particular subject will be found in the *Index to the Statutes*. This is unfortunately several years behind in publication, so it will be necessary to consult *Halsbury's Statutes* (**7–23**) or similar works to ensure that there have not been any recent changes.

The *Index to the Statutes* is comprehensive. It gives a complete list in subject order of all the statutes still in force. There is a detailed analysis of each subject, showing the section and subsections of all statutes which are relevant to that topic. Cross-references are given from one entry to another. (See the figure on p. 136.)

Where the law relating to England, Scotland and Northern Ireland is different, under some subject headings the topics are subdivided according to area. For instance, the law relating to agricultural holdings in England and Scotland is different, and there are therefore two main subject headings: "Agricultural holdings, England and Wales" and "Agricultural holdings, Scotland" (denoted by the abbreviations E & W, and S, respectively).

7–23 Halsbury's Statutes of England

Halsbury's Statutes provides the amended text of legislation which is still in force, along with annotations detailing, for example, statutory instruments made under the Act, case law, judicial interpretation of words and phrases and references to relevant sections of *Halsbury's Laws*.

The 50 volumes of the main work are arranged alphabetically by broad subject areas. Acts dealing with agriculture, for example, are found in Volume 1, whereas statutes on the subject of wills are found in Volume 50.

The annual *Table of Statutes and General Index* provides a comprehensive subject index to the volumes to enable you to find statutes on a particular topic. The Index will refer you to the appropriate *volume* and *page* number. In the *Table of Statutes and General Index* volume there is a separate subject index to the *Current Statutes Service*, which contains those Acts that were passed after the main volumes were issued. If you are looking for the latest Acts on a particular subject, look also in the subject index at the front of the looseleaf

Volume 1 of the *Current Statutes Service.* This indexes the material that has been added to the *Service* since the annual *Table of Statutes and General Index* was published.

Once you have identified those Acts which are of relevance to you, it is essential to consult both the *Cumulative Supplement* and the *Noter-Up* to see if there have been any changes in the law. An explanation of how to do this, along with further details of *Halsbury's Statutes*, can be found at **4–17**.

Other Sources for Tracing Legislation on a Subject   7–24

Halsbury's Laws (**7–3**) contains references to relevant statutes, although the text of the Acts is not printed. The *Current Law Monthly Digests* and *Year Books* (**7–11** and **7–12**) are arranged by subject and include entries for new statutes and statutory instruments as well as for cases on a subject. A brief summary appears under the appropriate subject heading. The text of statutes is printed in *Public General Acts* (**4–6**), *Law Reports: Statutes* (**4–14**) and *Current Law Statutes Annotated* (**4–15**).

HOW TO TRACE STATUTORY   7–25
INSTRUMENTS ON A SUBJECT

Statutory instruments on a particular subject can be traced by consulting:

Electronic sources (**7–26**);
Halsbury's Statutory Instruments (**7–27**);

For an explanation of the nature and purpose of statutory instruments, refer back to **4–26**.

Electronic Sources for Tracing Statutory Instruments   7–26

Most of the full-text databases of legislation listed in **4–8** provide access to statutory instruments and to statutes. Whether you are interested in finding statutory instruments or statutes, the standard legislation search for these databases will review both and place the results side by side. Consequently, the considerations noted for tracing statutes by subject in **7–20** also apply to searching for statutory instruments. If you wish to search only for statutory instruments use the "advanced search" or "select database" features.

The one exception among the commercial database providers is the JUSTIS *UK Statutory Instruments* database from Context, which comes as a separate individual subscription, rather than part of a package. The JUSTIS database is also an exception in that it contains the text of statutory instruments as originally published. Coverage is from 1987. The other commercial databases provide the text of legislation in force, as explained in **7–20**.

If you are seeking the text of statutory instruments on the free HMSO site, you can keyword search for statutory instruments using the "Search" link that appears on the HMSO legislation pages (at **www.legislation.hmso.gov.uk**). The HMSO website has a search engine which produces results using relevance ranking, as noted for legislation searches in **4–8**.

Unfortunately, it is not possible to search for statutory instruments only on the HMSO site. The search engine searches the text of both statutes and statutory instruments. The full (unamended) text of the statutory instruments is available from 1988.

The BAILII databases (at **www.bailii.org**) do not include U.K. statutory instruments, though the intention is to include the statutory instruments available on the HMSO site. The BAILII website should allow a keyword search to be restricted to statutory instruments, when they become available.

7–27   Halsbury's Statutory Instruments

Halsbury's Statutory Instruments is a series which covers every statutory instrument of general application in force in England and Wales. It reproduces the text of a selected number and provides summaries of others. The series is arranged alphabetically by subject and is kept up to date by looseleaf *Service* binders containing, in Binder 1, notes of changes in the law and, in Binder 2, the text of selected new instruments. A full description of the work can be found in **4–29**.

If you are looking for statutory instruments dealing with a particular subject, you should start by looking up your subject in the *Consolidated Index and Alphabetical List of Statutory Instruments*. This paper-covered volume is issued annually and indexes the contents of all the main volumes, along with the information in the *Annual Supplement* in Binder 1. The entries give you the volume number (in **bold** type) and page number in the main work and the number of the statutory instrument (in brackets). Where "S" appears instead of a volume and page number, you should refer to the *Chronological List* in Binder 1, which will direct you to the appropriate title in the *Annual Supplement*.

Occasionally you will find that the volume to which you are referred has been reissued since the latest *Consolidated Index* was published. The references from the *Consolidated Index* will no longer be correct and in this case you will need to refer to the subject index at the back of the new volume.

Once you have traced the relevant statutory instruments on your subject in the main volumes, it is important to turn to Binder 1 to find out if the information you have traced is still up to date. To do this, turn first to the *Annual Supplement* in Binder 1 and look up the relevant subject title. This shows new statutory instruments which have appeared since the main volume was compiled. It tells you which statutory instruments printed in the main volumes are no longer law and provides you with a page-by-page guide to changes made since the main volume was published.

For the most recent changes in the law, you should consult the *Monthly Survey—Key* in Binder 1. Under the appropriate subject titles, this lists new statutory instruments and any amendments or revocations of earlier instruments. Summaries of the new instruments are given in numerical order in the *Monthly Survey—Summaries*.

Summary: How to Use Halsbury's Statutory Instruments to find Information on a Subject

1. Consult the *Consolidated Index*. This tells you the volume, page number and statutory instrument numbers you require. Where "S" appears instead of a volume number, the instrument appears in the *Annual Supplement* in Binder 1.
2. To check if there have been any changes in the law, look in:
   the *Annual Supplement* and

the *Monthly Survey—Key*
under the appropriate title.

Tracing Recent Statutory Instruments on a Subject   7–28

Electronic

All draft statutory instruments awaiting approval are published in full-text form on the
HMSO web pages (at **www.legislation.hmso.gov.uk**) and they remain on the web site until
they are superseded by a statutory instrument or, indeed, until they are withdrawn.
Otherwise, recent statutory instruments are available on the website as soon as they are
published. There may be some delay before these appear in the databases of the
commercial database providers listed in **4–8**, but all of these are sources for recent
statutory instruments. Use keyword searches as noted in **7–26**.

Print

Statutory instruments may be traced by consulting the subject indexes in the bound
volumes of *Statutory Instruments*, and, for more recent changes, the monthly and annual
Lists of Statutory Instruments, which contain entries in subject order. If you suspect that
there has been a very recent change, it may be necessary to go through the *TSO Daily Lists*
(**6–14**) for the past few weeks, to bring the information in the latest monthly *List* up to date.
Recent instruments can also be traced by looking in the *Current Law Monthly Digests*, or in
the *Monthly Reviews* in *Halsbury's Laws* or by looking in *Halsbury's Statutory Instruments*
(**7–27**). New instruments are also noted weekly in the *Solicitors' Journal* and the *New Law
Journal*.

If you suspect that the text of an instrument has been changed or amended, *Halsbury's
Statutory Instruments*, or one of the specialist encyclopedias (if there is one available
covering your subject field), is probably the easiest place to trace the updated version of the
instrument. The *Current Law Legislation Citator* contains a numerical list of statutory
instruments passed since 1947, showing, for each one, whether it has been amended or
revoked.

FINDING BOOKS ON A SUBJECT   7–29

Your first task is to find out what suitable books are available in your own library. A
computerised catalogue allows you to search for keywords in the titles of books. This
means you can search for title words that match your subject. A keyword search on
"negligence", for example, picks up the titles "Introduction to negligence", "The law of
negligence" and so on. If you do not find books on your subject, try some alternative
headings or look under a more general, or a more specific subject. Negligence, for instance,
is part of the law of torts and there will be a chapter on negligence in all general textbooks
on the law of torts.

Many computerised library catalogues also have a subject search. This acts as an index to
the classification scheme. If you enter the word "negligence" using a subject search you are
shown the classification number (or classmark) for books on negligence. The catalogue
then links you to a list of books sharing that classmark. Such a subject search is a more
systematic approach to searching the catalogue, as the books listed represent all the books

in the library which share a common subject. If you searched on "negligence", you see a list of the general works on negligence, whether or not they have the word negligence in the title. Using a subject search is of particular help if you want to find books on a specific aspect of a subject, and are not sure where the classification scheme places the books on the library shelves. For medical negligence, for example, a subject search of this kind leads you to a classification which places books on medical negligence with other books on medical law, often some distance away from the general textbooks on negligence.

If your library catalogue does not have a subject search of this kind, an alternative approach is to search for keywords in book titles and note the classmark of a book that matches your subject interest, even if that book might be hopelessly out of date. Most computerised catalogues enable you to search by classmark. You can find a list of the books on a subject, usually showing the most recent first.

Remember also that footnotes and bibliographies (lists of books) in textbooks and journal articles refer you to other books, journals and cases on a subject. Check in the library catalogue to find out if these are available in your library. Government reports on a subject may not be entered on a subject, and you need to make use of other catalogues and indexes to trace these publications (see **6–14** and **6–18**).

You are not restricted to your own catalogue, if you wish to trace books on a subject. The online catalogues of all of the U.K. universities, along with the British Library, can be searched. COPAC (at **www.copac.ac.uk**) provides a particularly useful starting point for U.K. academic research libraries as it provides access to the merged catalogues of 20 of the largest research libraries in the U.K. and Ireland. This means that a single catalogue search can find details of a book held by, among others, the Cambridge University Library, the Bodleian Library, Trinity College Dublin and the Institute of Advanced Legal Studies. The Institute of Advanced Legal Studies collections can by searched via the Institute's own library pages (at **ials.sas.ac.uk/library.htm**). A complete listing of U.K. university library catalogues is available from the NISS (National Information Services and Systems) website (at **www.niss.ac.uk**). A directory of catalogues is at its "Library & Info services" link. The British Library catalogue (at **blpc.bl.uk**) includes both the main reference and document supply collections.

Many universities also have subscriptions to the OCLC FirstSearch service (at **firstsearch.uk.oclc.org**) which contains the WorldCat database, the largest online catalogue available. It has records which are based largely, though not exclusively, on U.S. university holdings. The Library of Congress catalogue (at **catalog.loc.gov**) provides another starting point for U.S. publications.

7–30   Legal Bibliographies

Bibliographies list books that have been published on a subject, both in this country and abroad. A number of possible sources are given below. All of them are print volumes that list books under legal subject headings. Not all of them may be available in your library. However, you will only need one or two of them to trace relevant books.

7–31   D. Raistrick—Lawyer's Law Books

Lawyers' Law Books (3rd ed. published by Bowker-Saur in 1997) provides probably the quickest and easiest way to find out what has been written on a particular subject. It is alphabetically arranged by subject (see the illustration on page 146). Under each subject heading it gives a list of textbooks written on that topic. There are also references to relevant government publications, such as reports issued by the Law Commission. At the beginning of each subject heading, there are references to alternative headings, and a list of the major legal reference works and journals that contain information on that topic. Full details of the authors, titles, publishers and dates of books are provided.

Current Law   7–32
At the back of each *Current Law Monthly Digest* is a list of new books published during that month (mainly British, with a few foreign works in English). When the *Monthly Digests* are replaced by the *Current Law Year Book*, a list of books published during the year is printed at the back of the *Year Book*.

Current Publications in Legal and Related Fields   7–33
Current Publications in Legal and Related Fields (published for the American Association of Law Libraries by Fred B. Rothman & Co.) is published in looseleaf parts which are replaced by annual volumes. There are entries under authors and titles in the looseleaf volume.

In the annual volume, a detailed subject index at the front of the volume guides you to relevant entries in the main (alphabetically arranged) part of the work. Each item has its own individual number.

Law Books 1876–1981   7–34
The first three volumes of *Law Books 1876–1981* are arranged by subject and cover books published mainly in the United States, although some British and other countries' publications are also included. The fourth volume contains some entries under authors, titles and serials. Rather than update the original work, the publishers, Bowker, now publish *Bowker's Law Books and Serials in Print: a Multimedia Sourcebook*, in three annual volumes (see **7–37**).

Other legal bibliographies   7–35
Sweet & Maxwell's *Legal Bibliography of the British Commonwealth* is especially useful for tracing older British Books. C. Szladits, *Bibliography on Foreign and Comparative Law* is a detailed bibliography covering books and articles on foreign and comparative law published in English.

Many other specialist legal bibliographies have also been published, *e.g.* P. O'Higgens and M. Partington, *Social Security Law in Britain and Ireland: a Bibliography* (1986); E. Beyerly, *Public International Law: a Guide to Information Sources* (1991); and R. W. M. Dias, *Bibliography of Jurisprudence* (1979). As you can see from their publication dates, such bibliographies do not always provide a guide to recent publications, but this does not exhaust their usefulness. Raistrick's *Lawyers' Law Books* (**7–31**) contains a useful list of more specialised legal bibliographies, under the heading "Bibliographies".

Library staff will help you to trace recent bibliographies. Remember too, that many textbooks will also contain a bibliography on their subject.

The British National Bibliography   7–36

The main source of information for British books which have been published since 1950 is the *British National Bibliography* (BNB). This is published weekly and the last issue of each month contains an index to books published that month. At the end of the year, an annual volume is produced containing details of British books published that year. Entries

Example Page from D. Raistrick, Lawyers' Law Books

BUSINESS TENANCIES

See also Landlord and Tenant.

Encyclopaedias and periodicals

Statutes in Force. Group: Landlord aand Tenant.
Halsbury's Laws of England. 4ed. vol.27(1).
Halsbury's Statutes of England and Wales. 4ed. vol.23.

Encyclopaedia of Court Forms in Civil Proceedings (Atkin). 2ed. vol.24.
Encyclopaedia of Forms and Precedents. 5ed. vol.22.
Estates Gazette. 1858–

Texts

ALDRIDGE, T.M.
Companion to the Law Society business lease. FT Law & Tax, 1991.

ALDRIDGE, T.M.
Letting business premises. 6ed. FT Law & Tax, 1990.

FOX-ANDREWS, J.
Business tenancies. 3ed. Estates Gazette, 1978.

HUGILL, C.
Business tenancies. 2ed. FT Law & Tax, 1994.

LAW REFORM ADVISORY COMMITTEE FOR NORTHERN IRELAND
Report no.1: business tenancies. HMSO, 1994 (LRAC no. 2).

LAW REFORM ADVISORY COMMITTEE FOR NORTHERN IRELAND
A review of the law relating to business tenancies in Northern Ireland. HMSO, 1992 (Discussion paper no.3).

LEWISON, K.
Drafting business leases. 4ed. FT Law & Tax, 1993.

SWEET, R.
Commercial leases: tenants' amendments. 2ed. FT Law & Tax, 1995.

WEBBER, G.
Possession of business premises. FT Law & Tax, 1992.

WILLIAMS, D., BRAND, C. & HUBBARD, C.
Handbook of business tenancies. Sweet & Maxwell. Looseleaf.

BY-LAWS

See also Delegated Legislation; Local Government.

Encyclopaedias

Halsbury's Laws of England. 4ed. see index vol.
Halsbury's Statutes of England and Wales. 4ed. vols.22,35.

Encyclopaedia of Court Forms in Civil Proceedings (Atkin). 2ed. see index vol.
Encyclopaedia of Forms and Precedents. 5ed. see index vol.

Texts

AULT, W.O.
Open field farming in Medieval England: a study of village by laws. Allen, 1972.

KNIGHT, C.
Annotated model byelaws. 11ed. Knight, 1953. 2 vols.

NATIONAL WATER COUNCIL
A guide to the model water byelaws. 1977.

SCHOFIELD, A.N.
Byelaws of local authorities. Shaw, 1939.

WELSH WATER AUTHORITY
Water byelaws. 1978.

WISDOM, A.S.
Local authorities' byelaws. 5ed. B.Rose, 1978.

are arranged by subject in a classification scheme. You will first need to look up your subject in the Subject Index, which refers you to the classification number under which the books can be found. Entries for law books are at the numbers 340–349.

The BNB is also available on CD-ROM, from the publishers, the British Library. Unlike the print version, the CD-ROM enables you to make highly specific searches using title keywords and author names. Access to the BNB using the British Library's Blaise online information service is no longer available, but a new BNB service should be available in the latter part of 2001 (for details on current services consult the British Library website at **www.bl.uk**).

Sources for Books in Print   7–37

A number of sources enable you to search for the titles of books in print. Among the electronic sources, the commercial books in print databases allow subject searching using keywords, and these have been supplemented by the catalogues of the internet booksellers. Publishers' websites also list current and forthcoming publications and many will organise their titles by subject. Among the print sources, *Law Books in Print* (see below) allows a subject approach.

Electronic
If you want to search the web pages of the major law publishers there are internet gateway sites (**2–16**) which provide a current listing. Sarah Carter's lawlinks site for example (at **library.ukc.ac.uk/library/lawlinks**) lists U.K. legal publishers. Many law school sites provide similar listings. Findlaw (at **www.findlaw.com**) also lists U.K. and American publishers, as does Hieros Gamos (at **www.hg.org**). An extensive listing of publishers of all kinds can be found using the AcqWebsite (at **acqweb.library.vanderbilt.edu**).

The internet bookseller Amazon (at **www.amazon.co.uk**) is a useful source for information for books in print, as most publishers supply the site with title information. Its listings can be searched using keywords. Other websites linked to conventional booksellers are the internet Bookshop (at **www.bookshop.co.uk**), linked to WHSmith, Blackwell's Online Bookshop (at **www.blackwells.co.uk**) and Waterstone's Online (at **www.waterstones.co.uk**).

The major database for U.K. books in print is *Whitaker's Books in Print*, available on CD-ROM as *Bookbank*. *Bookbank* provides a convenient single source for books in print information. The Book Data company also offers much the same information on its *Bookwise* CD-ROM.

The major American publication *Books in Print* is available in a variety of electronic formats. A number of CD-ROM publishers and database suppliers provide access to the database. The publishers of the print version, Bowker, have in addition launched booksinprint.com and globalbooksinprint.com as internet services directly available from the their website (at **www.bowker.com**). The latter service combines the *Bowker's Books in Print* database of American publications with the U.K. data available from Whitaker. As with *Bookbank*, your library will need to have a subscription before you can make use of these databases.

Print
Law Books in Print (8th ed., 1997) from the publishers Oceana covers British and American publications and is arranged by author, title, subject and publisher. It is updated

by *Law Books Published* which appears twice a year, the second volume being a cumulation for the year.

If *Law Books in Print* is not available, you might wish to make use of *Whitaker's Books in Print* which appears every year in five volumes and covers British books in print. Bowker's *Books in Print* provides an equivalent for American publications, this time in nine volumes.

7–38 # THESES

If you are undertaking a comprehensive piece of research, you may need to find out if any theses have already been written on that subject. The *Index to Theses*, more fully, the *Index to Theses Accepted for Higher Degrees by the Universities of Great Britain*, is, as the title suggests, the major source for tracing British and Irish theses. Coverage is extensive, but it does rely on universities to submit theses information. The *Index* is available online (at **www.theses.com**) and online coverage begins in 1970. The print version dates back to 1950. Another print source of information for U.K. law theses, *Legal Research in the United Kingdom, 1905–1984*, was published by the Institute of Advanced Legal Studies, and updated until 1988 by the *List of Current Legal Research Topics*. Publication has now ceased.

Details of the vast majority of North American theses can be found in *Dissertation Abstracts International*, which also includes some non-North American theses. Abstracts are available from 1980. The publishers, UMI, have made the *Dissertation Abstracts International* database available to a number of online database providers including DIALOG and OCLC FirstSearch. *Dissertation Abstracts International* is also available on CD-ROM using Proquest software. The Proquest Digital Dissertations link on the UMI website (at **www.umi.com**) offers free access to the most recent three months of the database.

Theses which have been completed at your own institution are normally available for consultation in the library. It is usually possible for the library staff to borrow, on inter-library loan, copies of theses completed in other universities in this country and abroad.

8 | Scots Law

INTRODUCTION 8–1

The advent of executive and legislative devolution in the United Kingdom has re-emphasised the separateness of the Scottish legal system. This was a feature preserved by the political settlement of 1707 and has been jealously guarded ever since. It is worth noting that administrative devolution may be traced back to the establishment of the Scottish Office in 1885; a brief but useful survey of developments will be found in C. M. G. Himsworth and C. R. Munro, *The Scotland Act 1998* (2nd ed., 2000). Scots law can differ markedly from the law elsewhere in the U.K., especially criminal law and certain areas of private law such as those concerning contract, the family, and property.

The Scotland Act 1998 devolved extensive legislative powers to a directly elected Scottish Parliament and these took effect on July 1, 1999. The Parliament's powers are not unlimited but it can enact primary legislation on a wide range of issues affecting Scotland. Those matters excluded from the legislative competence of the Scottish Parliament, and set out in full in Schedule 5 to the Act, are known as "reserved matters" because they are reserved to the U.K. Parliament. They include the Constitution, political parties, foreign affairs, the civil service, defence and treason, and specific powers in relation to aspects of central economic policies, home affairs, trade and industry, energy, transport, social security, employment, health and the media.

The Act also established the Scottish Executive which constitutes the government of Scotland in respect of devolved matters. It comprises a First Minister nominated from among the members of the Scottish Parliament, such ministers as the First Minister may appoint and the Scottish Law Officers (the Lord Advocate and the Solicitor General for Scotland). The members of the Executive are referred to collectively as the Scottish Ministers. The departments and agencies of the former Scottish Office transferred to the new administration and were renamed as part of the Scottish Executive.

Meanwhile the Scotland Office in Whitehall, headed by the Secretary of State, represents Scottish interests within the U.K. government on reserved matters and encourages co-operation between Edinburgh and London. Further information on its role and work will be found on the official website (at **www.scottishsecretary.gov.uk**).

Some useful textbooks on Scots law and the Scottish legal system are noted in **8–55**. In addition to those, the student with an interest in historical development may wish to investigate D. M. Walker, *A Legal History of Scotland* (1988–).

The rest of this chapter outlines sources of printed and electronic information including primary and secondary legislation from the U.K. and Scottish parliaments, other forms of legislation less frequently encountered, law reports old and modern, institutional writings, important secondary sources and the publications of the Scottish Parliament and Scottish Executive.

8-2 LEGISLATION

Legislation applying to Scotland may derive from its pre-1707 Parliament (**8–24**), from the United Kingdom Parliament (**8–3**), or from the Scottish Parliament (**8–8**).

8-3 LEGISLATION FROM THE U.K. PARLIAMENT

8-4 Public General Acts

The United Kingdom Parliament often passed primary legislation specific to Scotland. Sometimes this took the form of discrete provisions within an Act and sometimes it necessitated a separate Act. It should be noted that legislation on reserved matters will continue to be created in this way. There are no differences in the structure, method of citation, and means by which commencement, amendment and repeal are determined. The *Laws of Scotland* (**8–50**) is a good starting place for research and is also available online as a Butterworths *Scotland Direct* service (at **www.butterworths.co.uk**).

8-5 Sources

Acts applying to Scotland will be found in most of the standard collections mentioned in Chapter 4 with the notable exception of *Halsbury's Statutes*. In addition some libraries may have the collections issued by two Edinburgh publishing houses. In 1848 William Blackwood & Sons were granted a licence to publish annual volumes of Acts. *Public General Statutes Affecting Scotland* (known as "Blackwood's *Acts*") continued until 1947, and the period 1707–1847 was covered in three additional volumes published in 1876. Between 1899 and 1902, William Green & Sons published 10 volumes of *Scots Statutes Revised* covering the period 1707–1900, and these were continued by annual volumes of *Scots Statutes* from 1901 to 1948. *Scottish Current Law Statutes* first appeared in 1949, also published by W. Green but reproducing all Public General Acts. In 1991 this Scottish edition merged with *Current Law Statutes* (**4–15**) from which it differed only slightly. Electronic sources include the website of Her Majesty's Stationery Office (at **www.hmso.gov.uk),** the Statute Law Database, JUSTIS *UK Statutes* (at **www.justis.com**) and Westlaw UK (at **www.westlaw.co.uk**). The full amended text of the Scotland Act 1998 is available on *Scottish Legislation Direct* from Butterworths (at **www.butterworths.co.uk**).

8-6 Statutory Instruments

Secondary legislation might also be specific to Scotland. Such statutory instruments (S.I.s) were numbered as part of the sequence within a calendar year, but were given an additional number preceded by the letter S. Again note that legislation on reserved matters will still be created in this way. Cite in the usual manner without reference to the S. number, *e.g.* S.I. 2001/497. Amendment and revocation are traced through the *Table of Government Orders* and the *Current Law Statutory Instrument Citator* (**4–28**). The *Laws of Scotland* (**8–50**) whether in print or online may also be used to trace S.I.s on a subject.

Sources   8–7
General S.I.s applying to Scotland will be found in the volumes of *Statutory Instruments* (**4–28**) but not in *Halsbury's Statutory Instruments*. Electronic sources include the website of Her Majesty's Stationery Office (at **www.hmso.gov.uk**), the Statute Law Database (**4–7**), JUSTIS *UK Statutory Instruments* (at **www.justis.com**) and Westlaw UK (at **www.westlaw.co.uk**). Statutory instruments made under the authority of the Scotland Act 1998 are available on the Queen's Printer for Scotland website (at **www.oqps.gov.uk**) and *Scottish Legislation Direct* (at **www.butterworths.co.uk**).

LEGISLATION FROM THE SCOTTISH PARLIAMENT   8–8

Acts of the Scottish Parliament   8–9

When a Scottish Parliament Bill (**8–58**) has been passed and has received the Royal Assent, it becomes an Act of the Scottish Parliament (ASP). Most Acts will be Public Acts, applying throughout Scotland. ASPs may also amend or repeal pre-devolution legislation from the U.K. Parliament in so far as it affects Scotland.

Structure   8–10

An extract from the Transport (Scotland) Act 2001 is reproduced on page 153. All ASPs are structured in the same way, although some of the parts described are not present in every Act.

The parts of an ASP (see the illustration) are:

1. Running header. A useful aid to navigation within longer Acts.
2. Short title. The name by which the Act is known, including the year.
3. Calendar year citation. Acts are numbered consecutively within the calendar year and may be referred to in this way as a form of shorthand. The "asp number" is thus the equivalent of the "chapter number" of a U.K. Parliament Act.
4. Enactment formula. A standard form of words recording the Parliament's approval of the originating Bill and the granting of the Royal Assent.
5. Long title. Describes the purpose or purposes of the Act.
6. Number and title of part. The sections which comprise the main body of the Act may be grouped into parts.
7. Number and title of section. The text of the Act is divided into sections, consecutively numbered and individually titled. They in turn may be divided into two or more numbered subsections. Further subdivisions may be employed to make the text easier to follow, *e.g.* paragraphs.
8. Cross-heading. A further aid to navigation present in longer Acts.
9. Short title citation. The formal statement of the short title.
10. Commencement provisions. Recording the arrangements for bringing the Act into force.

Longer Acts also have a table of contents at the front. Many Acts have schedules which contain supplementary or consequential provisions.

8–11   Citation

An Act may be cited either by its short title, *e.g.* Transport (Scotland) Act 2001, or by the calendar year and asp number, *e.g.* 2001 asp 2. Reference may also be made to a specific section or subdivision, *e.g.* Transport (Scotland) Act 2001 s.1(1).

8–12   Sources

The official print version of an Act is published by The Stationery Office (TSO), on behalf of the Queen's Printer for Scotland, shortly after it receives the Royal Assent. Individual Acts are subsequently gathered into annual volumes of the *Acts of the Scottish Parliament*. Explanatory notes are issued separately for those Acts which originated as Executive Bills. ASPs are also published in a section of *Current Law Statutes* with brief introductions and, in some cases, useful annotations. The official electronic version of an Act appears on the Queen's Printer for Scotland website (at **www.oqps.gov.uk**). However it should be noted that this is the Act as it was when it received the Royal Assent. The Statute Law Database (**4–7**) will provide the official amended version. Commercial sources of the full amended text include *Scottish Legislation Direct* (at **www.butterworths.co.uk**) and Westlaw UK (at **www.westlaw.co.uk**). JUSTIS *UK Statutes* (at **www.justis.com**) and Lawtel (at **www.lawtel.co.uk**) reproduce the original text with the facility to link to amending legislation.

8–13   Checking whether an ASP is in force

An Act may come into force on a specified date, after a specified period has elapsed or by means of a "commencement order" published as a Scottish statutory instrument (**8–16**). The Act's commencement provisions will make this clear. *Is It In Force?* is the most convenient print source, ASPs and Public General Acts being listed in a single sequence by calendar year and thereafter by short title. If the Act comes into force in piecemeal fashion, the information will be presented section by section. The annual edition is updated by the noter-up services to both *Halsbury's Statutes* and the *Laws of Scotland*, but if these are not to hand use the table of statutory commencement dates in *Current Law Monthly Digest*. An electronic version of *Is It In Force?* is available as a Butterworths *Scotland Direct* service (at **www.butterworths.co.uk**) and the Statutory Status Table on Lawtel notes details of commencement. A U.K. Legislative Locator Quick Search on Westlaw UK will reveal the status of a given provision; an alternative is to select the Analysis option for a section already located and displayed. Repeals are traced as amendments.

8–14   Checking whether an ASP has been amended

The *Chronological Table of the Statutes* published by TSO will be the official consolidated record of amendments and repeals. The *Current Law Statute Citator* (see **4–19** for a fuller description) lists ASPs in a separate sequence and details changes section by section. It is the most up to date print source. Although *Is It In Force?* notes some amendments and repeals, it is not intended as a comprehensive record and is therefore not recommended for this purpose. Annotations to the electronic version of the amended text on *Scottish Legislation Direct* and Westlaw UK clearly state the nature of the amendment and its origin. The Statutory Status Table on Lawtel indicates the existence of amending legislation and provides links to the text. JUSTIS *UK Statutes* has a Crossref feature intended to do the same but, as not every amendment made by statutory instrument is included, its reliability is compromised.

Extract from the Transport (Scotland) Act 2001

Transport (Scotland) Act 2001 (asp 2)
Part 1 - Joint transport strategies

Transport (Scotland) Act 2001
2001 asp 2

The Bill for this Act of the Scottish Parliament was passed by the Parliament on 20th December 2000 and received Royal Assent on 25th January 2001

An Act of the Scottish Parliament to make provision about transport; to make provision as respects certain bridges; to amend section 21 of the Chronically Sick and Disabled Persons Act 1970; to amend section 40 of the Road Traffic Act 1988; to amend sections 26, 28 and 63 of the Road Traffic Regulation Act 1984; and for connected purposes.

PART 1

JOINT TRANSPORT STRATEGIES

1   Joint transport strategies

(1) The Scottish Ministers may by order require such public bodies as may be specified in the order to prepare, and submit to them, jointly a strategy-

   (a)   dealing with such matters; and

   (b)   for such purposes,

as may be so specified in relation to the discharge of the functions of those bodies relating to transport.

(2) Before making an order under this section the Scottish Ministers shall consult-

   (a)   the public bodies in respect of which they propose to make the order; and

   (b)   such other persons as they consider appropriate.

Road safety information and training: subsidies

76   Amendment of Road Traffic Act 1988

In section 40 of the Road Traffic Act 1988 (c.52) (power to subsidise certain authorities and bodies for giving road safety information and training)-

(a) the words "authorities or bodies other than" are repealed; and

(b) at the end there shall be inserted "or by other authorities or bodies".

84   Short title and commencement

(1) This Act may be cited as the Transport (Scotland) Act 2001.

(2) The provisions of this Act, other than this section, shall come into force on such day as the Scottish Ministers may by order appoint.

(3) Different days may be so appointed for different purposes.

8–15   Tracing ASPs on a subject

The *Laws of Scotland* (**8–50**) is a good starting place for research and will draw attention to any relevant legislation. *Current Law Yearbook* supplemented by *Current Law Monthly Digest* provides a broader approach but is more up to date. Electronic services such as Westlaw UK definitely have the edge here, their search engines permitting a level of detail which printed indexes cannot match. Lawtel and *Current Legal Information* however only search summaries of Acts. The *Laws of Scotland* is available online as a Butterworths *Scotland Direct* service (at **www.butterworths.co.uk**).

8–16   Scottish Statutory Instruments

The power to make secondary legislation on a devolved matter may derive from either an Act of the Scottish Parliament or a pre-devolution Public General Act. Such legislation takes the form of a Scottish statutory instrument (S.S.I.). Most S.S.I.s will be general in application but some, such as those dealing with roads and road traffic, will be classified as local and may not be published. Commencement orders are an important type of S.S.I.

8–17   Structure

An extract from the European Communities (Matrimonial Jurisdiction and Judgments) (Scotland) Regulations 2001 is reproduced on page 155. All S.S.I.s are structured in the same way.

The parts of an S.S.I. (see the illustration) are:

1. Citation. S.S.I.s are numbered sequentially within the calendar year. Commencement orders are given an additional number preceded by the letter C.
2. Subject. Words and phrases describing the subject of the instrument and used in the arrangement of the *List of Statutory Publications*.
3. Title. The name by which the instrument is known, including the year.
4. Dates. Including a statement of when the instrument comes into force.
5. Preamble and enabling powers. The enabling Act may have been passed by the Scottish Parliament or by the U.K. Parliament.
6. Title and number of division of text; these may be known as articles, regulations (as in the example given) or rules, depending upon the nature of the instrument.
7. Signature. Usually a member of the Scottish Executive.

Longer instruments may have a table of contents at the front. Many S.S.I.s will have schedules which contain provisions dependent upon one or more of the numbered divisions of the text. Explanatory notes are included but these do not form part of the legislative text.

8–18   Citation

An S.S.I. may be cited either by its title, *e.g.* European Communities (Matrimonial Jurisdiction and Judgments) (Scotland) Regulations 2001, or by the calendar year and sequence number, *e.g.* S.S.I. 2001/36. Reference may also be made to a specific division or subdivision, *e.g.* S.S.I. 2001/36 reg.2(2).

8–19   Sources

The official print version of an S.S.I. is published by The Stationery Office, on behalf of the Queen's Printer for Scotland. Individual general instruments are subsequently gathered into annual volumes of *Scottish Statutory Instruments*. The full text of selected S.S.I.s is

Extract from the European Communities (Matrimonial Jurisdiction and Judgments) (Scotland) Regulations 2001

SCOTTISH STATUTORY INSTRUMENTS

---

① **2001 No. 36**

FAMILY LAW

② # JUDGMENTS

③ The European Communities (Matrimonial Jurisdiction and Judgments) (Scotland) Regulations 2001

Made	*6th February 2001*
④ *Laid before the Scottish Parliament*	*7th February 2001*
Coming into force	*1st March 2001*

⑤ The Scottish Ministers, in exercise of the powers conferred by section 2(2) of the European Communities Act 1972 and of all other powers enabling them in that behalf, hereby make the following Regulations:

⑥ **Citation, commencement and extent**

1. - (1) These Regulations may be cited as the European Communities (Matrimonial Jurisdiction and Judgments) (Scotland) Regulations 2001 and shall come into force on 1st March 2001.

2. - (1) These Regulations extend to Scotland only.

Amendment of the Domicile and Matrimonial Proceedings Act 1973

2. - (1) The Domicile and Matrimonial Proceedings Act 1973 is amended in accordance with paragraphs (2) to (5) of this regulation.

(2) In section 7 -
    (a) in subsection (2) the words "divorce, separation or" are repealed;
    (b) after that subsection, insert-

. . .

Application

6. The amendments to the Domicile and Matrimonial Proceedings Act 1973 made by regulation 2 shall not apply in respect of proceedings before 1st March 2001.

⑦   *JAMES WALLACE*
A member of the Scottish Executive

St Andrew's House,
Edinburgh
6th February 2001

Crown copyright 2001 with the permission of the Queen's Printer for Scotland reproduced in *Green's Scottish Statutory Instruments Service*, but most are only summarised. The official electronic version of an instrument appears on the Queen's Printer for Scotland website (at **www.oqps.gov.uk**). Neither this site nor the Statute Law Database incorporates subsequent amendments. Commercial sources of the full amended text include *Scottish Legislation Direct* (at **www.butterworths.co.uk**) and Westlaw UK (at **www.westlaw.co.uk**). JUSTIS *UK Statutory Instruments* (at **www.justis.com**) reproduces the original text while Lawtel (at **www.lawtel.co.uk**) simply links to the version on the Queen's Printer site.

8–20 Checking whether an S.S.I. is in force
The date on which an S.S.I. comes into force is specified on the instrument itself. If this is not to hand a summary in *Current Law Yearbook*, *Current Law Monthly Digest*, or *Green's Scottish Statutory Instruments Service* will include the information. The Queen's Printer for Scotland website is the obvious electronic source as access is free of charge. Revocations are traced as amendments.

8–21 Checking whether an S.S.I. has been amended
With the *Table of Government Orders* in abeyance, no official consolidated record of amendments and revocations is published at present. The annual volumes of *Scottish Statutory Instruments* include a table recording effects on legislation, but as time passes this will be an unwieldy approach. The *Current Law Statutory Instrument Citator* lists S.S.I.s in a separate sequence and details changes division by division. Annotations to the electronic version of the amended text on *Scottish Legislation Direct* and Westlaw UK clearly state the nature of the amendment and its origin. The Status field on Lawtel notes amending legislation but the Crossref feature on JUSTIS *UK Statutory Instruments* is not reliable as only minimal cross referencing is implemented.

8–22 Tracing S.S.I.s on a subject
Researching an area of law in the *Laws of Scotland* (**8–50**) or identifying an appropriate subject heading in *Current Law Yearbook* and *Current Law Monthly Digest* will reveal the existence of secondary legislation. Specialist looseleaf services such as *Scottish Planning Encyclopedia* are another valuable source of information. The *List of Statutory Publications* presents details of S.S.I.s arranged by the broad subject headings allocated by the draftsmen, and indexes them by a combination of these headings and terms drawn from the titles of the instruments. Considerable detail can be specified when searching a full-text electronic service such as Westlaw UK, but *Current Legal Information* will only search in abstracts of S.S.I.s. The *Laws of Scotland* is available online as a Butterworths *Scotland Direct* service (at **www.butterworths.co.uk**).

8–23 OTHER LEGISLATION

8–24 Acts of the Parliaments of Scotland

Prior to the Union with England in 1707, Scotland was an independent kingdom with its own Parliament enacting laws. Some of these Scots Acts are still in force. The *Chronological Table of the Statutes* published by The Stationery Office is the official consolidated record of amendments and repeals but the *Current Law Statute Citator* (see **4–19** for a fuller description) is the most up to date source of information. The *Laws of Scotland* (**8–50**) both in print and online (at **www.butterworths.co.uk**) draws attention to

Scots Acts still extant. For those whose research is of a more historical nature, the final volume of *Acts of the Parliaments of Scotland 1124–1707* contains a general index.

Citation   8–25

The Statute Law Revision (Scotland) Act 1964 designated short titles for the Scots Acts it left in force. Such Acts should be cited either by short title, *e.g.* Royal Mines Act 1424, or by calendar year and chapter number, *e.g.* 1424 c.13. Regnal years are never used to cite Scots Acts. Those Acts repealed in or before 1964 are usually cited by reference to the volume, page and chapter number in *Acts of the Parliaments of Scotland 1124–1707*, *e.g.* APS III, 28, c. 20.

Sources   8–26

The most authoritative version is the 12-volume *Acts of the Parliaments of Scotland 1124–1707* (known as the "Record Edition" or "Thomson's *Acts*") published in the nineteenth century. Other, perhaps more accessible, sources include the one-volume *Acts of the Parliaments of Scotland 1424–1707* published by Her Majesty's Stationery Office in 1966. This only reproduces Acts in force at the time.

Private Legislation   8–27

The preceding description of legislation has concentrated upon public legislation; that is to say legislation of general application, affecting the community at large. Private legislation confers powers or benefits upon a particular body (such as a public authority) or person. The U.K. Parliament passed most legislation of this type specific to Scotland under procedures governed by the Private Legislation Procedure (Scotland) Act 1936. This involved application to the Secretary of State, an inquiry by commissioners if required, and an expedited passage in Parliament: see Erskine May, *Parliamentary Practice* (22nd ed., 1997), pp. 944–955. It should be noted that private legislation on reserved matters, or on a combination of devolved and reserved matters, will continue to be created in this way. Such Acts may be cited either by short title, *e.g.* Comhairle Nan Eilean Siar (Eriskay Causeway) Order Confirmation Act 2000, or by calendar year and chapter number, *e.g.* 2000 c. i. Amendments and repeals are charted by the *Chronological Table of Local Legislation*, and the *Index to the Local and Personal Acts* is an essential research tool. If the conferring of powers is wholly within the legislative competence of the Scottish Parliament, a promoter may seek to introduce a Private Bill. The procedures involved are fully explained in *Guidance on Private Bills* (2001). All Bills that are enacted become Acts of the Scottish Parliament (ASPs) irrespective of the public/private nature of the Bill.

Sources   8–28

Private legislation applying in Scotland is published in the series of *Local and Personal Acts* (**4–25**) and in *Current Law Statutes* from 1992. Electronic versions of Local Acts passed in and after 1991 are available on the website of Her Majesty's Stationery Office (at **www.hmso.gov.uk**). Private ASPs will be numbered and published in the same series as Public ASPs (**8–12**).

Local Statutory Instruments   8–29

The secondary legislation equivalents of Local and Personal Acts are statutory instruments classified as local. Not all such instruments are published and only a few are included in the annual editions of *Statutory Instruments* from 1990. To be included, the instrument must have been made under the authority of one of a handful of Acts, *e.g.* the Harbours Act 1964, and have an effect upon primary or secondary legislation; thus while the Scrabster (Forward Supply Base) Harbour Revision Order 1998 is reproduced, the Peterhead Harbours Revision Order 1998 is not. Local instruments can be identified through the *List of Statutory Publications* if the S.I. number is known and through a listing in the annual editions if only the title is known. Scottish statutory instruments classified as local will only be published if the Presiding Officer of the Scottish Parliament so directs, or if the responsible authority specifically requests it.

8–30   Sources
Electronic sources are particularly useful in that if a local instrument was published it remains available on the website of Her Majesty's Stationery Office (at **www.hmso.gov.uk**) and on JUSTIS *UK Statutory Instruments* (at **www.justis.com**). Westlaw UK (at **www.westlaw.co.uk**) is more selective but all such instruments from 2000 onwards will be retained.

8–31   Acts of Sederunt and Acts of Adjournal

Acts of Sederunt govern procedure in the civil courts and Acts of Adjournal govern procedure in the criminal courts. They generally take the form of statutory instruments or Scottish statutory instruments with titles such as Act of Sederunt (Ordinary Cause Rules) Amendment (Commercial Actions) 2001, which is S.S.I. 2001/8.

8–32   Sources
The sources for Acts of Sederunt and Acts of Adjournal are the same as for S.I.s (**8–7**) and S.S.I.s (**8–19**). Acts of Sederunt may also be reproduced in *Parliament House Book* and Acts of Adjournal in *Renton and Brown's Criminal Procedure Legislation*. Both were published in *Scottish Current Law Statutes* from 1949 until 1990, and still appear in *Scots Law Times*.

8–33   Byelaws, Management Rules and Orders

Rarely encountered by the law student, these are forms of secondary legislation made by local authorities and operative only in the local government area concerned, *e.g.* Dumfries and Galloway Regional Council Public Library Byelaws 1980. The offices of the relevant authority are the only reliable source; contact details are conveniently provided in the *Scottish Law Directory* and the *Blue Book*. An excellent introduction to this subject is the Local Government title in the *Laws of Scotland*, both in print and online.

8–34   CASE LAW

Civil cases are heard in the sheriff courts, the Court of Session and, as a final court of appeal, in the House of Lords. The Outer House of the Court of Session determines cases at first instance while the Inner House is mainly a court of appeal. Criminal cases are heard in the district courts, the sheriff courts and the High Court of Justiciary. The High Court is both a court of first instance and the court of appeal. Courts of special jurisdiction include the Court of the Lord Lyon and the Scottish Land Court, while the Crofters Commission, Lands Tribunal for Scotland and Children's Hearings are among the statutory tribunals. The Scotland Act 1998 cast the Judicial Committee of the Privy Council in the role of constitutional court, and "devolution issues" which arise in any court or tribunal may be referred or appealed to it. Such issues include whether the Scottish Parliament has exceeded its legislative competence, whether a member of the Scottish Executive has acted outwith devolved competence and whether an action is contrary to E.C. law or the "Convention rights" safeguarded by the Human Rights Act 1998.

Reports of cases may be found in published series of law reports and their direct electronic equivalents, via electronic services such as *Scottish Case Digests Online* and Westlaw UK, or on official court websites such as that of the Scottish Court Service.

Modern Law Reports 8–35

This section treats those series which are still extant, although they may have originated in the nineteenth century.

Structure 8–36

The structure of Scottish case reports is not markedly different from those of other U.K. jurisdictions. However different series of law reports may present the information in slightly different ways.

The parts of a case report (see the illustration on page 161) are:

1. The names of the parties as they will be used in the citation of the case. In a civil case the name of the pursuer (the person bringing the action) comes first, followed by the name of the defender. In this example the case went to appeal and the parties are therefore also described as appellant and respondent. Public prosecution in criminal cases is conducted in the name of the Lord Advocate (H.M.A. or H.M. Advocate) or a procurator fiscal. When referring to either category of case, the abbreviation v. is spoken as "against" and not "versus".

2. The date on which the decision was given. If the opinion of the court is delivered some time later it will be backdated. In this example the opinion was delivered at advising, *i.e.* when giving judgment.

3. The name of the court in which the case was heard. In this example the case was appealed from the Sheriff Court to the Inner House of the Court of Session. The Inner House sits in two permanent divisions known as the First and Second Division (of equal authority), but here three judges have been constituted as an Extra Division to assist in dealing with the volume of business. The judges are often named at this point but here they are named further on.

4. A fuller statement of the names and roles of the parties and, in italics, the names of their representatives in court.

5. A summary of the subject of the case and the main legal issues by the editor of the report. These are known as "catchwords".

6. A more detailed statement known as the "headnote" or "rubric", again prepared by the editor of the report. It includes the decision of the court.

7. A summary of previous proceedings.

8. A list of authorities referred to in the case. This may include textbooks.

9. Further details of the court, the judges and the hearing.

10. The opinion of the court and the most important part. In this example only one judge

explained the reasoning that led to the decision. Each judge may deliver an opinion or simply state that they concur. Any dissenting opinion will be reported.
11. The outcome of the case.
12. The names of the agents for the parties. In this example these are firms of solicitors.

The diligent student should never rely upon the headnote, which is the work of the editor of the report and has no authority, but should read the opinion itself, which is what the judge or judges said. Of course, the opinion made available on an official court website has none of the editorial paraphernalia.

8–37   Citation

A published report of a case may be cited by:

(a) the names of the parties, abbreviated for the purpose; plus
(b) the year of the volume in which the case was reported. Round brackets are not used when citing modern reports, and square brackets are never used. Citations of older reports may include a specific volume number and substitute the year when the case was decided; plus
(c) the abbreviation for the title of the series of law reports. It is common nowadays for these to be given without punctuation, *e.g.* SC rather than S.C.; plus
(d) the number of the page on which the report begins.

Thus for the report given as an illustration:

The Globe (Aberdeen) Ltd. v. *North of Scotland Water Authority*[a] 2000[b] S.C.[c] 392[d].

It should be noted that while the abbreviations for modern law reports are generally stable, and indeed most series clearly indicate the preferred form of citation, there is usually no sanctioned form of abbreviation for older reports and many variations may be encountered.

8–38   Session Cases

There is no official series of law reports in Scotland although *Session Cases*, which reports decisions in the superior courts, is regarded as having an authority beyond that of any alternative source. The present series (1907–) follows on from five series which appeared between 1821 and 1906 and are known by the names of five respective editors.

First series	Shaw	(S.)	1821–1838	16 vols.
Second series	Dunlop	(D.)	1838–1862	24 vols.
Third series	Macpherson	(M.)	1862–1873	11 vols.
Fourth series	Rettie	(R.)	1873–1898	25 vols.
Fifth series	Fraser	(F.)	1898–1906	8 vols.

Cases decided in the Court of Session are cited by the volume number, the initial letter of the editor's name and the page number. Thus the citation 5 R. 742 indicates that the case is reported in the fifth volume of the fourth series of *Session Cases*, edited by Rettie, and the report begins on page 742. It is now standard practice to include the calendar year in which the case was decided and this certainly helps to avoid confusion, *e.g.* (1878) 5 R. 742. From the advent of the present series, cases are cited by the volume year, the abbreviation S.C., and the page number, *e.g.* 2000 S.C. 69. House of Lords decisions in Scottish appeals from 1850 onwards appear in a separately paginated sequence, distinguishable by the form of citation, *e.g.* (1877) 4 R.(H.L.) 48. An equivalent citation is employed in the present series, *e.g.* 2000 S.C.(H.L.) 67. Cases decided in the High Court of Justiciary were added in 1874, again clearly differentiated by citation, *e.g.* (1880) 7 R.(J.) 11. Justiciary cases in the 1907 to

Extract from a Scottish Case Report

1 THE GLOBE (ABERDEEN) LTD v NORTH OF SCOTLAND
WATER AUTHORITY

2 No 41
10 March 2000

3 EXTRA DI
Sheri

4 THE GLOBE (ABERDEEN) LIMITED, Pursuers (Appellants) - *Macdonal*
NORTH OF SCOTLAND WATER AUTHORITY, Defenders (Respondents) - (

5 *Reparation - Nuisance - Remoteness of damage - Public house entrance obstructed d
nine months when water authority replacing underground sewer - Publicans sustaini
of profits - Water authority sued for failing to take reasonable care to avoid causing
- Whether loss of profits recoverable*

6 The pursuers, who carried on the business of a public house, sued their wate.
authority for nuisance caused by the water authority's obstructing the public street
outside their premises over a period of nine months while the water authority replaced
an underground sewer there. The pursuers averred that they had been told that the
works would be likely to take six weeks to complete. The pursuers claimed damages
for, *inter alia*, loss of profits sustained by them as a result of the water authority's
failure to take reasonable care to avoid causing a nuisance by fully planning the
works prior to commencing them. At debate the sheriff (Miller) dismissed the action
on the ground that the pursuer's claim was for pure economic loss and was
accordingly too remote. The pursuers appealed to the Court of Session.
Held (1) that since the proper angle of approach to a case of alleged nuisance was
from the victim's standpoint and that it was generally irrelevant as a defence for the
defender to plead that he was making a normal and familiar use of his own property,
it could not be affirmed that in a case of alleged nuisance it was necessarily too
remote to claim mere financial loss (pp 394I-395A); and (2) that, further, since the
pursuers' averments of nuisance had not been challenged at debate, it would be
inappropriate to allow further debate in the Inner House or before the sheriff and
accordingly the appropriate course was to allow a proof before answer (p 395B); and
appeal *allowed*.

7 THE GLOBE (ABERDEEN) LIMITED brought an action in the sheriffdom of Grampian,
Highland and Islands at Aberdeen against North of Scotland Water Authority, the statutory
successors to Grampian Regional Council, for damages for nuisance.
The cause came to debate before the sheriff (I H L Miller) on, *inter alia*, the defenders' plea
to the relevancy of the pursuers' averments.
On 18 February 1999 the sheriff dismissed the action.
The pursuers thereafter appealed to the Court of Session.

8 *Cases referred to:*
Dynamco Ltd v Holland & Hannen & Cubitts (Scotland) Ltd 1971 SC 257
East Lothian Angling Association v Haddington Town Council 1980 SLT 213
R H M Bakeries (Scotland) Ltd v Strathclyde Regional Council 1985 SC (HL) 17
Walker's Trustees v Caledonian Railway Co (1882) 9 R (HL) 19
Watt v Jamieson 1954 SC 56

9 The cause called before an Extra Division, comprising Lord Coulsfield, Lord Milligan and
Lord Cameron of Lochbroom, for a hearing on the summar role.
At advising, on 10 March 2000, the opinion of the court was delivered by Lord Coulsfield.

10 OPINION OF THE COURT - The pursuers and appellants carry on the business of a public
house at premises in North Silver Street, Aberdeen. The defenders and respondents are the
statutory successors to the Grampian Regional Council in regard to sewerage works. In this
action, the appellants are seeking to recover losses which they aver they sustained because of
the very substantial prolongation of certain sewer replacement work carried out by Grampian
Regional Council. On 18 February 1999, the sheriff sustained certain pleas in law for the
respondents and dismissed the action. The appellants have now appealed to this court.

...

In the whole circumstances, therefore, in our opinion the proper course is to allow the appeal
and remit the cause to the sheriff to proceed to a proof before answer.

11 THE COURT allowed the appeal and remitted to the sheriff to allow a proof
before answer.

12 *Drummond Miller, WS (for Lefevre Litigation, Aberdeen) - Ledingham Chalmers*

1916 volumes are cited S.C.(J.) but since then the accepted form has been J.C., *e.g.* 2000 J.C. 62. It is worth noting that some law libraries also have a 10-volume set of *Justiciary Cases* running from 1917 to 1965; this is simply a compilation of the relevant sections from *Session Cases* for the years concerned. The practice was briefly revived for the years 1995 and 1996. Cases decided in the Judicial Committee of the Privy Council (**8–34**) first appear in 2001, *e.g.* 2001 S.C.(P.C.) 37. It is important therefore to remember that although

    2001 S.C.(P.C.) 1   2001 J.C. 1   2001 S.C. 1

are three completely different case reports, they appear in sections of the same physical volume. *Session Cases* are published on behalf of the Scottish Council of Law Reporting, with five paperback parts issued during the year and a sixth incorporated into the annual bound volume.

There are cumulative indexes of cases by names of parties and by subject matter in the individual parts and in the annual bound volumes. As there is no consolidated index, the most convenient means of tracing cases on a subject across a number of years is the *Faculty Digest* (**8–43**). At present there is no electronic version of *Session Cases*, although many cases which were reported in the series do appear on Lexis (at **www.butterworths.co.uk**) and Westlaw UK (at **www.westlaw.co.uk**) by virtue of having been reported elsewhere, and a citation for *Session Cases* may be given.

8–39 **Scots Law Times**
The other major series of Scottish law reports is the *Scots Law Times*. This has been published weekly during session since 1893 and contains news, articles and case reports. The 40 weekly parts are cumulated into annual bound volumes. The Reports section has usually been the most substantial, and since 1989 has merited a volume to itself. Cases decided in the Court of Session, the High Court of Justiciary, the House of Lords and on occasion other superior courts are presented in a single sequence, unlike their counterparts in *Session Cases*. Apart from the early years when volumes were individually numbered (1893–1908) or when two bound volumes were issued annually (1909–21), cases are cited by the volume year, the abbreviation S.L.T. and the page number, *e.g.* 2000 S.L.T. 1393. However the *Scots Law Times* also contains the following case reports in sections which are paginated and cited separately:

    (a) Sheriff Court Reports, *e.g.* 2000 S.L.T. (Sh. Ct.) 60;
    (b) Reports of Cases decided in the Scottish Land Court and the Lands Tribunal for Scotland,
        e.g. 2000 S.L.T. (Land Ct.) 27 and 1997 S.L.T. (Lands Tr.) 14;
    (c) Reports of Cases decided in the Lyon Court, *e.g.* 2000 S.L.T. (Lyon Ct.) 3.

Before 1982 there was also a section entitled Notes of Recent Decisions to which reference may still be made, *e.g.* 1981 S.L.T. (Notes) 5. Thus, whether using the thin weekly parts or the burly annual volumes, remember that the citation always indicates the appropriate section to be consulted.

There are indexes of cases by names of parties and by subject matter in the annual bound volumes. These are built up throughout the year; they appear on blue paper in the weekly parts and are cumulated every 10 parts and published separately. Thus the third issue of the index covers the first 30 weekly parts, and the blue paper index printed in part 35 covers parts 31–34. Research involving more than one specific year is facilitated by a consolidated *Index* to cases reported between 1961 and 1990, with cumulative supplements issued annually.

Scots Law Times is no longer available on Lexis (although parallel citations persist) and has migrated to Westlaw UK (at **www.westlaw.co.uk**). Case reports are also available as *Scots Law Times Reports on CD-ROM*, which is updated monthly.

Other sources   8–40
The Law Society of Scotland is the moving force behind two series of law reports. *Scottish Criminal Case Reports* (*e.g.* 2000 S.C.C.R. 884) includes brief commentaries on selected cases from 1981 onwards, while otherwise unreported cases from 1950 to 1980 have been published as a supplement. The indexes in the annual bound volumes cumulate over a five-year period, *e.g.* 1991–95, and consolidated indexes have been published for 1981–90 and 1991–2000. *Scottish Civil Law Reports* (*e.g.* 2000 S.C.L.R. 1057) followed in 1987 and also includes brief commentaries. Again the indexes in the annual bound volumes cumulate over a five-year period, *e.g.* 1997–2001, and a consolidated *Index* has been published for 1987–96. Both are available on Lexis.

   Green's Weekly Digest (1986–   ), arranged by subject, summarises all decisions brought to the attention of the publishers, with judgments of legal significance reported subsequently in the *Scots Law Times*. As the 40 weekly parts are not cumulated, citation is by the volume year, and the part and paragraph numbers, *e.g.* 2000 G.W.D. 15–570. Blue paper indexes are issued at intervals throughout the year and a consolidated *Index* covers 1986–2000.

   There are relatively few specialised series of law reports. *Green's Family Law Reports* (1997–   ), *Green's Housing Law Reports* (1996–   ), and *Green's Reparation Law Reports* (1996–   ) include limited commentary. The coverage of Land Court decisions in *Scottish Land Court Reports* (new series 1982–   ) is more inclusive than that in *Scots Law Times*; the original series reported decisions from 1913 to 1963 and was published as a supplement to the *Scottish Law Review*. *Scottish Planning Appeal Decisions* (1976) contains only brief summaries of decisions. Scottish cases of wider significance may also appear in *Appeal Cases*, *Weekly Law Reports*, *All England Law Reports* or in a specialist series such as *Industrial Relations Law Reports*.

   Lexis includes transcripts of unreported (*i.e.* not published in print) decisions from the Scottish courts. Apart from this, the most useful electronic source is the website of the Scottish Court Service (at **www.scotcourts.gov.uk**) which provides full-text opinions of the Court of Session and High Court of Justiciary, and selected Sheriff Court decisions. However as the coverage only begins with 1998, the archive of unreported Inner House (1982–   ) and Outer House (1985–   ) decisions on Lexis still represents a valuable resource. *Scottish Case Digests Online* from Butterworths *Scotland Direct* (at **www.butterworths.co.uk**) offers a case digest service with headnotes and links to the full text on the Scottish Court Service website. The U.K. Parliament website (at **www.parliament.uk**) includes judgments in Scottish appeals to the House of Lords from late 1996 onwards. Judgments of the Judicial Committee of the Privy Council in devolution cases are available on that official website (at **www.privy-council.org.uk**). With effect from 2001 these are cited in a neutral format, *e.g.* [2001] U.K.P.C. D1. The abbreviations D.P. and D.R.A. which may be encountered refer to the procedure by which the devolution issue was raised, *i.e.* by "devolution petition" and by "devolution reference or appeal" respectively.

Older Law Reports   8–41

   The law reports familiar today have their origins in the "decision practicks" and printed collections of earlier times. A helpful summary is to be found in D. M. Walker, *The Scottish*

Legal System (8th ed., 2001), pp. 493–500. These are not available in all law libraries, but there are alternative sources for many of the most important decisions. The most widely used collection of cases from the mid-sixteenth to the early nineteenth centuries is Morison's *Dictionary*. Arranged by subject, the pages throughout its 38 volumes are numbered continuously from page 1 to page 17074; thus a typical citation might be: (1623) Mor. 14264. Various appendices, supplements and synopses were added and, most importantly, an index (Tait's *Index*) was issued in 1823. Between 1898 and 1909, William Green & Sons published 45 volumes of *Scots Revised Reports* which reprinted many pre-1873 decisions in similar fashion to the *English Reports*. These are drawn from Morison's *Dictionary*, the *Faculty Collection*, the House of Lords series (see below), the first three series of *Session Cases* and the *Scottish Jurist*.

House of Lords decisions in Scottish appeals for the period 1707–1873 are reported in ten series of private reports, again known by the names of the editors.

Robertson	Robert.	1707–1727	1 vol.
Paton	Pat.	1726–1821	6 vols
Shaw	Sh. App.	1821–1824	2 vols
Wilson & Shaw	W. & Sh.	1825–1834	7 vols
Shaw & Maclean	Sh. & Macl.	1835–1838	3 vols
Maclean & Robinson	Macl. & R.	1839	1 vol.
Robinson	Robin.	1840–1841	2 vols
Bell	Bell App.	1842–1850	7 vols
Macqueen	Macq.	1851–1865	4 vols
Paterson	Paters.	1851–1873	2 vols

Cases are cited by the volume number, an abbreviated form of the editor's name and the page number, *e.g.* 1 Pat. 44. It is now usual to include the calendar year in which the case was decided, *e.g.* (1730) 1 Pat. 44. A further 10 series by private reporters cover early criminal cases.

Shaw	P. Shaw	1819–1831	1 vol.
Syme	Syme	1826–1829	1 vol.
Swinton	Swin.	1835–1841	2 vols
Broun	Broun	1842–1845	2 vols
Arkley	Arkley	1846–1848	1 vol.
Shaw	J. Shaw	1848–1852	1 vol.
Irvine	Irv.	1852–1867	5 vols
Couper	Coup.	1868–1885	5 vols
White	White	1885–1893	3 vols
Adam	Adam	1893–1916	7 vols

Cases are cited as above, *e.g.* 7 Adam 732 or (1916) 7 Adam 732.

Three other defunct series are consulted often enough to be worth noting here. The *Scottish Jurist* reported cases from the Court of Session, High Court of Justiciary and the House of Lords from 1829 until it was incorporated into *Session Cases* in 1873. The *Scottish Law Reporter* covered the same courts from 1865 to 1924, and was then incorporated into *Scots Law Times*. *Sheriff Court Reports* appeared from 1885 until publication ceased in 1963; note that these were published as part of the *Scottish Law Review* and may be bound with that set.

Finding Case Law

It is relatively straightforward to find the report of a case with a full (and accurate) citation. Abbreviations can be deciphered with the aid of D. Raistrick, *Index to Legal Citations and Abbreviations* (2nd ed., 1993) and other publications (**3–5**). However there are occasions when alternative strategies are required. In addition to the sources mentioned below, textbooks, periodicals and the indexes to the individual series of law reports have their uses.

Tracing a Case by the Names of the Parties   8–43

It may be necessary to trace a case by the names of the parties because of a problem with the full citation, but it is also useful to be able to locate an alternative report of the case. This is also the means of tracking the subsequent judicial history of a case. Cases reported in Scotland or judicially considered in a Scottish court may be traced through the *Scottish Current Law Case Citator*. Two bound volumes were published, covering the years 1948–76 and 1977–88 respectively. The *Current Law Case Citator* for 1989–95 was the first to make the Scottish table available in the parent edition (see **3–14** for a fuller description) but some law libraries will have the consolidated and corrected 1977–97 citator which incorporates Scotland. It is important to note that the Scottish information always appears in a separate table, although Scottish cases considered in English courts will be listed in the main section. Indexes to Shaw's *Digest*, the *Scots Digest* and the *Faculty Digest* can be used for the pre-1948 period.

  Electronic services such as *Current Legal Information* (**3–14**) and Westlaw UK (at **www.westlaw.co.uk**) are very useful for tracing modern cases. *Current Legal Information* on CD-ROM has a case citator which covers cases digested or otherwise referred to in its database (but see **8–44** for issues relating to coverage of Scottish cases). A case locator document on Westlaw UK will also reveal subsequent judicial history.

Tracing a Case by Subject   8–44

A *Scottish Current Law Yearbook* was published for the years 1948–90. The greater part of the text is identical to that of the parent edition, digesting English cases, legislation only applying to England and Wales and legislation applying throughout the United Kingdom. Scottish cases and legislation only applying to Scotland appear in a separate sequence, summarised under subject headings adapted to reflect Scots terminology. No equivalent to the *Current Law Consolidation* was published in Scotland, but the 1956 volume was styled a "master volume" and integrates brief Scottish entries for 1948–55 with the full entries for that year. English and United Kingdom material for 1952–55 is treated in similar fashion. There were also master volumes in the years 1961, 1966 and 1971, each incorporating entries for the previous four years. It is however always necessary to refer to the original yearbook for the full entry. Cumulative subject indexes appeared in the volumes for 1949–52, followed by annual indexes in 1953–55, but were regarded as "an unnecessary luxury which is not justified by the considerable extra expense it involves" for the next 20 years ([1956] C.L.Y., p. 6). In 1976 Sweet & Maxwell's decision to abandon master volumes forced W. Green to produce a comprehensive subject index of entries in the 1972–76 Scottish sections. Cumulative indexes appeared in subsequent years, culminating in an index for 1972–86. The cumulative index to the English and United Kingdom section, which had remained a feature of the English edition, was first included in 1979. The final volume of *Scottish Current Law Yearbook* carried 1987–90 subject indexes to both sections. From 1991 onwards the Scottish section in *Current Law Yearbook* may be used.

To summarise the shortcuts for tracing Scottish cases and information in *Scottish Current Law Yearbook*:

1948–1956   look under the subject headings in the 1956 master volume;
1957–1961   look under the subject headings in the 1961 master volume;
1962–1966   look under the subject headings in the 1966 master volume;
1967–1971   look under the subject headings in the 1971 master volume;
1972–1986   use the cumulative Scottish subject index in the 1986 volume;
1987–1990   use the cumulative Scottish subject index in the 1990 volume.

To summarise the shortcuts for tracing English cases and U.K. information in *Scottish Current Law Yearbook*:

1948–1951   use the cumulative subject index in the 1951 volume;
1952–1956   look under the subject headings in the 1956 master volume;
1957–1961   look under the subject headings in the 1961 master volume;
1962–1966   look under the subject headings in the 1966 master volume;
1967–1971   look under the subject headings in the 1971 master volume;
1972–1986   use the cumulative main subject index in the 1986 volume;
1987–1989   use the cumulative main subject index in the 1989 volume;
1990   use the main subject index in the 1990 volume.

The *Faculty Digest* provides a subject approach to decisions of the superior courts but, as it is published in decennial instalments, it is perhaps more useful for its coverage of the years from 1868 to 1950. The predecessors of these publications were the *Scots Digest* and Shaw's *Digest*, which covered decisions in the supreme courts from 1800 and the House of Lords from 1707 and 1726 respectively. Morison's *Dictionary* permits research back to 1540. As a jumping-off point for subject research the *Laws of Scotland* (**8–50**) cannot be bettered, but it will be necessary to consult both the *Consolidated Index* and the indexes to any reissued titles which might be relevant.

Current *Legal Information* and Westlaw UK are again of considerable value. However it is important to note that *Current Legal Information* on CD-ROM is not a straightforward electronic version of the yearbooks. Although all the case digests from the 1986–90 volumes of *Scottish Current Law Yearbook* are included, the Scottish coverage for the period from 1947 to 1985 is derived from the parent edition, *i.e.* only those cases which were digested in the English/U.K. section are there. The internet version only covers cases digested from 1986 onwards anyway, so the issue does not arise.

8–45   Tracing Very Recent Cases
Green's Weekly Digest and *Current Law Monthly Digest* are the best printed sources. However the currency of official websites such as that of the Scottish Court Service cannot be matched. Westlaw UK has a current awareness feature with a Scottish section.

8–46   Tracing Journal Articles and Commentaries on a Case

Legal Journals Index (**5–4**), whether accessed in print form (1986–99 only), on CD-ROM (*Current Legal Information*) or on the internet (*Current Legal Information* and Westlaw UK), is the most comprehensive research source available. The *Scottish Current Law Case Citator* will also highlight articles and stretches back to 1948.

8–47   INSTITUTIONAL WRITINGS

The formal sources of Scots law include certain authoritative writings dating from the mid-seventeenth to the early nineteenth centuries. These include Viscount Stair,

Institutions of the Law of Scotland (6th ed., 1981), first published in 1681; J. Erskine, *Institute of the Law of Scotland* (8th ed., 1871), first published in 1773; D. Hume, *Commentaries on the Law of Scotland Respecting Crimes* (4th ed., 1844), first published in 1797; and G. J. Bell, *Commentaries on the Mercantile Law of Scotland* (7th ed., 1870), first published in 1800. These may be regarded as potentially decisive in the absence of legislation or clear precedent, but only in those areas of law where social change over the intervening period has not diminished their persuasiveness (see, for example, *S.* v. *H.M. Advocate* 1989 S.L.T. 469 on marital rape). A comprehensive listing of institutional writings, with a succinct appraisal of their current standing, will be found in R. M. White and I. D. Willock, *The Scottish Legal System* (2nd ed., 1999), at pp. 105–108.

REFERENCE BOOKS   8–48

Reference books, such as legal encyclopedias and dictionaries, can be of assistance when beginning the search for information on a subject. D. M. Walker, *The Oxford Companion to Law* (1980), though dated, is a useful source, referring to all manner of legal topics including persons and institutions. As it was written by a professor of law in Glasgow, there is much Scottish material which would not be found in a similar work compiled south of the border.

Encyclopedias   8–49

There is a tradition of comprehensive encyclopedias of Scots law and a landmark in the renaissance of Scottish legal publishing was the publication of the *Laws of Scotland* (8–50), also known by its subtitle of *Stair Memorial Encyclopaedia*. The three editions of the *Encyclopaedia of the laws of Scotland* edited by Chisholm (1896–1904 and 1909–14) and Dunedin (1926–35) are still occasionally of use.

Laws of Scotland   8–50
This is an essential component of legal research and probably the single most important starting point for ascertaining the law of Scotland on a given subject. The main body of the work was published between 1987 and 1996 and consists of subject "titles" organised alphabetically into 25 bound volumes. Each volume has tables of legislation and cases, and an index subdivided by the individual titles in that volume. A programme of issuing revised titles began in 1999 and these are published as separate booklets to be filed in looseleaf *Reissue* binders. Each reissued title has its own tables and index. It is important to note that some reorganisation of the original title scheme has taken place. An annual *Cumulative Supplement* updates the individual titles and the various tables, though it may exclude titles to be reissued in the near future. This in turn is updated by a looseleaf *Service* volume with two releases a year, but there is no new commentary. A *Consolidated Index* (1997) merges the title indexes published in the original volumes, with some revision, but has not been updated. However the *Consolidated Tables of Statutes etc* (1996) and *Consolidated Table of Cases* (2000) are updated by the *Cumulative Supplement* and the *Service* volume.

An online version of the encyclopedia is available through Butterworths *Scotland Direct* service (at **www.butterworths.co.uk**).

8–51   **How to use the Laws of Scotland**
To research a subject:

(a) Identify the title or titles that may be relevant. If you are adopting a "broad brush" approach, this can be done by consulting the complete list provided in the *Cumulative Supplement* and then examining the table of contents or index to the individual title selected. If the query is more specific, consult the *Consolidated Index*. Remember to check the *Reissue* binders to see if a revised version has been published and note that the *Consolidated Index* does not cover reissued titles.

(b) Check the entry for the title in the current *Cumulative Supplement* to see if there has been any updating. This will also draw attention to titles which have been reissued or are no longer in use.

(c) Check the entry for the title in the *Service* volume to see if there has been any recent legislation or case law which may have had an effect. Note that reissued titles are treated in a separate section at the back of the volume.

To research legislation:

(a) Identify references to the Act, statutory instrument or other enactment in the encyclopedia by consulting the *Consolidated Table of Statutes etc.*

(b) Check for more recent references in the tables of legislation in the current *Cumulative Supplement* and the *Service* volume.

To research a case:

(a) Identify references to the case in the encyclopedia by consulting the *Consolidated Table of Cases.*

(b) Check for more recent references in the tables of cases in the current *Cumulative Supplement* and the *Service* volume.

Remember that references are to paragraph numbers and not to page numbers. In the original bound volumes the paragraphs are numbered consecutively throughout each volume, but in reissued titles the paragraphs are numbered consecutively within each title. The *Cumulative Supplement* and *Service* volume are organised by reference to the paragraphs in the original volumes or, if appropriate, in the reissued titles. The tables of legislation and cases distinguish between original and reissued titles by referring to the one by volume number and the other by an abbreviation, *e.g.* Admn for Administrative Law.

The online version presents the text from the original or reissued title in split-screen format, with updating material in the lower part. With monthly updating, this is clearly more current than the information in the *Service* volume. However this means that sections of narrative which have been added or substituted are not integrated; for an online service this seems a missed opportunity and may confuse the unwary. The user can select the appropriate title and then navigate through a hierarchical menu which functions as the table of contents, or perform a search for a word or words either in a specific title or throughout the encyclopedia. References to cases can be located with relative ease by searching on the names of the parties, *e.g.* "Donoghue Stevenson" as words in any order in the same paragraph or "Donoghue v Stevenson" as words next to each other in order; it is important to note that the search engine does not recognise punctuation marks. References to Acts can be located by searching on the short title, and references to statutory instruments by searching on the title or the citation, *e.g.* "1977/1877". However pinpointing a specific provision, *e.g.* a section of an Act or a particular regulation, may prove more challenging. Hypertext links permit the user to follow up references to other parts of the *Laws of Scotland* and, if authorised, to certain other Butterworths Direct services.

Specialised Encyclopedias and Looseleaf Works

8–52

The number of Scottish looseleaf works is growing; some are also available on CD-ROM and may in time migrate to online services. Examples include *Butterworths Scottish Family Law Service* and the *Scottish Planning Encyclopedia*. *Green's Litigation Styles* and *Green's Practice Styles* are a valuable source of precedents (or "styles") for drafting legal documents. The *Encyclopaedia of Scottish Legal Styles* (1935–40) may occasionally be of use. The *Parliament House Book* is a compendium of primary and delegated legislation covering private law and court procedure. It includes practice notes, solicitors' rules, guidance notes and other information that can be hard to find. There is a limited amount of annotation. Sections may be reprinted and issued separately, *e.g. Green's Family Law Statutes*, and some have evolved into independent works, *e.g. Renton and Brown's Criminal Procedure Legislation*. Some of the English looseleaf works, *e.g. Palmer's Company Law*, have Scottish editors and take account of any differences in the law, but it is always advisable to check.

Dictionaries

8–53

The newcomer to law will be aided by J. A. Beaton, *Scots Law Terms and Expressions* (1982); A. G. M. Duncan, *Green's Glossary of Scottish Legal Terms* (3rd ed., 1992); or the *Glossary* which forms part of the *Laws of Scotland* and was published separately in 1992. The classic works remain W. Bell, *Dictionary and Digest of the Law of Scotland* (7th ed., 1890) and J. Trayner, *Latin maxims* (4th ed., 1894), reprinted in 1993. W. J. Stewart, *Scottish contemporary judicial dictionary of words and phrases* (1995) is a dictionary of the English language as it has been interpreted in the Scottish courts.

Directories

8–54

Two annual directories, the *Scottish Law Directory* (often known as the *White Book*) and the Law Society of Scotland's *Blue Book*, contain useful addresses and other information and will help trace an individual or a firm of solicitors. In addition, the larger Scottish practices are included in the *Legal 500*. The website of the Law Society of Scotland (at **www.lawscot.org.uk**) has searchable directories of solicitors, firms and accredited specialists and is a source of other information on Scots law.

TEXTBOOKS

8–55

W. Green (Sweet & Maxwell) and Butterworths are the main players in Scottish legal textbook publishing, though occasionally books are produced by the smaller independents such as Cavendish.

H. L. MacQueen, *Studying Scots Law* (2nd ed., 1999) is aimed primarily at those contemplating entry into the legal profession. R. M. White and I. D. Willock, *The Scottish Legal System* (2nd ed., 1999) is a useful alternative to D. M. Walker's long-established work with the same title (8th ed., 2001). W. M. Gloag and R. C. Henderson, *The Law of*

Scotland (11th ed., 2001) has long been a standard in universities, while E. A. Marshall, *General Principles of Scots Law* (7th ed., 1999) and N. Busby *et al.*, *Scots Law: a student guide* (2000) are favoured by those pursuing non-law degree courses. A. A. Paterson and T. St. J. N. Bates, *The Legal System of Scotland: Cases and Materials* (4th ed., 1999) is an important adjunct to any of the above.

Scottish legal publishing is in a healthy state with up to date textbooks in most subject areas. Due to the restricted size of the market, many older books tried to serve student, academic and practitioner, but there is now a better mix of introductory works, professional publications and scholarly tomes.

The Scottish Universities Law Institute (SULI) has promoted a distinguished series of texts on modern Scots law, *e.g.* F. P. Davidson, *Arbitration* (2000). These are generally regarded as the standard works in their respective areas. The Stair Society, founded in 1934 to encourage the study and advance the knowledge of the history of Scots law, makes valuable material available through its publications. *An Introductory Survey of the Sources and Literature of Scots Law* (1936) and *An Introduction to Scottish Legal History* (1958) are still convenient for information on older sources.

There is a growing body of literature on the new arrangements for the governance of Scotland, *e.g.* J. McFadden and M. Lazarowicz, *The Scottish Parliament: an introduction* (2nd ed., 2000) and C. M. G. Himsworth and C. R. Munro, *The Scotland Act 1998* (2nd ed., 2000).

The publication of new law books is noted by *Current Law Monthly Digest* and *Current Law Yearbook* under an appropriate subject heading and in a separate list arranged alphabetically by author.

8–56   PERIODICALS

As previously noted, the *Scots Law Times* includes news items, articles and book reviews. This section is cited as S.L.T. (News) which may belie the importance of the contributions from academic writers and practising lawyers. The annual bound volumes contain an index to the News section but it is not covered by the consolidated *Index*. Nor is the News section available in electronic format. The *Journal of the Law Society of Scotland* and the *Scottish Law Gazette* combine articles with professional news while *SCOLAG Legal Journal*, published by the Scottish Legal Action Group, has a crusading streak. The *Juridical Review*, *Scottish Law and Practice Quarterly* and the *Edinburgh Law Review* are more academic in character. A *Centenary Index* to the *Juridical Review* covers articles published between 1889 and 1988. *Scottish Planning and Environmental Law* and a series of bulletins published by W. Green, *e.g. Green's Business Law Bulletin*, provide surveys of current law and procedure.

All the above are covered by *Legal Journals Index* (**5–4**) in print form (1986–99 only), on CD-ROM (*Current Legal Information*), and on the internet (*Current Legal Information* and Westlaw UK). *Scottish Current Law Yearbook* also indexed articles. A consolidated index for 1947–56 appeared in the 1956 master volume, but thereafter it is necessary to use the annual indexes. *Current Law Yearbook* indexed articles until 1997.

8–57   SCOTTISH PARLIAMENT PUBLICATIONS

Within a relatively short time the Scottish Parliament has produced a substantial body of official publications. Not all law libraries will have a comprehensive collection, but it is worth noting that one in eight public libraries in Scotland has been designated a "partner library" and acts as a focal point for parliamentary information. The official website (at **www.scottish.parliament.uk**) represents a source for everyone with access to the internet, reflecting the Scottish Parliament's commitment to information and communications technologies as a vehicle for the promotion of openness, accountability and democratic participation.

Bills   8–58

As in the U.K. Parliament, a Bill is a draft version of an Act. Bills are published by The Stationery Office (TSO) and appear on the Scottish Parliament website. The majority of Bills will be Public Bills, introduced directly by a Member of the Scottish Parliament (MSP), and there are three main types. If the MSP is a member of the Scottish Executive, the Bill is known as an Executive Bill. A Committee Bill is one introduced on behalf of a committee of the Parliament, and a Member's Bill is one introduced by an MSP acting as an individual. A Private Bill may be promoted by an individual, a corporate body or an unincorporated association. Private legislation was the subject of a report by the Procedures Committee in November 2000 (*SP Paper* 204) which contained many recommendations. One notable effect was that the Parliament's Standing Orders were amended to permit the lodging of a Private Bill at any point in the parliamentary session (originally there had been only two opportunities a year). Such Bills are subject to substantially different procedures, fully described in *Guidance on Private Bills* (2001).

Stages in the passage of a Bill   8–59
Bills pass through three stages in the unicameral Parliament. The exact stage which any Bill has reached can be determined by consulting *What's Happening in the Scottish Parliament* (**8–61**) or the Parliamentary Business section of the official website. *Guidance on Public Bills* (1999), prepared by the Parliament's Clerking Services Directorate and published by TSO, provides more detailed information on procedure.

  (a) Stage 1—the general principles of the Bill are considered in committee and then debated in the Parliament. According to the subject matter of the Bill, one of the 17 all-purpose committees will have been designated the "lead committee", but other committees may also consider it and report to the lead committee. If the vote at the end of the Stage 1 debate is in favour of the Bill, it proceeds to Stage 2 and it is open to MSPs to lodge amendments. If the vote is not in favour, the Bill falls.
  (b) Stage 2—the details of the Bill are considered in committee and proposed amendments are accepted or rejected. Once this stage is completed it is open to MSPs to lodge further amendments.
  (c) Stage 3—the Bill is debated in the Parliament and proposed amendments are accepted or rejected. Finally there is a vote on whether to pass the Bill.

   If the Bill is passed, there follows a period of four weeks during which it is subject to legal challenge. The Advocate General for Scotland, the Lord Advocate and the Attorney General may refer questions of legislative competence to the Judicial Committee of the Privy Council. The Secretary of State for Scotland may also challenge the provisions of the Bill on certain statutory grounds. If a challenge is successful, the Parliament may resolve to reconsider contested provisions in proceedings similar to those at Stage 3 (known as the Reconsideration Stage). If there is no challenge, the Presiding Officer (the equivalent of the Speaker of the House of Commons) submits the Bill for Royal Assent and it will become an Act of the Scottish Parliament.

Bills are submitted for introduction with various accompanying documents: a statement from the Presiding Officer stating that its provisions are within the legislative competence of the Parliament; a financial memorandum estimating the costs to which its provisions will give rise; and an Auditor General's report if it contains any provision charging expenditure on the Scottish Consolidated Fund. In addition, Executive Bills are accompanied by: explanatory notes which summarise what each of the provisions does and explain the overall effect; and a policy memorandum which sets out the Scottish Executive's policy objectives, justifies the approach taken to meet those objectives, details what prior consultation took place and assesses the overall effect.

8–60 Citation of Bills

Bills and accompanying documents are printed by TSO in preparation for proceedings at Stage 1, and reprinted with revisions as required. As there is a hiatus between the passing of a Bill and its appearance as an Act, this includes the text as passed. Amendments moved at Stages 2 and 3 are published in the *Business Bulletin* (**8–65**) as they are lodged, and drawn together into "marshalled lists" before consideration. Each Bill is allocated a serial number which it retains throughout its passage, an alphabetical suffix indicating that revisions have been made, *e.g.*:

SP Bill 18   the Transport (Scotland) Bill as introduced;
SP Bill 18A   the Transport (Scotland) Bill as amended at Stage 2;
SP Bill 18B   the Transport (Scotland) Bill as passed.

The serial number appears in the bottom left-hand corner of the first page, with the session and calendar year shown at the right. Accompanying documents and marshalled lists of amendments are linked to the relevant version of the Bill, *e.g.*:

SP Bill 18-PM   the policy memorandum;
SP Bill 18-EN   the explanatory notes and other accompanying documents;
SP Bill 18-ML6   the sixth marshalled list of amendments for Stage 2;
SP Bill 18A-ML   the marshalled list of amendments selected for Stage 3.

A Bill may be cited by its number and short title, an indication of the version, the session number and the calendar year in which that version was published, *e.g.* SP Bill 18 Transport (Scotland) Bill [as introduced] Session 1 (2000).

8–61 Tracing current Bills

What's Happening in the Scottish Parliament (*WHISP*) has a Bills section, recording the short and long titles and the number of the Bill, indicating the M.S.P. who introduced it and the lead committee, and providing a full timetable of the Bill's progress. The official website hosts an electronic version of *WHISP*, while the full text of the various versions of Bills, marshalled lists of amendments and accompanying documents is available in the Parliamentary Business section. TSO's *Daily List* notes the bibliographic details of Bills and other Scottish Parliament publications. Basic information on the parliamentary progress of Bills is available in *Current Law Monthly Digest* and *Current Legal Information*. Lawtel (at **www.lawtel.co.uk**) also provides links to the full text of Bills and accompanying documents. Plenary debates and committee discussions on the Bill are published in the *Official Report* (**8–64**) and reports from committees appear in the series of *SP Papers* (**8–63**).

Tracing older Bills   8–62

An interesting innovation is the *Passage of the Bill* series which is intended to provide an authoritative record of proceedings leading to the enactment of every Act of the Scottish Parliament. Each volume gathers together all the versions of a Bill, the accompanying documents, marshalled lists of amendments, committee reports, and relevant extracts from the *Official Report*. This will be a very convenient source for those seeking to understand the background to a particular Act. The annotations to the version of an Act published in *Current Law Statutes* include information on the progress of the original Bill. The Scottish Parliament website retains an archive of enacted, fallen and withdrawn Bills.

Papers   8–63

Committee reports and other important documents laid before the Parliament are published by The Stationery Office in the *SP Papers* series. These are numbered consecutively within the parliamentary session and the serial number appears in the bottom left-hand corner of the cover and first page, with the session and calendar year shown at the right, *e.g.* SP Paper 171 Session 1 (2000). Papers are listed by committee or as miscellaneous publications in the Bibliography section of *WHISP*; this information cumulates throughout the parliamentary term. The bibliography is eventually superseded by the biannual *Scottish Parliamentary and Statutory Publications* which lists papers in numerical order and provides a subject index. Electronic versions are distributed across the official website, committee reports being accessed via the pages relating to that committee. The *Daily List* notes the bibliographic details of Papers and other Scottish Parliament publications. Abstracts appear in *Current Legal Information* and the current awareness section of Westlaw UK (at **www.westlaw.co.uk**).

Official Report   8–64

This substantially verbatim report of proceedings in the Parliament is published in three parts, covering the plenary debates, the committee discussions held in public and written answers respectively. An unrevised report of a full meeting of the Parliament is published on the following working day. The report of a committee meeting will always be available before the next meeting of that committee. The written answers report appears weekly. The plan to publish revised and indexed bound volumes of the *Official Report* has been abandoned in favour of an archive edition on CD-ROM. This is to be issued approximately three times a year. The unrevised and (later) the definitive versions of the text are also available on the official website. As with *Hansard*, each column (rather than each page) of the *Official Report* is numbered, and debates are cited by reference to these column numbers, *e.g.* SP OR 9. 20 December 2000, col 1164. The use of volume and part numbers was discontinued in April 2001 and the citation simplified accordingly. A reference to the committee series incorporates the official abbreviation for that committee, *e.g.* SP OR TE 22 November 2000, col 1255. However the written answers report is not set in columns and is therefore cited by page number, *e.g.* SP WA 14 March 2001, p. 186. Again volume and part numbers are no longer used.

Other parliamentary publications   8–65

For information on the current, future and past business of the Parliament, the *Business Bulletin* is a prime source. Published daily it includes: announcements; the programme of business; agendas of committee meetings; oral and written questions; motions and amendments to Bills; information on Bills and other documents; petitions; and an overview of the progress of parliamentary business. The *Minutes of Proceedings* is a formal record of the decisions made. *What's Happening in the Scottish Parliament* (*WHISP*) is compiled by the Scottish Parliament Information Centre (SPICe) and published each week that the Parliament is sitting. It is probably the single most useful publication on the activities of the Parliament and the documentation it generates. Regular features include: an overview of forthcoming and recent business; lists of Bills, papers and petitions; lists of SPICe research publications; and lists of other parliamentary publications. The lists cumulate throughout the parliamentary term. Occasional features include: profiles of M.S.P.s; profiles of committees; profiles of Scottish regions and parliamentary constituencies. A cumulative index is published at the end of the parliamentary year, with interim cumulations at the end of each term. Miscellaneous publications include procedural guides, *e.g. Detailed Guidance on Parliamentary Questions* (2001), and SPICe's research papers, *e.g. Freedom of Information in Scotland* (2000). These are all available in print or on the Scottish Parliament website.

8–66 ## SCOTTISH EXECUTIVE PUBLICATIONS

U.K. official publications are covered in Chapter 6. The range of publications emanating from the Scottish Executive reflects its responsibility for all devolved matters. The majority are published and/or sold by The Stationery Office (TSO) in Edinburgh, and should be available on the Scottish Executive website (at **www.scotland.gov.uk**). Circulars and consultation papers are only available from the appropriate department of the Executive.

Many papers are laid before the Scottish Parliament and these are numbered sequentially, *e.g.* SE/2000/45. Some are laid before both the U.K. and Scottish parliaments, and these display a Command Paper (Cm.) number and an SE number. Laid papers will not be available on the Scottish Executive website unless they were prepared by one of its departments; however they may be freely available on another site and the public sector information website (at **www.ukonline.gov.uk**) acts as a gateway with alphabetical indexes of central and local government services and a search facility.

The Central Research Unit (CRU), which forms part of the Justice Department, investigates a broad spectrum of socio-legal and other issues on behalf of the Scottish Executive and allied agencies such as the Crown Office. Its *Research Findings* are available free in print and on the CRU section of the Executive website (at **www.scotland.gov.uk/cru**), while full reports are sold by TSO and may also be on the website.

The Executive's Library and Information Service produces an annual *Scottish Executive Publications List* in hard copy and on the website; publications are arranged by the issuing department, with separate sections for consultation papers and circulars, and there is an index. The biannual *Scottish Parliamentary and Statutory Publications* lists laid papers in numerical order.

8–67 ## OTHER IMPORTANT PUBLICATIONS

The sources of information directly or indirectly related to the study of law are legion. These are just some which may be of use or interest.

Law Reform

8–68

The Scottish Law Commission was established in 1965 to promote reform of the law of Scotland. It issues very useful discussion papers, usually followed by reports proposing changes to particular aspects of the law. Such reports are now laid before the Scottish Parliament by the Scottish Ministers, and are accordingly Scottish Executive publications. Some are published jointly with the Law Commission in England and therefore are also published as Command Papers or House of Commons Papers (**6–3**). Annual reports list recent publications and indicate which proposals have been implemented. The Commission's website (at **www.scotlawcom.gov.uk**) includes the full text of discussion papers and reports from late 2000 onwards.

Statistics

8–69

The Scottish Executive publishes criminal statistics through its *Statistical Bulletin: Criminal Justice Series*. Individual issues focus on particular topics, *e.g.* criminal proceedings in Scottish courts, motor vehicle offences, prisons and recorded crime. These are sold on behalf of the Executive by The Stationery Office (TSO) bookshop in Edinburgh, and are also available on the Justice section of the Scottish Executive website (at **www.scotland.gov.uk**). Statistics on juvenile justice and the Children's Hearings system were previously published as part of the *Statistical Bulletin: Social Work Series*, but publication was suspended in 1997. However the Scottish Children's Reporter Administration intends to remedy this in the near future. Statistics relating to the business of the civil courts and legal and public departments, compiled by the Scottish Executive Justice Department (and previously by the Scottish Courts Administration), are published annually by TSO as *Civil Judicial Statistics, Scotland*. Statistics are often an important feature of annual reports (**8–70**).

A wider portal to the world of Scottish statistics is provided by the Statistics section of the Executive website (at **www.scotland.gov.uk/stats**).

Annual Reports

8–70

Virtually all Scottish government and public bodies publish annual reports, and many are also available in electronic form, *e.g.* the Crown Office and Procurator Fiscal Service (at **www.crownoffice.gov.uk**), the Scottish Committee of the Council on Tribunals (at **www.council-on-tribunals.gov.uk**), the Scottish Court Service (at **www.scotcourts.gov.uk**), the Scottish Criminal Cases Review Commission (at **www.sccrc.co.uk**), the Scottish Law Commission (at **www.scotlawcom.gov.uk**), the Scottish Legal Aid Board (at **www.slab.org.uk**), the Scottish Legal Services Ombudsman (**at www.scot-legal-ombud.org.uk**), the Scottish Prison Service (at **www.sps.gov.uk**) and the Police (at **www.scottish.police.uk**).

Continuing Education

8–71

The papers from all the seminars and conferences organised as part of the Law Society of Scotland's Update programme are published and represent a useful source of information, particularly for practitioners. They may be purchased direct from the Law Society's headquarters in Edinburgh.

9 | Northern Ireland Law

INTRODUCTION

Throughout Northern Ireland's existence as a political entity, legislation in a number of key areas has taken a form which applies exclusively to Northern Ireland. Some of this legislation has been passed by its own Parliament, or now Assembly. A great deal of the legislation has originated in Westminster, either as an Act of Parliament, or much more commonly, as delegated legislation. The key areas include health and social services, education, planning and the environment, industrial development and agriculture. To take some examples from education law: the main provisions of the Education Reform Act 1998 did not apply to Northern Ireland, but were instead duplicated in the Education Reform (N.I.) Order 1999. When the Labour government introduced its School Standards and Framework Act 1998, similar proposals for Northern Ireland where included in the Education (N.I.) Order 1998. Post-war education reforms were introduced in Northern Ireland by the Education Act (N.I.) 1947. Education is now one of the areas for which the Northern Ireland Assembly can legislate, and it is intended that future legislation in this area will take the form of Acts of the Northern Ireland Assembly. These may or may not follow the precedent set by Westminster.

However, legislation applying exclusively to Northern Ireland forms only part of the picture. A great deal of legislation passed in Westminster applies to Northern Ireland in just the same way as it does to the rest of the United Kingdom. Legislation in the areas of general taxation, foreign policy and intellectual property would be examples. The Capital Allowances Act 2001 for example, applies completely to Northern Ireland. Other legislation may apply in part, *e.g.* the Learning and Skills Act 2000. Usually, the last or penultimate section of a recent Act will tell you whether it applies to Northern Ireland.

If the law which interests you applies in Northern Ireland as it does in the rest of the United Kingdom, you will need to use the resources described in Chapters 3 to 7 of this book to find a statement of that law. If you discover that a particular Westminster Act does *not* apply to Northern Ireland, use the editions of statutes and finding aids described in the rest of this chapter. You will now need to discover what the law might be in Northern Ireland. The case law of the courts of Northern Ireland is also relevant and indexes and databases covering Northern Ireland case law are noted in **9–9**.

For a general introduction to the legal system, read Brice Dickson's *The Legal System of Northern Ireland* (4th ed., 2001). The constitutional background to legislation in Northern Ireland is described in the following section.

9-2 THE CONSITUTIONAL BACKGROUND

Northern Ireland came into being in 1921. Its Parliament could legislate on a range of transferred matters and these became the areas in which Northern Ireland built up its own statute book. Although the transferred powers were not listed in the Government of Ireland Act 1920, which established the jurisdiction, the Act did list excepted and reserved matters, on which only the Westminster Parliament could legislate. The Northern Ireland (Stormont) Parliament had the power to legislate on all other matters. As a result, in the period following its first meeting in 1921, until 1972, it was the Stormont Parliament which legislated on matters of law and order, local government, health and social services, education, planning, internal trade, industrial development and agriculture. For the most part the Stormont Parliament legislated along the same lines as Westminster during this period, though it did not always follow changes introduced in Westminster and introduced new legislation of its own. By convention, the Westminster Parliament did not legislate for Northern Ireland on transferred matters. This, and the duplication of the Westminster model of a Prime Minister and bi-cameral Parliament, gave Northern Ireland the appearance of being a semi-autonomous province, even a mini state, within the United Kingdom.

Following the suspension of executive powers and the proroguing of the Northern Ireland Parliament in 1972, previously transferred matters were legislated for by means of Orders in Council. Technically a form of delegated legislation, they constituted what, for the rest of the United Kingdom, would have been primary legislation and were given both a Statutory Instrument number and a Northern Ireland chapter number, *e.g.* the Children (N.I.) Order 1995, S.I. 1995/755 (N.I.2). Again, this Northern Ireland legislation tended to keep in step with legislation for the rest of the U.K., though as before, Northern Ireland did not always follow legislative changes made for the rest of the United Kingdom. Although Orders in Council were used for the vast majority of previously transferred matters, a small amount of key legislation took the form of Acts of the Westminster Parliament. Legislation created in this way could then receive the full Parliamentary debate denied to Orders in Council. The Fair Employment (Northern Ireland) Act 1989 is a significant example.

Direct rule lasted from 1972 until 1999, with the exception of the first five months of 1974, when again a system of devolution operated. The then Northern Ireland Assembly, set up under the Northern Ireland Constitution Act 1974, passed four Measures (not Acts), before being prorogued following the collapse of the so-called "power-sharing" Executive. An experiment in "rolling devolution" also lead to the creation of an Assembly under the Northern Ireland Act 1982. This time, full legislative devolution did not occur. The Assembly met from 1983 until 1986.

The Northern Ireland Act 1998, which followed the Belfast (or "Good Friday") Agreement, once again established a legislative Assembly, and again used the terminology of excepted, reserved and transferred matters introduced by the Government of Ireland Act 1920. The excepted matters listed in Schedule 2 to the 1998 Act include, for example, taxes, trade and immigration and asylum law. Reserved matters listed in Schedule 3 include public order, policing and criminal law. The Assembly can only legislate on these reserved matters with the consent of the Secretary of State for Northern Ireland and Westminster. The draft Life Sentences (N.I.) Order 2001 continues the system of legislating by Orders in Council in a reserved area. A Westminster Act was used for the Police (N.I.) Act 2000. The Assembly has powers to legislate in the transferred areas of health and social services, education, planning and the environment, industrial development and agriculture.

The brief suspension of the current Executive in early 2000 meant a reversion to Orders in Council for a few matters, but the first Act of the current phase of devolution received the Royal Assent in February of that year. This was the Financial Assistance for Political Parties Act (Northern Ireland) 2000.

LEGISLATION

9–3

The statute law which affects, or has affected, Northern Ireland comes from more than one source and in more than one form. Post-1921 statute law has already been mentioned. The full list is as follows:

(a) Acts passed by the Irish Parliament in Dublin from 1310 to 1800,
   e.g. Sale of Cattle Act (Ireland) 1703.
(b) Acts passed by the Parliaments of England (1226 to 1707) and Great Britain (1707 to 1800) and by the United Kingdom Parliament thereafter,
   e.g. Public Processions (Northern Ireland) Act 1998.
(c) Acts passed by the Parliament of Northern Ireland from 1921 to March 1972,
   e.g. Wild Birds Protection Act (Northern Ireland) 1931.
(d) Orders in Council made in 1972 and 1973 under section 1(3) of the Northern Ireland (Temporary Provisions) Act 1972,
   e.g. Education and Libraries (Northern Ireland) Order 1972.
(e) Measures passed by the Northern Ireland Assembly in 1974,
   e.g. Financial Provisions Measure (Northern Ireland) 1974.
(f) Orders in Council made from 1974 to 1999 under paragraph 1 of Schedule 1 to the Northern Ireland Act 1974,
   e.g. Water (Northern Ireland) Order 1999.
(g) Acts passed by the Northern Ireland Assembly from 2000 onwards,
   e.g. Electronic Communications Act (Northern Ireland) 2001.

Sometimes it is possible to tell by the date whether an Act was passed at Westminster, Dublin or Northern Ireland. However, a more useful indicator of the source is generally the position of the words "Ireland" or "Northern Ireland" in relation to the word "Act". As can be seen from the examples used above, if "Ireland" or "Northern Ireland" in the title comes before "Act", the source is Westminster, *e.g.*

   the Bills of Exchange (Ireland) Act 1828
   the Fair Employment (Northern Ireland) Act 1989.

If "Ireland" appears after "Act", and directly before the date, the source is Dublin, *e.g.*

   The Landlord and Tenant Act (Ireland) 1741

If "Northern Ireland" appears after "Act", and directly before the date, the source is either the Northern Ireland Parliament or the Northern Ireland Assembly, *e.g.*

   Factories Act (Northern Ireland) 1949
   Ground Rents Act (Northern Ireland) 2001

9–4 Editions of Statutes

The statute law of Northern Ireland has been published in various forms. *The Statutes, Measures and Orders in Council of Northern Ireland* were published by HMSO, Belfast, singly at first and later in annual bound volumes from 1921 to 1981 and in looseleaf binders after that date (as *The Northern Ireland Statutes*). The Northern Ireland legislation page of the HMSO website (at **www.northernireland-legislation.hmso.gov.uk**) includes links to Northern Ireland Orders in Council from 1987 onwards. TSO Belfast has published Acts of the current Assembly singly from 2000, and like the more recent Orders in Council, these are available from the Northern Ireland legislation page of the HMSO website (see illustation on page 181). There have also been significant editions of the revised text of legislation affecting Northern Ireland, published first in 1956 and then in 1982.

The *Statutes Revised Northern Ireland* (2nd ed.), published in 1982, reprinted legislation in force in Northern Ireland on March 31, 1981 in 12 looseleaf binders. The Acts or sections of Acts or Orders in force on that date are printed, together with a note of any repealing legislation. Volumes A–D cover all pre-1921 legislation from whatever source and include Acts of the Dublin Parliament along with Westminster Acts. Volumes 1–6 cover Acts of the Northern Ireland Parliament, Volumes 7–8, Orders in Council from 1973 to 1981. Post-1920 Westminster Acts are omitted. There has been no further edition of *The Statutes Revised*, and so for the period after 1981, you need to use the legislation published in the looseleaf binders of *The Northern Ireland Statutes*. These binders match those of *The Statutes Revised* but differ from *The Statutes Revised,* in that they contain the text of post-1981 legislation as published. Acts of the Northern Ireland Assembly are now included in the *Northern Ireland Statutes* binders.

TSO Belfast publishes a cumulative supplement to *The Statutes Revised*, listing the sources of amendments, repeals, etc., which have occurred since 1981 to the legislation printed in both *The Statutes Revised* and the subsequent *Northern Ireland Statutes*. The last appeared in 2001 as *The Statutes Revised Northern Ireland: Cumulative supplement to 31 December 2000.*

Your library may also keep bound volumes of all Northern Ireland legislation as originally published along with *The Statutes Revised*, so that library users can find the full unamended text of pre-1982 legislation. The most comprehensive edition of the statutes of the Dublin Parliament 1310 to 1800 is *The Statutes at Large Passed in the Parliaments Held in Ireland from AD 1310 to 1786 inclusive* (13 volumes), continued to 1800 in seven additional volumes, printed in Dublin by George Grierson, 1786 to 1810.

The BAILII website (at **www.bailii.org**) has made the text of *The Statutes Revised Northern Ireland* (2nd ed.) available in a straightforward alphabetical arrangement. However, the notes of repealing and amending legislation carried in *The Statutes Revised Northern Ireland: Cumulative Supplement* are absent. BAILII presents the legislative picture as it was in 1981.

9–5 Delegated Legislation

The rules, regulations and orders made by Northern Ireland rule-making authorities are called *statutory rules and orders* (S.R. & O.s) up to the end of 1973 and *statutory rules* (S.R.s) thereafter. *Statutory rules* from 1991 onwards are available from the HMSO Northern Ireland legislation web pages (at **www.northernireland-legislation.hmso.gov.uk**), listed by year and number. The print versions, now published by TSO in Belfast, occupy two or more bound volumes per year. Annual indexes are available

Acts of the Assembly on the HMSO website

Acts of the Northern Ireland Assembly   http://www.northernireland-legisl...ation/northernireland/ni-acts.ht

Acts of the
Northern Ireland
Assembly

All Acts of the Northern Ireland Assembly will be published in full text
form on the Internet and will be accessible from this Web page. They will
appear as originally enacted by the Northern Ireland Assembly.

The aim is to publish these documents on the Internet simultaneously or at
least within 24 hours of their publication in printed form. However, any
document which is especially complex in terms of its size or its
typography may take longer to prepare.

The search engine has been designed to help identify the document that
you wish to browse and will search the text of all documents on this site.

2000

- Financial Assistance for Political Parties Act (Northern Ireland)
  2000 c.1

- Appropriation Act (Northern Ireland) 2000 c.2

- Allowances to Members of the Assembly Act (Northern Ireland)
  2000 c.3

- Child Support, Pensions and Social Security Act (Northern
  Ireland) 2000 c.4

- Weights and Measures (Amendment) Act (Northern Ireland)
  2000 c.5

2001

- Dogs (Amendment) Act (Northern Ireland) 2001 c.1

- Planning (Compensation, etc.) Act (Northern Ireland) 2001 c.2

- Health and Personal Social Services Act (Northern Ireland)
  2001 c.3

- Fisheries (Amendment) Act (Northern Ireland) 2001 c.4

- Ground Rents Act (Northern Ireland) 2001 c.5

- Government Resources and Accounts Act (Northern Ireland)
  2001 c.6

- Budget Act (Northern Ireland) 2001 c.7

on publication of the final volume. Recently published *statutory rules* (S.R.s) are listed in the TSO *Daily List* (**6–14**). Later they appear in the monthly and annual editions of the *List of Statutory Instruments together with the List of Statutory Rules of Northern Ireland for* ....

A Westminster statutory instrument applying solely to Northern Ireland can be distinguished from a Northern Ireland statutory rule by the relative positions of "Northern Ireland" and "Order" or "Regulations". The Legal Aid (Financial Conditions) Regulations (Northern Ireland) 2001 constitutes a Northern Ireland statutory rule, cited as S.R. 2001 No. 111. The Maximum Number of Judges (Northern Ireland) Order 2001 is a statutory instrument, cited as S.I. 2001 No. 958. As noted in **9–2**, Orders in Council are also technically statutory instruments and carry both Northern Ireland chapter numbers and statutory instrument numbers.

9–6 Finding Legislation

Some Northern Ireland legislation constitutes an exact or near-exact enactment of earlier Westminster legislation. The Children (N.I.) Order 1995, for example, largely replicates the provisions of the Children Act 1989. However, there is no sure way of moving from a statement of the law for England and Wales, to the discovery of equivalent legislation for Northern Ireland. In order to be sure of the state of the law in Northern Ireland, you need to use the finding aids available for Northern Ireland legislation.

A chronological approach to the law affecting Northern Ireland is provided by *The Chronological Table of the Statutes of Northern Ireland*, which is constructed in much the same way as the *United Kingdom Chronological Table of the Statutes*, and lists all legislation which affects or has affected Northern Ireland since 1310. The *Table* is published every three years by TSO in Belfast, the last appearing in 1999 as *The Chronological Table of the Statutes Northern Ireland: covering legislation to 31 December 1998*.

A subject approach is provided by the *Index to the Statutes: Northern Ireland*. This two-volume work is constructed in the same way as the *Index to the Statutes* covering U.K. legislation, although it does not use precisely the same subject headings. The *Index* includes references to both Northern Ireland legislation and Westminster Acts under each of its subject headings. All relevant legislation is listed under a main heading followed by a series of subheadings listing the relevant sections or articles of particular Acts or Orders. The *Index* is published by TSO in Belfast, again every three years, the last appearing in 1998 as the *Index to the Statutes Northern Ireland: covering legislation to December 31, 1996*.

The delegated legislation of Northern Ireland can be found using the *Index to the Statutory Rules and Orders of Northern Ireland*, published, like the other indexes, every three years by TSO in Belfast. It was last published in 2001 as the *Index to the Statutory Rules and Orders of Northern Ireland: in force on 31st December 2000 showing the statutory powers under which they were made*.

The availability of Northern Ireland legislation on the HMSO website (see **9–4**) also makes it possible to search for legislation using a keyword search engine. Unfortunately, the search results include all the legislation on the website, making it difficult to trace the legislation specifically relevant to Northern Ireland. *UK Statutory Instruments*, available online from Justis.com (at **www.justis.com**) or on CD-ROM from Context, provides subscribers with an alternative means of keyword searching Orders in Council from 1987 onwards.

A Library subscription to UKOP online (at **www.ukop.co.uk**) will enable keyword searches to be made for legislation by title for the period from 1980 to the present. The TSO websites can also be used to trace legislation by title (see **6–14**).

Checking whether Legislation Is in Force   9–7

The means to check whether Northern Ireland legislation is still in force are relatively limited. The cumulative supplement to the *Statutes Revised Northern Ireland* (**9–4**) shows amendments and repeals to legislation printed in both the *Statutes Revised* and the *Northern Ireland Statutes*. The *Current Law Legislation Citator* (**4–19**) can be used to check amendments to Orders in Council as they appear in the statutory instrument section of the citator.

The *Chronological Table of the Statutes Northern Ireland* (**9–6**) lists the initial amending legislation for a statute where applicable, but can be up to three years out of date. The *Index to the Statutes: Northern Ireland* (**9–6**) lists legislation in force by subject, but again can be up to three years out of date.

LAW REPORTS   9–8

Although the Northern Ireland jurisdiction came into existence in 1921, the Incorporated Council of Law Reporting for Northern Ireland only started publishing the *Northern Ireland Law Reports* in 1925. Reports of cases in the Northern Ireland courts between 1921 and 1924 can be found in the *Irish Reports* and the *Irish Law Times Reports*.

The *Northern Ireland Law Reports* are the official law reports for Northern Ireland. However, because of the inconvenience caused by the time lag before publication of the reports, the *Northern Ireland Law Judgments Bulletin* (which has had several minor changes of title over the years) was produced from 1970 onwards. They are cited as: [year] number N.I.J.B.

The full text of reports from both the *Northern Ireland Law Reports* and the *Northern Ireland Judgments Bulletin* is available online from Lexis-Nexis (**2–7**). The Lexis Northern Ireland cases database also includes unreported Northern Ireland cases. These are transcripts of judgments supplied by the Northern Ireland Court Service. The Court Service also plans to include transcripts of judgments on its own website (at **www.nics.gov.uk/pubsec/courts/courts.htm**). These should be available from late 2001. A selection of cases is available on the BAILII website (at **www.bailii.org**).

Indexes to Law Reports   9–9

Butterworths has published an *Index to Northern Ireland Cases, 1921–1997* in association with the Incorporated Council of Law Reporting for Northern Ireland. It indexes cases reported in both the *Northern Ireland Law Reports* and the *Northern Ireland Judgments Bulletin*. It also includes Northern Ireland cases reported in the *Irish Law Times Reports*, the *Irish Jurist Reports,* the *Irish Reports*, the *Law Reports: Appeal Cases*, the *Criminal Appeal Reports* and *Tax Cases*. The main body of the *Index* lists cases (with headnotes) under alphabetical subject headings (see page 184). Other sections list statutes judicially considered and words and phrases judicially considered.

Index to Northern Ireland Cases, 1921–1997

Subject Index

ELECTORAL LAW
Broadcast

Plaintiff on electoral register for constituency of Foyle — Detained as remand prisoner in Belfast — Whether Chief Electoral Officer had power or duty to provide voting facilities for plaintiff in Belfast — Whether Governor under duty to take plaintiff to his constituency — Electoral Law Act (Northern Ireland) 1962, s 65(6) — Prison Act (Northern Ireland) 1953, s 16(1)

McCartney v Chief Electoral Officer [1984] 14 NIJB

Proposed election broadcast in which certain candidates allocated more time than plaintiff and others — Plaintiff refused consent to broadcast — Whether broadcast unlawful — Whether British Broadcasting Corporation under duty to secure a fair balance — Whether injunction will be granted to restrain broadcast — Representation of the People Act 1969, s 9(1)

McAliskey v British Broadcasting Corporation [1979] 4 NIJB
[1980] NI 44

Illegal Practice

Election expenses — Failure to make statutory return and declaration — Whether through inadvertence or reasonable cause of a like nature — Good faith — Representation of the People Act 1949 (12 & 13 Geo 6, c 68), s 74(3)(d)

In re Devlin NIJB January 1970

Jurisdiction of election court

Local election held under Electoral Law (NI) Order 1972 — Whether election court has jurisdiction to hear petition relating thereto under Electoral Law Act (NI) 1962 (c 14), ss 78, 79(1) — Electoral Law (NI) Order 1972 (SI No 1264 (NI 13)) — Electoral Law (Local General Election 1973) Regulations (NI) 1973 (SR & O (NI) 1973, No 122)

Hutchinson v McCusker [1973] NI 244

Parliament of United Kingdom

Member of Royal Ulster Constabulary — Whether entitled to vote at election for members of Parliament of the United Kingdom — Constabulary (Ir) Act 1836 (6 & 7 Will 4, c 13), s 18 — Constabulary (Ir) Act 1922 (12 & 13 Geo 5, c 55) — Constabulary Act (NI), 1922 (12 & 13 Geo 5, c 8), s 1(3)

Hunter v M Kinley [1923] 2 IR 165

Whether votes for candidate known by electors to have been disqualified to be regarded as null and void — Forfeiture Act 1870 (33 & 34 Vict, c 23), s 2 — Representation of the People Act 1949 (12, 13 & 14 Geo 6, c 68), Part III

In re Mid–Ulster Election Petition [1958] NI 143

In re Fermanagh and South Tyrone Election Petition [1958] NI 151

See also PARLIAMENT OF NORTHERN IRELAND (Electoral law)

The *Index to Cases Decided in the Courts of Northern Ireland and Reported during the period 1921 to 1970*, edited by Desmond Greer and Brian Childs (Incorporated Council of Law Reporting for Northern Ireland, 1975) had previously covered the same range of case reporting as Butterworth's *Index to Northern Ireland Cases, 1921–1997*. It also used the same section headings. The *First Interim Supplement, 1971 to 1975* to the *Index* was published in 1976, a *Second Supplement, 1975–1985*, edited by Robert Miller, was published in 1989.

The *Bulletin of Northern Ireland Law* (**9–17**) digests cases in the official law reports and in the judgments bulletins from 1981 onwards. It has also digested some otherwise unreported cases.

The *Irish Digest* consists of a number of volumes published in Dublin covering the years 1867 onwards. Coverage includes the *Northern Ireland Law Reports*.

Decisions of Tribunals   9–10

The *Northern Ireland Digest of Case-law (NIDOC)*, available free from the Department for Social Development website (at **www.dsdni.gov.uk**), contains both reported and unreported decisions given by Northern Ireland's Social Security and Child Support Commissioners on benefit, child support and compensation recovery appeals. The database contains all decisions from 2000 and most of the important decisions dating back to 1972. Reported decisions are prefixed "R", so that R1/96(IB), for example, represents a reported decision which was the first decision on Incapacity Benefit for 1996. Unreported decisions are prefixed "C".

Reported Northern Ireland Decisions 1978–1999 is also available free on the Department for Social Development website. This is the electronic version of *Reported Decisions of the Social Security Commissioners under the Northern Ireland Family Allowances, Social Security, Industrial Injuries, Child Support and Compensation Recovery Acts and Orders 1978 to 1999*. The print volume is published by TSO. HMSO published a previous volume of decisions in 1978 as *Reported Decisions of the Commissioners under the Family Allowances, National Insurance and Industrial Injuries Acts (N.I.) and the Social Security Acts (N.I.) April 1961 to December 1977*. This volume in turn succeeded the *Reported Decisions of the Umpire under the Family Allowances, National Insurance and Industrial Injuries Acts (N.I.) 1948 to 1961*, published by HMSO in 1963.

Selected decisions of the Fair Employment Tribunal are digested in the *Bulletin of Northern Ireland Law* (see **9–17**). The Fair Employment Commission for Northern Ireland also published *Fair Employment case law: religious and political discrimination in employment* (4th ed., 1999). The Commission's role has now been superseded by the Equality Commission for Northern Ireland.

The *Reports of Decisions of the Industrial Tribunals* were published with a limited circulation from 1966 to 1978. An example of their citation is I.T.R. 135 (N.I.). The reports are no longer published but are held in the Bar Library and are available from the Central Office of Industrial Tribunals. The *Industrial Court (Northern Ireland) Awards* were published between 1963 and 1978.

Reports of appeals to the Lands Tribunal for Northern Ireland are distributed to a number libraries in Northern Ireland and are available on request from the Tribunal.

The *Bulletin* of the Planning Appeals Commission has been published since 1974, and is available from 2000 onwards on the Planning Appeals Commission website (at **www.pacni.gov.uk**). It is issued monthly and contains digests of cases.

9-11 PARLIAMENTARY AND ASSEMBLY PUBLICATIONS

The Parliament of Northern Ireland produced its own Official Report (Hansard) volumes and Parliamentary Papers from 1921 onwards, along the same lines as the Westminster Parliament. These were published by HMSO in Belfast. The Command papers ("Presented by Command of His Excellency the Governor of Northern Ireland") were numbered from Cmd. 1 and cited, for example, as *Higher Education in Northern Ireland Cmd. 475*. There were also *Northern Ireland House of Commons Papers*, numbered from H.C.1 and a small number of Senate Papers, numbered from S.1. The primary reference source for this period is Arthur Maltby's *The Government of Northern Ireland 1922–1972: a Catalogue and Breviate of Parliamentary Papers*, published by the Irish University Press in 1974.

The Northern Ireland Assembly set up under the Northern Ireland Constitution Act 1974 also produced Hansard volumes, again following a Westminster model, and Northern Ireland Assembly Papers were published, numbered N.I.A.1–N.I.A.29. The Northern Ireland Assembly subsequently set up under the Northern Ireland Act 1982 began its Hansard volume numbering at number 4, picking up where the previous Assembly had left off, and Northern Ireland Assembly papers were numbered from N.I.A.30. Unlike other Parliamentary and Assembly papers, these consisted only of reports and minutes of evidence from the Assembly's committees.

The current Northern Ireland Assembly began meeting in September 1998, producing Hansard volumes, this time numbered from volume 1. Assembly papers appeared at this stage numbered N.N.I.A. 1–12, denoting the New Northern Ireland Assembly, as the previous Assembly still had a technical existence prior to the full devolution of powers. Northern Ireland Assembly Papers succeeded these in 1999, numbered from N.I.A.1. The Northern Ireland Assembly Papers, like the Assembly Hansard volumes, are published by The Stationery Office and are available from the Stationery Office Bookshop in Belfast.

The Hansard Official Report can also be found on the Northern Ireland Assembly website (at **www.ni-assembly.gov.uk**). The site also provides access to the full-text of Assembly reports from N.I.A.1 and some of the earlier N.N.I.A. reports.

Some Assembly papers are available on the Assembly website under "Publications" as Assembly reports. A selection of committee reports is also available. These include reports on the committee stages of Northern Ireland Bills, *e.g.* the *Report on the Electronic Communications Bill* (N.I.A. Bill 9/00). The "Minutes of Proceedings" page on the website contains the weekly minutes of proceedings themselves, followed by "Papers presented to the Assembly" and "Northern Ireland Legislation (Assembly)". The last section lists Northern Ireland Bills for the session with a note of the stage each Bill has reached. The Bills themselves are not available on the website. They are published in print by TSO in Belfast.

The *Weekly Information Bulletin* published by TSO for the Assembly also contains lists of Bills before the Assembly, and papers presented to the Assembly. Other sections include a list of Northern Ireland statutory rules with dates for referral to Assembly Committees, notes on Committee business, and contact information for the Assembly.

9–12 # ANNUAL REPORTS AND STATEMENTS OF ACCOUNTS

Between 1922 and 1972, Northern Ireland Parliamentary Papers included the annual reports and statements of accounts of government departments and agencies. Reports published in 1973 and 1974 appeared as Northern Ireland Assembly papers. After 1974 departmental annual reports were published individually for the departments by HMSO and then (for the most part) by TSO. Some agency reports appeared as Westminster House of Commons Papers or Command Papers (see **6–2**). The *Eighteenth Annual Report of the Standing Advisory Committee on Human Rights*, for example, was published as H.C. 1992–93, 739, the *Accounts of the Northern Ireland Housing Executive for the year ended 31 March 1998* were published as Cm. 4268.

From 2000 onwards annual reports of activities and statements of accounts for both government departments and agencies have been published as Northern Ireland Assembly Papers. The *Accounts of the Northern Ireland Housing Executive for the year ended 31 March 2000* were published for the 2000/2001 session as N.I.A. 43/00.

FINDING NORTHERN IRELAND GOVERNMENT PUBLICATIONS

9–13

HMSO (now TSO) in Belfast has acted as publisher for the Northern Ireland Parliament and Assemblies and the various Northern Ireland government departments throughout the existence of Northern Ireland. TSO Belfast publications can be traced through TSO Daily and Weekly Lists and website (see **6–14**). Annual reports of government agencies published as House of Commons or Command Papers can also be traced though TSO sources. The UKOP online database (at **www.ukop.co.uk**) includes Northern Ireland publications along with U.K. government publications generally and allows keyword searches for material published after 1980. Separate lists of Northern Ireland publications were issued by the Belfast HMSO until 1987. However, not all departmental material is published by TSO, and it may be necessary to contact departments directly or refer to their websites. Such material will also include circulars, press releases, etc., which are not otherwise easy to find. Links to the Northern Ireland government departments can be found on the Northern Ireland Executive home page (at **www.northernireland.gov.uk**).

Publications by the Northern Ireland agencies include those of the Equality Commission for Northern Ireland (at **www.equalityni.org**), set up under the Northern Ireland Act 1998, which took over the responsibilities of the Fair Employment Commission, the Equal Opportunities Commission (N.I.), and the Disability Council. The Northern Ireland Act 1998 also established the Northern Ireland Human Rights Commission (at **www.nihrc.org**), which took over from the Standing Advisory Commission on Human Rights. Other significant bodies include the Labour Relations Agency (at **www.lra.org.uk**) and the Northern Ireland Housing Executive (at **www.nihe.gov.uk**).

BOOKS AND PAMPHLETS

9–14

A number of books have been published on the law of Northern Ireland, many by S.L.S. Legal Publications (N.I.), which produces books and pamphlets on various aspects of the

Northern Ireland legal system. It concentrates on areas of Northern Ireland law and practice which differ substantially from that in England and Wales. The current catalogue is found on the S.L.S. website (at **wwwsls.law.qub.ac.uk**). Titles include: Laura Lundy's *Education Law, Policy and Practice in Northern Ireland* (2000), the source of the education law examples used in **9–1**, and Barry Valentine's *Civil Proceedings: the County Court* (1999). S.L.S. also publishes the *Digest of Northern Ireland Law*, a series of booklets designed to provide reliable, practical guidance on Northern Ireland law, and written in a style suitable for those without formal legal training. Thirteen booklets have been published, the most recent being the booklets on *Child Law* (2nd ed., 1996) and *Discrimination Law* (1996).

A small number of books on Northern Ireland law have been produced by other publishers, and these include, for example, John Stannard's *Northern Ireland Criminal procedure: an Introduction* (2000) and *Northern Ireland: Politics and the Constitution* (1992), edited by Brigid Hadfield, which, though outdated, contains useful background articles on constitutional issues.

Various agencies and departments in Northern Ireland publish pamphlets on aspects of the law in Northern Ireland and these include, for example, the Labour Relations Agency (at **www.lra.org.uk**), the Equality Commission for Northern Ireland (at **www.equalityni.org**), the Department of Higher & Further Education, Training & Employment (at **www.northernireland.gov.uk/hfe.htm**) and the Department for Social Development (at **www.dsdni.gov.uk**).

9–15 JOURNALS

The Northern Ireland Legal Quarterly (1936–1961, 1964 onwards), published by S.L.S., is a general legal journal containing articles, notes, comments and book reviews on a wide variety of legal topics. It does not confine itself to Northern Ireland law, but contains articles of worldwide legal interest. From 1993, articles appearing in N.I.L.Q. on European law are indexed in the *European Legal Journals Index*, and not in the *Legal Journals Index*.

The *Gazette of the Incorporated Law Society of Northern Ireland* was published irregularly between 1964 and 1982. It was succeeded by *The Writ; Journal of the Law Society of Northern Ireland* (August 1986 onwards), primarily for members of the Society, but containing items of general interest.

The Law Centre (N.I.) publishes a social welfare law quarterly which was entitled *Welfare Rights News* (Nos 1–21) from December 1983 to April 1991, and is now entitled *Frontline*, published from June 1991 (No. 1) onwards.

Fortnight: an Independent Review, published since 1970, is primarily concerned with local politics and current affairs but frequently contains articles or commentary relevant to the study of the Northern Ireland legal system.

Articles on Northern Ireland law appear, from time to time, in journals published outside Northern Ireland, *e.g.* the articles contained in a special issue of the *Fordham International Law Journal* (volume 22, number 4, 1999), published as an "analysis of the Northern Ireland peace agreement".

9–16 Indexes to Journals

A Bibliography of Periodical Literature Relating to Irish Law by Paul O'Higgins is an invaluable guide to articles published up to 1981. The original volume was published in

1966 and was followed by two supplements in 1973 and 1983. It covers articles in journals published anywhere in the world, non-legal journals, and articles on foreign law by Irish authors.

The *Legal Journals Index*, the *Index to Legal Periodicals*, the *British Humanities Index* and other electronic and print sources mentioned in Chapter 4 frequently contain references to articles on Nothern Ireland law.

THE BULLETIN OF NORTHERN IRELAND LAW   9–17

The *Bulletin of Northern Ireland Law*, published by S.L.S. and appearing 10 times a year, provides a regular, comprehensive digest of legal developments in Northern Ireland and is therefore an invaluable current awareness work. Included under broad subject headings are:

(a) summaries of all new legislation applicable to Northern Ireland with commencement dates.
(b) digests of written judgments and awards in the courts.
(c) selected tribunal decisions and tax cases.
(d) Practice Directions and Court Service notices; and
(e) selected recent developments in Great Britain and the Republic of Ireland and in E.C. law.

(See the figure on p. 190.)

Current Law (**7–11**) uses "Northern Ireland" as one of its subject headings, further subdivided alphabetically by subject.

Example Page from Bulletin of Northern Ireland Law

30   Professional negligence - failure to provide accurate information in house purchase - measure of damages

McBLAIN v McCOLLUM, QBD (Coghlin J), 27 October 2000

The plaintiffs, a married couple, instructed the defendants, a firm of solicitors, in the purchase of a house, which they intended as a long-term home. The price was £90,000. After the completion the plaintiffs discovered that no Building Control Certificate, Final Architect's certificate or National House Building Council warranty had been issued for the house. After a month serious defects became manifest. The plaintiffs had not yet carried out the necessary repairs due to lack of funds and the non-admission of liability but would not have bought the house if they had been aware of the absence of the certificates. On the evidence of experts the market value of the house without the certificates was £60,000. The cost of repairing the defects was £40,000. The defendants admitted liability on the morning of the trial and the judge had to decide quantum of damages.

HELD:

For breach of duty of care to provide accurate information, as opposed to breach of warranty that information is accurate, the damage is the loss caused by the inaccuracy, which the plaintiff has suffered by reason of having entered the transaction on the assumption that it was accurate. The question is 'what loss has he suffered that he would not have suffered of he had not entered the transaction and what element of it is attributable to the inaccuracy?'

The plaintiffs should not be awarded £40,000 damages because that would be the basis of compensation for breach of warranty. They should be awarded £30,000, being the difference in value of the house at the date of purchase. As the plaintiffs have not proved that they intend to leave the house, no damages should be awarded for money expended on the house moving and decoration of the house.

The charges of the expert who examined the defects and assessed the cost of repair is part of the costs of the action. £2,000 was also awarded for the distress and inconvenience in not being able to use some rooms affected by damp.

DISCRIMINATION

31   Disabled persons

DISABILITY DISCRIMINATION ACT 1995 (COMMENCEMENT NO 7) ORDER (NI) 2001 (SR 2001/163)

The Order brings into operation ss 37 and 38 of the Disability Discrimination Act 1995 (noted 95/10/40) on 1 June 2001 in respect of certificates and 1 August 2001 for general purposes.

S 37 of the Act imposes a duty on taxi drivers to carry in their taxis a guide dog, hearing dog or other prescribed category of dog when it accompanies the hirer. It also provides for a taxi driver to be exempted from that duty on medical grounds if a certificate of exemption has been issued to him by the Department of the Environment.

S 38 of the Act provides for a right of appeal against the refusal of the Department to issue certificate of exemption. (£2.00)

32   Equality - proposed legislation - consultation paper

PROMOTING EQUALITY OF OPPORTUNITY - A SINGLE EQUALITY BILL FOR NORTHERN IRELAND, A consultation paper by the Office of the First Minister and Deputy First Minister.

The Office of the First Minister and Deputy First Minister has published an initial consultation paper which describes the present equality framework in NI and seeks views on the scope and content of the proposed Bill for the NI Assembly. The Office is engaged in a primary consultation which seeks to identify the issues to be addressed in the Bill and it is anticipated that a further consultation, incorporating the draft Bill, an Equality Impact Assessment and Regulatory Impact Assessment, will take place next year. This consultation paper addresses areas such as the scope of a Single Equality Bill, exemptions, discrimination, addressing under-representation, structures and investigations, complaints and enforcement. The paper also has an attached questionnaire which consultees are asked to complete and return by 3 August 2001.

Copies of the consultation paper are available from the Single Equality Bill Unit, Office of the First Minister and Deputy First Minister, FREEPOST 3900, Belfast, BT4 3BR, which is also the address for comments on the proposals before the above date.

10 Irish Law

INTRODUCTION 10–1

Having the complex historical background that Ireland does, it is generally accepted that Irish law is difficult to find. Irish legal history very much consists of English law in Ireland, as with the importation of English law from the twelfth century onwards, the existing Brehon law was effectively eradicated. Apart from the few brief intervals of legal independence, until 1922 the Irish legal system was heavily influenced by English authority. In 1800, after the Act of Union, the Irish Parliament was dissolved. In 1920, the Government of Ireland Act provided for devolved governments in both the North and South, but this was never implemented in the South. The Anglo-Irish Treaty of 1922 established the Irish Free State with dominion status within the British Commonwealth. A considerable amount of nineteenth-century English law is still in force in Ireland. It was only in the second half of the twentieth century that there was a move away from dependence on English law and legal literature. This divergence from English law has seen a new era of Irish legal publishing, with the production of textbooks in all the main subject areas together with an array of law journals. However, as with many former Commonwealth countries, early editions of secondary materials published in the United Kingdom are frequently of great interest. The later editions which contain current United Kingdom legislation are now too far removed to be relied on as heavily as they were. Consequently, many textbooks based on legislation now amended in England are still relevant to the law in Ireland.

LEGISLATION 10–2

Bunreacht na hEireann (the Constitution) 10–3

The written Constitution of Ireland embodies the most important constitutional laws. Legislation which conflicts with the Constitution may be declared invalid by the courts. If a Bill is introduced to amend the Constitution, it can only become an Act after a public referendum.

In 1922, the Constitution of the Irish Free State, or Saorstat Eireann, was enacted and established the foundations for the machinery of government for the new State. In 1937, a

Parts of an Act

①   *Number 27 of* 2000

②   **ELECTRONIC COMMERCE ACT, 2000**

AN ACT TO PROVIDE FOR THE LEGAL RECOGNITION OF
ELECTRONIC CONTRACTS, ELECTRONIC WRITING,
ELECTRONIC SIGNATURES AND ORIGINAL INFOR-
③ MATION IN ELECTRONIC FORM IN RELATION TO
COMMERCIAL   AND   NON-COMMERCIAL   TRANS-
ACTIONS AND DEALINGS AND OTHER MATTERS, THE
ADMISSIBILITY OF EVIDENCE IN RELATION TO SUCH
MATTERS, THE ACCREDITATION, SUPERVISION AND
LIABILITY OF CERTIFICATION SERVICE PROVIDERS
AND THE REGISTRATION OF DOMAIN NAMES, AND TO
PROVIDE FOR RELATED MATTERS.

[10*th July*, 2000]   ④

⑤   BE IT ENACTED BY THE OIREACHTAS AS FOLLOWS:

PART 1
PRELIMINARY AND GENERAL

1.—(1) This Act may be cited as the Electronic Commerce Act,   Short title and
2000.   commencement.

(2) This Act shall come into operation on such day or days as the
Minister, after consultation with the Minister for Enterprise, Trade
and Employment, may appoint by order or orders, either generally or
with reference to any particular purpose or provision, and different
days may be so appointed for different purposes or different
provisions.

⑥

2.—(1) In this Act, unless the context otherwise requires—   Interpretation.   ⑦

"accreditation" means an accreditation under *section 29(2)*;

"addressee", in relation to an electronic communication, means a
person or public body intended by the originator to receive the
electronic communication, but does not include a person or public
body acting as a service provider in relation to the processing, receiving
or storing of the electronic communication or the provision of other
services in relation to it;

"advanced electronic signature" means an electronic signature—

(*a*) uniquely linked to the signatory,

new Constitution was adopted by plebiscite. This Constitution in the main provided a stabilising and reforming continuation of the 1922 Constitution, but also established a Constitution free from all elements of subservience to the British Crown.

The latest edition of the Constitution was published in bilingual format by the Stationery Office in 2000. It contains a list of amending acts up until 1999, along with the dates of their signature. There is an alphabetical subject index at the rear.

Primary Legislation   10–4

Before a Bill can become law, it must be approved by both Houses of the Irish Parliament—Dáil and Seanad Eireann—and signed by the President. Once this has happened, the Bill becomes an Act immediately. Unless otherwise specified, the date of commencement is the date of signature by the President.

Parts of an Act   10–5
The various parts of an Act can be seen on the copy reproduced in the figure on p. 192, and are as follows:

1. official citation;
2. short title;
3. long title;
4. date of signature by the President;
5. enacting formula;
6. section and subsection;
7. marginal note.

Citation   10–6
Acts are commonly referred to by their short title and the year of publication, *e.g.* the Finance Act 2000. Acts are numbered within the year, and may also be cited in this way. Thus the Finance Act 2000 is cited officially as 3/2000. Private Acts are numbered in a similar way *e.g.* Trinity College, Dublin (charters and letters patent amendment) Act, 1P/2000. Prior to 1922, the British method of citation in use at that time applies, so that statutes are referred to by regnal year and by chapter number (**4–3**).

For the last few years there has been a choice of electronic services providing legislation from 1922:

1. The *Irish Statute Book* (ISB) on CD-ROM published by the Office of the Attorney General. The most recent version of ISB uses Folio software and contains the full text of all Acts and statutory instruments from 1922 to 1998 and includes chronological tables to the Acts for that period.
2. BAILII (at **www.bailii.org**) contains all the material from the ISB as well as the texts of Acts since 1998. The hypertext links and added power of the Sino search capacity make this a very useful service.
3. The ISB on the Attorney General's website (at **www.irlgov.ie/ag**).

10–7   Publication of Irish Acts

The *Acts of the Oireachtas* are the official source of Irish legislation and are published by the Stationery Office. In addition to the electronic versions already mentioned they are available in two printed formats:

1. Acts as promulgated (A4 format). This is a re-print on cream paper of the Bill as passed by both houses, with the addition of an Act title, number and date of signature by the President. These Acts are in the language as enacted, almost always English. If enacted in Irish an English translation is provided. This monolingual version is bound in annual volumes.
2. Bilingual texts (quarto format). It is this version that eventually appears as the official annual bound volume.

For years there was a backlog in the translation of Acts into Irish, but with the allocation of extra resources such delays should be eliminated. At present the texts in Irish are also available on the Oireachtas website (at **www.irlgov.ie/oireachtas**).

Since 1984 Sweet & Maxwell have produced an annotated edition of the Irish Acts, entitled *Irish Current Law Statutes Annotated* (ICLSA) modelled on the English *Current Law Statutes Annotated*. This looseleaf publication is issued in several parts each year. Each part cover several Acts and is published some months after the Acts contained in it have been passed. Most Acts are extensively annotated and any that are not have a general note giving the background to the Act. There is a subject index, which is updated with each issue. The table of contents at the front of the volume lists the Acts both alphabetically and chronologically within each year.

10–8   Tracing an Irish Act

Apart from the electronic versions described above, there is also a commercial current awareness service called FirstLaw. This service covers legislation, case law and general articles on Irish Law since 1998.

Since 1993, the most comprehensive and current print service for searching legislation is the Legislation Update section of ICLSA. The citators index the effects on all Acts and Statutory Instruments (amendments, repeals, etc.) together with details of any cases that have considered them. The Update includes tables detailing: dates of commencement of Acts and how they were commenced; legislation not yet in force; E.U. directives implemented.

Irish Current Law Monthly Digest (ICLMD) is published 11 times a year (and then consolidated as an annual yearbook). It provides: a table on Progress of Bills and the stages; a list of Acts for that year and dates of commencement of Acts within the period covered by the issue; short descriptions of each Act.

The ISB contains the Chronological Tables of the Statutes from 1922 to 1998 but 1922 to 1995 is the most recent printed version. The Chronological Tables detail:

1. year and number of the Act;
2. short title;
3. how the Act has been affected;
4. the affecting provision relating to 3 (see the figure on p. 195).

The following chronological tables are also included:

Example Page of Chronological Table of Statutes in the Irish Statute Book 1922–1998

Year and Number	Short Title	How Affected	Affecting Provision
1992 1.-*contd.*	**Patents Act, 1992.** -*contd.*	S. 97(1), subsec. substit.	28/1998, ss. 5(a), 6(2)
		S. 97(3), subsec. substit.	28/1998, ss. 5(b), 6(2)
		S. 97(3A), subsec. ins.	28/1998, ss. 5(c), 6(2)
		S. 97(4A), subsec. ins.	28/1998, ss. 5(d), 6(2)
		S. 97(5), subsec. substit.	28/1998, ss. 5(e), 6(2)
		S. 97(6), subsec. substit.	28/1998, ss. 5(f), 6(2)
		S. 105(1) am.	S. I. No. 179 of 1992, rl. 79, sch. 2, Form 5
		S. 107(1)(a) am.	S. I. No. 179 of 1992, rl. 81
		S. 108(4) am.	S. I. No. 180 of 1992, rl. 13
		S. 109(3) am.	S. I. No. 179 of 1992, rl. 80(2)
		S. 110 am.	S. I. No. 179 of 1992, rl. 82
		S. 119(6)(b) am.	S. I. No. 179 of 1992, rl. 83
		S. 120(6) am.	S. I. No. 179 of 1992, rl. 84
		S. 121(3) am.	S. I. No. 179 of 1992, rl. 85
		S. 122(2)(a)(b)(i) am.	S. I. No. 179 of 1992, rl. 86
		S. 131 am.	S. I. No. 179 of 1992, rl. 88
2.	**Merchant Shipping Act, 1992.**	S. 2, defs. am.	20/1998, s. 4(a)
		Pt. 3 (ss. 14-18) am.	S. I. No. 295 of 1992, rl. 3
		S. 14(3), subsec. ins.	20/1998, s. 4(b)
		S. 14A, new s. ins.	20/1998, s. 4(c)
		S. 26 appl.	S. I. No. 549 of 1998, reg. 4(7)
3.	**Oireachtas (Allowances to Members) and Ministerial and Parliamentary Offices (Amendment) Act, 1992.**	S. 3, allowance under exempted.	39/1997, ss. 836(1), 1097

Irish Statute Book 1922 - 1998 © Irish Government 1999

1. lists of Irish Private Acts;
2. pre-Union Irish statutes, English statutes, pre-Union British statutes; British local statutes; Local Government (Adaptation of Irish Enactments) Order 1899; and the Local Government (Application of Enactments) Order 1898;
3. table of expressions used in British statutes or in Saorstat Eireann statutes which have been adapted by orders made under the Adaptation of Enactments Act 1922 or the Constitution (Consequential Provisions) Act 1937;
4. list of Regulations made under section 3 of the European Communities Act 1972;
5. list of orders made under section 6(1) of the Ministers and Secretaries (Amendment) Act 1939.

The last subject index published was for 1922 to 1982 with a supplement covering 1983 to 1985 and annual supplements to 1989.

The Bills Office of the Oireachtas issues an annual alphabetical list of Acts from 1922 to date.

10–9   Older Irish Acts
Prior to 1922, there are two principal sources of legislation:

A. Irish or pre-Union Statutes passed in the Parliaments held in Ireland between 1310 and 1800
These were published by Grierson in the nineteenth century in two editions:

1. folio edition of 20 volumes entitled *The Statutes at Large Passed in the Parliaments Held in Ireland*;
2. octavo edition of 12 volumes, entitled *Statutes Passed in the Parliaments Held in Ireland*.

A two-volume *subject index* accompanying the octavo edition contains a table showing the correspondence between the two.

Acts which were in force in 1885 were presented in a much more convenient one-volume format by HMSO as the *Irish Statutes Revised 1310–1800*. This work was reprinted by Round Hall Press in 1985 with the addition of a useful introduction by Professor N. Osborough. This contains a chronological table which gives details of:

1. the regnal year, statute title and chapter number;
2. subject matter;
3. reason for total or partial omission (usually that it has been repealed in full or in part);
4. page number in the volume if in force in 1885.

There is a subject index at the back of the volume.

B. United Kingdom of Great Britain and Ireland 1801–1921
During this period Ireland, being governed directly from Westminster, had no separate legislation. The sources for the years 1801–1921 are therefore the same as for British statutes and have been described in Chapter 4.

Oulton's *Index to the Statutes at Present in Force in, or affecting Ireland, from the year 1310 to 1839 inclusive,* 2nd edition with eight supplements to the year 1846, is a useful guide to early Irish legislation.

Another source of Irish legislation which should be mentioned is the *Green Book* or Vance, *Reading made Easy of the Irish Statutes*. Published in 1862, it contains an account of

Parts of a Statutory Instrument

<h1 style="text-align:center">S.I. No. 279 of 2000 ②</h1>

<h2 style="text-align:center">① LIVESTOCK MARTS REGULATIONS, 1968 (AMENDMENT)
REGULATIONS, 2000</h2>

④

I, JOE WALSH, Minister for Agriculture, Food and Rural Development, in
③ exercise of the powers conferred on me by section 6 of the Livestock Marts
Act, 1967 (No. 20 of 1967) (as adapted by the Agriculture and Food
(Alteration of Name of Department and Title of Minister) Order, 1999 (S.I.
No. 307 of 1999)), hereby make the following regulations:

1.   These Regulations may be cited as the Livestock Marts Regulations,
      1968 (Amendment) Regulations, 2000.

2.   Regulation 19 of the Livestock Marts Regulations, 1968 (S.I. No. 251
      of 1968), is revoked.

⑤ GIVEN under my Official Seal,
this 11th day of September, 2000.

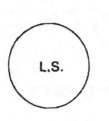

L.S.

JOE WALSH
Minister for Agriculture, Food & Rural
Development.

Explanatory Note

(This note is not part of the Instrument and does not purport to be a legal
interpretation)

These Regulations revoke Regulation 19 of the Livestock Marts Regulations, 1968
(S.I. No. 251 of 1968) requiring marts to have conditions of sale approved by the
Minister.

Pn 9003

Published by the Stationery Office, Dublin 2.

Price £0.40.

the principal decisions of Irish statutes, Rules and Orders of Court from 1224 to 1860, and any amendments made to them. A Subject Index is found at the rear of the volume.

10–10   Secondary Legislation

In order to avoid the necessity of passing a huge amount of primary legislation, certain ministers or government departments are given powers under various Acts to make detailed rules and regulations. These are known as *statutory instruments*, and fulfil the same function as their British counterparts.

However they are also extremely important as a vehicle for the implementation into Irish law of E.U. obligations under the European Communities Act 1972.

10–11   Parts of a Statutory Instrument

The following elements can be seen on the statutory instrument reproduced on p. 197:

1. title;
2. statutory instrument number;
3. enabling Act;
4. minister responsible;
5. date of signature.

10–12   Citation

During the year, every statutory instrument published is given its own number; for example, the Electronic Commerce Act 2000 (Commencement) Order 2000 is cited as S.I. No. 293 of 2000.

10–13   Publication

In addition to electronic versions (see **10–7**) statutory instruments are available in two print formats:

1. loose typescript A4 issued by the relevant department;
2. printed quarto format (later bound in volumes and published by the Stationery Office).

Bound volumes of *Statutory Instruments* are published annually from 1948. They are arranged numerically within each year, and recently there has been more than one volume for each year. Prior to 1948, statutory instruments were known as *statutory rules and orders*. These were published by the Stationery Office in 1948 as a subject collection of 39 volumes, entitled *Statutory Rules, Orders and Regulations*.

10–14   Tracing statutory instruments

The electronic services described above in relation to tracing Acts also provide searching for statutory instruments. Although it is not an official source, since 1993 the statutory instruments citator in the Legislation Update of ICLSA is the best print service to use.

Indexes produced by the Stationery Office are available up until 1999. Entitled the *Index to the Statutory Instruments*, they are published in 10 volumes and cover the years 1922 to 95.

The Indexes have two tables listing statutory instruments by title or under their enabling authority.

The most comprehensive single index is the *Index of Statutory Instruments 1922–1986* by

Richard Humphreys. However, as the index only covers statutory instruments until 1986 this is now considerably out of date. The three-volume index allows searching by title (Volume I); by enabling authority (Volume II); and by subject (Volume III).

CASE LAW   10–15

Irish law reporting dates from 1615 with the publication of *Irish Equity Cases 1604–1612*, by Sir John Davis, Attorney-General. Originally in Norman French (*Le Primer Report des Cases en Ley en les Courts de Roy en Ireland*), it was reprinted in London in 1628 but was not published in English until 1762. Little else was published until the mid-eighteenth century. 1782–1800 saw a brief period of independence of the Irish courts and Parliament and an increase in the publication of reports, including Ridgeway's three-volume work on cases in the Irish House of Lords 1784–1792. From this date until the mid-nineteenth century, over 50 series of reports were published covering case law in Ireland. These reports were reprinted in the Revised Reports. In 1866 the Incorporated Council of Law Reporting for Ireland was established and in 1867 began publication of "official" reports: The Irish Common Law Series and The Irish Reports Equity Series. These two series later joined to become *The Law Reports (Ireland)* in 1878 after the Judicature (Ireland) Act 1877. In 1894, they were to become the *Irish Reports* and the volume numbers were replaced by the year of issue.

Hence the reporting of Irish case law goes back to the seventeenth century and is continued with varying levels of coverage down to the two major series of today—the *Irish Reports* and the commercial service *Irish Law Reports Monthly*, the latter providing coverage from 1976.

As with legislation there is a choice of electronic services available for case law:

1. BAILII (at **www.bailii.org**) is now receiving a regular supply of judgments and is the only free searchable database of judgments for Irish law. The facility to jump direct to the text of legislation referred to in the judgment has made this service unique in Irish Legal research.
2. The electronic Irish Reports (eIR) 1919 to date, published on CD-ROM four times a year by the Incorporated Council of Law Reporting for Ireland and Context. Running on JUSTIS software the eIR contains the full text of all cases in the *Irish Reports* and the abstracts from the *Irish Digests* for the period. This means that one may search for cases in the *Digest* not just for those reported in the *Irish Reports*—most significantly the *Irish Law Reports Monthly* (ILRM) and the *Northern Ireland Law Reports* are digested.
3. LEXIS (in IRCAS) provides access to: the *Irish Reports* from 1950; the *Irish Law Times*, 1950 to 1980; Frewen (Court of Criminal Appeal), 1950 to 1983; selected unreported judgments from 1986 onwards.
4. Electronic Irish Weekly Law Reports (eIWLR), published by FirstLaw and Lendac, was originally on CD-ROM, but is now also on the web. Starting in 1998 eIWLR promises "An end to unreported judgments" as they intend to report all written judgments circulated by the Courts Service.

Citation of Law Reports   10–16
This resembles the British method of citation:

e.g. Wildgust[1] v. *Bank of Ireland*[2] [2001][3] 1 I.L.R.M.[4] 24[5;]

Constituent Parts of a Law Report

① **Paula Kealy,** Appellant v. **The Minister For Health,** Respondent [1998 No. 5 CT]

② High Court   19th April, 1999

③ *Damages - Assessment - Personal injuries - Hepatitis C Tribunal - Whether general damages awarded by Tribunal sufficient in circumstances - Hepatitis C Compensation Tribunal Act, 1997 (No. 34), s. 5.*

④   The appellant was injected with contaminated anti-D blood products in June, 1977. She subsequently developed hepatitis which the Court learned was likely to cause cirrhosis within 10 years and decompensation within a further five years necessitating a liver transplant at that stage. The Hepatitis C Compensation Tribunal made an award to the appellant and her husband of £50,000 jointly for loss of earnings and awarded the appellant £165,000 for general damages of which £15,000 was for out of pocket expenses such as travel. The appellant appealed to the High Court.

⑤   *Held* by the High Court (Morris P.), in allowing the appeal and increasing the award from £150,000 general damages (exclusive of out of pocket expenses) to £250,000, 1, that as no omnibus sum was being taken into account there was no obligation on the court to look at the overall sum being awarded to see whether it was out of proportion in all of the circumstances.
    Sinnott v. Quinnsworth Ltd. [1984] I.L.R.M. 523 distinguished.
    2. That the value of an award had to be looked at in the light of the prevailing economic conditions.
    Sinnott v. Quinnsworth Ltd. [1984] I.L.R.M. 523 distinguished.

⑥ Cases mentioned in this report:-
    Reddy v. Bates [1983] I.R. 141; [1984] I.L.R.M. 197.
    Sinnott v. Quinnsworth Ltd. [1984] I.L.R.M. 523.

    Motion on notice.
    The facts have been summarised in the headnote and are fully set out in the judgment of Morris P., *infra.*
    The appellant issued an originating notice of motion by way of an appeal on the 15th April, 1998, from the decision of the Hepatitis C Compensation Tribunal of the 13th March, 1998.
    The action was heard by the High Court (Morris P.) on the 12th April, 1999.

⑦   *John Rogers* S.C. (with him *Richard McDonnell*) for the appellant.

    Michael O'Donoghue S.C. (with him *Gráinne Clohessy*) for the respondent.

                                                    Cur. adv. vult.

⑧ **Morris P.**   19th April, 1999
    This matter comes before the Court by way of an appeal from an award made by the Hepatitis C Compensation Tribunal which was heard on the 13th March, 1998. Under the terms of the award communicated to the appellant's solicitors on the 18th March, 1998, the appellant was awarded £165,000 for general damages of which £15,000 were to represent out of pocket expenses. Accordingly, the award for general damages for personal injuries was £150,000.

[1] plaintiff or applicant;
[2] defendant or respondent;
[3] year in which the case is reported;
[4] abbreviated name of reports series;
[5] page number at which report begins.

Format of Law Reports   10–17
The various parts of a law report (see the figure on p. 200) are:

1. names of the parties;
2. name of the court(s) in which the case was heard, and the date;
3. summary in italics;
4. headnote;
5. ruling of the court;
6. cases mentioned during the hearing;
7. names of counsel appearing for the parties;
8. judgment(s).

Often the High Court and the Supreme Court judgments will be reported together.

Recent and Unreported Judgments   10–18
The coverage and currency of law reports has improved since both major series (IR and ILRM) began publishing multiple volumes each year. However, as there are still a significant number of cases remaining unreported in print format each year, the written judgment itself is of great importance with regard to case law in Ireland.

Since 1976, following a recommendation of the Committee on Court Practice and Procedure, the courts have circulated copies of the written judgments from the superior courts (the Supreme Court, the Court of Criminal Appeal and the High Court) to a variety of bodies including: the judiciary; government agencies; the professions and the universities. It is expected that judgments will be available on the courts website (at **www.courts.ie**).

In addition to the electronic services mentioned in **10–15**, FirstLaw provide the full texts of the judgments before they are reported in the eIWLR.

Citation of Unreported Cases   10–19

These are cited by:

1. names of parties;
2. judge;
3. record number;
4. date.

e.g. *Forbes*[1] v. *Tobin*[1] McCracken J.[2] 1999/5327P[3] 8.3.01[4]

Where the judgment is delivered in the Supreme Court, "Supreme" appears instead of the name of the judge.

10–20 **Format of Unreported Judgments**

Unreported judgments are produced in typescript format on A4 paper (see p. 203). They are cited by:

1. plaintiff or applicant;
2. defendant or respondent;
3. judge;
4. record number;
5. court;
6. date.

10–21   Indexes and Digests

Irish Digests are available covering the period up until 1999 in print or as part of eIR.

The *Digests* are indexes to Law Reports and do not cover unreported written judgments (see **10–25**). The *Digests* are as follows:

O'Donnell and Brady, *Analytical Digest of all the Reported Cases in Equity* (1840);
Brunker, *Digest of All the Unreported Cases Decided in the Superior Courts of Common Law in Ireland and in Admiralty* (1865);
Gamble and Barlow, *Index to Irish Equity Cases* (2 volumes) (1838–1867);
Green and Manders, *The Law Reports Digest of Cases* (1890);
Stubbs, *Irish Law Times Digest of Cases* (1867–1893);
Murray and Dixon, *Digest of Cases* (1867–1893);
Maxwell, *Digest of Cases* (1894–1918);
Ryland, *Digest of Cases* (1919–1928);
Ryland, *Digest of Cases* (1929–1938);
Harrison, *Digest of Cases* (1939–1948);
Harrison, *Digest of Cases* (1949–1958);
Ryan, *Digest of Cases* (1959–1970);
de Blaghd, *The Irish Digest* (1971–1983);
Clancy and Ryan, *The Irish Digest* (1984–1988);
Clancy, *The Irish Digest* (1989–1993);
Clancy, *The Irish Digest* (1994–1999).

10–22   Irish Digests

These index cases in the following ways:

1. by name of parties;
2. by subject matter;
3. citator approach—this lists case law and legislation followed, overruled or considered by the reports so digested.

10–23   Irish Current Law Monthly Digest

Since 1995 *Irish Current Law Monthly Digest* (ICLMD) has provided digests of recent case law arranged by subject. ICLMD is published 11 times a year and also contains a cumulating table of all cases digested in the current year together with all the cases judicially considered in those summaries.

Format of Unreported Judgments

⑤

THE HIGH COURT

④

1999 No. 1606p

IN THE MATTER OF THE PROCEEDS OF CRIME ACT 1996

BETWEEN

① **MICHAEL F MURPHY**

PLAINTIFF/APPLICANT

AND

② **M. C., J. W., P. C.**

(OTHERWISE KNOWN AS P. C.) AND

J. C.

DEFENDANTS/RESPONDENTS

③

JUDGMENT of O'Sullivan J. delivered the 13th of March 2001. ⑥

The first named defendant seeks an order dismissing the plaintiff's claim against him for failure to furnish a statement of claim.

An interlocutory order has already being made under Section 3 of the Proceeds of Crime Act and a receiver appointed over the assets of the defendants pursuant to Section 7 thereof. These proceedings were commenced by plenary summons and it is submitted on behalf of the defendant that the Rules of the Superior Courts impose a mandatory requirement on the plaintiff to deliver a statement of claim within specified time limits. This has not been done and the first defendant now seeks an order dismissing the proceedings. The relevant

10–24   Pink Sheets

From 1976 to 1996 a subject index to the written judgments was published entitled *Index to Superior Courts*, or pink sheets as they are commonly called. Published originally by the Law Reporting Council and then jointly by the Bar Council and the Law Society, they were issued separately as well as circulated as an insert to the *Law Society Gazette*. In 2001 it is intended that the pink sheets will again be published by the Bar Council and Law Society.

10–25   Indexes to superior court judgments

These cover the years 1966–1989 in three volumes:

1. *Index to Unreported Judgments of the Irish Superior Courts 1966–1975* (*Green Index*)—published by the Irish Association of Law Teachers;
2. *Index to Irish Superior Court Written Judgments 1976–1982* (*Red Index*)—published by the Irish Association of Law Teachers;
3. *Index to Irish Superior Court Written Judgments 1983–1989* (*Blue Index*)—published by the General Council of the Bar of Ireland.

The *Red* and *Blue Indexes* each contain two sections; the first part is an alphabetical index by party to all the cases summarised in each volume. The subject index, which forms the second part, consolidates all the entries from the original pink sheets.

All written judgments from the years 1976–1989, whether reported or not, should therefore appear in these *Indexes*.

The *Green Index* differs slightly, in that it covers only unreported judgments and lacks case summaries in its subject index. It does, however, have a statute citator.

10–26   Tracing a Judgment

For help in tracing a judgment, use the flow chart, "Finding Irish Cases", on page 205.

10–27   Government Agencies

Among the government agencies that make decisions are:

1. *Employment Appeals Tribunal*
    Established under the Redundancy Payments Act 1967, the Tribunal determines matters of dispute under the entire range of employment legislation. The Tribunal issues its decisions on A4 paper and circulates them to the universities, professions and other interested bodies.
2. *Valuation Tribunal*
    Established under the Valuation Act 1988, the Tribunal hears and determines appeals against rateable valuations set by the Valuation Office. Decisions of the Tribunal have been published in print as *Journal of Valuation Tribunal Judgments* in two volumes covering 1988 to 1998 as well as on CD-ROM.

Other government agencies that make decisions include: the Competition Authority; the Information Commissioner; the Equality Commissioner. Their decisions are available on paper or on the agency's websites and on BAILII where they may be searched at the same time as case law or legislation.

The Office of the Director of Telecommunications Regulation usually publishes decision notices on its website (at **www.odtr.ie**) The offices of the Data Protection

Finding Irish Cases

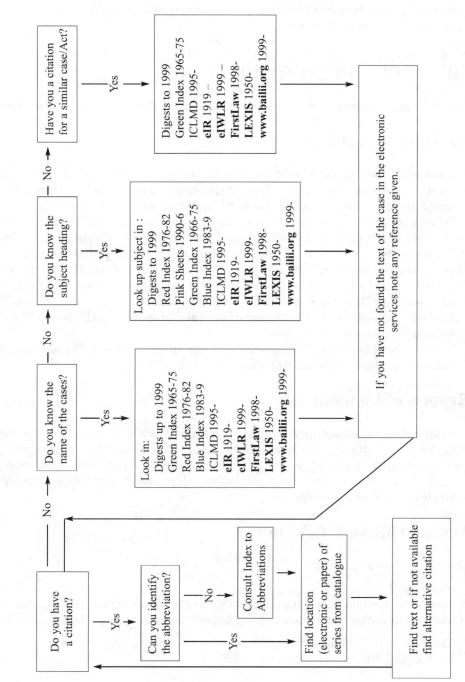

Commissioner, Ombudsman and Insurance Ombudsman publish case summaries in their Annual Reports and on their websites.

10–28 OFFICIAL PUBLICATIONS

Acts, Bills and statutory instruments have already been dealt with in earlier sections.

10–29 Parliamentary Debates

The debates of the Dáil and Seanad are available on the Oireachtas site (at **www.irlgov.ie/ oireachtas**). The entire series from 1919 is available on the site and is fully searchable. It is intended that the whole series will also be published on CD-ROM and DVD.

Debates are published in daily parts which are unrevised. Corrections or amendments may be included in the bound volume a year later. The bound volumes are each indexed and contain a list of ministers, deputies and senators. Each volume is assigned a running number. At the start of 2001, the Dáil Debates had reached Volume 512 and the Seanad Debates Volume 161, so it should not be assumed that the volume number for the Dáil Debates would be the same as that for the Seanad Debates of the same date. *Consolidated Indexes* are published for Dáil Debates in six volumes for the years 1922–56 and for Seanad Debates in two volumes for 1922–48.

Irish Current Law Statutes Annotated lists the volume and column number of the Debates in each house for each Act since 1984.

10–30 Reports of Committees

Committees are appointed by either House, usually to consider technical or specialised Bills, which may then go to report stage before the House. For major Bills Joint Committees of the Dáil and Seanad may be appointed. Certain committees appointed regularly have produced a significant number of reports. Reports of Committees are also available on the Oireachtas site.

10–31 Tracing Official Publications

This is done by way of:

1. *Iris Oifigiúil*
A weekly list of publications from the Stationery Office is listed in the Friday issue of this bi-weekly publication. Reprints are available from the Stationery Office on subscription.

2. *Catalogue of Government Publications*
These are published by the Stationery Office:

    (a) quarterly—published in typescript;
    (b) annual catalogue of government publications;
    (c) consolidated catalogues in nine volumes for the years 1922–60.

Information given is as follows:

    (a) order number;

(b) title;

(c) price and postage charge;

and is grouped into the following sections:

(a) Acts;

(b) Bills;

(c) Dáil Reports;

(d) Oireachtas Reports;

(e) Stationery Office publications—alphabetically by department;

(f) Statutory instruments;

(g) general literature.

3. Maltby and McKenna, *Irish Official Publications: A Guide to Republic of Ireland Papers with a Breviate of Reports 1922–1972.*
Here, the reports are grouped under broad subject headings and summarised. There are separate name and subject indexes at the end.

JOURNALS

10–32

Journals provide the main outlet for Irish legal scholarship, and are also an important source of current developments in legislation.

There are three major professional journals:

1. the *Bar Review*;

2. the *Gazette of the Law Society*;

3. the *Irish Law Times* (I.L.T.).

These provide articles and commentaries on legislation, relevant E.C. and English legal developments, information on legal education and the role of the lawyer in Ireland, and reviews of recent publications. The *Bar Review* and the I.L.T. also provide useful updates on the progress of legislation, both primary and secondary, and of recent superior court decisions and journal articles.

The other type of Irish journal available tends toward the learned journal, providing a more scholarly dimension, or concentrating on a particular aspect of the law. The titles listed below fall into this category:

Title	Abbreviation
Annual Review of Irish Law	
Bar Review	BR
Commercial Law Practitioner	CLP
Contemporary Issues in Irish Politics	CILP
Dublin University Law Journal	DULJ
Family Law Journal (I)	FLJ
Garda Review	
Gazette of Law Society of Ireland	GLSI
Hibernian Law Journal	HLJ
Irish Business Law	IBL

Irish Conveyancing & Property Law Journal	ICPLJ
Irish Criminal Law Journal	ICLJ
Irish Current Law Monthly Digest	ICLMD
Irish Journal of European Law	IJEL
Irish Journal of Family Law	IJFL
Irish Jurist	IJ
Irish Law Times	ILTR
Irish Planning & Environment Law Journal	IPELJ
Irish Student Law Review	ISLR
Irish Tax Review	ITR
Journal of University of Limerick	JUL
Medico-Legal Journal of Ireland	MLJI
Practice & Procedure	P & P
Technology & Entertainment Law Journal	T & ELJ

10–33 Citation

The citation of journal articles follows the same format as that used in England. Abbreviations commonly used are given above.

10–34 Tracing Journal Articles

The Legal Journals Index described in **5–4** also indexes Irish journal articles. FirstLaw include abstracts of journal articles in their current awareness service.

For recent coverage on paper the *Irish Current Law Monthly Digest* (modelled on the English *Current Law* service) provides abstracts arranged by subject of: journal articles; judgments; Acts and Statutory Instruments.

Paul O'Higgins' *A Bibliography of Periodical Literature Relating to Irish Law* (N.I.L.Q. 1966, supplements published in 1973 and 1983) provides excellent historical coverage of around 5,000 articles from over 130 journals. The titles are arranged within broad subject headings with cross-references. Alphabetical subject and other indexes are provided, along with a list of journals cited and their abbreviations.

10–35 TEXTBOOKS AND BIBLIOGRAPHIES

When searching for textbooks on a given topic, your own library catalogue will probably provide the best starting point. However, bibliographies provide an important source, and can often be more effective in narrowing down a search strategy. Most textbooks provide comprehensive bibliographies, and many give lists of possible further reading. An excellent subject guide to Irish legal textbooks can be found in T. O'Malley's *Round Hall Guide to the Sources of Law: an introduction to legal research and writing* (2nd ed., 2001). Bibliographic information relating to Ireland and Irish law may also be found in:

Twining and Uglow, *Law Publishing and Legal Information: Small Jurisdictions of the British Isles* (1981);

Alan Eager, *Guide to Irish Bibliographic Material: Bibliography of Irish Bibliographies and Sources of Information* (2nd ed., 1980);

A. G. Donaldson, *Some Comparative Aspects of Irish Law* (1957);

A Legal Bibliography of the British Commonwealth of Nations Vol. 4, "Irish Law to 1956" (2nd ed., 1957).

11 European Community Law

INTRODUCTION

European Community law is as much part of the law of this country as the laws passed by the United Kingdom Parliament. For this reason, U.K. legal sources should, and often will, include references to the relevant E.C. rules. However, because this is not always so and because E.C. law is organised in a different way from English law, students also need to become familiar with the sources of E.C. law.

The use of the term "E.C. law" in this chapter needs to be explained at the outset. The Treaty of Maastricht or Treaty on European Union, which came into force in 1993, made the European Communities the first "pillar" of the European Union. This chapter is concerned with the body of law based around these Communities. Hence the term "E.C. law". The three communities are the European Community, the European Coal and Steel Community (ECSC) and the European Atomic Energy Community (EURATOM). These remain distinct legal entities. Before Maastricht, the European Community was referred to as the European Economic Community (EEC).

Some textbooks and articles discuss "European Union law". The term "European Union" (E.U.) is used in this chapter to refer to the institutional framework of the European Union. The European Commission, for example, is an institution of the E.U. Many of the sources of information you will be using when studying E.C. law have been provided by the institutions of the E.U.

The sources of E.C. law, along with a great deal of other information, are made available in both electronic and print form by the E.U. Most, if not all of the printed sources will be available in your law library, especially if it is a designated European Documentation Centre (E.D.C.). E.D.C.s are part of the European Information Relay Network and receive copies of publicly available documents from the European Commission. Details of the U.K. E.D.C.s and other sources of E.U. information are found on the website of the European Commission Representation office in the U.K. (at **www.cec.org.uk)**. Details can also be found in the print publication, *European Union Information: Directory of UK sources*.

The online information provided by the E.U. comes from three main sources: the Europa website (**11–2**), Celex (**11–3**) and EUR-Lex (**11–4**). Links to the second two sources can be found on the Europa website. CD-ROM versions of the *Official Journal* are also supplied to E.D.C.s.

11-2   EUROPA

EUROPA (at **europa.eu.int**) is the main E.U. website on the internet, providing a wealth of information from the E.U. institutions. It contains 1.5 million pages. From EUROPA, it is possible to access the home pages of all the E.U. institutions and their departments. Overviews of the activities of the E.U. and links to legislation and key official documents are available, along with links to official databases such as CELEX, SCAD and ECLAS (found via "Information Sources").

Having accessed EUROPA and selected the language of your choice, you will find that the opening page of EUROPA presents seven sections: "News", "Activities", "Institutions", "ABC", "Official documents", "Information sources" and "What's new on EUROPA?"

Each section leads to further subsections. For example the "News" section provides access to recent press releases, details of events and entries on current "Key issues". Key issues at the time of writing include the recently published draft of the Treaty of Nice which follows the Intergovernmental Conference held in December 2000. Heads of State and Government reached agreement at Nice on the draft of a new treaty proposing institutional reforms.

The "Activities" section provides a very useful overview of the current policy areas of the E.U. There are links to legislation and case law by subject and to the European Commission Directorate-General responsible for each subject area. Summaries of the main policy areas of the E.U. with details of key legislation are included on EUROPA (at **europa.eu.int/scadplus/scad_en.htm**).

EUROPA has a search engine, found under the "Search" link. Although it does not provide the search facilites of databases such as Lexis-Nexis or CELEX, searches on one or more keywords can be conducted and there is a "Help" section. However, the sheer amount of information on EUROPA can overwhelm users, so it may save time if you use other sources to begin your research.

11-3   CELEX

CELEX is the official multilingual legal database of the E.U. It is the key source for legislation and case law. It will often be the first source to use. It contains the full text of the treaties, the *Official Journal* L series, and the *European Court Reports* (see **11–18**), along with the full text of the merger decisions of the Commission. The coverage of the nine "sectors" (categories) of the database varies; some cover the period from 1952 onwards. The merger decisions are covered from 1990.

CELEX is available via EUROPA to subscribing libraries and institutions. European Documentation Centres are also able to provide access. There is a menu search facility allowing searching by keywords, citations or title. CELEX contains the text of the *Official Journal* L series and it is intended to add the full text of the C Series during 2001, beginning with 1995–2000.

CELEX is also available on CD-ROM or online from commercial publishers. It is available as Justis CELEX from Context, Eurolaw from ILI and OJ Online from Ellis Publications. These are non-official sources and offer the CELEX data in a re-packaged format. Law libraries are likely to have one of these databases available for you to conduct a personal search.

EUR-LEX

In 1998, the E.U. launched a daily update service called EUR-Lex (at **europa.eu.int/eur-lex/en**), providing access to both legislation and case law. It contains the full text of the following legislation:

treaties as amended by the Treaty of Amsterdam;

legislation in force—adopted legislation and the consolidated texts of secondary legislation;

legislation in preparation;

documents of public interest—this is a newly added section which includes European Commission Communications, White papers, Green papers, working documents and reports.

The full text of the *Official Journal* C and L series is available for the last 45 days. If you have a reference to a recent issue you can select and display the text. The current issue is available by about midday on the day of publication.

The final section, "Case law", provides a link to the website of the Court of Justice of the European Communities where the full text of recent judgments is available (see **11–20**).

The launching of EUR-Lex has meant that a large amount of legal information of the E.U. is now available to anyone with access to the internet.

THE COMMUNITY TREATIES

The principal source of Community law is the E.C. Treaty (the Treaty Establishing European Union). However, there are many other related treaties, including:

— the ECSC Treaty, 1951;

— the EURATOM Treaty, 1957;

— the Single European Act, 1986;

— the Treaty on European Union, 1992;

— the Treaty of Amsterdam, 1997.

The current form of the E.C. Treaty is the result of changes made by the Single European Act, the Treaty on European Union (the Maastricht Treaty) and the Treaty of Amsterdam. These amended the text of the original EEC Treaty, 1957. The Treaty on European Union was responsible for the change in name from EEC Treaty to E.C. Treaty.

The E.C. Treaty performs two main tasks. The first is that it represents a system of substantive rules which are binding on the Member States, and whose aim is to foster social and economic integration among the Member States. Secondly, and equally importantly, the Treaty creates a set of institutions and a procedural framework through which these institutions can create secondary Community legislation and take other measures which have a legally binding effect.

One of the amendments made by the Treaty of Amsterdam, of which you should be aware, is the renumbering of the provisions of the E.C. Treaty (and the Treaty on European Union). For example, Article 119 E.C. of the E.C. Treaty is now Article 141 E.C.

A useful booklet published by the European Commission, *The ABC of Community Law* by Dr Klaus-Dieter Borchardt (2000) provides an introduction to Community law and provides a table of the old and new numbering scheme referred to in Article 12 of the Treaty of Amsterdam. The web pages of the Court of Justice and the Court of First Instance have a useful Notes section setting out the new form of citation (at **curia.eu.int/en/ jurisp/renum.htm**).

The consolidated text of the founding treaties can be found on the EUR-Lex website (at **europa.eu.int/eur-lex/en**), incorporating the amendments made by the Treaty of Amsterdam. EUR-Lex has also added the text of the Treaty of Nice, signed on February 26, 2001, which will amend the existing Treaties. It will enter into force once all 15 Member States have ratified it. Both original and present versions of the Treaties are published on CELEX. Links to the texts of the Treaties are provided via the "ABC" section of EUROPA.

The text of primary legislation is published by the E.U. publisher, the Office for Official Publications of the European Communities (OOPEC), or EUR-OP (at **eur-op.eu.int**). The latest printed version, *EU—Selected instruments taken from the Treaties* (1999) includes the Treaty of Amsterdam. Book I, Volume I contains the texts currently in force including the Treaty of Amsterdam, the Treaty on European Union and the Treaty establishing the E.C. in its amended form. Volume II contains the full documentation of the treaties establishing the ECSC, and the EURATOM treaties.

Primary legislation which has not yet been brought together in an official set is generally published in the *Official Journal of the European Communities* (see **11–8**) in either the C series or the L series according to its official status. Primary legislation can often be located as separately published documents or even as United Kingdom Command Papers. The Treaty of Nice was published both in the *Official Journal* C series on March 10, 2001 and as Command Paper (Cm. 5090).

In addition to these official sources, you will find many of the important texts of primary materials published in student textbooks. Examples include *Blackstone's Statutes on E.C. Legislation* (2000/2001 edition), edited by Nigel Foster; and Rudden and Wyatt, *Basic Community laws* (1999). The *Encyclopedia of European Union Laws* also contains the texts of the treaties.

11–6   SECONDARY LEGISLATION

Secondary legislation is that which is created by the institutions of the European Communities in implementing the powers granted to them in the Community treaties. There are different types of legislative acts, and these are given different names depending on whether they are made under the E.C. and EURATOM Treaties or under the ECSC Treaty. The following table lists the different types:

ECSC	*E.C./EURATOM*
Decisions (general)	Regulations
Recommendations	Directives
Decisions (individual)	Decisions
	Recommendations
Opinions	Opinions

Article 249 (previously Article 189) of the E.C. Treaty explains the different kinds of act made under it. It is with these you will be most concerned.

The legislative process of the European Union is very different from that of the United Kingdom. Draft legislation or proposals are put forward by the Commission and the final versions are published as *Commission Documents* (known as *COM Docs*). They are also published in the *Official Journal* C series. Proposals are then considered by the European Parliament and the Economic and Social Committee (ESC) or the Committee of the Regions (CoR), which publish *Reports* or *Opinions*.

COM Docs, European Parliament Reports, Economic and Social Committee Opinions and *Committee of the Regions Opinions* are available as series and may be taken by your library. Recent *COM Docs* are also included on EUR-Lex under "Legislation in Preparation" or "Documents of Public Interest" . *ESC* and *CoR Opinions* are published in the *Official Journal* C series. Selected recent *ESC Opinions* are available on their website (at **www.ces.eu.int**). *CoR Opinions* in progress are also available (at **www.cor.eu.int**). Resolutions of the European Parliament (but not the full report) are published in the *Official Journal* C series and since 1997, *European Parliament Reports* have been made available on the Parliament's website, Europarl (at **www.europarl.eu.int**). *Common Positions* of the Council are published in the *Official Journal* C series and are included on Europarl. All of the above can be located in CELEX, but the full text is not always given.

Once the various suggestions from these bodies have been considered, and the original proposals amended if necessary (in some cases there will have to be a second reading in the European Parliament), the Council will adopt the directive or regulation and it will be published in the *Official Journal* L series. Directives must then be implemented in the law of the Member States.

Procedures that are used in the legislative process, *e.g.* consultation, co-operation, co-decision and approval procedures are outlined in *The ABC of Community Law* (see **11–5**).

Citation of E.C. Legislative Acts   11–7

The formal citation of a European Communities legislative act is made up of the following elements:

1. The institutional origin of the act (Commission or Council).
2. The form of the act (regulation, directive, decision, etc.).
3. An act number.
4. The year of the enactment.
5. The institutional treaty basis (E.C., ECSC, EURATOM).
6. The date the act was passed.

Regulation numbers are written with the number first and the year following. Decisions and directives are written the other way round, with the year first and the number following. All indexes will therefore always list regulations first and decisions and directives afterwards. Two examples follow:

1. Commission Regulation (EEC) No. 896/93 of 16 April 1993, setting the indicative yield for hemp seed for the 1992/93 marketing year. (This can be abbreviated to Reg. (EEC) 896/93.)

2. 93/209/EEC Commission Decision of 6 April 1993, amending Decision 93/144/EEC on certain protective measures in respect of salmon from Norway. (This can be abbreviated to Dec. 93/209/EEC.)

Between 1958 and 1967, this citation form varied. The variations are laid out in *Halsbury's Statutes* (4th ed.), Vol. 50, pp. 211–212. From 1992, directives and decisions were given separate numerical sequences, with the consequence that a directive and a decision can both be given the same number. Thus there exist both Dir. 93/12/EEC and Dec. 93/12/EEC.

A legislative act is given a date of enactment but this does not indicate the date when the act is published in the *Official Journal*: this can be up to several months later.

11–8 The Official Journal

The *Official Journal*, published by the European Communities, is the official and authoritative source of legislation. It carries the text of proposed and enacted legislation and official announcements, as well as information on the activities of Community institutions.

The *Official Journal* is published about six times a week in the following separate parts:

1. *L series* (*Legislation*): this consists of the texts of enacted legislation. This legislation is divided into two sequences.

   (a) acts whose publication is obligatory (primarily regulations, directives addressed to all Member States, ECSC Decisions and acts concerning the European Economic area);
   (b) acts whose publication is not obligatory (all other legislation).
   In effect, this means that all legislative acts are published in the *Official Journal*; but note that they are listed in two sequences in the *Official Journal: Index*.
2. *C series (Information and Notices)*: this is arranged in three parts, as follows:
   (a) Part I, *Information* from the various Community institutions including:
      (i) *Commission*—EURO exchange rates, communications and notices concerning Community policy and notifications from companies and governments applying Community law.
      (ii) *Court of Justice*—a list of new cases brought before this court and the Court of the First Instance, summaries of judgments of the Court of Justice and the Court of First Instance.
      (iii) *European Parliament*—minutes of the plenary sessions and written questions from members of the European Parliament.
      (iv) *Economic and Social Committee*—Opinions.
   (b) Part II, Preparatory Acts: the texts of proposed legislation.
   (c) Part III, *Notices* of invitation to tender for commercial and research contracts and notices of staff vacancies in Community institutions.
3. *S series (Supplement)*: this publishes details of public contracts open to competitive tender.
4. *Official Journal: annex—debates of the European Parliament*: this contains the full text of the debates of the plenary sessions of the European Parliament and oral questions.
5. *Official Journal: Special Edition*—this gives an official English translation of the legislation enacted between 1952 and 1972 which was still in force at the time of the United Kingdom's accession.

Two parts are no longer published in paper format—the S series and the Annex. The S series has been published on CD-ROM since 1997. *Tenders Electronic Daily* (*TED*) (at **ted.eur-op.eu.int**) is the E.U.'s internet version of the S series. TED is updated daily and provides an archive of the last five years of the S series. The Annex to the *Official Journal* ceased to be published in paper in 2000 and has been published on CD-ROM since summer 2000 by EUR-OP. The *Debates* of the Parliament are also available on the European Parliament website Europarl (at **www.europarl.eu.int**).

EUR-OP has issued a monthly CD-ROM version of the *Official Journal* C and L series since 1999. An *Official Journal* C E edition was also launched in 1999. It contains the text of preparatory acts and is only available on the EUR-Lex website or as part of the monthly *Official Journal* CD-ROM. The full text of these legislative proposals no longer appears in the printed *Official Journal* C series. The full text of the *Official Journal* C series from 1990 onwards is also available from Context, either on CD-ROM or via their webservice, Justis.com. It should be noted that although electronic versions are widely and publicly available, the printed edition of the *Official Journal* remains the authoritative source of legislation.

The citation of references to the *Official Journal* is not standardised, but the usual form is: O.J. L73 26.3.93 p. 12. An alternative form is [1993] O.J. L73/12. This refers you to the *Official Journal* L series issue 73, dated March 26, 1993, at page 12.

The Official Journal Index   11–9

The key to any substantial source of legislative information is its index. Unfortunately, the *Official Journal Index* is less helpful than you would wish. It only indexes the adopted legislation published in the L series and the cases (by subject and number) in the C series. It is issued monthly with an annual cumulation. It is divided into two sections:

Volume I—Alphabetical Index;
Volume II—Methodological Table (numerical index).

The *Methodological Table* gives the *Official Journal* reference to all the legislative acts in numerical order. It also lists the cases brought before, and the judgments of, the European Court of Justice and the Court of First Instance for the period which is indexed. If, for example, you are given a reference to a legislative act such as Reg. (EEC) 990/93 or a case C–77/93, the *Methodological Table* gives you the reference in the *Official Journal*.

The *Alphabetical Index* is used in a different way. If you have no reference, or it is incomplete or incorrect, but you know, for example, what subject you are dealing with, use the alphabetical subject index to find the required references.

These volumes are used in tandem, the indexed items in the *Alphabetical Index* referring to the titles of the documents in the *Methodological Table*.

Other Sources of E.C. Legislation   11–10

In addition to the official electronic sources, CELEX and EUR-Lex, various commercially published sources provide access to E.C. legislation. Lexis-Nexis and Westlaw UK both provide full-text coverage of legislation and case law as well as current awareness information.

In Lexis-Nexis, the Source Directory will help you locate the files under "European Union". Lexis-Nexis is one of the commercial hosts to CELEX and therefore sources include the *Official Journal* L and C series, SEC and COM Docs The Directory within Westlaw UK lists the contents under "EU materials". Eurolaw, Justis CELEX, OJ Online, and Eurocat are additional electronic sources that can be used to trace legislation.

A useful printed source for legislation is *The Encyclopedia of European Community Law (Secondary Legislation)* published by Sweet & Maxwell. It is a looseleaf collection of all significant legislation in force. It has both subject and chronological indexes.

11–11   Indexes to E.C. Legislation

If access to CELEX is not available, and you are looking for references to E.C. legislation in force, in addition to the *Official Journal Index* (**11–9**), there is the *Directory of Community legislation in force*, published as part of the *Official Journal* L series. It is available both in print and on the EUR-Lex service under "Community legislation in force".

The print version is published in two volumes and updated every six months. Volume I, the *Analytical Register*, is a subject listing of all the acts in force together with amending legislation. *Official Journal* references are given. Volume II has a chronological and an alphabetical index by subject to Volume I. The acts in the *Chronological Index* are arranged under a notation derived from CELEX and are not immediately recognisable as a chronological listing of directives and regulations. The "Information to readers" section of the print version explains how to translate the numbers used into standard citations (see also **11–12**). The *Directory* provides references to initial texts and any amendments. It also includes references to agreements and conventions made by the E.U.

The *Directory* on EUR-Lex provides links to both the original and consolidated texts (where available) of legislation currently in force. Consolidated texts are not legally binding but are convenient for use as they incorporate the original text with any amending legislation. It has an alphabetical index listing subject terms. The "Consolidated legislation" section on EUR-Lex includes both a "Chronological Index" and, like the print version, a subject listing, the "Analytical Structure". The most recent additions to EUR-Lex can be seen under "Latest deliveries".

European Communities Legislation: Current Status, generally referred to as *Current Status*, is a non-official source for finding references to E.C. legislation, published by Butterworths. It consists of two annual volumes, kept up to date by quarterly *Cumulative Supplements* and a fortnightly updating sheet. It lists in chronological order references to all E.C. secondary legislation. There is also a *subject index*.

Current Status combines the work of both the *Official Journal Index* and the *Directory* in one consecutive numerical listing. It also has the advantages of being more up to date and of noting amendments to legislative acts, giving the appropriate *Official Journal* reference.

11–12   How to Trace the Text of an E.C. Regulation or Directive

How would you look for Directive 93/104/E.C. on the organisation of working time? The directive covers the right to have regular rests and to work a maximum 48 hour week.

Electronic
The best source to use if available is CELEX. Regardless of whether you are accessing CELEX via EUROPA or one of the commercial hosts, enter the directive number in the document number search box. You will need to use all four digits of the relevant year.

Along with the text of a directive on CELEX, you will also see a number, *e.g.* 31993L0104. This is the CELEX document number and was originally for internal use, but an understanding of these numbers can help when searching for documents on CELEX or EUR-Lex. The number is made up of the file sector within the database (*e.g.* legislation), the year, type of legal act and the document number (based on the natural number of the document). Thus, Directive 93/104/E.C. is 31993L0104. "3" is sector number for adopted legislation, "1993" is the year of the act, "L" signifies that the act is a directive and "0104" is the 104th directive of 1993. Before 1999, the year was noted in two digits not four, and you may still see these older references.

On the EUR-Lex web pages, use the "Search" facility to find Directive 93/104/E.C. A "Simple Search" will enable you to input the type of legislation (directive or regulation), year and number. An alternative approach is to select "Legislation in force" and then *Consolidated legislation* to access the Chronological Index. The directives are listed numerically after the decisions. However, not all legislation in force is available in a consolidated version. The directive you are looking for may also not have been amended and, if this is so, it will not feature in the consolidated section.

Remember that EUR-Lex covers legislation in force. If the directive you are seeking is no longer in force, it will not be on EUR-Lex. CELEX is the source that covers both historical and current legislation.

Print
If you are using printed indexes to locate Directive 93/104/E.C., the easiest index to use is *European Communities Legislation: Current Status* (**11–11**). Here, E.C. legislation is arranged by year and then by type of act. At the relevant page for Directive 93/104/E.C., you will see the entry:

> **93/104 [Cl Dir (E.C.)]**
> *OJ L 307 13.12.1993 p.18*

You can then find the full text of the directive in the appropriate issue of the *Official Journal*.

Alternatively, use the *Official Journal Annual Index* for 1993. In the *Methodological Table,* there is a section entitled "Acts whose publication is not obligatory", where directives are listed, alongside decisions, in numerical order. All references will be to the *Official Journal* L series.

If your reference is to legislation made during the current year, you need to refer to the *Official Journal: Monthly Index.* Then look at the *Methodological Table* in each monthly issue until you locate your reference.

How to Trace E.C. Legislation on a Subject without a Reference

11–13

If you have been told, for example, that there is a directive on working time or parental leave, but you do not have a number or a date, you will need to use a subject approach. Databases can be searched by keyword. Various printed subject indexes are also available.

Whether you use electronic or print approaches, choosing the correct terminology can be a problem. Directives are commonly given colloquial titles such as the "Working Time Directive" or the "Parental Leave Directive", but these are not official titles. Searching for these colloquial terms in sources will not necessarily locate them. It is possible in certain electronic databases such as Justis CELEX to search on the colloquial term, but not all are indexed. As a result it is necessary to consider the keywords that might be used to index the directive. The "Parental Leave Directive" has the official title "Council Directive 96/34/E.C. of 3 June 1996 on the framework agreement on parental leave concluded by UNICE, CEEP and the ETUC".

Electronic

Electronic sources such as CELEX have the advantage that you can search using any subject term that appears in the title or text of a directive. This provides the quickest method of tracing E.C. legislation by subject. If you know there is a directive on working time, you can find all directives which have "working time" in the title. "Working hours" could also be used in a search of words in title or text. Searching for words in the text, rather than the title, of a document will widen your search results.

A search using "parental leave" on the EUR-Lex website will find the consolidated text of Council Directive 96/34/E.C. and the amending directive 97/75/E.C. The directive can also be found using the analytical structure or the alphabetical index. The directive on the organisation of working time is to be found in "chapter 05 Freedom of movement for workers and social policy" under the subsection "Wages, income and working hours". You will find the entry:

> **Consolidated text 1993L0104**
> Council Directive 93/104/E.C. of 23 November 1993 concerning certain aspects of the organization of working time

Print

Among the print indexes, *Current Status*, if available, provides a comprehensive approach. Begin with the subject entries in the *Supplement* volume. However, if you are looking, for example, for the directive on parental leave, you will not find an entry under "parental leave", so you must think of wider terms to search the index. Under "social policy", there is a sub-heading "parental leave" and a further sub-heading "equal treatment" referring you to 96/34 and 97/75. When you go to the volumes to look up the first directive, you will find that it is called "Council Directive on the framework agreement on parental leave concluded by UNICE, CEEP and the ETUC". You will be given the *Official Journal* reference needed to find the text. The second reference in the index refers to an amending directive.

If you do not have access to *Current Status*, use the *Official Journal's Annual Indexes* (but you will have to go through each one to find a directive as you do not know the year). If you are searching, for example, for directives on copyright of computer software, then in the 1991 *Alphabetical Index*, you will find the following entry:

Keywords/expressions	Document number	OJ reference	Legal form
international organization, legal status, market supervision, UNO	91/179	L2/89/39	D/CS
metal product, Mexico, restoration of customs duties	2250/91	L1/204/36	R/COM
copyright			
approximation of laws, computer piracy, data-processing law, software	91/250	L2/122/42	L/CS
broadcasting, information medium, television	70/89	C1/201/13	2/T
	76/89	C1/201/14	2/T
monopoly, public prosecutor's department, tax	270/86	C1/12/4	2/CJ

The document number heading tells you the Directive number: 91/250 and the *Official Journal* reference tells you that it will be found in the 1991 *Official Journal*, at page 42.

If you still cannot find your piece of legislation, then it may be that it is too recent to be in any of the printed indexes. If so, then current awareness services may provide the reference. Electronic services such as *European Access plus* published by Chadwyck-Healey, Butterworths *EU Direct* service or Lawtel may be available. *European Access* is also available in print and is published six times a year. Press releases of the E.U. institutions are available via EUROPA under "News".

Other sources you can use are the *Encyclopedia of European Community Law (Secondary Legislation)*; *Halsbury's Laws of England*, Vols 51 and 52 (or its equivalent, Vaughan, *Law of the European Communities Service*); the E.U.'s *General Report on the Activities of the European Union*; and the *Bulletin of the European Union*. The last two are official sources and are available on the EUROPA website from 1997 onwards. To locate them on EUROPA, select "Official Publications".

The contents pages of the *General Report on the Activities of the European Union*, list broad headings such as "Company law". In the 1999 *Report*, this heading comes under Chapter IV—The Community economic and social area and Section 5—Internal market, though this may differ in earlier *Reports*. By reading a succession of *General Reports*, you can build up a history of the subject.

The *General Report* is published annually. For more up-to-date information, turn to the *Bulletin of the European Union*, which is a monthly review of the Union's work. It is arranged in a standard format in each issue. Here company law will be dealt with in the section on the Internal Market and then under the sub-heading "Company Law". For example, the *Bulletin* of the European Union for December 2000 has an entry for company law reporting the "Amended proposal for a thirteenth European Parliament and Council Directive on company law concerning takeover bids" and lists the document references at its various stages of consultation with the citations for the *Official Journal* plus a summary.

Alternatively, use *Halsbury's Laws of England* to find out the E.C. law on a subject. At the back of Volume 52 of the fourth edition of *Halsbury's Laws of England*, you will find an Index to Volumes 51 and 52. Under the heading "Company", there are various sub-headings including "EEC law. See E.C. company law". Under that heading, you will find a large number of sub-headings, such as "Draft directive—fifth directive, 11.62". By turning to paragraph 11.62, in Volume 51 you will find the history of that directive. To bring the information up to date, you will need to refer to the *Cumulative Supplement* and looseleaf *Current Service* volumes. *Halsbury's Laws* is also available electronically via the Butterworths Direct services as *Halsbury's Laws Direct* (see **7–4**).

Since 1992 Butterworths have published a review of the year which is part of the annual cumulation of the *EU Brief*, entitled *Butterworths Annual European Review*. It is an index to all key community legislation and case law for each year.

11–14 How to Trace if E.C. Legislation Is Still in Force

How do you discover if Directive 90/387/EE.C., dealing with the establishment of the internal market for telecommunications services, is still in force?

Electronic
You can find the directive most easily by number using EUR-Lex. Restrict your search to the section "Legislation in force". EUR-Lex displays the text of the directive along with links to any amending legislation and the consolidated text. The reference to the appropriate issue of the *Official Journal* is also given. If the legislation is not in force, it does not appear.

Print
Use the print *Directory of Community Legislation in force* if you do not have access to EUR-Lex. Refer to Volume II of the latest edition of the *Directory* and use the *Chronological Index.* The acts are arranged by year and type of act, but not in a notation which is instantly recognisable. The notation is that given by CELEX, as described in **11–12**.

Once you have worked out how to convert your directive number into a CELEX document number, you can find it in the *Chronological Index*, where you will be referred to a page in Volume I of the *Directory*. There you will find a list of all E.C. legislation on telecommunications in force. There is also a reference to the *Official Journal*. Amendments to the legislation are listed. As with EUR-Lex, legislation not in force is not printed.

11–15 How to Know if a Proposal Has Become Law

In the United Kingdom, draft legislation is introduced into Parliament and becomes law during the same parliamentary session. This is not the case with E.C. legislation, which may take years to either become law or ultimately fail to become law. How, for example, would you know if the Commission's proposal for a directive on parental leave has become law? The Commission introduced a proposal on this subject in 1996, published as COM (1996) 26/Final.

Electronic
Tracing a proposal through the stages in the legislative process is possible through two websites, the Legislative Observatory (OEIL) on the European Parliament pages (at **wwwdb.europarl.eu.int/dors/oeil/en**), or PreLex on the EUROPA pages (at **europa.eu.int/prelex**).

The Legislative Observatory (OEIL) is a database provided by the European

Parliament which contains the details of all procedures or proposals still ongoing, along with those concluded since the beginning of the fourth legislative term in July 1994. It is possible to search by specific reference, or by keywords in titles or abstracts. To do this select the "Legislative Dossiers: Search" section and select your search option. To trace COM (1996) 26, search by document reference and enter the number required. The search displays a reference to a procedure identified by a number, *e.g.* "COS/1996/0033 Framework agreement on parental leave concluded by UNICE, CEEP and the ETUC". On displaying the procedure, you see a section "Stages in the procedure". You will discover that a European Parliament Report PE A4–0064/1996 was tabled on February 27, 1996 and that the final act was published in the *Official Journal* L series (O.J.L 145) on June 19, 1996, page 5 as Council Directive 96/34/E.C. of June 3, 1996. Links are available both to the text of the European Parliament Report and to the directive. Background information at the various stages is also supplied.

Pre-Lex was launched by the European Commission in 2000 and has a similar purpose to the Legislative Observatory. It can be used in much the same way. PreLex follows all Commission proposals and communications from the Council or European Parliament through to adoption or rejection. Using the standard search option on PreLex, a search can be conducted by COM Doc reference or by keyword. A search for the COM Doc, COM (1996) 26 FINAL, again presents the stages of the decision-making process, with dates and references for each stage, ending with a reference to the directive itself. (Both the Legislative Observatory and PreLex use the CELEX number 31996L0034 for the directive reference.) Links are provided to online versions of documents where available.

Print

Another way of tracing a proposal's progress is to use the *General Report on the Activities of the European Union.* If you do not know the date when the proposal was introduced, it is necessary to go to the latest *General Report* and work backwards. If you know the date of the proposal, then begin with the *General Report* of that year and work forwards. The *Bulletin of the European Union* will bring you up to date. The *General Report* for 1996 gives the complete legislative history and sources for all stages of the proposal on parental leave.

Alternative sources include Volumes 51 and 52 of *Halsbury's Laws.* Once Halsbury's has identified the proposal, you can check the Cumulative Supplement and the Service volume at the same paragraph number to see if the proposal has progressed. You can use *Vaughan* in the same way, with the advantage that, under each subject, there is a list of adopted and proposed legislation, to enable you to find the correct reference.

How to Trace whether a Directive Has Been Implemented in the United Kingdom
11–16

Directives, once adopted by the Council of the European Union, must be implemented by Member States by the most appropriate method for each country. In the United Kingdom, this is generally done by passing an Act of Parliament or issuing a statutory instrument. Member States are given a set period of time in which to do this.

Electronic

CELEX is the main source for information on the implementing legislation of Member States. However, the information provided on CELEX is supplied by the Member States, and there is no guarantee that the information is complete.

Print

The main printed source for the United Kingdom is *Butterworths E.C. Legislation Implementator*. This lists all directives in chronological order and gives an *Official Journal* reference for each, along with the target date by which it must be implemented and the Act or statutory instrument which implements it. The *Implementator* is issued twice yearly and is kept up to date by the fortnightly updating sheets which come with its sister publication, *Current Status*.

11–17   CASE LAW

There are two courts which interpret and enforce E.C. law. The first, the European Court of Justice (ECJ), has been in existence since the Communities were founded. The second, the Court of First Instance (CFI), gave its first judgments in 1990. The ECJ hears all types of cases, including appeals from the CFI, but the CFI hears only competition, anti-dumping and staff cases. The case law of both courts has assumed a position of great importance.

The *Official Journal* C series carries notices of cases pending before the courts. Brief details of the nature of the proceedings and the judgment are provided.

11–18   European Court Reports

The official source of European Court judgments is the *Reports of Cases before the Court*. These are more commonly known as the *European Court Reports* (abbreviated to E.C.R.). In this series, the opinion of the Advocate General is given alongside the judgment. This is an important stage in the proceedings before the European Court of Justice. The Advocate General's opinion is not binding on the court, but it is of great use to students of Community law in that it will include a thorough analysis of the facts and legal arguments in the case. There is an English language set of the *Reports* covering the judgments of the courts since 1954. Since 1990, the *Reports* have been split into two parts in each issue. Part I contains ECJ cases and Part II contains CFI cases. Since 1994 staff cases are being published in a separate series known as *Reports of European Community Staff Cases* (ECS-SC), and are not all translated into other languages.

Although the E.C.R. is the official series, it suffers from major delays in publication. Precise and accurate translation into the various Community languages results in delays of up to two years which makes it impossible to use it for recent cases. However for the 1994 *Reports* onwards, English translations are appearing much earlier although there is still a delay in translating cases into English before this date. The indexing for this series is also poor and late. Older indexes (before 1985) allow you to trace the case by the names of the parties, by subject and by case number. Since 1985, only indexes by subject and by date are available for each year. From 1990 onwards, these are again divided by court.

11–19   Citation of European Court of Justice and Court of First Instance Cases

The case citation is made up as follows:

1. case number;

2. year;
3. name of parties;
4. citation: indicating where the case can be found in the *European Court Reports* (E.C.R.):

e.g. Case C–59/89 *Commission* v. *Germany* [1991] E.C.R. I–2607 Case T–12/90 *Bayer* v. *Commission* [1991] E.C.R. II–219.

Alternatively the citations for the European Court Reports can be written as follows: [1991] I E.C.R. 2607 and [1991] II E.C.R. 219.

Note that each case after 1990 is preceded by the letter C (European Court of Justice) or the letter T (Court of First Instance). Also note that a case with a reference ... /89, for example, means that the application or reference to the court was made in 1989. The judgment was not necessarily given in that year. This means that you cannot automatically go to the E.C.R. for the year 1989 to find the judgment.

Other Sources of E.C. Case Law

11–20

CELEX is the main electronic source to use when tracing E.C. case law. It contains all the judgments and opinions delivered by the European Court of Justice since 1970. Judgments appearing in CELEX will be published, after some delay, in the *European Court Reports*. Both online and printed judgments appear more quickly in their French versions. All the available versions of CELEX can be used for tracing and retrieving the full text of E.C. case law by case name, number or subject.

The website of the Court of Justice and Court of First Instance (at **curia.eu.int/en**) is the source to use for recent case law. The site includes full case lists that can be browsed by year in numerical order. Coverage is from 1953 onwards with links to judgments where available. There is also a diary of pending cases, and press releases from the Court from 1996 onwards. The full text of the judgments and opinions can be searched from June 1997 onwards by case number, date, party name or keywords. Dates have to be input by year, month, day (1999–04–28). Judgments are made available in all E.U. languages on the day on which they are delivered.

Some libraries subscribe to *Judgments or orders of the Court and Opinions of the Advocates General.* These are printed in a typescript format, and are sent out in regular batches. They are issued on the day of judgment. They are not considered authoritative.

The *Proceedings of the Court of Justice* is a weekly bulletin giving a summary of the judgments and opinions of the court during the week in question. It is primarily a current awareness service and is available on the Court of Justice website from 1996 onwards in the "Press and Information" section. At the end of the year, the *Synopsis of the judgments delivered by the Court of Justice for the year......* is issued, which is an index to the contents of the year's issues. This arranges the judgments, but not the opinions, under headings such as "social policy" and "free movement of goods". The *Proceedings* are also available in the JUSTIS range of databases from Context as *ECJ Proceedings.* Daily newspapers such as *The Times* and the *Financial Times* also report significant European Court judgments in their Law Reports section.

The *Common Market Law Reports* (C.M.L.R) is the main alternative to the *European Court Reports.* It is published by Sweet & Maxwell and also covers the cases with an E.C dimension in national courts. C.M.L.R. appears sooner than the *European Court Reports* with a full, if not official, report. Although it does not report all cases, it does report all cases of significance. It has a similar range of indexes to the *European Court Reports*. The series is available on CD-ROM from 1962 onwards from Context and online from Westlaw UK.

The *All England European Cases* (All ER (EC)) from Butterworths has published decisions from the Court of Justice and the Court of First Instance since 1995. It is also available via the web service *EU Direct* from Butterworths and online from Lexis-Nexis. *European Community Cases* (C.E.C.) is another source of E.C. case law. Originally published by CCH as part of the *Common Market Reporter*, it is now published by Sweet & Maxwell. Only very important cases are covered. Specialist law report series such as *Fleet Street Reports* or *Industrial Relations Law Reports* also include relevant significant E.C. case law.

If you are specifically interested in decisions relating to competition there are further sources. The website of the Directorate-General for Competition (at **europa.eu.int/comm/competition**) publishes antitrust and merger cases and liberalisation decisions. Merger decisions can be searched by case number, company name or NACE code and coverage is from 1990 onwards. Merger decisions are also included on CELEX. The C.M.L.R. Antitrust Reports have been published since 1988.

11–21   Tracing Cases with an E.C. Dimension

For recent judgments, use CELEX or the ECJ website. The published sets of law reports mentioned above also produce their own indexes. The *Current Law Case Citator* indexes selected cases, as does its sister publication, *European Current Law. Current Legal Information* (**2–12**) can also be used to trace some European cases. Both Westlaw UK and Lexis-Nexis contain the full text of cases from the ECJ and the CFI. Both begin coverage from 1954 and in addition to the official *European Court Reports* from the ECJ, they include the full text of some commercially published law report series.

Butterworths EC Case Citator and Service covers most E.C. case law from 1954. Cases are indexed by case number, first party name, subject keywords, legislation covered and "nicknames". The *Citator* is published twice a year and fortnightly updating sheets are issued. Very recent cases can be traced by subject, name of party and case number. Sources given are the *European Court Reports* and the *Common Market Law Reports*, but where a case has not yet been published in either of these, the transcript date or *Official Journal* reference is given.

Another cumulative index is the *Gazetteer of European Community Law* 1953–1983 with two *Annual Supplements* in 1989 and 1990. This is an index to the whole of the E.C. case law for the years covered, plus much national case law with an E.C. dimension. It allows you to trace cases by the names of the parties, by case numbers and by subject. There is also a "Case Search" in the original volumes and a "Case/Law Tracker" for 1989 and 1990.

The ECJ's own *Digest of Case-law relating to the European Communities* consists of two series. The A series (most ECJ cases) covers case law from 1977 and was published in looseleaf format. The French version is currently available on the Court's website (at **www.curia.eu.int/en**), but not the English. The D series (cases relating to the Brussels Conventions) covers the case law of the Court of Justice from 1976 to 1991, and case law of the courts of the Member States from 1973 to 1990. The website also contains an *Alphabetical index of subject matter* in English.

How to Find a Court of Justice Judgment if you Have the Reference

Suppose you are given the following case reference: Case C–196/89 *Nespoli* v. *Crippa*. How do you find it?

Electronic

Searching CELEX on either the case number, or one or both of the party names, finds the full text of the case. If a free-text search is conducted on the case number or names, in addition to the original case, later cases which refer to it will also be retrieved. CELEX cites the *European Court Reports* reference for the *Nespoli* case, [1990] ECR I–3647. However, the case will not be found on the European Court website, as it is prior to 1997. A search for Nespoli in the "word in the text field" box locates references to the case in later judgments. The judgment could also be located from the numerical list. If you do not have access to CELEX, use the European Court's website for judgments made from 1997 onwards, *e.g.* for the judgment delivered on February 8, 2001 for case C–350/99, *Wolfgang Lange* v. *Georg Schünemann GmbH*.

Westlaw UK and Lexis-Nexis also provide access to the full text of cases. Search by name or number within the European case files. Journal indexes such as *Legal Journals Index* will enable you to trace full references to recent developments in various U.K. law journals (see Chapter 5).

Print

If using print sources, turn to the *Butterworths EC Case Citator*, as this covers every year.

A judgment for a case with the number 290/83 may have been given in any year subsequent to 1983, and therefore it is best to use the *Butterworths EC Case Citator* to find a case where you do not know the year of judgment. When you have a case number, *e.g.* Case C–196/89, go to the numerical list of cases. By the side of number C–196/89 there are two citations: one for the official *European Court Reports* and the other for the *Common Market Law Reports*. If you do not have a full reference for your case but were only given the names of the parties "Nespoli" and "Crippa", look up the first name in the alphabetical list of names. You will not find the case under the second name. The full citation will be given in all cases.

Alternatively, particularly for older cases, you should use the *Gazetteer of European Law*. You can use it in much the same way as the *Butterworths EC Case Citator*.

If these reference works are not available, there are alphabetical and numerical indexes to important cases at the front of Volume 52 of *Halsbury's Laws* (4th ed.). Recent cases need to be traced in the (separate) index contained in the Table of Cases, first in the *Cumulative Supplement* and then in the *Current Service* binder.

Law journals, *e.g. European Law Review*, often have alphabetical and numerical indexes to cases.

How to find a Judgment of the Court of Justice on a Subject

What can you do if you want to find cases on, for instance, the Common Customs Tariff?

Electronic

Using CELEX, you can search for the phrase "Common Customs Tariff" wherever it occurs in the text of the document to find relevant cases. As mentioned before, be aware of the different ways and different terms which all databases and printed indexes can use.

Using the Court of Justice website and searching for the names in the "words in the text" section also finds references to judgments which refer to a case if the judgment was made after 1997.

Print

In *Butterworths EC Case Citator*, there is a long list of cases on the Common Customs Tariff under that heading, but there is no such heading in the *Gazetteer*. You will find them there, however, under the main heading "Customs", sub-headed "Classification". Also note that *Butterworths EC Case Citator* does not aim to index all its cases by subject.

The Digest summarises cases on E.C. law under appropriate subject headings. Volume 21 contains the main collection of cases on E.C. law, with alphabetical and case number indexes. You can update it by referring to the *Cumulative Supplement* and *Quarterly Surveys*.

11–24 How to Trace Cases which Refer to the Leading Case

You may want to know if a European Court case, such as Case 139/79, has been referred to in a later judgment.

Electronic

As mentioned in **11–23**, a free-text search on the case name using a database such as CELEX will find references to the case in the text of other judgments. If you are using the E.U.'s version of CELEX display the original case and use the option to display all documents referring to it.

Print

The *Gazetteer of European Law* is useful for older cases with coverage from 1953 to 1983 and there are further volumes for 1989 and 1990. In Volume II, the section called "Case search", Part IV, lists cases in numerical order. Under Case 139/79, there are nine cases listed. In the two later volumes the section "Case Tracker" lists seven more cases. Those in bold type are considered to be the most important.

Current Law includes key European judgments and indexes cases considered in the English courts. *European Current Law* digests selected cases from the European courts and the national courts of the Member States. References in the two publications will be given to the *European Court Reports* and any commercially published law report series.

11–25 How to Trace Cases on E.C. Primary or Secondary Legislation

Commonly in research, there is a need to trace cases which are concerned with specific provisions of Community law. For example, how do you find out what cases have been heard in the European Court of Justice on Directive 93/96/EEC on the right of residence for students?

Electronic

A free-text search using CELEX using a directive number, or the title of the directive, is the quickest way to retrieve references to judgments referring to legislation. On the European Court of Justice website, it is possible to search for the directive number using the word search option.

Print

Butterworths EC Case Citator lists cases by treaty provision, regulations, directives and decisions. The *Gazetteer* for the 1989 and 1990 volumes has a section called "Law Tracker" which has the same purpose of tracking cases by legal provision. You may find that coverage in these two print sources varies. Neither are comprehensive.

How to Trace Recent Judgments   11–26

The European Court of Justice website should be the first place you turn to. The judgment of case C–123/00 delivered on April 5, 2001 was available at the end of April 2001. Use the search facility for recent case law and search by case name or number. If it does not appear, there is a list of pending cases included on the site.

The Court press releases may help in tracing recent cases. The judgment in *Germany v. European Parliament* (C–376/98) annulled Directive 98/43 regarding the advertising and sponsorship of tobacco products and was delivered on October 5, 2000. Details can be found in Press Release no. 72/00 issued on October 5, 2000. It announced the annulment of the directive and referred to *Germany v. European Parliament* and a related case, C–74/99, *R. v. Secretary of State for Health, ex parte Imperial Tobacco Ltd*. A substantial summary appeared in Issue 26/00 of the *Proceedings of the European Court of Justice and the Court of the First Instance*, published both on the web and in print. The print version of the *Proceedings* may take longer to appear in libraries.

Current Law indexed cases C–376/98 and C–74/99 in the November 2000 issue and cited the report published in *All England European Cases* at [2000] All E.R. (E.C.) 769. Although at the time of writing, the case had not been published in the authoritative *European Court Reports,* it was available on CELEX.

LEGAL ENCYCLOPEDIAS   11–27

Volumes 51 and 52 of *Halsbury's Laws of England* (4th ed.) cover the European Communities. They are a comprehensive account of institutional and policy developments up to the middle of the 1980s. The information in these volumes is kept up to date by the *Cumulative Supplement* and looseleaf *Service* binders. The *Current Service* contains developments at the back of each *Monthly Review*, including a separate index. You may find that your library has the electronic version, *Halsbury's Laws Direct*.

Other encyclopedic works include *Vaughan: Law of the European Communities Service,* edited by David Vaughan (Butterworths), a four-volume work arranged by subject comprehensively covering E.C. law, and Smit and Herzog, *Law of the European Communities.*

The Encyclopedia of European Community Law (Secondary Legislation) published by Sweet & Maxwell is a collection of all significant E.C. legislation in force, consolidated with annotations. It has checklists and tables for locating legislation and covers all areas of E.C. law.

The Encyclopedia of European Union Laws (also Sweet & Maxwell) provides coverage of all E.C. constitutional texts. There are four sections: the Treaties, the Institutions, Ancillary texts, and the Union Pillars.

11-28 BOOKS

The European Commission publishes a wealth of material providing introductions, overviews and summaries of topics. All these are available at your European Documentation Centre (see **11-1**). The library catalogue can help you locate them. Commission monographs on the legal system include *The Court of Justice of the European Communities* (1998) and *The ABC of Community Law* (5th ed., 2000).

A wide range of textbooks explaining the institutions of the E.U. and their part in the legislative process and the substantive law of the E.C. has also been published. These include, for example, Wyatt and Dashwood, *European Union Law* (4th ed., 2000). Many will be available from your own library. Because of the reforms introduced by the Treaty of Amsterdam, it is important to use the latest editions.

Current awareness services such as *European Access plus* (see **11-31**) include references to recent official and non-official publications. Remember also that E.C. law becomes part of English law either with direct effect (regulations and decisions) or after being implemented as Acts or statutory instruments (directives). This means that books on English law often include a chapter or section on Community law.

ECLAS, the European Commission's own library catalogue available via EUROPA (at **europa.eu.int**), is useful for tracing publications, journals and internet sites. Details of selected journal articles from European related journals are being added from 2001 onwards. The E.U. publisher, EUR-OP, also gives details of its publications on its website and in the bulletin *EUR-OP News*.

United Kingdom government publications of particular relevance to E.C. law include the *Reports of the House of Lords Select Committee on the European Communities*. These very often discuss proposed E.C. legislation in great detail. See Chapter 6 for help in tracing British government publications.

11-29 JOURNALS

Many legal journals cover E.U. topics in a selective manner. Major English-language journals that specialise in the subject include the *Common Market Law Review*, the *European Law Review*, the *European Business Law Review*, the *European Competition Law Review*, *International and Comparative Law Quarterly* and the *Yearbook of European Law*.

Publishers are increasingly publishing electronic journals so you will find some journals available in your library both in print and electronically (see **5-2**).

11-30 How to Find Articles on E.C. Law

If you are looking for recent articles on the "Working Time Directive", the best source is the Legal Journals Index (**5-4**) for coverage in U.K. law journals. Entries can be located by using the phrase "working time" or the directive number.

The European Commission's SCAD database is an excellent place to start research on E.U. topics for articles published between 1983 and 2001. It is available via EUROPA (at **europa.eu.int/scad**). It provides references to both official E.U. publications (including acts and proposals published in the *Official Journal* L and C series and the *Bulletin of the European Union*) and non-official publications (over 2,000 European related academic journals). It is available free on the EUROPA website, as well as from Context on CD-ROM as *European References*. ILI also include SCAD in *EU Infobase*. In March 2001, it was announced that due to reorganisation, SCAD was no longer being updated. Alternative sources for the information provided in SCAD are the legislation and proposals on CELEX and EUR-Lex and the articles to be included on ECLAS.

CURRENT INFORMATION   11–31

It is important to keep up to date with developments in the E.U. EUROPA has a "What's New" section and a "News" section. The Commission's press release database, Rapid, provides access to press releases from the early 1980s onwards. You can access the press releases of each E.U. institution from the "News" pages.

European Access plus is an excellent online information service published by Chadwyck-Healey. It includes information on key documents published by the E.U., summaries of activities, references to recent information sources—books, journal or newspaper articles—along with links to full-text material on the internet where available. A particularly useful section is "Europe on the internet", a frequently updated listing of key European internet sites. This is invaluable as websites change and develop. This section is also available online from another Chadwyck-Healey service, *Know Europe*.

The print version of *European Access* is published six times a year. Other current information services include *EU Direct* from Butterworths, Lexis-Nexis Direct, *EU Aware* from Ellis Publications, and *EU Interactive* from Lawtel. In addition to providing current and frequently updated information, these electronic services contain full text materials, including cases and legislation. *Butterworths EU Brief* is now published electronically. All these are subscription services.

News services such as those provided by Lexis-Nexis and Reuters Business Briefing can be used for news coverage in the European press. *The Times*, *The Financial Times*, *The Independent* and *The Guardian* are available on CD-ROM and have internet editions. *Europe*, a briefing service more familiarly known as *Agence Europe*, is available on Reuters Business Briefing. *European Report* is a twice-weekly publication begun in 1972 highlighting E.U. developments.

12 | Public International Law

INTRODUCTION

Early definitions of international law described it as "a body of rules governing the relations between states." In modern times, this definition has been expanded so that the concept now includes regulation of the relationships not only between states, but also between international organisations and individuals.

This chapter helps you find the international law materials in the library. Remember that public international law should be distinguished from private international law, or conflict of laws, which deals with the interrelationship of domestic municipal law of different states, rather than regulating the international relations between different states.

International law has no legislature, and no system of binding precedent in its judicial forums. Its observance therefore depends on the adherence by nations to its principles, which are mainly embodied in international treaties and international custom. The rules of international law only have binding effect from their inclusion in a treaty or convention or because they have been recognised as an international custom. States which do not ratify a particular treaty are not bound by its provisions. With the growth of international organisations, another body of international law is being created by them and it is therefore necessary for you to know how to find the legal publications of the major international organisations. You should also be aware of the way in which international law is constantly developing and expanding into new areas. Subjects now include environmental law, human rights, law of armed conflict and related issues such as humanitarian intervention, international economic and trade law, intellectual property and maritime law (both shipping law and the law of the sea). There is a constant flow of new publications in all these subjects.

As a student of international law, you will need to look well beyond the confines of the traditional law library to locate the various materials you will need, as they will also be found in international relations and official publications collections. To help you in your researches, this chapter describes the various generally accepted sources of international law and tells you about the materials comprising each source.

Electronic Sources for International Law

As explained in Chapter 2, electronic legal sources began to be produced on CD-ROM, but there is a gradual but ever faster migration to internet versions. Sometimes a particular database exists in both formats, possibly with differences in either content or software or both.

Websites fall into several categories. Examples are: (1) Worldwide or regional organisations producing their own documents (*e.g.* United Nations, Council of Europe); (2) specialist organisations with collections of documents on their particular subject (*e.g.* World Trade Organisation, International Committee of the Red Cross); (3) national government websites with foreign relations information (*e.g.* the U.K. Foreign Office, U.S. Department of State), and (4) research organisations and university departments offering a mixture of collected texts and link pages to other relevant websites (*e.g.* the Max Planck Institute; University of Minnesota Human Rights Library). Online library catalogues are also a source of information about publications relating to international law.

Starting points for electronic research
A well-organised and extensive site is that of the American Society of International Law (at **www.asil.org**). In particular you should look at its *Guide to Electronic Sources for International Law*, which is divided into sections dealing with various topics including human rights, environmental law and treaties. The Law Library of New York University (**www.law.nyu.edu/library/index.html**) also has a web page of links to internet sources for international law in general, and special subjects such as international trade law and international criminal law. The Social Sciences Information Gateway (SOSIG) (at **www.sosig.ac.uk**) has a section for international law, with links to various sources under about a dozen categories ranging from books, documents and articles to mailing lists, research centres and governmental organisations.

General legal databases
The major legal onine databases Lexis and Westlaw, now available in the U.K. as Westlaw UK, have materials that they describe as "international law", but you should be aware that this quite often means foreign domestic law. An example of true international law is the Westlaw database of judgments of the International Court of Justice (INT-ICJ).

12–3   SOURCES

The most frequently accepted definition of the sources of international law can be found in Article 38(1) of the Statute of the International Court of Justice which states that disputes submitted to it will be decided according to the principles of international conventions, international custom, general principles of law, judicial decisions and the writings of leading commentators.

12–4   TREATIES

As defined in the Vienna Convention on the Law of Treaties, a treaty is a written agreement concluded between two or more states or international organisations and governed by international law. Treaties come in many different disguises, such as protocols, conventions, charters, statutes, accords, etc. In this modern technological age, with its vastly improved communications, the huge growth of international trade and the growth of international interdependence, the volume of treaty publishing has become enormous and it is often difficult to trace particular treaties.

GENERAL COLLECTIONS

12–5

The first major category of treaty publishing is the general collection, of which there are three major series. The *Consolidated Treaty Series* (CTS) (1969–1986) edited by Clive Parry, and published in 231 volumes by Oceana, covers the years 1648 to 1920. It attempts to reprint the original text and official translations (if any) of all treaties published during that period. The treaties are arranged chronologically, with French or English translations where available. There is a multi-volume *Index-Guide* which contains a general chronological list of treaties, plus a party/country Index.

How to use the Consolidated Treaty Series **12–6**

Start with the *Index-Guide* volumes, which can be distinguished by the colour binding on the spine. They are divided into three sections. The *Party Index* is black. This lists countries alphabetically, and within each country gives a chronological list of the treaties concluded by that country, the names of the parties and the volume and page number within *CTS* where the treaty is published. The *General Chronological List* is red. This lists all treaties from 1648 to 1920 by date. It is a useful listing of all the treaties traced by the editors of *CTS*. It not only gives the *CTS* reference, but also references to the publication of treaties in other collections. The *Special Chronology* is green. This deals with colonial and other less important treaties and you will probably not need to use it.

Let's suppose that you are looking for a bilateral treaty between Great Britain and Belgium, setting the boundary between Uganda and the Congo. You know that the date of the treaty was 1910; you can therefore go straight to the *Chronological List* and under 1910 you will find the following entry:

> 1910: 14 May Agreement between Belgium and Great Britain settling the boundary dispute between the Congo and Uganda, Signed at Brussels.
> 211 CTS 103
> CVII B.S.P. 348 (Eng)

You will therefore be able to find the Treaty in the *Consolidated Treaty Series*, Vol. 211, at page 103. The reference to B.S.P. is to *British and Foreign State Papers* (see **12–10**).

If you do not know the date of the treaty, go to the *Party Index* and in the entries under Belgium you will find:

> 1910 May 14
> Belgium Great Britain
> 211 CTS 103

The *Consolidated Treaty Series* ends in 1920, because this is the first year covered by the *League of Nations Treaty Series*. This series continues until 1946 and contains over 4,000 treaties in 205 volumes. There are *Subject* and *Chronological Index* volumes interspersed between the texts.

United Nations Treaty Series and United Nations Treaty Collection

12–7

The third important series is the *United Nations Treaty Series* which started publication in 1946 when the UN took over the functions of the dissolved League of Nations. The UN publishes the text of every treaty entered into by any of its members, as all treaties have to be registered with the Secretariat. They are published in order of registration, and not by date of conclusion, which can make them extremely difficult to locate. So far, nearly 2,000 volumes have been published, at the rate of over 40 a year. The series is very late in publication, current issues covering a period seven or eight years ago.

This delay in publication can be remedied to some extent if your library has access to the corresponding online archive called the *United Nations Treaty Collection* (UNTC) (at **untreaty.un.org**). The database includes not only the *United Nation Treaty Series* itself, but also a database of the *Status of Multilateral Treaties Deposited with the Secretary General*. This gives the current status (signatures, ratifications, reservations, etc.) of over 500 treaties. The paper version of the *Status* part, entitled *Multilateral Treaties Deposited with the Secretary General*, is published annually in two volumes, but the online version is updated daily.

UNTC is a subscription service requiring a password, so you will need to find out whether your library subscribes. Notice that the treaty collection is not a searchable database but an image archive. Only indexed data such as title, date of signature or adoption, subject descriptors, registration number, etc., can be searched.

If you do not have access to the online version, then to locate a treaty you need to use the *Index* volumes of the printed series. Each *Index* contains a *Chronological Index* listing treaties in order of the date on which they were signed, plus an *Alphabetical Index*. If you need to find the countries that ratified the 1980 convention on child abduction during 1989, check in the *Chronological Index* for that period (Volume 27). The entry is shown in the figure on page 237. The first column indicates the languages of the authentic text, the second the treaty number, and the third the volume number in the *UN Treaty Series*.

If you are unsure of the date of the original treaty, check in the subject section of the *Alphabetical Index* under "Children—Minors—Youth", subsection MULTILATERAL. This entry appears in the figure on page 238.

Treaty numbers have four possible prefixes: I denotes a treaty *registered* with the UN Secretariat, II is a treaty *filed and recorded* with the Secretariat. A and B are subsequent instruments related to treaties in category I and II respectively.

The *Multilaterals Project* (at **fletcher.tufts.edu/multilaterals.htm**) was set up in 1992 at Tufts University in the U.S.A. It aims to provide free online access to the texts of international conventions. Originally limited in scope to environmental agreements, it now includes treaties on human rights, trade, armed conflict and other subjects, as well as some important historical documents.

12–8 National Collections

The second method of publication of texts of treaties is by country, many countries publishing separate collections of treaties. There is not yet an electronic database of the texts of United Kingdom treaties. The Foreign and Commonwealth Office web page (at **fco.gov.uk/directory/treaty.asp**) has only a list of the 30 or so multilateral treaties for which the U.K. is a depository, plus status information about them. So you will have to rely on the official printed source, the *United Kingdom Treaty Series*. Treaties are published in this series only after ratification. They may have appeared earlier as *Command Papers* (see **6–3**). The *Treaty Series* forms a sub-series to the Command Paper series and every treaty has both a Command Paper number and a Treaty Series number followed by the year of issue.

Example Page from UN Treaty Series Chronological Index

1980   **Chronological Index**

		Lang	Reg	Vol
10 Oct	**Multilateral:** Convention on Prohibitions or Restrictions on the Use of Certain Conventional Weapons which may be deemed to be Excessively Injurious or to have Indiscriminate Effects (with Protocols I, II and III) (with protocols). Geneva, 10 October 1980. Entry into force: 2 December 1983.	Arabic, Chinese, English, French, Russian, Spanish	I-22495	*(1342)*
	ACCESSION			
	Benin, 27 Mar 1989		A-22495	1527
	Cyprus, 12 Dec 1988 (With declaration)		A-22495	1520
	RATIFICATION			
	Liechtenstein, 16 Aug 1989		A-22495	1543
15 Oct	**United States of America and Mexico:** See 30 Jul 1980		I-26489	
17 Oct	**Spain and Equatorial Guinea:** Agreement on technical co-operation for the implementation of a social affairs and labour programme, especially in the field of vocational training and employment in Equatorial Guinea. Malabo, 17 October 1980. Entry into force: provisionally, on 17 October 1980 and definitively, on 25 June 1981.	Spanish	I-20358	*(1248)*
	Exchange of notes constituting an agreement amending the above-mentioned Agreement. Malabo, 22 May 1986 and 25 September 1986. Entry into force: 16 February 1988.	Spanish	A-20358	1505
17 Oct	**Multilateral:** European Agreement concerning the provision of medical care to persons during temporary residence (with procès-verbal of rectification). Geneva, 17 October 1980. Entry into force: 1 February 1983.	English, French, German, Russian, Spanish	I-21609	*(1301)*
	RATIFICATION			
	Italy, 4 Aug 1989 (With declaration)		A-21609	1547
	Norway, 6 Jun 1989		A-21609	1541
17 Oct	**Austria and Hungary:** Agreement on co-operation in the field of tourism. Vienna, 17 October 1980. Entry into force: 16 December 1980.	German, Hungarian	I-25930	1504
25 Oct	**Multilateral:** Convention on the Civil Aspects of International Child Abduction. The Hague, 25 October 1980. Entry into force: 1 December 1983.	English, French	I-22514	*(1343)*
	ACCEPTANCE			
	Australia, 7 Dec 1987 (ACCEPTANCE of the accession of Hungary)		A-22514	1504
	Canada, 26 Jan 1988 (ACCEPTANCE of the accession of Hungary)		A-22514	1504
	United Kingdom of Great Britain and Northern Ireland, 21 Jul 1989 (ACCEPTANCE OF THE ACCESSION OF BELIZE)		A-22514	1543
	United States of America, 29 Apr 1988 (ACCEPTANCE of the accession of Hungary)		A-22514	1504
	United States of America, 14 Aug 1989 (ACCEPTANCE OF THE ACCESSION OF BELIZE)		A-22514	1548
	ACCESSION			
	Belize, 22 Jun 1989 (With reservation)		A-22514	1541
	APPLICATION TO A TERRITORIAL UNIT			
	Canada, 26 Jan 1988 (With reservation) (application to North-west Territories)		A-22514	1504
	North-west Territories, 26 Jan 1988		A-22514	1504
	RATIFICATION			
	Austria, 14 Jul 1988		A-22514	1510
	Norway, 9 Jan 1989 (With reservations)		A-22514	1523
	Spain, 16 Jun 1987		A-22514	1504
	Sweden, 22 Mar 1989 (With reservation)		A-22514	1529
	United States of America, 29 Apr 1988 (With reservations)		A-22514	1504

CHEMICAL PRODUCTS

SEE ALSO INDUSTRY

CHINA

International Bank for Reconstruction and Development: Loan Agreement--Fertilizer Rationalization Project. Washington, 28 Dec 1987. (I-26046)

FRANCE

Switzerland: Agreement concerning the removal of phosphates from the waters of Lake Geneva. Berne, 20 Nov 1980. (I-20939)

INTERNATIONAL BANK FOR RECONSTRUCTION AND DEVELOPMENT

China: Loan Agreement--Fertilizer Rationalization Project. Washington, 28 Dec 1987. (I-26046)

Jordan: Guarantee Agreement--Shidiya Phosphate Mine Project. Washington, 10 Feb 1988. (I-26052)

JORDAN

International Bank for Reconstruction and Development: Guarantee Agreement--Shidiya Phosphate Mine Project. Washington, 10 Feb 1988. (I-26052)

MULTILATERAL

European Agreement on the restriction of the use of certain detergents in washing and cleaning products. Strasbourg, 16 Sep 1968. (I-11210)

SWITZERLAND

France: Agreement concerning the removal of phosphates from the waters of Lake Geneva. Berne, 20 Nov 1980. (I-20939)

CHILDREN-MINORS-YOUTH

SEE ALSO LABOUR; UNITED NATIONS CHILDREN'S FUND (UNICEF); HEALTH AND HEALTH SERVICES

ALGERIA

France: Convention relating to children born from separated parents of mixed French and Algerian nationalities. Algiers, 21 Jun 1988. (I-26445)

FEDERAL REPUBLIC OF GERMANY

France: Convention concerning the carrying out of an exchange of juveniles and adults undergoing basic or advanced vocational training. Paris, 5 Feb 1980. (I-20335)

FRANCE

Algeria: Convention relating to children born from separated parents of mixed French and Algerian nationalities. Algiers, 21 Jun 1988. (I-26445)

Federal Republic of Germany: Convention concerning the carrying out of an exchange of juveniles and adults undergoing basic or advanced vocational training. Paris, 5 Feb 1980. (I-20335)

GHANA

United Nations (United Nations Children's Fund): Agreement concerning the activities of UNICEF in Ghana. New York, 12 Aug 1958. (I-4469)

ITALY

United Nations (United Nations Children's Fund): Agreement for the establishment of an international child development centre in the "Istituto degli Innocenti" in Florence. New York, 23 Sep 1986. (I-26123)

LESOTHO

United Nations (United Nations Children's Fund): Agreement concerning the activities of UNICEF in Lesotho. Lusaka, 29 Oct 1971 and Maseru, 7 Apr 1972. (I-11699)

MULTILATERAL

Convention (No. 10) concerning the age for admission of children to employment in agriculture, as modified by the Final Articles Revision Convention, 1946. Geneva, 16 Nov 1921. (I-593)

Convention (No. 124) concerning medical examination of young persons for fitness for employment underground in mines. Geneva, 23 Jun 1965. (I-8873)

Convention (No. 15) fixing the minimum age for the admission of young persons to employment as trimmers or stokers, as modified by the Final Articles Revision Convention, 1946. Geneva, 11 Nov 1921. (I-598)

Convention (No. 16) concerning the compulsory medical examination of children and young persons employed at sea, as modified by the Final Articles Revision Convention, 1946. Geneva, 11 Nov 1921. (I-599)

Convention (No. 33) concerning the age for admission of children to non-industrial employment, as modified by the Final Articles Revision Convention, 1946. Geneva, 30 Apr 1932. (I-615)

Convention (No. 5) fixing the minimum age for admission of children to industrial employment, as modified by the Final Articles Revision Convention, 1946. Washington, 28 Nov 1919. (I-588)

Convention (No. 58) fixing the minimum age for the admission of children to employment at sea (revised 1936), as modified by the Final Articles Revision Convention, 1946. Geneva, 24 Oct 1936. (I-635)

Convention (No. 59) fixing the minimum age for admission of children to industrial employment (revised 1937), as modified by the Final Articles Revision Convention, 1946. Geneva, 22 Jun 1937. (I-636)

Convention (No. 7) fixing the minimum age for admission of children to employment at sea, as modified by the Final Articles Revision Convention, 1946. Genoa, 9 Jul 1920. (I-590)

Convention concerning the powers of authorities and the law applicable in respect of the protection of infants. The Hague, 5 Oct 1961. (I-9431)

Convention on the Civil Aspects of International Child Abduction. The Hague, 25 Oct 1980. (I-22514)

European Agreement on travel by young persons on collective passports between the member countries of the Council of Europe. Paris, 16 Dec 1961. (I-7909)

European Convention on the legal status of children born out of wedlock. Strasbourg, 15 Oct 1975. (I-17868)

UNITED NATIONS (UNITED NATIONS CHILDREN'S FUND)

Ghana: Agreement concerning the activities of UNICEF in Ghana. New York, 12 Aug 1958. (I-4469)

Italy: Agreement for the establishment of an international child development centre in the "Istituto degli Innocenti" in Florence. New York, 23 Sep 1986. (I-26123)

Lesotho: Agreement concerning the activities of UNICEF in Lesotho. Lusaka, 29 Oct 1971 and Maseru, 7 Apr 1972. (I-11699)

CHILE

France: Agreement relating to air services between and beyond their respective territories. Paris, 6 Dec 1979. (I-26545)

EXTRADITION

[Royal Crest omitted]

Italy No. 1 (1986)

Extradition Treaty

between the
United Kingdom of Great Britain and Northern Ireland
and the Italian Republic

Florence, 12 March 1986

[Instruments of ratification have not been exchanged]

*Presented to Parliament
by the Secretary of State for Foreign and Commonwealth Affairs
by Command of Her Majesty
June 1986*

LONDON
HER MAJESTY'S STATIONERY OFFICE
£1·90 net

Cmnd. 9807

The Agreement was
previously published as
China No. 1 (1984),
Cmnd. 9247

CHINA

[Royal Crest
omitted]

Treaty Series No. 14 (1985)

Agreement

between the Government of the
United Kingdom of Great Britain and Northern Ireland
and the Government of the People's Republic of China

on the Establishment of a British Consulate-General at Shanghai and a Chinese Consulate-General at Manchester

Peking (Beijing), 17 April 1984

[The Agreement entered into force on 14 January 1985]

*Presented to Parliament
by the Secretary of State for Foreign and Commonwealth Affairs
by Command of Her Majesty
April 1985*

LONDON
HER MAJESTY'S STATIONERY OFFICE
£1·75 net

Cmnd. 9472

The figure on p. 239 shows the first publication in the Command Paper series of an Extradition Treaty with Italy which had not been ratified.

The figure on p. 240 shows an agreement with China, published in the *Treaty Series*, which has been ratified. The heading on the top right-hand corner gives the name of the country as it is a bilateral treaty (if it were a multilateral treaty, then the subject matter would be printed here). The number on the top left-hand corner refers to the original, pre-ratification, Command Paper number.

How to use the United Kingdom Treaty Series 12–9

Start with the *Indexes to Treaty Series* which appear under three titles:

(a) the *General Index to Treaty Series*, of which the latest issue to appear was for 1977–79;
(b) the *Annual Index to Treaty Series*; and
(c) the *Supplementary List of Ratifications, Accessions, Withdrawals etc.*, which appears about four times a year.

Each *Index* is divided into numerical and subject sequences. The subject headings chosen are wide and slightly idiosyncratic, but once mastered are useful.

If you need to trace the Convention relating to a Uniform Law on the International Sale of Goods of 1964 and to find out if the United Kingdom is a signatory, then it can be found in the *Index to Treaty Series* under "Private International Law" as illustrated on p. 243. The entry gives details of the signatories to the Convention, its Treaty Series number and its Command Paper number.

It is possible, but not particularly easy, to extract treaty references from *UKOP*, the CD and online index of British official publications (see 6–18).

British and Foreign State Papers 12–10

This series was produced by the Foreign Office Library between 1812 and 1968. It contains the text of important treaties and conventions, not only between Great Britain and other countries, but also a selection of those made between other countries. Treaties are sometimes presented as part of a collection of all existing treaties on a particular topic, and the years indicated on the volume do not necessarily mean that the volume only contains material for those years. For example, Volume 1 has the years 1812–1814 on the spine but among its contents are "the treaties of alliance and commerce between Great Britain and Portugal subsisting in ... 1814". The earliest of these treaties is dated 1373.

The best way of finding material in *British and Foreign State Papers* is by using the cumulative general *Indexes*, which are numbered volumes in the series. The index volumes are numbers 64, 93, 115, 138, 165 and 170. They contain both a chronological and an alphabetical subject index.

Other national collections 12–11

More and more countries are making their treaties available on the internet. As yet this does not include the United States government, although the two major online databases both have full-text files of U.S. treaties. LEXIS has a complete file going back to 1776 and including texts of treaties no longer in force. From the source directory choose Area of Practice, then International Law, then Treaties, then U.S Treaties. Coverage on Westlaw begins with 1979. The legal publishers Oceana also provide an online database of United

States Treaties under the title TIARA. The full text database and index are subscription services, but the *Quick U.S. Treaties Index* is available free on registration with the website (at **www.oceanalaw.com**).

The official printed source is *United States Treaties and Other International Agreements* (U.S.T.), published by the Department of State since 1950. There is a long delay in publication, the fourth part of volume 35 covering 1983–84 being published in 1998. Even the individual pamphlet series T.I.A.S. *(Treaties and other International Acts Series)*, from which U.S.T. is compiled, is about five years behind. U.S. treaties before 1950 are published in C. Bevans, *Treaties and other International Agreements of the U.S.A. 1776–1949*, in 12 volumes plus an *Index*.

The most complete official online collection of treaties appears to be the *Australian Treaties Library* (at **austlii.edu.au/au/other/dfat**). This can also be used as a free source for the text of some historical multilateral treaties to which Australia is a party.

The *European Treaty Series*, containing the texts of treaties concluded by the Member States of the Council of Europe is described in **12–46**.

12–12   Hague Conventions

You may sometimes be referred to "The Hague Convention on …" While there are numerous treaties which happen to have been signed at The Hague, this very often refers to those drafted at sessions of The Hague Conference on Private International Law. The texts of these conventions are available on the Hague Conference website (at **hcch.net/e/**). As well as the full text of each convention, there is an explanatory report, status report (signatures, ratifications, etc.), bibliography and list of translations. A paperback *Collection of Conventions (1951–1996)* contains all but the most recent (2000) convention. It does not include status information; for an annual printed statement you need to consult the *Netherlands International Law Review*.

12–13   Subject Collections

There are several special-interest websites, which provide the text of relevant treaties and other documents. An example is ECOLEX (at **www.ecolex.org**). This is a joint project of the UN Environmental Program and IUCN (the World Conservation Union). It has the full text of multilateral environmental treaties. Paper sources continue to be published, for instance Burhenne's *International Environmental law: Multilateral Treaties*, a looseleaf set in eight binders. On a smaller scale, there is Philippe Sands's *Principles of International Environmental Law*, of which Volumes II and III contain international and European documents respectively. Tax treaties are made available by the International Bureau of Fiscal Documentation. The looseleaf supplements to its *European Taxation* contain texts of all tax treaties between European countries and the rest of the world. Its complete *Tax Treaties Database* is sold as a CD-ROM, but is also available on Lexis.

12–14   Finding Treaties

If you cannot trace a treaty in the Indexes to the various collections described above, then there are other Indexes, both national and international, which can provide some extra help.

	Date	Treaty Series No.	Command No.
PRIVATE INTERNATIONAL LAW (continued)—			
Convention relating to a Uniform Law on the International Sale of Goods	The Hague, 1 July, 1964– 31 Dec., 1965	74/1972	Cmnd. 5029
Signatures—			
Belgium	6 Oct., 1965		
France	31 Dec., 1965		
Germany, Federal Republic of*	1 July, 1964		
Greece (ad referendum)	3 Aug., 1964		
Holy See*	2 Mar., 1965		
Hungary	31 Dec., 1965	74/1972	Cmnd. 5029
Israel*	28 Dec., 1965		
Italy	23 Dec., 1964		
Luxembourg	7 Dec., 1965		
Netherlands	12 Aug., 1964		
San Marino	24 Aug., 1964		
United Kingdom	21 Aug., 1964		
* With reservation in respect of ratification.			
Ratifications—			
Belgium (with reservations)	12 Dec., 1968	74/1972	Cmnd. 5029
Germany, Federal Republic of (also applies to Berlin (West)) (with declaration) ...	16 Oct., 1973	121/1973	Cmnd. 5586
Israel	3 Dec., 1971		
Italy (with declaration)	22 Feb., 1972		
Netherlands (for Kingdom in Europe) (with declaration)	17 Feb., 1972	74/1972	Cmnd. 5029
San Marino (with declarations)	24 May, 1968		
United Kingdom (with declarations) ...	31 Aug., 1967		
Convention relating to a Uniform Law on the Formation of Contracts for the International Sale of Goods	The Hague, 1 July, 1964– 31 Dec., 1965	75/1972	Cmnd. 5030
Signatures—			
Belgium	6 Oct., 1965		
France	31 Dec., 1965		
Germany, Federal Republic of*	1 July, 1964		
Greece (ad referendum)	3 Aug., 1964		
Holy See*	2 Mar., 1965		
Hungary	31 Dec., 1965	75/1972	Cmnd. 5030
Israel*	28 Dec., 1965		
Italy	23 Dec., 1964		
Luxembourg	7 Dec., 1965		
Netherlands	12 Aug., 1964		
San Marino	24 Aug., 1964		
United Kingdom	8 June, 1965		
* With reservation in respect of ratification.			
Ratifications—			
Belgium	1 Dec., 1970	... 75/1972	Cmnd. 5030
Germany, Federal Republic of (also applies to Berlin (West)) (with declaration) ...	16 Oct., 1973	121/1973	Cmnd. 5586
Italy	22 Feb., 1972		
Netherlands (for Kingdom in Europe) (with declaration)	17 Feb., 1972	75/1972	Cmnd. 5030
San Marino (with declaration)	24 May, 1968		
United Kingdom	31 Aug., 1967		
Convention on the Service Abroad of Judicial and Extrajudicial Documents in Civil or Commercial Matters	The Hague, 15 Nov., 1965	50/1969	Cmnd. 3986

150

12–15 National Indexes

12–16 United Kingdom

For treaties concluded by the United Kingdom, there are two main sources. Parry and Hopkins, *Index of British Treaties* was first published in three volumes in 1970, and covered treaties concluded by the United Kingdom between 1101 and 1968. Volumes 2 and 3 contain a *Chronological List of Treaties*, giving details of the place and date of signature, entry into force and termination (where applicable). The references given in brackets at the end of the entry show where the treaty can be found. This Index covers both bilateral and multilateral treaties to which the United Kingdom is a party. Volume 1 is an *Index*, divided into separate indexes to bilateral and multilateral treaties. A fourth volume covering 1969 to 1988 appeared in 1991.

The *Index to Treaty Series*, which forms part of the Treaty Series, has already been mentioned (**12–9**).

12–17 United States

The best known American index is *Treaties in Force*, published annually by the Department of State. It lists all treaties and ageeements which are in force in the United States on January 1 of each year. Part 1 lists bilateral treaties by country and by subject; Part 2 lists multilateral treaties in an alphabetical subject arrangement. It is available online in PDF format on the U.S. Department of State website (at **www.state.gov/www/ global/legal_affairs/tifindex.html**). The Oceana *Quick U.S. Treaty Index* has already been mentioned (**12–10**) The corresponding paper version is *United States Treaty Index. 1776–1990 consolidation*. This is in 12 volumes with supplementation.

12–18 International Indexes

A most welcome addition to treaty indexes was *Multilateral Treaties: Index and Current Status*, edited by Bowman and Harris and published in 1984. A product of the Treaty Research Centre at the University of Nottingham, it offers status information on over 800 major treaties. Unfortunately the project terminated on publication of the 11th cumulative supplement in 1995. Everyone hopes it can be revived, perhaps in online form.

12–19 How to use Bowman and Harris

A helpful feature of this index is the word index within the Subject Index. If you need to find the Convention relating to a Uniform Law on the Formation of Contracts for the International Sale of Goods, check in the word index and under "Goods, Sale" you will find references by number to the relevant entries.

The figure below shows the entry for this treaty. The entry gives the full title, the date and place of conclusion, the date of entry into force, the duration, the language of the authentic text and a most useful "Notes" section, which gives the purpose of the treaty and, in this instance, tells you that it is due to be replaced by a new UN Convention (which has in fact been in force since 1988). This section also gives details of any periodical articles about the treaty.

```
┌─────────────────────────────────────────────────────────────────────────┐
│ TREATY 462            CONVENTION RELATING TO A UNIFORM LAW ON THE          │
│                       FORMATION OF CONTRACTS FOR THE INTERNATIONAL SALE    │
│                       OF GOODS                                            │
│                                                                           │
│ CONCLUDED             1 Jul 64, The Hague                                  │
│ LOCATION              834 UNTS 169; UKTS 75(1972), Cmnd 5030; 45 Vert A 615; 3 ILM │
│                       864; 13 AJCL 453                                     │
│ ENTRY INTO FORCE      23 Aug 72.  Later acceptances effective 6 months after │
│                       deposit: Art 8                                       │
│ DURATION              Unspecified.  Denunciation permitted on 1 year's notice: Art │
│                       10                                                   │
│ RESERVATIONS          Certain declarations and derogations permitted under Arts 2- │
│                       4.  Withdrawal of same effective 3 months after      │
│                       notification: Art 5                                  │
│ AUTHENTIC TEXTS       E F                                                  │
│ DEPOSITARY            Netherlands                                          │
│ OPEN TO               As for treaty 463: Arts 6, 7                         │
│ PARTIES (9)           BELGIUM 1 Dec 70; GAMBIA 5 Mar 74; GFR* 16 Oct 73; ISRAEL 30 │
│   May 80; ITALY 22 Feb 72; LUXEMBOURG* 6 Feb 79; NETHERLANDS* 17 Feb 72; SAN MARINO* │
│   24 May 68; UK 31 Aug 67                                                  │
│ TERRITORIAL SCOPE     See Art 11.  Declared applicable: GFR - Berlin (West); │
│   NETHERLANDS - Kingdom in Europe                                         │
│ SIGNATORIES          FRANCE 31 Dec 65; GREECE 3 Aug 64; HUNGARY 31 Dec 65; │
│   VATICAN CITY 2 Mar 65                                                    │
│ NOTES                 This Convention, to which the Uniform Law is annexed, will │
│   be replaced by the 1980 UN Convention on the Sale of Goods (treaty 775) for the │
│   parties to both.                                                        │
└─────────────────────────────────────────────────────────────────────────┘
```

To check whether the information in the original entry is still correct, look in the *Cumulative Supplement*. Using the same example, you will see that Germany, Italy and the Netherlands have withdrawn from the treaty.

If you need to find a bilateral or multilateral treaty agreed between two obscure parties, probably the best source is the *World Treaty Index*, the second edition of which was published in 1983 to 1984. It is a massive computer-generated index, covering the years from 1920 to 1984 and lists the treaties by subject, by parties and chronologically. Once again, this has not been updated, nor is it available online.

Other Sources of Treaty Information

12–20

Finding treaties can be difficult, especially as some of the official series take so long to print a document, and there are some other helpful sources apart from the collections noted above. A handy and manageable source for about 25 of the most well-known international conventions is *Blackstone's international law documents* (4th ed., 1999). For greater coverage (about 50 documents), look at von Münch and Buske, *International law: the essential treaties and other relevant documents* (1985).

International Legal Materials, published by the American Society of International Law, is very useful. It is a bi-monthly periodical which provides up-to-date information on legal aspects of public and private international relations. It frequently reproduces the texts of treaties and other agreements before they are published elsewhere. Issues also include such items as decisions of international arbitral tribunals and important UN Security Council Resolutions. It has annual Indexes, as well as two *Cumulative Indexes* which together cover Volumes 1–18 (1962–1979). ILM documents from 1990 onwards can also be traced using ASILEX, the online index to ASIL publications (at **www.asil.org/asilex.htm**).

Government bulletins, press releases and circulars often contain the texts of treaties shortly after they are signed. The U.S. Department of State provides information on recent treaty actions on its web site (at **state.gov**) (being reorganised at the time of writing). The information was formerly published in its monthly newsletter entitled *Dispatch* (1990–1999) and its predecessor the *Department of State Bulletin*.

National official gazettes also sometimes contain the texts of treaties by that country and some gazettes have special sections devoted to such texts, for example, the German *Bundesgesetzblatt*, Part II. Other countries like the United Kingdom have separate treaty series, *e.g.* the Netherlands *Tractatenblad*. The British Library Official Publications Library in London has the best collection of such gazettes in the United Kingdom.

12–21   LAW REPORTS

12–22   Court Reports

As stated above, international law does not have a system of binding precedent, although international tribunals are reluctant to change principles which they have laid down in earlier decisions. Because it is a permanent institution operating independently under its own statute, the International Court of Justice has developed a considerable body of case law and has thus been instrumental in the development of international law. The I.C.J. web site (at **www.icj-cij.org**) contains full texts of recent judgments of the Court (from about 1990) in PDF format. Earlier judgments back to 1946 are summarised. The printed version of the official reports of the Court is entitled *Reports of Judgments, Advisory Opinions and Orders*; this is published in parts, which are cumulated into an annual volume. Each volume has a subject index. A second series is entitled *Pleadings, Oral Arguments and Documents*. It contains the documents filed in each case heard by the Court, and appears on an irregular basis, usually several years after the corresponding decision. The ICJ also publishes the *Yearbook of the International Court of Justice* which contains useful information on cases that the Court has heard during the year under review.

You may also sometimes be referred to the reports of the ICJ's predecessor, the Permanent Court of International Justice which was set up by the League of Nations and operated between 1922 and 1940. Its publications had a complicated numbering system; the main series to mention being series A: *Judgments* and series B: *Advisory opinions*, which were amalgamated in 1931 into series A/B containing both types of document. The *Pleadings* appear in series C.

A recent development has been the establishment of international criminal courts and tribunals. The war crimes tribunals for Rwanda (at **www.ictr.org/**) and the former Yugoslavia (at **www.un.org/icty/index.html**) each have online collections of their judgments. The new International Criminal Court was set up in 1998 but has not yet heard any cases. Its constitutional documents are available (at **www.un.org/law/icc/index.html**).

12–23   General Reports

Because it is difficult to isolate cases relating to international law from the mass of domestic cases published each year, various series of specialised international law reports are published, the most important one being the *International Law Reports*. This covers reports from several countries, and includes the decisions of international tribunals as well as of international courts. Cases are published in full in their original form and where necessary translations of foreign judgments are provided. There are summaries following each report. The series is arranged according to a comprehensive classification scheme. Some volumes cover one topic, others cover several. Four volumes a year are published and a two-volume set of consolidated tables and indexes to volumes 1–80 was published in

1990–1. You will see that I.L.R. was originally published as the *Annual Digest of Public International Law Cases*, as it was then just a digest (summary) of the cases. As the reports grew longer, this was reflected in 1950 in a change of title. I.L.R is not yet available in electronic form, though there is indication from the publishers that this is planned.

National Series

12–24

Some countries produce national series of international law reports. In the U.K. *British International Law Cases* covers cases from 1607 to 1970. This series is designed to complement I.L.R. Cases are published in full, but no headnotes are added. Each volume gives a cumulative list of the cases published giving full references to the original reports. There is an index in each volume, plus a cumulative index for the last eight volumes. Unfortunately it is doubtful whether any further volumes are ever likely to be published. Another useful source of information on law reports is the *British Yearbook of International Law* which every year contains a section entitled "Decisions of British Courts . . . involving questions of Public or Private International Law". You should also remember that many of the leading textbooks contain comprehensive lists of cases.

In America the major series is *American International Law Cases*, which contains full reprints of both federal and state cases involving international law.

Reports of Arbitrations

12–25

The awards of international arbitral tribunals have always been of importance as a source of international law. The most important series is the *Reports of International Arbitral Awards* published by the United Nations Office of Legal Affairs. There are also various series of reports covering arbitrations before specific tribunals, for example the Iran–U.S. Claims Tribunal. A.M. Stuyt's *Survey of International Arbitrations 1794–1989* (1990) is a useful source of information. The figure on page 248 shows a sample page.

Example page from A. M. Stuyt's Survey of International Arbitrations 1794–1989

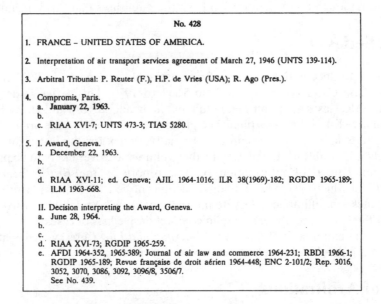

```
                              No. 428

1.  FRANCE – UNITED STATES OF AMERICA.

2.  Interpretation of air transport services agreement of March 27, 1946 (UNTS 139-114).

3.  Arbitral Tribunal: P. Reuter (F.), H.P. de Vries (USA); R. Ago (Pres.).

4.  Compromis, Paris.
    a.  January 22, 1963.
    b.
    c.  RIAA XVI-7; UNTS 473-3; TIAS 5280.

5.  I. Award, Geneva.
    a.  December 22, 1963.
    b.
    c.
    d.  RIAA XVI-11; ed. Geneva; AJIL 1964-1016; ILR 38(1969)-182; RGDIP 1965-189;
        ILM 1963-668.

    II. Decision interpreting the Award, Geneva.
    a.  June 28, 1964.
    b.
    c.
    d.  RIAA XVI-73; RGDIP 1965-259.
    e.  AFDI 1964-352, 1965-389; Journal of air law and commerce 1964-231; RBDI 1966-1;
        RGDIP 1965-189; Revue française de droit aérien 1964-448; ENC 2-101/2; Rep. 3016,
        3052, 3070, 3086, 3092, 3096/8, 3506/7.
        See No. 439.
```

The arbitrations are listed by parties and by subject matter. Details of the award are also given including the date, the party in whose favour the award was made, whether it was accepted and where the text may be found. There are also references to the *Encyclopedia of Public International Law* and to another important collection edited by Professors Coussirat-Coustère and Eisemann, the *Repertory of International Arbitral Jurisprudence 1794–1988*, published in four volumes in 1989–90. This consists of extracts from awards in a classified arrangement. The source for each extract is given by a coded reference, and using this you can look up the full details in the chronological Table of Awards.

12–26   Digests of Case Law

During the early years of its existence, it was often difficult to obtain copies of the ICJ's decisions and this prompted some commentators to produce digests of its reports. One of the most important of these is *World Court Digest*, produced by the Max Planck Institute for Comparative Public Law and International Law. This is a continuation of a previous series having various titles, most recently *Digest of the Decisions of the International Court of Justice*. This covered not only the ICJ itself (volumes 5–7), but also its predecessor the Permanent Court of International Justice, as well as the Permanent Court of Arbitration (volumes 1–4). The two volumes of *World Court Digest* so far published are available on the Institute's website (at **virtual-institute.de**).

STATE PRACTICE/CUSTOMARY INTERNATIONAL LAW

12–27

Custom is regarded as the second source of international law. This term is generally defined as state practice. State practice comprises a wealth of sources of law and is the body of materials which together illustrate the type of action taken by a state in an international situation. These materials include national legislation, diplomatic correspondence, legal opinions, evidence given before courts and tribunals, parliamentary proceedings, etc.

Digests

12–28

Several states produce digests of these materials to make them more readily accessible. In the United Kingdom, the *British Digest of International Law* began publication in the 1960s but it is still incomplete and unlikely to be finished in the foreseeable future.

The corresponding American series is the U.S. Department of State's annual *Digest of United States Practice in International Law*, covering the years 1973 to 1980. There is also a cumulative set covering the years 1981–1988, and the International Law Institute in Washington DC is planning to revive the annual series.

A historical source of state practice is Clive Parry, *Law Officers' Opinions to the Foreign Office 1793–1860*, published by Oceana in 95 volumes, with Volumes 96 and 97 containing *Indexes*. It is a collection of opinions, principally of the Advocate General (a forerunner of the Legal Adviser to the Foreign Office) on policy matters relating to the foreign and colonial affairs of the United Kingdom during that period. Opinions delivered between 1861 and 1939 were issued by the same publisher on microfilm.

The *British Yearbook of International Law* contains a section entitled "U.K. materials on international law", which is an excellent survey of items published during the year under review relating to international law. It includes extracts from parliamentary debates, answers given to parliamentary questions, evidence given to committees, and speeches given by U.K. representatives at international meetings. It also gives details of any U.K. legislation involving international law.

British and Foreign State Papers contains a wealth of international material. From 1812 to 1968, there are selections from diplomatic papers and circulars. These provide valuable background material to international events that is not easily obtainable elsewhere.

Collections of Documents

12–29

Other useful starting places for retrieving information relating to state practice are the commercially published multi-volume series on particular areas of international law. They are rather like vastly overgrown "cases and materials" books, but each series covers only one area of international law. They contain extracts from treaties, law reports, proceedings, background papers and documents from international organisations. Good examples are Durante and Rodino, *Western Europe and the Law of the Sea*, Ruster and Bruno, *International Protection of the Environment; Treaties and Related Documents*, and *New Directions in the Law of the Sea*. The advantage of these series is that you can find in one place extracts from all the different materials on a particular subject, plus information on where the original documents can be found. One of the most comprehensive printed collections is Weston, *International Law and World Order: Basic Documents*, now in seven looseleaf binders.

12–30   TREATISES

12–31   Textbooks

The writings of leading commentators, or jurists, are accepted as another source of international law. There is a very distinguished history of academic scholarship in international law. Famous writers include Grotius, Gentili, Pufendorf and Savigny. The Carnegie Endowment for International Peace has collected many of these works together and reprinted them in a series entitled *Classics of International Law*. Among later writers in this country, Oppenheim, *International Law* has been described as being "as nearly official as anything of the kind can be". A ninth edition of Volume 1: "Peace" appeared in 1992 in two parts. Volume 2: "Disputes, War and Neutrality" was last published in 1952. Of similar importance is Brownlie, *Principles of Public International Law* (5th ed., 1998).

12–32   Students' Textbooks

There are many good students' textbooks, including *Akehurst's Modern Introduction to International Law* (7th rev. ed., 1997), *Starke's International Law* (11th ed., 1994) and Shaw, *International law* (4th ed., 1997). The leading casebook is that by D. J. Harris, *Cases and Materials on International Law* (5th ed., 1998).

12–33   SECONDARY SOURCES

12–34   Journals

The first international law journal was the *Revue de Droit International et de Législation Comparée*, which initially appeared in 1869, almost 40 years before the American Society of International Law started publication of the *American Journal of International Law* (1907). There are now large numbers of journals worldwide, devoted to international law in general and to particular topics. The Institute of Advanced Legal Studies (IALS) library has over 150 journal titles in general international law, and over 70 in international economic law. An increasing number of international law journals is now available online, but in varying ways. Both Lexis and Westlaw include a large number of American university law journals in specialised topics, which may not otherwise be available even at IALS. There are web versions of individual journals, sometimes providing only tables of contents, sometimes the full text of the latest issue and sometimes the entire journal. On the SOSIG law gateway (at **www.sosig.ac.uk**) you can see a list of electronic international law journals. Select "International Law", then from the "Resource type" list, choose either Journals (contents and abstracts) or Journals (full text). A similar list can be seen on the Findlaw site (at **findlaw.com**). Start with the Students section and look for "Law Reviews: International". Some web-based online library catalogues can now link to electronic as well as paper sources, but as explained in Chapter 2, access can depend on your status and whether you are on campus or not.

12–35   Newsletters and Bulletins

To trace very recent information on international law, newsletters and bulletins can be useful. The *Bulletin of Legal Developments* is published fortnightly by the British Institute of International and Comparative Law and contains a wealth of useful information on legal developments and forthcoming legislation in both the United Kingdom and abroad. Unfortunately it is not yet available online. The American Society of International Law produces its *ASIL Newsletter* bi-monthly; the extracts available online (at **www.asil.org/ news.htm**) include its regular "What's Online" column noting developments in online sources in international law.

Yearbooks   12–36

Yearbooks, which normally contain a collection of articles and documents relating to international law, are another useful source of information and several countries publish them, including Australia, Canada, France, Germany, Italy, Japan and Switzerland. The *British Yearbook of International Law* is an excellent example of the genre. It contains not only the various items mentioned earlier in this chapter but also summaries of the decisions of leading international tribunals, such as the European Court of Human Rights, together with a comprehensive book review section, and digests of national cases relating to international law.

Yearbooks are also published in particular subject areas, for example, the *Yearbook: Commercial Arbitration*.

Proceedings   12–37

Other useful sources of articles on international law are proceedings of courses, conferences and other international meetings. The most notable of these are the *Recueil des Cours* (collected courses) of The Hague Academy of International Law, which contains the texts of lectures given each year by leading international law scholars from all over the world. There are regularly published indexes, and a useful biography and bibliography for each person delivering the lectures. The proceedings of the conferences of the International Law Association are also important.

FINDING BOOKS AND JOURNALS   12–38

Bibliographies   12–39

The available printed general bibliographies of international law are now very out of date, being published in the 1970s. The lists at the beginning of each chapter of Oppenheim's *International law* (1992) are still a good starting point. For current information, you will need to use online library catalogues or the indexes described in **12–40**, which include books as well as articles. Elizabeth Beyerly, *Public International Law: A Guide to Information Sources* (1991) is a well-annotated guide, which includes primary as well as secondary sources.

A more recent publication, produced by staff of the George Washington University Journal of International Law and Economics, is *A guide to International Legal Research* (3rd ed., 1998).

There are several specialist institutes within universities devoted to research into particular areas of international law and they frequently produce excellent bibliographical tools. The Centre for the Study of the Law of the Sea at Dalhousie University in Halifax,

Nova Scotia, produces a *Marine Affairs Bibliography*. The Centre for Air and Space Law at McGill has published Kuo Lee Li, *Worldwide Space Law Bibliography* (1978) and the Centre for the Study of Human Rights at Columbia has published *Human Rights: A Topical Bibliography*.

12–40   Library Catalogues

The catalogues of most of the larger national and university libraries across the world can now be accessed on the internet. American university libraries such as Harvard, Yale and the various campuses of the University of California can all be sources of bibliographical information for published materials on international law. The most wide-ranging list of law library catalogues is provided by Washburn University in the U.S.A. (at **washlaw.edu/ lawcat.html**). Sometimes it will link to an out-of-date telnet version of a catalogue. British academic law libraries' web pages can be traced from the University of Warwick website (at **www.law.warwick.ac.uk/cti/lawschools.html**).

12–41   Indexes of Journal Articles

As well as the general legal periodical indexes, *Index to Legal Periodicals*, *Index to Foreign Legal Periodicals* and *Legal Journals Index* mentioned in Chapter 5, there are two specialist indexes worth consulting. One is a web-based index called RAVE (at **www.jura.uni-dueseldorf.de/rave/e/englhome.htm**), based at the University of Düsseldorf. It indexes court decisions and periodical articles in public international law and European law. Over 180 journals are indexed, beginning in 1995. There are links to full text if this is available. The Max-Planck Institute for Comparative Public Law and International Law has produced its *Public International Law: a Current Bibliography of Books and Articles* since 1975. It covers over 1,000 journals. Since 1996, references to articles in journals held by the Institute's Library have been entered in its online catalogue (at **www.virtual-institute.de**).

12–42   INTERNATIONAL ORGANISATIONS

There is no agreed scientific classification of international organisations. The term "international intergovernmental organisation" is usually used to describe an organisation set up by agreement between two or more states, as distinct from "non-governmental" organisations set up by individuals.

There are currently over 4,000 international organisations in existence, of which one alone, the United Nations, produces over 180,000 items of documentation a year. The total number of publications produced by international organisations each year is therefore massive.

It is extremely difficult to trace the publications of international organisations, not only because there are so many of them, but also because the organisations themselves frequently do not produce comprehensive catalogues or lists of their publications. These publications can be most conveniently divided into two main groups: sales publications and documents. You are most likely to need material in the first group, which includes all those publications issued in printed form and generally available. The second group comprises documents which are mainly produced for internal use by the organisation concerned and are not normally of wide outside interest. Obviously, sales publications cover a vast subject area and legal documents form only a small part of the total output of international orgnisations.

United Nations   12–43

The largest and most important of international organisations is of course the United Nations. Its central institutions include the General Assembly, the Security Council, the Secretariat, the Economic and Social Council and the International Court of Justice, which has already been mentioned. The UN also operates through a large number of specialised agencies with wide-ranging interests, some of which you may not realise are part of the United Nations system. They include the International Civil Aviation Organisation, the International Labour Organisation, UNCITRAL, UNCTAD, the World Intellectual Property Organisation and the World Trade Organisation (successor to the GATT). Two bodies particularly concerned with international law are the International Law Commission, charged with the development and codification of international law, and the UN Commission on International Trade Law (UNCITRAL), which works on the harmonisation and unification of the law of international trade.

All these bodies produce an overwhelming number of documents and sales publications. One starting point on the internet is the UN home page (at **www.un.org**). Although it is mainly aimed at the general public, there are some useful links to sites of the major UN organs. For a full alphabetical list of websites of the UN system, follow the link to "Other UN Sites" and then to "Official WEB Locator for the UN system". You will reach sites for all the organisations mentioned above, and many more. Each has links to information about its publications. The most comprehensive official online source for UN documents is the *United Nations Optical Disk System* (at **www.ods.un.org**). This is a subscription service providing the full text of resolutions of the General Assembly, the Security Council and the Economic and Social Council back to 1946, and all official documents in PDF format beginning with 1992. Individual documents are usually only to be found in larger libraries, particularly depository libraries which receive them automatically and reasonably quickly. Luckily most of the more important UN agencies publish a *Yearbook*, which contains not only an annual report on activities, but reprinted working documents, drafts of treaties, summaries of meetings and special reports. There is for example an *UNCITRAL Yearbook* and an *International Law Commission Yearbook*. The UN Secretariat publishes the *United Nations Juridical Yearbook*. These are important sources for official versions of documents which may not be recent enough to appear in online databases.

The UN frequently convenes conferences on legal topics and then publishes the proceedings. Such proceedings often contain the texts of conventions or other agreements reached at the conference, usually as part of the "Final Act". The United Nations Conferences on the law of the sea are a good example. There is also a *United Nations Legislative Series*, which contains materials on legal matters. These are normally compiled following a resolution from the General Assembly asking for further information on a particular topic.

Bibliographies to UN materials   12–44
The most wide-ranging index to UN documents is the *United Nations Documents Index*, published in its present form since 1998. Its predecessor, UNDOC, began in 1979. They provide broad subject access, but have the disadvantage of being in annual cumulations.

The UN Dag Hammarskjold Library in New York and the Library of the UN office in Geneva produce UNBISnet, an online index to UN documents published since 1979, as well as non-UN materials collected by both libraries. A CD-ROM index called UNBIS Plus combines the *UN Documents Index* with indexes to proceedings and speeches, as well as a guide to document series symbols. This will help you for instance to identify "A/CN4/219" as an International Law Commission document. The printed version of this is *United Nations Document Series Symbols 1946–1996*, published in 1998. A rival service to UNBIS Plus is provided by Readex in conjunction with their microform collection of UN documents. The CD-ROM version is called *Index to United Nations Documents and publications*, and the web version *AccessUN*. For each version there are several subscription options, giving different years of coverage between just the last three years and all the way back to 1956. You will need to check with any library that subscribes.

12–45   Council of Europe

The Statute of the Council of Europe was signed in 1949 by 10 European states. By early 2001 there were 43 Member States, with others such as Bosnia-Herzegovina having "guest" status. Its objectives are, broadly, European co-operation in the fields of human rights, social, cultural, legal and administrative matters. Its main organs are the Committee of Ministers, formed from the foreign ministers of Member States, and the Parliamentary Assembly. The Secretariat is divided into four Directorates-General. I: Legal Affairs, II: Human Rights, III: Social Cohesion and IV: Education, Culture, Youth & Sport, and Environment.

12–46   Treaties

A major part of the work of the Council is the preparation of Conventions, some signed by all Member States and others, so-called "partial agreements", by smaller groups of Member States. They are collected together in the *European Treaty Series*, which is available online (at **conventions.coe.int**). This includes a complete list of treaties in numerical order (approximately 180), as well as the full text of each treaty in both html and Word format. Associated documents include the corresponding charts of signatures and ratifications, lists of declarations, reservations etc., and the useful *Explanatory Reports*. Each treaty in the series continues to be published individually in hard copy; the looseleaf edition of the *Chart of Signatures and Ratifications* has been overtaken by its online version and has not been updated for some time.

12–47   Documents

The texts adopted by the Committee of Ministers comprise Declarations, *Resolutions,* and *Recommendations to Member States*. They are available on the Committee's own website (at **cm.coe.int**) from various dates (resolutions being complete from 1949). Since January 1999 these have appeared in the monthly *Official Gazette of the Council of Europe: Committee of Ministers Part Volume*. Its immediate predecessor was *Texts adopted by the Committee of Ministers* 1996/97 to 1998/99, with various annual bound volumes before that.

The Parliamentary Assembly issues three series: The *Official Reports of Debates* are in three volumes a year, with a brief annual Subject Index. *Texts adopted* comprise the equivalent of legislation, namely opinions, recommendations, resolutions and orders, each in their own continuous numbered sequence. The *Documents (Working Papers)* include written questions, reports from subject committees, and reports from the Committee of Ministers to the Assembly. Again, a single numbered sequence is carried over from session to session.

At present (2001) there is little full-text material on the Assembly's website (at **stars.coe.int**), other than an incomplete set of the verbatim debates starting in 1998. There are searchable lists of texts adopted.

Reports   12–48
A general overview of the year's work of the Council of Europe can be found in the *Annual Report on the Activities of the Council of Europe*, published by the Secretariat. It contains useful lists of texts adopted by each organ during the year, including judgments of the European Court of Human Rights. Also listed are the reports of conferences such as the Standing Conference of European Ministers of Education and the proceedings of the Colloquy on European Law. Individual reports and other publications of the various directorates are best traced from the Council of Europe publishing web site (at **book.coe.int**). You can choose to browse the catalogue or perform a search either by keywords or free text.

European Convention on Human Rights   12–49
The most well-known work of the Council of Europe is in the field of human rights. The Convention for the Protection of Human Rights and Fundamental Freedoms (otherwise known as the European Convention on Human Rights) was drawn up in 1950 and came into force in 1953. The European Commission on Human Rights was formed in 1953 to investigate complaints against states said to be in breach of the Convention. The European Court of Human Rights (ECHR), which hears cases referred to it by the Commission, was set up in 1959.

There have been two important recent developments regarding the Convention. First, the European Court of Human Rights has been reconstituted following the coming into force of the 11th Protocol to the Convention in 1998. The effect of this is that the European Commission of Human Rights has been abolished, and its work is now done by committees of judges in the Court itself. Secondly, the U.K. has incorporated the Convention into domestic law, by means of the Human Rights Act 1998 which came into force on October 2, 2000. This means that British courts must now apply rather than simply take account of the Convention. As a result, online services such as Lexis-Nexis, Westlaw UK and Lawtel now have specialised human rights areas in their databases.

Text   12–50
The text of the Convention itself is accessible from the *European Treaty Series* web page mentioned in section **12–46** (search for treaty number 005), or you can use the link on the front page of the European Court of Human Rights website (at **www.echr.coe.int**). The main official printed source is *Human Rights Today: European Legal Texts*, published by the Council of Europe in 1999. This also includes the European Convention for the Prevention of Torture and the Framework Convention for the Protection of National Minorities with all the related protocols and procedural rules of the respective bodies.

The *Collected Edition of the Travaux Préparatoires* (preparatory documents) leading up to the promulgation of the Convention was published in eight volumes between 1975 and 1985.

12–51 Reports

As well as the Convention, the website of the European Court of Human Rights includes HUDOC, a database of both its own judgments and the decisions and reports of the Commission until it ceased to function in 1999. All of the Court's judgments are available, but not all Commission decisions. Notice that the default search mode in HUDOC is for Court judgments *only*; you need to tick more boxes to find other documents.

Until 1995, the decisions of the Court appeared in *Publications of the European Court of Human Rights, Series A: Judgments and Decisions.* Series B contained pleadings, oral arguments and other documents. Since 1996 there has been the series *Reports of Judgments and Decisions.* The Commission had its own series of *Decisions and Reports*, decisions being on the admissibility of a case, and reports being the final word when cases were not passed on to the Court. The *European Human Rights Reports* are a commercially published series containing all judgments of the Court, selected reports and decisions of the Commission and resolutions of the Committee of Ministers relating to human rights. They are available on Westlaw.

12–52 Digests

In addition to the online HUDOC database, there are printed digests of European human rights case law. The *Digest of Strasbourg Case-law Relating to the European Convention on Human Rights* covers the period 1955–82, the main body of it arranged in order of the Articles of the Convention. Volume 6 of the set contains Indexes. Looseleaf supplements to the first two volumes first appeared in 1988. Vincent Berger, *Case Law of the European Court of Human Rights*, Vol. 1: 1960–1987; Vol. 2: 1988–1990; Vol. 3: 1991–1993, gives two- to three-page summaries of all the decisions of the Court in chronological order, and includes an index by Convention Article and a bibliography. The Commission's *Decisions and Reports* series has cumulative indexes every 10 volumes, the last one covering 1985–89.

12–53 Yearbook

The *Yearbook of the European Convention on Human Rights* summarises the year's activity of the Commission, the Court and the Committee of Ministers in the human rights area. Summaries of the main decisions of each are given, together with lists of other relevant documents (*e.g.* working papers of the Parliamentary Assembly) and a bibliography.

Appendix I Abbreviations of Reports, Series and Journals

This alphabetical list contains a selection of the more commonly used abbreviations in the **A1–1** United Kingdom, the E.C. and the Commonwealth. It is not exhaustive and further information can be found in D. Raistrick, *Index to Legal Citations and Abbreviations* and in the I.A.L.S. *Manual of Legal Citations*, Vols. I and II, the *Index to Legal Periodicals*, the *Legal Journals Index. The Digest (Cumulative Supplement)* and the *Current Law Citators* also contain lists of abbreviations, at the front.

A.C.—Law Reports Appeal Cases 1891–
A.J.—Acta Juridica
A.J.I.L.—American Journal of International Law
A.L.J.—Australian Law Journal
A.L.R.—American Law Reports Annotated
A.L.R.—Australian Law Reports, formerly Argus Law Reports
All E.R.—All England Law Reports 1936–
All E.R. Rep.—All England Law Reports Reprint 1558–1935
Am. J. Comp. L.—American Journal of Comparative Law
Anglo-Am. L.R.—Anglo-American Law Review
Ann. Dig.—Annual Digest of Public International Law Cases (1919–1949). (From 1950 this series has been published as the International Law Reports—I.L.R.)
App. Cas.—Law Reports Appeal Cases 1875–1890

B.C.L.C.—Butterworths Company Law Cases
B.D.I.L.—British Digest of International Law
B.F.S.P.—British and Foreign State Papers
B.I.L.C.—British International Law Cases
B.J.A.L.—British Journal of Administrative Law
B.J. Crim.—British Journal of Criminology
B.J.L.S.—British Journal of Law and Society
B.L.R.—Building Law Reports
B.L.R.—Business Law Review
B.N.I.L.—Bulletin of Northern Ireland Law
B.T.R.—British Tax Review

B.Y.I.L.—British Yearbook of International Law
Bull. E.C.—Bulletin of the European Communities
Business L.R.—Business Law Review

C.A.R.—Criminal Appeal Reports
C.A.T.—Court of Appeal Transcript (unpublished)
C.B.R.—Canadian Bar Review
C.D.E.—Cahiers de Droit Européen
C.J.Q.—Civil Justice Quarterly
C.L.—Current Law
C.L.J.—Cambridge Law Journal
C.L.P.—Current Legal Problems
C.L.R.—Commonwealth Law Reports (Australia)
C.M.L.R.—Common Market Law Reports
C.M.L. Rev.—Common Market Law Review
C.P.D.—Law Reports Common Pleas Division 1875–1880
C.T.S.—Consolidated Treaty Series
Calif. L. Rev.—California Law Review
Camb. L.J.—Cambridge Law Journal
Can. B.R.—Canadian Bar Review
Ch.—Law Reports Chancery Division 1891–
Ch.D.—Law Reports Chancery Division 1875–1890
Co. Law.—Company Lawyer
Colum. L. Rev.—Columbia Law Review
Com. Cas.—Commercial Cases 1895–1941
Constr. L.J.—Construction Law Journal
Conv.; Conv.—N.S.—Conveyancer and Property Lawyer
Cox C.C.—Cox's Criminal Law Cases
Cr. App. R.; Cr. App. Rep.—Criminal Appeal Reports
Cr.App.R.(S.)—Criminal Appeal Reports (Sentencing)
Crim. L.R.—Criminal Law Review

D.L.R.—Dominion Law Reports (Canada)
D.U.L.J.—Dublin University Law Journal

E.C.R.—European Court Reports
E.G.—Estates Gazette
E.G.L.R.—Estates Gazette Law Reports
E.H.R.R.—European Human Rights Reports
E.I.P.R.—European Intellectual Property Review
E.L. Rev.—European Law Review
E.R.—English Reports
Eng. Rep.—English Reports
Eur. Comm. H.R. D.R.—European Commission for Human Rights Decisions and
    Reports
Eur. Court H.R. Series A/Series B—European Court of Human Rights Series A & B
Euro C.L.—European Current Law
Ex.D.—Law Reports Exchequer Division 1875–1880

F.L.R.—Family Law Reports
F.L.R.—Federal Law Reports
F.S.R.—Fleet Street Reports
F.T.—Financial Times
Fam.—Law Reports Family Division 1972–
Fam. Law—Family Law

Grotius Trans.—Transactions of the Grotius Society

H.L.R.—Housing Law Reports
Harv. L. Rev.—Harvard Law Review

I.C.J. Rep.—International Court of Justice Reports
I.C.J.Y.B.—International Court of Justice Yearbook
I.C.L.Q.—International and Comparative Law Quarterly
I.C.R.—Industrial Cases Reports 1975–
I.C.R.—Industrial Court Reports 1972–1974
I.J.; Ir. Jur.—Irish Jurist
I.L.J.—Industrial Law Journal
I.L.M.—International Legal Materials
I.L.Q.—International Law Quarterly
I.L.R.—International Law Reports
I.L.R.M.—Irish Law Reports Monthly
I.L.T.; Ir.L.T.—Irish Law Times
I.R.—Irish Reports
I.R.L.R.—Industrial Relations Law Reports
I.R.R.R.—Industrial Relations Review & Reports
Imm.A.R.—Immigration Appeal Reports
Ir. Jur.—Irish Jurist
I.T.R.—Industrial Tribunal Reports

J.B.L.—Journal of Business Law
J.C.—Session Cases: Justiciary Cases (Scotland)
J.C.L.—Journal of Criminal Law
J.C.M.S.—Journal of Common Market Studies
J.I.S.E.L.—Journal of the Irish Society for European Law
J.I.S.L.L.—Journal of the Irish Society for Labour Law
J.L.S.—Journal of Law and Society
J.L.S.—Journal of the Law Society of Scotland
J. Legal Ed.—Journal of Legal Education
J.O.—Journal Officiel des Communautés Européennes
J.P.—Justice of the Peace Reports (*also* Justice of the Peace (journal))
J.P.I.L.—Journal of Personal Injury Litigation
J.P.L.—Journal of Planning and Environment Law
J.R.—Juridical Review
J.S.P.T.L.—Journal of the Society of Public Teachers of Law
J.S.W.L.—Journal of Social Welfare Law

K.B.—Law Reports: King's Bench Division 1901–1952

K.I.R.—Knight's Industrial Reports

L.A.G. Bul.—Legal Action Group Bulletin
L.G.C.—Local Government Chronicle
L.G.R.—Knight's Local Government Reports
L.J.—Law Journal 1866–1965 (newspaper)
L.J. Adm.—Law Journal: Admiralty N.S. 1865–1875
L.J. Bcy.—Law Journal: Bankruptcy N.S. 1832–1880
L.J.C.C.R.—Law Journal: County Courts Reports 1912–1933
L.J.C.P.—Law Journal: Common Pleas N.S. 1831–1875
L.J. Ch.—Law Journal: Chancery N.S. 1831–1946
L.J. Eccl.—Law Journal: Ecclesiastical Cases N.S. 1866–1875
L.J. Eq.—Law Journal: Equity N.S. 1831–1946
L.J. Ex.—Law Journal: Exchequer N.S. 1831–1875
L.J. Ex. Eq.—Law Journal: Exchequer in Equity 1835–1841
L.J.K.B. (or Q.B.)—Law Journal: King's (or Queen's) Bench N.S. 1831–1946
L.J.M.C.—Law Journal: Magistrates' Cases N.S. 1831–1896
L.J.N.C.—Law Journal: Notes of Cases 1866–1892
L.J.N.C.C.R.—Law Journal Newspaper: County Court Reports 1934–1947
L.J.O.S.—Law Journal (Old Series) 1822–1831
L.J.P.—Law Journal: Probate, Divorce and Admiralty N.S. 1875–1946
L.J.P.D. & A.—Law Journal: Probate, Divorce and Admiralty N.S. 1875–1946
L.J.P. & M.—Law Journal: Probate and Matrimonial Cases N.S. 1858–1859, 1866–1875
L.J.P.C.—Law Journal: Privy Council N.S. 1865–1946
L.J.P.M. & A.—Law Journal: Probate, Matrimonial and Admiralty N.S. 1860–1865
L.J.R.—Law Journal Reports 1947–1949
L. Lib.J.—Law Library Journal
L.M.C.L.Q.—Lloyd's Maritime and Commercial Law Quarterly
L.N.T.S.—League of Nations Treaty Series
L.Q.R.—Law Quarterly Review
L.R.A. & E.—Law Reports: Admiralty and Ecclesiastical Cases 1865–1875
L.R.C.C.R.—Law Reports: Crown Cases Reserved 1865–1875
L.R. C.P.—Law Reports: Common Pleas Cases 1865–1875
L.R. Ch. App.—Law Reports: Chancery Appeal Cases 1865–1875
L.R. Eq.—Law Reports: Equity Cases 1866–1875
L.R. Ex.—Law Reports: Exchequer Cases 1865–1875
L.R.H.L.—Law Reports: English and Irish Appeals 1866–1875
L.R. P. & D.—Law Reports: Probate and Divorce Cases 1865–1875
L.R.P.C.—Law Reports: Privy Council Appeals 1865–1875
L.R.Q.B.—Law Reports: Queen's Bench 1865–1875
L.R.R.P.; L.R. R.P.C.—Law Reports: Restrictive Practices Cases 1957–1973
L.S.—Legal Studies
L.S. Gaz.—Law Society Gazette
L.T.—Law Times
L.T.R.; L.T. Rep.—Law Times Reports (New Series) 1859–1947
L.T.Jo.—Law Times (newspaper) 1843–1965
L.T.O.S.—Law Times Reports (Old Series) 1843–1860
L. Teach.—Law Teacher
Law & Contemp. Prob.—Law and Contemporary Problems

Lit.—Litigation
Liverpool L.R.—Liverpool Law Review
Ll. L.L.R.; Ll.L.R.; LL.L. Rep.—Lloyd's List Law Reports *later* Lloyd's Law Reports
Lloyd's L.R.; Lloyd's Rep.—Lloyd's List Law Reports *later* Lloyd's Law Reports

M.L.J.—Malayan Law Journal
M.L.R.—Modern Law Review
Man. Law—Managerial Law
Med. Sci. & Law—Medicine, Science & the Law
Mich. L. Rev.—Michigan Law Review

N.I.—Northern Ireland Law Reports
N.I.J.B.—Northern Ireland Law Reports Bulletin of Judgments
N.I.L.Q.—Northern Ireland Legal Quarterly
N.I.L.R.—Northern Ireland Law Reports
N.L.J.—New Law Journal
N.Y.U.L. Rev.—New York University Law Review
N.Z.L.R.—New Zealand Law Reports
New L.J.—New Law Journal

O.J.—Official Journal of the European Communities
O.J.C.—Official Journal of the European Communities: Information and Notices
O.J.L.—Official Journal of the European Communities: Legislation, *e.g.* 1972, L139/28
O.J.L.S.—Oxford Journal of Legal Studies

P.—Law Reports: Probate, Divorce and Admiralty 1891–1971
P. & C.R.—Planning (Property from 1968) and Compensation Reports
P.C.I.J.—Permanent Court of International Justice Reports of Judgments
P.D.—Law Reports: Probate Division 1875–1890
P.L.—Public Law
P.N.—Professional Negligence

Q.B.—Law Reports: Queen's Bench Division 1891–1901, 1952–
Q.B.D.—Law Reports: Queen's Bench Division 1875–1890

R.D.E.—Rivista di Diritto Europeo
R.G.D.I.P.—Revue Générale de Droit International Public
R.M.C.—Revue du Marché Commun
R.P.C.—Reports of Patent, Design & Trade Mark Cases
R.R.—Revised Reports
R.R.C.—Ryde's Rating Cases
R.T.R.—Road Traffic Reports
R.V.R.—Rating & Valuation Reporter
Rec.—Recueil des Cours
Rec.—Recueil de la Jurisprudence de la Cour (Court of Justice of the European
    Communities)

S.A.—South African Law Reports
S.C.—Session Cases (Scotland)

S.C. (H.L.)—Session Cases: House of Lords (Scotland)
S.C.(J.)—Session Cases: Justiciary Cases (Scotland)
S.C.C.R.—Scottish Criminal Case Reports
S.I.—Statutory Instruments
S.J.—Solicitors Journal
S.L.R.—Law Reporter/Scottish Law Review
S.L.T.—Scots Law Times
S.R.—Statutory Rules (Northern Ireland)
S.R. & O.—Statutory Rules and Orders
S.T.C.—Simon's Tax Cases
Scolag.—Bulletin of the Scottish Legal Action Group
Sol. Jo.—Solicitors Journal
St. Tr.; State Tr.—State Trials 1163–1820
Stat.L.R.—Statute Law Review
State Tr. N.S.—State Trials (New Series) 1820–1858

T.C.—Reports of Tax Cases
T.L.R.—Times Law Reports
TSO—The Stationery Office, 1996–
Tax Cas.—Reports of Tax Cases
Tul. L. Rev.—Tulane Law Review

U. Chi. L. Rev.—University of Chicago Law Review
U.K.T.S.—United Kingdom Treaty Series
U.N.T.S.—United Nations Treaty Series
U.N.J.Y.—United Nations Juridical Yearbook
U.N.Y.B.—Yearbook of the United Nations
U. Pa. L. Rev.—University of Pennsylvania Law Review
U.S.—United States Supreme Court Reports
U.S.T.S.—United States Treaty Series

V.A.T.T.R.—Value Added Tax Tribunal Reports
V.L.R.—Victorian Law Reports (Australia)

W.I.R.—West Indian Reports
W.L.R.—Weekly Law Reports
W.N.—Weekly Notes
W.W.R.—Western Weekly Reporter

Y.B.—Yearbook (old law report), *e.g.* (1466) Y.B.Mich. (the term) 6 Edw. 4, pl. 18, fol.7
  (plea, folio)
Y.B.W.A.—Yearbook of World Affairs
Yale L.J.—Yale Law Journal
Yearbook E.C.H.R.—Yearbook of the European Convention on Human Rights

   More detailed information on legal and law-related materials can be found in the
following publications.

D. Butcher, *Official Publications in Britain* (2nd ed., London: Library Association, 1991).

R. G. Logan (ed.), *Information Sources in Law* (London: Butterworths, 1986).

D. D. Mackey, *How To Use a Scottish Law Library* (Edinburgh: W. Green, 1992).

E. M. Moys (ed.), *Manual of Law Librarianship: The Use and Organization of Legal Literature* (2nd ed., London: Gower, 1987).

J. E. Pemberton, *British Official Publications* (2nd ed., Oxford: Pergamon, 1973).

Glanville Williams, *Learning the Law* (11th ed., London: Stevens, 1982).

Appendix II   Words and Abbreviations in English and Latin

This alphabetical list contains some of the more commonly used words and abbreviations **A2–1** (in English and Latin) which you may encounter in textbooks and law reports. There is a separate list of abbreviations for the names of law reports in Appendix I.

A.G. or Att. Gen.—Attorney-General
A.G.—German incorporated company
Ab initio—from the beginning
Abstracts—summary of journal articles, books, etc. Usually arranged in subject order
Ad valorem—according to the duty. A duty levied
Aliter—otherwise
Amicus curiae—a friend of the court (a bystander who informs the judge on points of law or fact)
Annotations—notes
Anon.—anonymous
Applied (apld.)—the principle in a previous case has been applied to a new set of facts in another case
Approved—the case has been considered good law
Art.—Article (in an international Treaty or Convention)
Article—an essay published in a journal
Autrefois acquit—previously acquitted
Autrefois attaint—previously attained
Autrefois convict—previously convicted

B.—Baron (Exchequer)
B.C.—Borough Council
Bibliography—a list of books
Bills—draft versions of proposed legislation, laid before Parliament for its approval
Blue Book—a government publication, issued with blue covers to protect it because of its length

c.—chapter (Act)
C.—Command Paper 1836–1899
C.A.—Court of Appeal
C.A.T.—Court of Appeal Transcript (unreported)

C.A.V. (*curia advisari vult*)—the court deliberated before pronouncing judgment
C.B.—Chief Baron
C.C.—County Council
C.C.A.—Court of Criminal Appeal
C.C.R.—County Court Rules
c.i.f. (cost, insurance, freight)—a contract for the sale of goods in which the price quoted includes everything up to delivery
C.J.—Chief Justice
Cd.—Command Papers 1900–1918
CD-ROM—Compact Disc—Read Only Memory
cf. (confer)—to compare or refer to
Chronological—arranged in order of date
Cie.—French abbreviation for company (compagnie)
Citation—(1) a reference to where a case or statute is to be found; (2) the quotation of decided cases in legal arguments
Citator—a volume containing a list of cases or statutes with sufficient details to enable them to be traced in the volumes of law reports or statutes
Cl.—clause (in Bills)
Classification number (classmark)—a system of numbers, or letters and numbers, used to indicate the subject matter of the book. In many libraries the books are arranged on the shelves in the order indicated by this number
Cm.—Command Papers 1986–
Cmd.—Command Papers 1919–1956
Cmnd.—Command Papers 1956–1986
Command Paper—a form of parliamentary paper, issued "by Command of Her Majesty". Every Command Paper has its own individual number
Comrs.—Commissioners
Considered—the case was considered but no comment was made
Cumulative; Cumulation—combining the information in a number of previous publications into one sequence
Cur. adv. vult.—the court deliberated before pronouncing judgment

D.C.—Divisional Court
D.P.P.—Director of Public Prosecutions (whose name appears in criminal appeals to the House of Lords, and certain other circumstances)
De facto—in fact
De jure—by right
De novo—anew
Deb.—Debates
Dec.—Decision (E.C.), *e.g.* Dec. 82/112/EEC
Decd.—deceased
Delegated legislation—rules created by subordinate bodies under specific powers delegated by Parliament
Digest—a summary
Digested—summarised
Dir.—Directive (E.C.), *e.g.* Dir. 82/262/EEC
Distinguished—some essential difference between past cases and the present case has been pointed out
Doubted—the court's remarks tend to show case was inaccurate

E.A.T.—Employment Appeal Tribunal
E.C.—European Community
ECHR—European Convention on Human Rights
ECJ—Court of Justice of the European Community
ECSC—European Coal & Steel Community
Et seq. (*et sequentes*)—and those following
Ex cathedra (from the chair)—with official authority
Ex officio—by virtue of an office
Ex p. (*ex parte*)—the person on whose application the case is heard
Ex post facto—by a subsequent act; retrospectively
Ex rel. (*ex relatione*)—report not at first hand
Explained—previous decision is not doubted, but the present decision is justified by calling attention to some fact not clear in the report

ff.—and what follows
f.o.b. (free on board)—cost of shipping to be paid by vendor
Folio—technically this refers to the way in which a book is made up; usually used to denote a large book, often shelved in a separate sequence
Followed—same principle of law applied

GmbH.—German incorporated private company
Green Book—a term sometimes used to refer to *The County Court Practice*
Green Paper—a government publication setting out government proposals, so that public discussion may follow before a definite policy is formulated

H.C. Deb.—House of Commons Debate
H.L.—House of Lords
HMSO—Her Majesty's Stationery Office
Hale P.C.—Hale, *Historia Placitorum Coronae* (Pleas of the Crown)
Hansard—Parliamentary Debates
Headnote—a brief summary of a case found at the beginning of the law report

ICJ—International Court of Justice
I.R.C.—Inland Revenue Commissioners
Ibid. (*ibidem*)—in the same place
Id. (*idem*)—the same
In b. (*in bonis*)—in the goods of
In camera—hearing in private
In curia—in open court
In re—in the matter of
Infra—below
Inter alia—amongst other things
Inter vivos—during life: between living persons
Ipso facto—by the mere fact

J. (plural JJ.)—judge
JANET—Joint Academic Network
J.P.—Justice of the Peace

K.C.—King's Counsel

L.C.—Lord Chancellor

L.C.B.—Lord Chief Baron
L.C.J.—Lord Chief Justice
L.J. (plural L.JJ.)—Lord Justice
LPC—Legal Practice Course
L.V.App.Ct.—Lands Valuation Appeal Court (Scotland)
Legislation—the making of law: any set of statutes
Loc. cit. (*loco citato*)—at the passage quoted

M.R.—Master of the Rolls
M.V.—motor vessel
Microfiche; Microfilm—a photographic reduction of an original on to a sheet of film
(microfiche) or a reel of film (microfilm). A reading machine (which enlarges the image)
is needed to consult microfilm or fiche

N.V.—Dutch incorporated company
Nisi prius—unless before
Nolle prosequi—unwilling to prosecute
Non-parliamentary papers—government publications which are not required to be laid
before Parliament for their approval. They are usually entered in the library catalogue
under the name of the government department which publishes them

O.H.—Outer House of the Court of Session (Scotland)
Obiter dictum—a judicial observation on a point not directly relevant to the case (not
binding as precedent)
Op. cit.—the book or reference previously cited
Ord.—Order (Rules of the Supreme Court)
Orse—otherwise
Overruled—a higher court holds the decision to be wrong

P.C.—Privy Council
PCIJ—Permanent Court of International Justice
Pace—by permission of
Pamphlet—a small booklet usually less than 50 pages in length. It may be shelved in a
separate sequence
Pari passu—on equal footing; proportionately
Parl. Deb.—Parliamentary Debates
Parliamentary papers—papers required by Parliament in the course of their work. These
include: House of Lords and House of Commons Papers and Bills, Debates, Command
Papers and Acts
Per—as stated by
Per curiam—a decision arrived at by the court
Per incuriam—through want of care (a mistaken court decision)
Periodical—a publication with a distinctive title which appears regularly
Per pro. (*per procurationem*)—as an agent; on behalf of another
Per se (by itself)—taken alone
Periodicals index—(1) an index to the contents of a particular journal; (2) a subject index
to articles in a number of journals
Post—after (a later line or page)

Q.C.—Queen's Counsel
Q.S.—Quarter Sessions

q.v. (*quod vide*)—which see
Quantum meruit—as much as he had earned/deserved

r.—rule
R( )—Decision of administrative tribunal—letter in brackets indicates the appropriate
 tribunal, *e.g.* R(SB) 15/84
R. v.—Rex, Regina (the King, Queen) against
R.S.C., Ord.—Rules of the Supreme Court, Order
Ratio decidendi—the ground of a decision
Re—in the matter of
Rec.—Recueil
Reg.—Regina (the Queen)
Reg.—Regulation (E.C.), *e.g.* Reg. 467/82/EEC
Regnal year—the year of the monarch's reign

s. (plural ss.)—section of Act
S.A.—French company (société anonyme)/South Africa
s.c.—same case
S.G.—Solicitor-General
S.I.—Statutory Instrument
S.R. & O.—Statutory Rules and Orders
S.S.—steamship
Sched.—schedule (to an Act)
Scienter—knowingly
Semble—it appears
Sessional papers—a collection of all parliamentary papers published during a particular
 session of Parliament
Sessional set—a collection of all parliamentary papers issued during a particular session of
 Parliament, bound up into volumes
Statutes—Acts of Parliament
Sub judice—in course of trial
Sub nom. (*sub nomine*)—under the name
Sub voce—under the title
Supra—above

T.S.—Treaty series
Table of cases/statutes—a list of cases or statutes in alphabetical order
Treaty—(1) negotiations prior to an agreement; (2) an agreement between nations

Ultra vires—beyond the powers granted
Union catalogue/union list—a catalogue of the contents of a number of libraries

v.—versus
V.C.—Vice-Chancellor
Venire de novo—motion for a new trial
Viz. (*videlicet*)—namely; that is to say

White Book—a term sometimes used to refer to *The Supreme Court Practice*
White Paper—a parliamentary paper, usually containing a statement of government policy

Appendix III   How Do I Find? A Summary of Sources for English Law

ABBREVIATIONS (3–5) A3–1

D. Raistrick, *Index to Legal Citations and Abbreviations*.
Sweet & Maxwell's Guide to Law Reports and Statutes.
University of London Institute of Advanced Legal Studies, *Manual of Legal Citations*.
The front pages of: *Current Law Case Citator*; *The Digest*, Vol. 1 and the *Cumulative Supplement*; *Index to Legal Periodicals*; *Halsbury's Laws of England*, Vol. 1; *Legal Journals Index*.

BOOKS A3–2

Tracing Books on a Subject

Use the library catalogue (**7–29**).
Consult bibliographies (see below).

Tracing Books by Author or Title
Use the library catalogue (**7–29**).
Consult bibliographies (see below).

BIBLIOGRAPHIES A3–3

D. Raistrick, *Lawyers' Law Books* (**7–31**).
Current Publications in Legal and Related Fields (authors, titles and subjects) (**7–33**).
Legal Bibliography of the British Commonwealth (useful for older books) (**7–35**).
Bibliography on Foreign and Comparative Law (**7–35**).
British National Bibliography (**7–36**).
Law Books 1876–1981 (**7–34**).
Specialist legal bibliographies (**7–35**)—ask the library staff for advice.
The catalogues of large specialist and national libraries (**7–29**)

Sources for books in print (**7–37**)

A3–4   FINDING CASES

If you Know the Name of the Case (Summary: after **3–18**)
Current Law Case Citators (**3–14**).
The Digest (**3–15**).
English Reports (for English cases *before* 1865) (**3–10**).
Full-text databases (**2–7, 2–8, 7–8**).
For Very Recent Cases (3–18)
Current Law (**3–18**).
Daily Law Reports Index (**3–18**).
Cases in recent copies of *The Times* and other newspapers.
Summaries of cases in weekly journals, *e.g. Solicitors Journal, New Law Review.*
For Very Recent Unreported Cases (3–17)
Butterworths *Law Direct* (**3–17**).
Daily Law Notes (**3–17**).
Full-text databases of judgments (**3–12**).
Lawtel (**3–17**).

Scottish Cases

Current Law Case Citators (**3–14**).
The Digest (**3–15**).
Faculty Digest (**8–43, 8–44**).
Greens Weekly Digest (**8–45**).
Shaw's *Digest* (**8–43, 8–44**).
Scottish Current Law Case Citator (**8–43**).
Scottish Current Law Yearbook (**8–44**).
Scottish Court Service web site (**8–40**).

Irish Cases

BAILII website (**10–15**).
The Digest (**3–15**).
Index to Northern Ireland Cases (**9–9**).
Indexes to Superior Court Judgments (**10–25**).
Irish Digests (**10–22**).
Irish Law Monthly Digest (**10–23**).
Lexis-Nexis (**2–7**).
Pink Sheets (**10–24**).

Commonwealth Cases

The Digest (**3–15**).
Lexis-Nexis (**2–7**).

Tracing Cases on a Subject

Current Law (**7–9**, **7–11**, **7–12**).
The Digest (**3–15**, **7–14**).
Full-text case law databases (7–8).
Halsbury's Direct (**7–4**).
Halsbury's Laws of England (**7–4**).
Databases providing summaries of cases (**7–10**).

Tracing the Subsequent Judicial History of a Case (7–17)

Current Law (**7–9**, **7–11**, **7–12**).
The Digest (**3–15**, **7–14**).
Full-text case law databases (**7–8**).
Law Reports Index (table of cases judicially considered) (**7–16**).

Are there any Journal Articles on this Case?

Latest issue of *Current Law Monthly* (entries in the Cumulative Table of Cases).
Lawtel *Journals Index* (**5–7**).
Legal Journals Index (**5–4**).
Indexes to individual journals, *e.g. Modern Law Review; Law Quarterly Review.*

GENERAL STATEMENTS OF THE LAW A3–5

Textbooks (**A3–2**).
Halsbury's Laws of England (**7–3**).
Specialised legal encyclopedias (**7–5**).

GOVERNMENT PUBLICATIONS A3–6

Tracing Government Publications
BOPCRIS database (pre-1995 publications) (**6–18**).
General Index to Accounts and Papers (**6–18**).
  Subject Catalogue of House of Commons Parliamentary Papers (or *Index to House of Commons Papers* on CD-ROM) (**6–18**).
TSO *Daily Lists* and catalogues (HMSO pre-1996) (**6–14**).
Parlianet database (**6–18**).
UKOP database (and print equivalents) (**6–18**).

JOURNAL ARTICLES A3–7

Articles on a Subject

Legal Journals Index (**5–4**).
Lawtel *Journals Index* (**5–7**).
Index to Legal Periodicals (**5–6**).
Index to Foreign Legal Periodicals (**5–8**).

Current Law Monthly Digests (under appropriate subject heading) (**5–5**) and *Current Law Year Books* (at the back of the volumes) (**5–5**).
Index to Periodical Articles Related to Law (**5–12**).
Other non-legal journal indexes (**5–11** *et seq.*)

Articles on a Case

Articles on a Case
Latest issue of *Current Law Monthly* (entries in the Cumulative Table of Cases).
Lawtel *Journals Index* (**5–7**).
Legal Journals Index (**5–4**).
Indexes to individual journals, *e.g. Modern Law Review; Law Quarterly Review.*

Articles on an Act

Legal Journals Index (**5–4**).
Current Law Statute Citators (**4–19**).
Indexes to journals (under the appropriate subject heading).

Tracing Journals

Consult the library's periodicals catalogue (**1–9**).
If the journal is not available in your library, use other catalogues as for books (**7–29**)—ask the library staff for advice.

A3–8 STATUTES

Collections of the Statutes

Older statutes
Statutes of the Realm (**4–22**).
Statutes at Large (various editions) (**4–23**).
Acts and Ordinances of the Interregnum (**4–24**).

Modern statutes
Public General Acts and Measures (**4–6**).
Butterworths Legislation Direct (**4–9**).
Justis *UK Statutes* (**4–10**).
Lexis-Nexis (**4–11**).
Westlaw UK (**4–12**).
Law Reports: Statutes (**4–14**).
Current Law Statutes Annotated (**4–15**).
Butterworths Annotated Legislation Service (**4–16**).
Halsbury's Statutes (**4–17, 7–23**).

Collections of Acts by subject
Halsbury's Statutes (**4–17, 7–23**).

Annotated editions of statutes
Current Law Statutes Annotated (**4–15**).
Butterworths Annotated Legislation Service (**4–16**).
Halsbury's Statutes (**4–17, 7–23**).

Statutes in force
Lexis-Nexis (**4–11**).
Westlaw UK (**4–12**).
Halsbury's Statutes (**4–17, 7–23**).
Index to the Statutes (**7–22**).
Chronological Table of the Statutes (**4–20**).
Current Law Statute Citators (**4–19**).
Is It In Force? (**4–18**).

Tracing Statutes on a Subject

Halsbury's Statutes (**4–17, 7–23**).
Full-text databases of legislation (**7–20**) (other electronic sources **7–21**).
Index to the Statutes (**7–22**).
Halsbury's Laws (**7–3**).

Indexes to the Statutes

Chronological Table of the Statutes (shows whether Acts of any date are still in force) (**4–20**).
Is It In Force? (**4–18**).
Index to the Statutes (alphabetically arranged by subject, and lists all the Acts dealing with that subject) (**7–22**).
Halsbury's Statutes (alphabetically arranged by subject. Consult alphabetical list of statutes, then look in the *Cumulative Supplement* and *Noter-Up* service to check if an Act is still in force) (**7–23**).
Public General Acts: Tables and Index (annual—brings the information in the *Chronological Table of Statutes* up to date) (**4–6**).

Local and Personal Acts—Indexes

Index to Local and Personal Acts 1801–1947 (**4–25**).
Supplementary Index to the Local and Personal Acts 1948–1966 (**4–25**).
Local and Personal Acts; Tables and Index (annual) (**4–25**).

Is this Act Still in Force? Has it Been Amended?
Is It In Force? (shows whether Acts passed since 1961 are still in force) (**4–18**).
Chronological Table of the Statutes (indicates if an Act of any date is in force) (**4–20**).
Current Law Statute Citators (**4–19**).
Full-text databases (**4–8**).
Public General Acts: Tables and Index (annual—brings the information in the *Chronological Table* up to date—see the table "Effects of Legislation") (**4–6**).
Halsbury's Statutes (consult the main volumes, the *Cumulative Supplement and* the looseleaf *Service* volume) (**4–17**).

Lawtel (**4–18**).

What Cases Have there Been on the Interpretation of this Act?

Current Law Statute Citators (**4–19**).
Halsbury's Statutes (**7–23**).

What Statutory Instruments Have Been Made under this Act?

Current Law Statute Citators (**4–19**).
Halsbury's Statutes (**4–17**).

Have any Journal Articles Been Written about this Act?

Current Law Statute Citators (**4–19**).
Legal Journals Index (**5–4**).
Other indexes to journal articles (see heading "Journal Articles", above).

Has this Act Been Brought into Force by a Statutory Instrument?

Halsbury's Statutes (**4–17**).
Current Law Statute Citators (**4–19**).

A3–9   STATUTORY INSTRUMENTS

Collections of Statutory Instruments

Statutory Rules and Orders and Statutory Instruments Revised (all statutory instruments in
force in 1948) (**4–28**).
Statutory Instruments (annual volumes—subject index in last volume of each year) (**4–28**).
Halsbury's Statutory Instruments (selective—arranged by subject) (**4–29**).
UK Statutory Instruments database (**4–28**).
Full-text databases of legislation (**4–8**).

Is this Statutory Instrument in Force? Has it Been Amended?

Halsbury's Statutory Instruments (**4–29**).
Full-text databases of legislation (**4–8**)

What Statutory Instruments Have Been Made under this Act?

Current Law Statute Citator (**4–19**).
Halsbury's Statutes (**4–17**).
Lawtel (**4–31**).

Has this Act Been Brought into Force by a Statutory Instrument?

Is It in Force? (**4–18**).

Current Law Statute Citators (**4–19**).

Indexes to Statutory Instruments

Halsbury's Statutory Instruments (chronological, alphabetical and by subject) (**4–29, 7–27**).
Lists of Statutory Instruments (monthly and annually—entries by subject, and under the numbers of the Instruments) (**4–28**).
TSO Daily Lists (includes all new Instruments as they are published) (**6–14**).

THESES   A3–10

Index to Theses (**7–38**).
Dissertation Abstracts (**7–38**).

WORDS AND PHRASES   A3–11

For the meaning of words and phrases, use legal dictionaries (**1–12**).
For Latin phrases, use legal dictionaries and Broom's *Legal Maxims* (**1–12**).

Judicial and Statutory Definitions of Words and Phrases

Words and Phrases Legally Defined (**7–18**).
Stroud's Judicial Dictionary (**7–18**).
The entry "Words and Phrases" in: *Law Reports: Consolidated Index*; *Current Law Monthly Digests* and *Current Law Year Books*; and indexes to the *All England Law Reports*, *Halsbury's Laws*, and *The Digest*.

Appendix IV Creating a Search Strategy for Online Information Retrieval[1]

THE EXAMPLE OF WESTLAW UK

A4-1

Westlaw UK is a collection of over 17,000 databases of international legal content including cases, legislation and journals from the United Kingdom. United Kingdom materials are the default for any search. The materials available on Westlaw UK contain hypertext linking to related cases, journals and legislation, and the service is updated three times a day.

Westlaw UK offers three levels of searching:

(a) Searching at the "Welcome to Westlaw UK" screen allows basic intuitive searches of case law, legislation and abstracts from legal journals.
(b) Searching using "Quick Searches", which allow you to search case law, legislation and both abstracts and full text journal articles in greater detail than the "Welcome to Westlaw UK" screen.
(c) "Advanced Searches", which can be found via the "Directory" or using the links available on any of the "Quick Search" screens.

This appendix is concerned with developing a search strategy for an advanced search on Westlaw UK

Planning a Search Strategy

A4-2

In order to make the most effective use of online databases, you should plan, in advance, what you are going to do when connected to that service. This is known as planning the *search strategy*. The methods illustrated below are relevant to all the levels of searching (see above) available on Westlaw UK.

Westlaw UK allows you to search quickly through thousands of cases, statutes, statutory instruments and journal articles. It can rapidly trace cases in which a particular case or Act has been mentioned and find, within seconds, *all* cases, statutes or journal articles which

[1] This appendix has been compiled by David M. Holmes, Academic Account Manager, Westlaw UK.

mention a particular word, or words. Let us suppose, for example, that you want *all* cases on terrorism. As Westlaw UK contains the full text of each case, you need to know how the judges, in talking about terrorism, would phrase their judgments. They might talk about "terrorist" and about "terrorism". Cases using either of these words would probably be of interest to you. Westlaw UK allows you to look for both words:

TERRORIST or TERRORISM

[*Search tip*: Westlaw UK will interpret a space between two words as "or" (advanced searching only). You could search for terrorist or terrorism as follows: terrorist terrorism.]

What if you have a more complicated problem? Suppose you want to find out what cases deal with the negligence of surveyors. Prepare your search strategy by deciding what words judges use for this issue. The words "surveyor" or "valuer" might equally apply in the judgment, so you must tell Westlaw UK to search for both terms:

SURVEYOR or VALUER

If you type in these terms, Westlaw UK will discover all cases that mention either of these words. However, this information is far too general for your problem. You want to know about negligence of surveyors. Here judges might use words such as:

NEGLIGENCE or NEGLIGENT or NEGLIGENTLY

So, you can type in these words as alternatives for Westlaw UK to work on. You can see that these words have a common root or stem, "Negligen...". As a short cut, you can instruct Westlaw UK to search for any words which begin Negligen.... This is done by using a "truncation mark". The truncation mark in Westlaw UK is ! (an exclamation mark). If you type in "NEGLIGEN!" Westlaw UK will search for any word beginning with "negligen...". You must be cautious with this method if searching, as you may end up with words that you do not want, or simply had not thought about. For example, if you type "TERROR!" in the search for the words terrorist or terrorism it would also retrieve cases mentioning "terrorstricken", "terrorise" and, of course, "terror".

In Westlaw UK, you need to add a truncation mark to a singular word in order to include the plural. For example, if you wish to obtain both the singular and the plural of the word SURVEYOR, type SURVEYOR! Westlaw UK will now search for "surveyor", "surveyors", "surveyor's", and "surveyors'".

You can instruct Westlaw UK to link the two parts of the search by telling it to search for cases in which surveyor or valuer *and* negligence (or the alternative words) are mentioned in the same case. You can do this by typing in:

(SURVEYOR or VALUER) and NEGLIGEN!

Westlaw UK will respond by giving you results of cases that mention surveyor or valuer and negligen. The results will be displayed in reverse chronological order with the citations for those cases shown in the left-hand frame on the screen. The left-hand frame also tells you the number of cases you have retrieved which helps you narrow down the number of cases that you might want to read.

You can refine this strategy by looking for words that appear close together in the law report. For example, let us suppose that you want to find all cases that mention *Laker Airways* v. *Department of Trade*. If you type in:

LAKER /5 TRADE

you are asking Westlaw UK to find every mention of Laker within five words of Trade. Therefore "/", followed by a number, instructs Westlaw UK to search for words which occur within so many words of each other.

You can use this technique to link negligence more closely with surveyor. This will make sure that there is a relevant connection between the two words "negligence" and "surveyor". Otherwise both the words may appear somewhere within the same case but be unassociated with the issue of the negligence of surveyors. If you specify that the two words should appear fairly close to each other, say with 15 words, then you are likely to find that there is a relevant connection for your purposes:

SURVEYOR /15 NEGLIGEN!

However, this short cut also runs the danger of missing relevant cases where the key words do not occur within the stated 15-word proximity. Practice will help you develop a search strategy that will retrieve all the relevant cases and avoid picking up too many irrelevant results.

Summary: Search Strategy   A4–3

Although different command languages use different words and symbols, all languages have the same features to enable words to be linked by an "and" or "or" connection and allow words to be truncated. When using Westlaw UK, the four most useful words and symbols that you are likely to need when planning your search strategy are:

(a) **OR:** This tells Westlaw UK to look for alternative words. Doctor OR Surgeon; Surveyor OR Valuer; Negligence OR Negligently OR Negligent. It has the effect of widening the search and increasing the number of possible cases that may be relevant.

(b) **AND:** This tells Westlaw UK to link together two (or more) words and to refer you only to the cases that contain *both* words. Surveyor AND Negligence; Elephant AND Circus. Both words must appear in the same case. Westlaw UK will not report on cases that deal only with an elephant or only with a circus. "And" has the effect of *narrowing down* (or limiting) your research. "And" retrieves fewer cases than the word "or".

(c) **/5:** "/" means "Within so many words of". This example instructs Westlaw UK to find two words when they are located in the case within five words of each other. You can choose any number between 1 and 100. Do not bring the words too close together as you may miss relevant cases. The effect of using "/" is again to *narrow down* (or limit) your search.

(d) **!:** In Westlaw UK this is the "truncation mark". It instructs Westlaw UK to search for words that have the same beginning (stem) but different endings, *e.g.* "negligen!" will retrieve negligent, negligence, etc. Its effect is to widen the search.

There are other commands that you may need to use from time to time. For example, each law report, statute and journal article is divided up into parts (or segments) called "Fields". Law reports can be searched by looking for all cases heard within a particular court, or all judgments by a particular judge. The most common segment to search is called the "Title field"; this allows you to retrieve a specific case on Westlaw UK. For example, if you want to retrieve the case of *Pearce* v. *Ove Arup Partnership Ltd*, A search for *Pearce /5 Ove* will retrieve the *Pearce* case itself, and also other cases in which the *Pearce* case has been referred to. If you only want to retrieve the *Pearce* case itself, the best way to do this is within a segment search of the title field. Our search would be TI(*Pearce /5 Ove*). This would retrieve only the *Pearce* case. Full details of segment searches can be found in the *Westlaw UK User Guide*.

A4–4   Accessing Westlaw UK

There are currently two methods by which you may access Westlaw UK: passwords and IP authentication. Details of the latter method of access vary from institution to institution. Generally, IP authentication allows you to access the service from your library home page if you an enrolled member of an institution which subscribes to Westlaw UK. You do not require a password for such access. Your librarian will be able to help you with any questions.

If you have a Westlaw UK password open a browser on your computer such as Internet Explorer or Netscape. In the address field, type **www.westlaw.co.uk**. Select "Search Westlaw UK" from the options listed. You will now be shown a page with a password field and a client ID field. Enter your password in either upper or lower case in the field reserved for passwords. In the second field which is titled "Client ID", enter any series of letters, *e.g.* your name. Now select "Go". You will be taken to the "Welcome to Westlaw UK" screen at which point you can commence searching.

If you wish to use the advanced search method, select "Directory" at the top of the "Welcome to Westlaw UK" screen. In the right-hand frame of the screen select "UK Materials". The screen will show you a list of different files. Do you want cases, legislation or journals? Let us assume you wish to search cases. Select cases. A further list of files will appear, select "All Reports". You will now be taken to the advanced search screen for this database.

Let us return to our search for information on terrorism. You will have decided before using Westlaw UK that you are searching for all cases that mention terrorism or terrorist. So you type in:

TERRORISM or TERRORIST

and select Search. Westlaw UK will search through all of the cases in the "All Reports" database looking for any mention of *either* of these two words in its full-text case reports. After a few seconds, you will be shown the cases that mention the words you have asked for. You can look at these cases (to see if they are relevant) by pressing the right-hand arrow of the *term* button at the bottom of the right-hand frame. This shows you the search word (terrorism/terrorist) together with the surrounding sentences in the law report.

This gives you the context in which the word is found. Normally this is enough to let you decide whether the case is relevant. All results are in reverse chronological order. The citation list for all of the cases you have found, together with the number of cases found, can be seen in the left-hand frame of the screen. You can print any of the materials on Westlaw UK or email them to yourself. Ask your librarian or tutor for details.

Modifying and Editing your Search Strategy

It could be that, at your first attempt, you are unsuccessful with your search strategy and fail to find the information you need. If, for example, you key in a command which produces 500 cases which refer to the word you are searching for, then you must rethink your search strategy. It is very likely that you have defined the search far too widely. You must limit the search by adding another word or words to your command. For example, if you put in "NEGLIGEN!" on its own then you would be informed of thousands of cases that are concerned with various aspects of negligence. Therefore you must narrow the search by asking for negligence *and* surveyors. This command would reduce the number of cases significantly.

If you wish to edit or modify your search strategy select "Edit Query"from the top of the left-hand frame on Westlaw UK. You can now type in a new search word or words. If you are still having difficulty in retrieving helpful material you can telephone Westlaw UK's legally trained Customer Support team using the freephone telephone number listed at the bottom of their website address (**www.westlaw.co.uk**).

This appendix provides only the briefest outline of the type of searches that Westlaw UK can undertake. Further details can be found in the *Westlaw UK User Guide* and obtained from the Westlaw UK academic account management team who are responsible for the Westlaw UK academic training programme. The *Guide,* for example, will tell you how to find all cases discussing the interpretation of a particular section of an Act, and what statutory instruments brought sections of an Act into force; it will also enable you to discover whether a case has been overruled; and in which cases named barristers, solicitors or judges were involved.

If a statute has been amended by subsequent legislation, Westlaw UK will display the amended, up-to-date version of the Act. It will retrieve all references to statutes or statutory instruments on a subject, and provide you with the full text of the Act or statutory instrument. If you remember the facts of a case but not its name, or if you know the name of only one of the parties in the dispute, Westlaw UK can find the case. Sometimes such a search would be impossible with conventional printed sources. Almost always Westlaw UK will be faster than conventional methods. Further, Westlaw UK is the only online legal research tool that can provide both *primary* sources such as cases and legislation as well as *secondary* sources such as journal and newspaper articles written about the law in the United Kingdom. Finally, Westlaw UK is not an inexhaustible legal research tool. Other databases exist which contain information relevant to lawyers. Your librarian can tell you which of these are available and can, where relevant, get access to the information on your behalf.

Index